The Reading Teacher's BOOK OF LISTS

Third Edition

Edward Bernard Fry, Ph.D.

Jacqueline E. Kress, Ed.D.

Dona Lee Fountoukidis, Ed.D.

**THE CENTER FOR APPLIED
RESEARCH IN EDUCATION**
West Nyack, New York 10994

Library of Congress Cataloging-in-Publication Data

Fry, Edward Bernard, 1925–
    The reading teacher's book of lists / Edward Bernard Fry.
Jacqueline E. Kress, Dona Lee Fountoukidis.—3rd ed..
        p.   cm.
    Includes index.
    ISBN 0-13-762014-4
    1. Reading—Miscellanea.   2. Curriculum planning—Miscellanea.
3. Tutors and turoring—Miscellanea.   4. Handbooks, vade-mecums.
etc.   I. Kress, Jacqueline E.   II. Fountoukidis, Dona, 1938–.
III. Title
LB1050.2.F79   1993   93-9256
428.—dc20   CIP

Printed in the United States of America

10 9 8 7 6 5 4

ISBN 0-13-762014-4

**THE CENTER FOR APPLIED RESEARCH
IN EDUCATION**
West Nyack, NY 10994
A Simon & Schuster Company

On the World Wide Web at http://www.phdirect.com

Prentice-Hall International (UK) Limited, *London*
Prentice-Hall of Australia Pty. Limited, *Sydney*
Prentice-Hall Canada Inc., *Toronto*
Prentice-Hall Hispanoamericana, S.A., *Mexico*
Prentice-Hall of India Private Limited, *New Delhi*
Prentice-Hall of Japan, Inc., *Tokyo*
Simon & Schuster Asia Pte. Ltd., *Singapore*
Editora Prentice-Hall do Brasil, Ltda., *Rio de Janeiro*

About the Authors

Edward Bernard Fry, Ph.D., was director of the Reading Center and Professor of Education at Rutgers University for 24 years. Dr. Fry taught courses for graduate and undergraduate students and served on dissertation committees. As the Reading Center director, he provided instruction for children with reading problems, conducted statewide reading conferences, and provided teacher-training courses. Currently, he is authoring curriculum materials and working as a reading consultant.

Dr. Fry has authored a number of practical guides for reading teachers, including *Elementary Reading Instruction* (McGraw-Hill, 1977) and *Reading for Classroom and Clinic* (McGraw-Hill, 1972), coauthored the *Jamestown Heritage Reading Series* (1991), and edited *The Ten Best Ideas for Reading Teachers* (Addison Wesley, 1991). He has also developed a variety of curriculum materials, including typing courses for children, filmstrips, overhead transparencies, card reader programs on phonics and basic vocabulary, reading improvement drill books, criterion-referenced tests, and videotape reading-improvement programs for industries and universities. Dr. Fry is world-renowned for his Readability Graph.

Jacqueline E. Kress, Ed.D. is an experienced teacher, teacher-trainer, educational program designer, and administrator. Her research in reading comprehension strategies earned her the 1987 Evelyn Headley Award from Rutgers University, where she earned her doctorate in reading. She has taught developmental and remedial reading, and language arts in urban elementary schools as well as in several New Jersey colleges. She also served as a coordinator of elementary school reading and testing and as a college reading faculty member.

Dr. Kress has designed numerous educational programs for at-risk students with special instructional needs, including gifted and talented, underprepared, learning disabled, and visually or auditorily impaired students. She is the author of *The ESL Teacher's Book of Lists* (Prentice Hall, 1993) and co-author of *The Readability Machine* (Prentice-Hall, 1986). Currently, Dr. Kress directs the Office of Total Quality Management at the New Jersey Department of Higher Education.

Dona Lee Fountoukidis, Ed.D., has held a variety of teaching positions. In Japan, she taught English to Japanese junior and senior high school students. In the United States, she has taught, primarily at the college level, courses in developmental reading and study skills, content area reading and reading methods courses, as well as courses in statistics and educational psychology. Dr. Fountoukidis is currently Director of Planning, Research and Evaluation at William Paterson College, where she conducts research on student learning.

Preface
to the Third Edition

This Third Edition of *The Reading Teacher's Book of Lists* is quite different from the first edition published in 1984. But the premise upon which we based the book still holds—we believe reading teachers have a wealth of creative ideas about what to teach and how to teach it effectively. What they don't have is the time they need to gather or develop materials from many different sources for their classes. To fill a need, we created and put together what we thought were the most used and useful lists into a single desktop reference—a time-saving treasure chest we hoped would be looted over and over again.

One teacher we know has worn out two copies of the Second Edition and is now on her third. Others complain because they are borrowed all the time. Some of the biggest publishers in the nation, and some of the best-known authors of curriculum materials and tests, use these lists. In fact, they are used in some university reading courses as a supplement to the required test. We are continually delighted by the letters we receive from reading and language teachers, curriculum developers, librarians, and even children's book editors attesting to the usefulness of our book. Many of their ideas and suggestions have been incorporated into this edition, and we invite you to share your thoughts and comments with us, too.

Now, a few words about many of the new features of the Third Edition. First, many of the original lists from our earlier versions are included but they have been substantially updated, reorganized, and expanded. For example, the **Core Subject Words** are completely redone to reflect the content found in textbooks published in 1990 and later. There are now more **Phonograms, Homophones, Literary Terms, Similes, Proverbs, Idioms, Computer Terms,** and **Propaganda Techniques,** to name just a few. Several new lists focus on teamwork, cooperative learning, and problem solving, while others focus on increasing the effectiveness of students' learning skills. Two new lists in our *Phonics* Section will appeal to language and ESL teachers, and our list on **Alternative Assessment Techniques** reflects an important move in student evaluations across the nation. Additions to the *Using Language Arts* Section provide a multitude of ideas to boost every student's writing and research skills. And last, but not least, **People to Know, Native American Symbols,** and the revised book lists will update your reading curriculum and integrate gender as well as multicultural perspectives.

We guarantee that you will get some new and interesting ideas just by browsing through a few pages of this book. If you need to find something specific, such as **Story Starters** or **Predictable Books,** use our new Index. If you want to find a broad category, such as *Word Origins* or *Learning and Study Skills,* simply use the Contents page. And when you find what you need, notice the cross-referencing at the bottom of the list to see if a related list can further help you.

Finally, we would like to thank the more than one hundred thousand users of ***The Reading Teacher's Book of Lists*** for making it so popular. We hope you enjoy using this edition as much as we enjoyed working on it.

Edward Bernard Fry
Jacqueline E. Kress
Dona Lee Fountoukidis

A User's Guide

The wide diversity of lists in this book makes it possible for teachers to pick and choose those that meet specific classroom and teaching needs. Some lists may be appropriate for different types of teaching (ESL) or for various grade levels (primary). The following suggestions are designed to help you and to make this book of lists even more useful.

PRIMARY: GRADES K–2
(or any beginning reader)

4 Instant Words
5 Picture Nouns
46 Initial Consonant Sounds
47 Phonograms
48 Phonics Example Words
50 Sound Awareness Books
51 Speech Sound Development
100 Activities for Language Development
101 Games and Methods
113 Picture Books
114 Predictable Books
116 Books Most Frequently Read Aloud
143 Handwriting Charts

ELEMENTARY: GRADES 3–6

1 Homophones
2 Homographs
9 Collective Nouns
10 Mathematics Vocabulary
13 Measurement
15 Science Vocabulary
19 Social Studies Vocabulary
22 Synonyms
32 Clipped Words

33 Portmanteau Words
34 Compound Words
39 Onomatopoeia
43 Prefixes
44 Suffixes
47 Phonograms
60 Story Graphs
79 Story Starters
80 Descriptive Words
84 Basic Sentence Patterns
85 Punctuation Guidelines
86 Capitalization Guidelines
89 Proofreading Checklist
94 Spelling Demons-Elementary
98 Interest Inventory
102 Oral Reading Alternatives
104 Hink Pinks
116 Books Most Frequently Read Aloud
117 Book Interest Arousers
121 Book Report Alternatives
124 State Abbreviations

JUNIOR AND SENIOR HIGH SCHOOL

12 Mathematics Vocabulary
14 Geometry Vocabulary
16 General Science Vocabulary

Contents

IX. ENRICHMENT AND DISCOVERY ACTIVITIES   265

X. BOOKS   295

SECTION I
Foundation Words

1. *Homophones*

Homophones are usually words that sound the same but have different meanings and usually different spellings. This list was combined from many teachers' lists and secretaries' spelling wordbooks. We think that it is one of the most complete in existence. We omitted only rarely used words. Homophones are used in many reading and spelling games, jokes, and workbook drills. Homophones are particularly important as spelling words now that so many people are using "spell check" programs on word processors. The spell check program will not notice any word spelled correctly even though you used the homophone.

This list includes only homophones that have different spellings. If homophones have the same spelling (example, *bat* meaning a flying mammal and *bat* meaning a club) they are listed with homographs.

Many people would call this list *homonyms*, and they are not wrong. The term *homonym*, however, suffers from varying definitions and can include both what we are calling homophones (same sound) and homographs (same spelling).

ad (advertisement)
add (addition)

ads (advertisements)
adz (axlike tool)

aid (assistance)
aide (a helper)

ail (be sick)
ale (beverage)

air (oxygen)
heir (successor)

aisle (path)
I'll (I will)
isle (island)

all (everything)
awl (tool)

already (previous)
all ready (all are ready)

allowed (permitted)
aloud (audible)

altar (in a church)
alter (change)

ant (insect)
aunt (relative)

arc (part of a circle)
ark (boat)

ascent (climb)
assent (agree)

assistance (help)
assistants (those who help)

ate (did eat)
eight (number)

attendance (presence)
attendants (escorts)

aural (by ear)
oral (by mouth)

away (gone)
aweigh (clear anchor)

awful (terrible)
offal (entrails)

aye (yes)
eye (organ of sight)
I (pronoun)

bail (throw water out)
bale (bundle)

bait (lure)
bate (to decrease)

ball (round object)
bawl (cry)

band (plays music)
banned (forbidden)

bard (poet)
barred (having bars)

bare (nude)
bear (animal)

bark (dog's sound)
barque (ship)

base (lower part)
bass (deep tone)

bases (plural of *base*)
basis (foundation)

bazaar (market)
bizarre (odd)

be (exist)
bee (insect)

beach (shore)
beech (tree)

bearing (manner)
baring (uncovering)

bear (animal; carry)
bare (uncovered)

beat (whip)
beet (vegetable)

beau (boyfriend)
bow (decorative knot)

been (past participle of *be*)
bin (box)

beer (drink)
bier (coffin)

bell (something you ring)
belle (pretty woman)

The Reading Teacher's Book of Lists, Third Edition, © 1993 by Prentice Hall

berry (fruit)
bury (put in ground)

berth (bunk)
birth (born)

better (more good)
bettor (one who bets)

bight (slack part of rope)
bite (chew)
byte (computer unit)

billed (did bill)
build (construct)

blew (did blow)
blue (color)

block (cube)
bloc (group)

boar (hog)
bore (drill; be tiresome)

board (lumber)
bored (uninterested)

boarder (one who boards)
border (boundary)

boll (cotton pod)
bowl (dish; game)

bolder (more bold)
boulder (big stone)

born (delivered at birth)
borne (carried)

borough (town)
burro (donkey)
burrow (dig)

bough (of a tree)
bow (of a ship)

bouillon (clear broth)
bullion (uncoined gold or silver)

boy (male child)
bouy (floating object)

brake (stop)
break (smash)

bread (food)
bred (cultivated)

brewed (steeped)
brood (flock)

brews (steeps)
bruise (bump)

bridal (relating to bride)
bridle (headgear for horse)

Britain (country)
Briton (Englishman)

broach (bring up)
brooch (pin)

but (except)
butt (end)

buy (purchase)
by (near)
bye (farewell)

cache (hiding place)
cash (money)

callous (unfeeling)
callus (hard tissue)

cannon (big gun)
canon (law)

canvas (cloth)
canvass (survey)

capital (money; city)
capitol (building of U.S. Congress)

carat (weight of precious stones)
caret (proofreader's mark)
carrot (vegetable)

carol (song)
carrel (study space in library)

cast (throw; actors in a play)
caste (social class)

cede (grant)
seed (part of a plant)

ceiling (top of room)
sealing (closing)

cell (prison room)
sell (exchange for money)

cellar (basement)
seller (one who sells)

censor (ban)
sensor (detection device)

cent (penny)
scent (odor)
sent (did send)

cereal (relating to grain)
serial (of a series)

cession (yielding)
session (meeting)

chased (did chase)
chaste (modest)

cheap (inexpensive)
cheep (bird call)

chews (bites)
choose (select)

chic (style)
sheik (Arab chief)

chilly (cold)
chili (hot pepper)

choral (music)
coral (reef)

chorale (chorus)
corral (pen for livestock)

chord (musical notes)
cord (string)

chute (slide)
shoot (discharge gun)

cite (summon to court)
sight (see)
site (location)

claws (nails on animal's feet)
clause (part of a sentence)

click (small sound)
clique (group of friends)

climb (ascend)
clime (climate)

close (shut)
clothes (clothing)

The Reading Teacher's Book of Lists, Third Edition, © 1993 by Prentice Hall

coal (fuel)
cole (cabbage)

coarse (rough)
course (path; school subject)

colonel (military rank)
kernel (grain of corn)

complement (complete set)
compliment (praise)

coop (chicken pen)
coupe (car)

core (center)
corps (army group)

council (legislative body)
counsel (advise)

cousin (relative)
cozen (deceive)

creak (grating noise)
creek (stream)

crews (groups of workers)
cruise (sail)
cruse (small pot)

cruel (hurting)
crewel (stitching)

cue (prompt)
queue (line up)

currant (small raisin)
current (recent; fast part of a stream)

curser (one who curses)
cursor (moving pointer)

cymbal (percussion instrument)
symbol (sign)

deer (animal)
dear (greeting; loved one)

desert (abandon)
dessert (follows main course of meal)

die (expire)
dye (color)

dine (eat)
dyne (unit of force)

disburse (pay out)
disperse (scatter)

discreet (unobtrusive)
discrete (noncontinuous)

doe (female deer)
dough (bread mixture)
do (musical note)

do (shall)
dew (moisture)
due (owed)

done (finished)
dun (demand for payment; dull color)

dual (two)
duel (formal combat)

duct (tube)
ducked (did duck)

earn (work for)
urn (container)

ewe (female sheep)
yew (shrub)
you (personal pronoun)

eyelet (small hole)
islet (small island)

fain (gladly)
feign (pretend)

faint (weak)
feint (pretend attack)

fair (honest; bazaar)
fare (cost of transportation)

fawn (baby deer)
faun (mythical creature)

faze (upset)
phase (stage)

feat (accomplishment)
feet (plural of *foot*)

find (discover)
fined (penalty of money)

fir (tree)
fur (animal covering)

flair (talent)
flare (flaming signal)

flea (insect)
flee (run away)

flew (did fly)
flu (influenza)
flue (shaft)

flour (milled grain)
flower (bloom)

for (in favor of)
fore (front part)
four (number)

foreword (preface)
forward (front part)

forth (forward)
fourth (after third)

foul (bad)
fowl (bird)

franc (French money)
frank (honest)

friar (brother in religious order)
fryer (frying chicken)

gilt (golden)
guilt (opposite of innocence)

gnu (antelope)
knew (did know)
new (opposite of *old*)

gorilla (animal)
guerrilla (irregular soldier)

grate (grind)
great (large)

groan (moan)
grown (cultivated)

guessed (surmised)
guest (company)

hail (ice; salute)
hale (healthy)

hair (on head)
hare (rabbit)

hall (passage)
haul (carry)

handsome (attractive)
hansom (carriage)

hangar (storage building)
hanger (to hang things on)

halve (cut in half)
have (possess)

hart (deer)
heart (body organ)

hay (dried grass)
hey (expression to get attention)

heal (make well)
heel (bottom of foot)
he'll (he will)

hear (listen)
here (this place)

heard (listened)
herd (group of animals)

heed (pay attention)
he'd (he would)

hertz (unit of wave frequency)
hurts (pain)

hew (carve)
hue (color)

hi (hello)
hie (hasten)
high (opposite of *low*)

higher (above)
hire (employ)

him (pronoun)
hymn (religious song)

hoarse (husky voice)
horse (animal)

hole (opening)
whole (complete)

holey (full of holes)
holy (sacred)
wholly (all)

horde (crowd)
hoard (hidden supply)

hostel (lodging for youth)
hostile (unfriendly)

hour (sixty minutes)
our (possessive pronoun)

hurdle (jump over)
hurtle (throw)

idle (lazy)
idol (god)
idyll (charming scene)

in (opposite of *out*)
inn (hotel)

insight (self knowledge)
incite (cause)

instance (example)
instants (short periods of time)

intense (extreme)
intents (aims)

its (possessive pronoun)
it's (it is)

jam (fruit jelly)
jamb (window part)

knead (mix with hands)
need (require)

knew (remembered)
new (not old)
gnu (animal)

knight (feudal warrior)
night (evening)

knit (weave with yarn)
nit (louse egg)

knot (tangle)
not (in no manner)

know (familiar with)
no (negative)

lam (escape)
lamb (baby sheep)

lain (past participle of *lie*)
lane (narrow way)

lay (recline)
lei (necklace of flowers)

lead (metal)
led (guided)

leak (crack)
leek (vegetable)

lean (slender; incline)
lien (claim)

leased (rented)
least (smallest)

lessen (make less)
lesson (instruction)

levee (embankment)
levy (impose by legal authority)

liar (untruthful)
lyre (musical instrument)

lichen (fungus)
liken (compare)

lie (falsehood)
lye (alkaline solution)

lieu (instead of)
Lou (name)

lightening (become light)
lightning (occurs with thunder)

load (burden)
lode (vein of ore)

loan (something borrowed)
lone (single)

locks (plural of lock)
lox (smoked salmon)

loot (steal)
lute (musical instrument)

low (not high; cattle sound)
lo (interjection)

made (manufactured)
maid (servant)

mail (send by post)
male (masculine)

main (most important)
Maine (state)
mane (hair)

maize (Indian corn)
maze (confusing network of passages)

mall (courtyard)
maul (attack)

manner (style)
manor (estate)

mantel (over fireplace)
mantle (cloak)

marry (join together)
merry (gay)
Mary (name)

marshal (escort)
martial (militant)

massed (grouped)
mast (support)

meat (beef)
meet (greet)
mete (measure)

medal (award)
meddle (interfere)

might (may; strength)
mite (small insect)

miner (coal digger)
minor (juvenile)

missed (failed to attain)
mist (fog)

moan (groan)
mown (cut down)

mode (fashion)
mowed (cut down)

morn (early day)
mourn (grieve)

muscle (flesh)
mussel (shellfish)

naval (nautical)
navel (depression on abdomen)

nay (no)
neigh (whinny)

none (not any)
nun (religious sister)

oar (of a boat)
or (conjunction)
ore (mineral deposit)

ode (poem)
owed (did owe)

oh (exclamation)
owe (be indebted)

one (number)
won (triumphed)

overdo (go to extremes)
overdue (past due)

overseas (abroad)
oversees (supervises)

pail (bucket)
pale (white)

pain (discomfort)
pane (window glass)

pair (two of a kind)
pare (peel)
pear (fruit)

palate (roof of mouth)
palette (board for paint)
pallet (tool)

passed (went by)
past (former)

patience (composure)
patients (sick persons)

pause (brief stop)
paws (feet of animals)

peace (tranquility)
piece (part)

peak (mountaintop)
peek (look)
pique (offense)

peal (ring)
peel (pare)

pearl (jewel)
purl (knitting stitch)

pedal (ride a bike)
peddle (sell)

peer (equal)
pier (dock)

per (for each)
purr (cat sound)

pi (Greek letter)
pie (kind of pastry)

plain (simple)
plane (flat surface)

plait (braid)
plate (dish)

pleas (plural of *plea*)
please (to be agreeable)

plum (fruit)
plumb (lead weight)

pole (stick)
poll (vote)

pore (ponder; skin gland)
pour (flow freely)

pray (worship)
prey (victim)

presents (gifts)
presence (appearance)

principal (chief)
principle (rule)

profit (benefit)
prophet (seer)

rack (framework; torture)
wrack (ruin)

rain (precipitation)
reign (royal authority)
rein (harness)

raise (put up)
raze (tear down)
rays (of sun)

rap (hit; talk)
wrap (cover)

read (peruse)
reed (plant)

read (perused)
red (color)

real (genuine)
reel (spool)

reek (give off strong odor)
wreak (inflict)

rest (relax)
wrest (take from)

right (correct)
rite (ceremony)
write (inscribe)

rime (ice, or rhyme)
rhyme (same end sound)

ring (circular band)
wring (squeeze)

road (street)
rode (transported)
rowed (used oars)

roe (fish eggs)
row (line; use oars)

role (character)
roll (turn over; bread)

root (part of a plant)
route (highway)

rose (flower)
rows (lines)

rote (by memory)
wrote (did write)

rude (impolite)
rued (was sorry)

rumor (gossip)
roomer (renter)

rung (step on a ladder; past of *ring*)
wrung (squeezed)

rye (grain)
wry (twisted)

sail (travel by boat)
sale (bargain)

scene (setting)
seen (viewed)

scent (smell)
sent (past of *send*)
cent (penny)

scull (boat; row)
skull (head)

sea (ocean)
see (visualize)

seam (joining mark)
seem (appear to be)

sear (singe)
seer (prophet)

serf (feudal servant)
surf (waves)

sew (mend)
so (in order that)
sow (plant)

shear (cut)
sheer (transparent)

shoe (foot covering)
shoo (drive away)

shone (beamed)
shown (exhibited)

side (flank)
sighed (audible breath)

sign (signal)
sine (trigonometric function)

slay (kill)
sleigh (sled)

sleight (dexterity)
slight (slender)

slew (killed)
slue (swamp)

soar (fly)
sore (painful)

sole (only)
soul (spirit)

some (portion)
sum (total)

son (male offspring)
sun (star)

staid (proper)
stayed (remained)

stair (step)
stare (look intently)

stake (post)
steak (meat)

stationary (fixed)
stationery (paper)

steal (rob)
steel (metal)

step (walk)
steppe (prairie of Europe or Asia)

stile (gate)
style (fashion)

straight (not crooked)
strait (channel of water)

suite (connected rooms)
sweet (sugary)

tacks (plural of *tack*)
tax (assess; burden)

tail (animal's appendage)
tale (story)

taught (did teach)
taut (tight)

tea (drink)
tee (holder for golf ball)

teas (plural of *tea*)
tease (mock)

The Reading Teacher's Book of Lists, Third Edition, © 1993 by Prentice Hall

team (crew)
teem (be full)

tear (cry)
tier (level)

tern (sea bird)
turn (rotate)

their (possessive pronoun)
there (at that place)
they're (they are)

theirs (possessive pronoun)
there's (there is)

threw (tossed)
through (finished)

throne (king's seat)
thrown (tossed)

thyme (herb)
time (duration)

tic (twitch)
tick (insect; sound of clock)

tide (ebb and flow)
tied (bound)

to (toward)
too (also)
two (number)

toad (frog)
towed (pulled)

toe (digit on foot)
tow (pull)

told (informed)
tolled (rang)

trussed (tied)
trust (confidence)

vain (conceited)
vane (wind indicator)
vein (blood vessel)

vale (valley)
veil (face cover)

vary (change)
very (absolutely)

vice (bad habit)
vise (clamp)

wade (walk in water)
weighed (measured
   heaviness)

wail (cry)
whale (sea mammal)

waist (middle)
waste (trash)

wait (linger)
weight (heaviness)

waive (forgive)
wave (swell)

want (desire)
wont (custom)

ware (pottery)
wear (have on)
where (what place)

way (road)
weigh (measure heaviness)
whey (watery part of milk)

ways (plural of way;
   shipyard)
weighs (heaviness)

we (pronoun)
wee (small)

weak (not strong)
week (seven days)

weal (prosperity)
we'll (we will)
wheel (circular frame)

weather (climate)
whether (if)

weave (interlace)
we've (we have)

we'd (we would)
weed (plant)

weir (dam)
we're (we are)

wet (moist)
whet (sharpen)

which (what one)
witch (sorceress)

while (during)
wile (trick)

whine (complaining sound)
wine (drink)

who's (who is)
whose (possessive of who)

wood (of a tree)
would (is willing to)

worst (most bad)
wurst (sausage)

yoke (harness)
yolk (egg center)

you (pronoun)
ewe (female sheep)
yew (evergreen tree)

you'll (you will)
yule (Christmas)

your (possessive pronoun)
you're (you are)

See also List 2, Homographs and Heteronyms, and List 3, Near Misses.

2. *Homographs and Heteronyms*

Homographs are words that are spelled the same but have different meanings and different origins. Many other words have multiple meanings, but according to dictionary authorities, what makes these words homographs is that they have different origins as well. Some homographs are also heteronyms, which means that they have a different pronunciation—these are marked with an asterisk (*).

*affect (influence)
affect (pretend)

alight (get down from)
alight (on fire)

angle (shape formed by two connected lines)
angle (to fish with hook and line)

arch (curved structure)
arch (chief)

arms (body parts)
arms (weapons)

*august (majestic)
August (eighth month of the year)

*axes (plural of *ax*)
axes (plural of *axis*)

bail (money for release)
bail (handle of a pail)
bail (throw water out)

ball (round object)
ball (formal dance)

band (group of musicians)
band (thin strip for binding)

bank (mound)
bank (place of financial business)
bank (row of things)
bank (land along a river)

bark (tree covering)
bark (sound a dog makes)
bark (sailboat)

base (bottom)
base (morally low)

*bass (low male voice)
bass (kind of fish)

baste (pour liquid on while roasting)
baste (sew with long stitches)

bat (club)
bat (flying animal)
bat (wink)

batter (hit repeatedly)
batter (liquid mixture used for cakes)
batter (baseball player)

bay (part of a sea)
bay (aromatic leaf used in cooking)
bay (reddish brown)
bay (alcove between columns)
bay (howl)

bear (large animal)
bear (support; carry)

bill (statement of money owed)
bill (beak)

bit (small piece)
bit (tool for drilling)
bit (did bite)

blaze (fire)
blaze (mark a trail or a tree)
blaze (make known)

blow (hard hit)
blow (send forth a stream of air)

bluff (steep bank or cliff)
bluff (fool or mislead)

bob (weight at the end of a line)
bob (move up and down)
Bob (nickname for Robert)

boil (bubbling of hot liquid)
boil (red swelling on the skin)

boom (deep sound)
boom (long beam)
boom (sudden increase in size)

boon (benefit)
boon (merry)

bore (make a hole)
bore (make weary)
bore (did bear)

bound (limit)
bound (obliged)
bound (spring back)
bound (on the way)

*bow** (weapon for shooting arrows)
bow (forward part of a ship)
bow (bend in greeting or respect)

bowl (rounded dish)
bowl (play the game of bowling)

box (four-sided container)
box (kind of evergreen shrub)
box (strike with the hand)

bridge (way over an obstacle)
bridge (card game)

brush (tool for sweeping)
brush (bushes)

buck (male deer)
buck (slang for *dollar*)

buffer (something that softens)
buffer (pad for polishing)

*buffet** (cabinet for dishes and linens)
buffet (self-serve meal)
buffet (strike)

butt (thicker end of a tool)
butt (object of ridicule)

can (able to)
can (metal container)

capital (money)
capital (punishable by death)

carp (complain)
carp (kind of fish)

case (condition)
case (box or container)

chap (crack or become rough)
chap (boy or man)

chop (cut with something sharp)
chop (jaw)

chop (irregular motion)
chop (cut of meat)

chord (two or more musical notes)
chord (together)
chord (an emotional response)

chow (breed of dog)
chow (slang for *food*)

chuck (throw or toss)
chuck (cut of beef)

cleave (cut)
cleave (hold on to)

clip (cut)
clip (fasten)

*close** (shut)
close (near)

clove (fragrant spice)
clove (section of a bulb)

cobbler (one who mends shoes)
cobbler (fruit pie with one crust)

cock (rooster)
cock (tilt upward)

colon (mark of punctuation)
colon (lower part of the large intestine)

*commune** (talk intimately)
commune (group of people living together)

*compact** (firmly packed together)
compact (agreement)

compound (having more than one part)
compound (enclosed yard)

con (swindle)
con (against)

*console** (cabinet)
console (ease grief)

*content** (all things inside)
content (satisfied)

*converse** (talk)
converse (opposite)

corporal (of the body)
corporal (low-ranking officer)

count (name numbers in order)
count (nobleman)

counter (long table in a store or restaurant)
counter (one who counts)
counter (opposite)

crow (loud cry of a rooster)
crow (large black bird)
Crow (tribe of American Indians)

cue (signal)
cue (long stick used in a game of pool)

curry (rub and clean a horse)
curry (spicy seasoning)

date (day, month, and year)
date (sweet dark fruit)

defer (put off)
defer (yield to another)

demean (lower in dignity)
demean (humble oneself)

*****desert** (dry barren region)
desert (go away from)
desert (suitable reward or punishment)

die (stop living)
die (tool)

*****do** (act; perform)
do (first tone on the musical scale)

dock (wharf)
dock (cut some off)

*****does** (plural of *doe*)
does (present tense of *to do*)

*****dove** (pigeon)
dove (did dive)

down (from a higher to a lower place)
down (soft feathers)
down (grassy land)

dredge (dig up)
dredge (sprinkle with flour or sugar)

dresser (one who dresses)
dresser (bureau)

drove (did drive)
drove (flock; herd; crowd)

dub (give a title)
dub (add voice or music to a film)

duck (large wild bird)
duck (lower suddenly)
duck (type of cotton cloth)

ear (organ of hearing)
ear (part of certain plants)

egg (oval or round body laid by a bird)
egg (encourage)

elder (older)
elder (small tree)

*****entrance** (going in)
entrance (delight; charm)

*****excise** (tax)
excise (remove)

fair (beautiful; lovely)
fair (just; honest)
fair (showing of farm goods)
fair (bazaar)

fan (device to stir up the air)
fan (admirer)

fast (speedy)
fast (go without food)

fawn (young deer)
fawn (try to get favor by slavish acts)

fell (did fall)
fell (cut down a tree)
fell (deadly)

felt (did feel)
felt (type of cloth)

file (drawer; folder)
file (steel tool to smooth material)
file (material)

fine (high quality)
fine (money paid as punishment)

firm (solid; hard)
firm (business; company)

fit (suitable)
fit (sudden attack)

flag (banner)
flag (get tired)

The Reading Teacher's Book of Lists, Third Edition, © 1993 by Prentice Hall

flat (smooth)
flat (apartment)

fleet (group of ships)
fleet (rapid)

flight (act of flying)
flight (act of fleeing)

flounder (struggle)
flounder (kind of fish)

fluke (lucky stroke in games)
fluke (kind of fish)

fly (insect)
fly (move through the air with wings)

foil (prevent carrying out plans)
foil (metal sheet)
foil (long narrow sword)

fold (bend over on itself)
fold (pen for sheep)

forearm (part of the body)
forearm (prepare for trouble ahead)

forge (blacksmith shop)
forge (move ahead)

*****forte** (strong point)
forte (loud)

found (did find)
found (set up; establish)

founder (sink)
founder (one who establishes)

frank (hotdog)
frank (bold talk)
Frank (man's name)

fray (become ragged)
fray (fight)

fresh (newly made; not stale)
fresh (impudent; bold)

fret (worry)
fret (ridges on a guitar)

fry (cook in shallow pan)
fry (young fish)

fuse (slow-burning wick)
fuse (melt together)

gall (bile)
gall (annoy)

game (pastime)
game (lame)

gauntlet (challenge)
gauntlet (protective glove)

gin (alcoholic beverage)
gin (apparatus for separating seeds from cotton)
gin (card game)

gore (blood)
gore (wound from a horn)
gore (three-sided insert of cloth)

grate (framework for burning fuel in a fireplace)
grate (have an annoying effect)

grave (place of burial)
grave (important; serious)
grave (carve)

graze (feed on grass)
graze (touch lightly in passing)

ground (soil)
ground (did grind)

grouse (game bird)
grouse (grumble; complain)

gull (water bird)
gull (cheat; deceive)

gum (sticky substance from certain trees)
gum (tissue around teeth)

guy (rope; chain)
guy (fellow)

hack (cut roughly)
hack (carriage or car for hire)

hail (pieces of ice that fall like rain)
hail (shout of welcome)

hamper (hold back)
hamper (large container or basket)

hatch (bring forth young from an egg)
hatch (opening in a ship's deck)

hawk (bird of prey)
hawk (peddle goods)

haze (mist; smoke)
haze (bully)

heel (back of the foot)
heel (tip over to one side)

hide (conceal; keep out of sight)
hide (animal skin)

hinder (stop)
hinder (rear)

hold (grasp and keep)
hold (part of ship or plane for cargo)

husky (big and strong)
husky (sled dog)

*****impress** (have a strong effect on)
impress (take by force)

*****incense** (substance with a sweet smell when burned)
incense (make very angry)

*****intern** (force to stay)
intern (doctor in training at a hospital)

*****intimate** (very familiar)
intimate (suggest)

*****invalid** (disabled person)
invalid (not valid)

jam (fruit preserve)
jam (press or squeeze)

jar (container of glass)
jar (rattle; vibrate)

jerky (with sudden starts and stops)
jerky (strips of dried meat)

jet (stream of water, steam, or air)
jet (hard black coal)
jet (type of airplane)

jig (dance)
jig (fishing lure)

*****job** (work)
Job (Biblical man of patience)

jumper (person or thing that jumps)
jumper (type of dress)

junk (trash)
junk (Chinese sailing ship)

key (instrument for locking and unlocking)
key (low island)

kind (friendly; helpful)
kind (same class)

lap (body part formed when sitting)
lap (drink)
lap (one course traveled)

lark (small songbird)
lark (good fun)

lash (cord part of a whip)
lash (tie or fasten)

last (at the end)
last (continue; endure)

launch (start out)
launch (type of boat)

*****lead** (show the way)
lead (metallic element)

league (measure of distance)
league (group of persons or nations)

lean (stand slanting)
lean (not fat)

leave (go away)
leave (permission)

left (direction)
left (did leave)

lie (falsehood)
lie (place oneself in a flat position; rest)

light (not heavy)
light (not dark)
light (land on)

like (similar to)
like (be pleased with)

lime (citrus fruit)
lime (chemical substance)

limp (lame walk)
limp (not stiff)

line (piece of cord)
line (place paper or fabric inside)

list (series of words)
list (tilt to one side)

The Reading Teacher's Book of Lists, Third Edition, © 1993 by Prentice Hall

*live (exist)
live (having life)

loaf (be idle)
loaf (shaped as bread)

lock (fasten door)
lock (curl of hair)

long (great measure)
long (wish for)

loom (frame for weaving)
loom (threaten)

low (not high)
low (cattle sound)

lumber (timber)
lumber (move along heavily)

mace (club; weapon)
mace (spice)

mail (letters)
mail (flexible metal armor)

maroon (brownish red color)
maroon (leave helpless)

mat (woven floor covering)
mat (border for picture)

match (stick used to light fires)
match (equal)

meal (food served at a certain time)
meal (ground grain)

mean (signify; intend)
mean (unkind)
mean (average)

meter (unit of length)
meter (poetic rhythm)
meter (device that measures flow)

might (past of *may*)
might (power)

mine (belonging to me)
mine (hole in the earth to get ores)

*minute (sixty seconds)
minute (very small)

miss (fail to hit)
miss (unmarried woman or girl)

mold (form; shape)
mold (fungus)

mole (brown spot on the skin)
mole (small underground animal)

mortar (cement mixture)
mortar (short cannon)

mount (high hill)
mount (go up)

mule (cross between donkey and horse)
mule (type of slipper)

mum (silent)
mum (chrysanthemum)

nag (scold)
nag (old horse)

nap (short sleep)
nap (rug fuzz)

net (open-weave fabric)
net (remaining after deductions)

nip (small drink)
nip (pinch)

*object (a thing)
object (to protest)

pad (cushion)
pad (walk softly)

page (one side of a sheet of paper)
page (youth who runs errands)

palm (inside of hand)
palm (kind of tree)

patent (right or privilege)
patent (type of leather)

patter (rapid taps)
patter (light, easy walk)

pawn (leave as security for loan)
pawn (chess piece)

*peaked (having a point)
peaked (looking ill)

peck (dry measure)
peck (strike at)

pen (instrument for writing)
pen (enclosed yard)

pile (heap or stack)
pile (nap on fabrics)

pine (type of evergreen)
pine (yearn or long for)

pitch (throw)
pitch (tar)

pitcher (container for pouring liquid)
pitcher (baseball player)

poach (trespass)
poach (cook an egg)

poker (card game)
poker (rod for stirring a fire)

pole (long piece of wood)
pole (either end of the earth's axis)

policy (plan of action)
policy (written agreement)

pool (tank with water)
pool (game played with balls on a table)

pop (short, quick sound)
pop (dad)
pop (popular)

post (support)
post (job or position)
post (system for mail delivery)

pound (unit of weight)
pound (hit hard again and again)
pound (pen)

present (not absent)
present (gift)

press (squeeze)
press (force into service)

prime (chief)
prime (prepare)

*__primer__ (first book)
primer (something used to prepare another)

prune (fruit)
prune (cut; trim)

pry (look with curiosity)
pry (lift with force)

pump (type of shoe)
pump (machine that forces liquid out)

punch (hit)
punch (beverage)

pupil (student)
pupil (part of the eye)

quack (sound of a duck)
quack (phony doctor)

racket (noise)
racket (paddle used in tennis)

rail (bar of wood or metal)
rail (complain bitterly)

rank (row or line)
rank (having a bad odor)

rare (unusual)
rare (not cooked much)

rash (hasty)
rash (small red spots on the skin)

rear (the back part)
rear (bring up)

ream (500 sheets of paper)
ream (clean a hole)

*__record__ (music disk)
record (write down)

recount (count again)
recount (tell in detail)

reel (spool for winding)
reel (sway under a blow)
reel (lively dance)

refrain (hold back)
refrain (part repeated)

*__refuse__ (say no)
refuse (waste; trash)

rest (sleep)
rest (what is left)

rifle (gun with a long barrel)
rifle (ransack; search through)

ring (circle)
ring (bell sound)

The Reading Teacher's Book of Lists, Third Edition, © 1993 by Prentice Hall

The Reading Teacher's Book of Lists, Third Edition, © 1993 by Prentice Hall

root (underground part of a plant)
root (cheer for someone)

*****row** (line)
row (use oars to move a boat)
row (noisy fight)

sage (wise person)
sage (herb)

sap (liquid in a plant)
sap (weaken)

sash (cloth worn around the waist)
sash (frame of a window)

saw (did see)
saw (tool for cutting)
saw (wise saying)

scale (balance)
scale (outer layer of fish and snakes)
scale (series of steps)

school (place for learning)
school (group of fish)

scour (clean)
scour (move quickly over)

scrap (small bits)
scrap (quarrel)

seal (mark of ownership)
seal (sea mammal)

second (after the first)
second (one-sixtieth of a minute)

*****sewer** (one who sews)
sewer (underground pipe for wastes)

shark (large meat-eating fish)
shark (dishonest person)

shed (small shelter)
shed (get rid of)

shingles (roofing materials)
shingles (viral disease)

shock (sudden violent disturbance)
shock (thick bushy mass)

shore (land near water's edge)
shore (support)

shot (fired a gun)
shot (worn out)

size (amount)
size (preparation of glue)

*****slaver** (dealer in slaves)
slaver (salivate)

sledge (heavy sled)
sledge (large hammer)

slip (go easily)
slip (small strip of paper)

*****slough** (swamp)
slough (shed old skin)

slug (small slow-moving animal)
slug (hit hard)

smack (slight taste)
smack (open lips quickly)
smack (small boat)

snare (trap)
snare (strings on bottom of a drum)

snarl (growl)
snarl (tangle)

sock (covering for foot)
sock (hit hard)

soil (ground; dirt)
soil (make dirty)

sole (type of fish)
sole (only)

*****sow** (scatter seeds)
sow (female pig)

spar (mast of a ship)
spar (argue)
spar (mineral)

spell (say the letters of a word)
spell (magic influence)
spell (period of work)

spray (sprinkle liquid)
spray (small branch with leaves and flowers)

spruce (type of evergreen)
spruce (neat or trim)

squash (press flat)
squash (vegetable)

stable (building for horses)
stable (unchanging)

stake (stick or post)
stake (risk or prize)

stalk (main stem of a plant)
stalk (follow secretly)

stall (place in a stable for one animal)
stall (delay)

staple (metal fastener for paper)
staple (principal element)

stay (remain)
stay (support)

steep (having a sharp slope)
steep (soak)

steer (guide)
steer (young male cattle)

stem (part of a plant)
stem (stop; dam up)

stern (rear part of a ship)
stern (harsh; strict)

stick (thin piece of wood)
stick (pierce)

still (not moving)
still (apparatus for making alcohol)

stoop (bend down)
stoop (porch)

story (account of a happening)
story (floor of a building)

strain (pull tight)
strain (group with an inherited quality)

strand (leave helpless)
strand (thread or string)

strip (narrow piece of cloth)
strip (remove)

stroke (hit)
stroke (pet; soothe)

stunt (stop growth)
stunt (bold action)

sty (pen for pigs)
sty (swelling on eyelid)

swallow (take in)
swallow (small bird)

tap (strike lightly)
tap (faucet)

*__tarry__ (delay)
tarry (covered with tar)

tart (sour but agreeable)
tart (small fruit-filled pie)

*__tear__ (drop of liquid from the eye)
tear (pull apart)

temple (building for worship)
temple (side of forehead)

tend (incline to)
tend (take care of)

tender (not tough)
tender (offer)
tender (one who cares for)

tick (sound of a clock)
tick (small insect)
tick (pillow covering)

till (until)
till (plow the land)
till (drawer for money)

tip (end point)
tip (slant)
tip (present of money for services)

tire (become weary)
tire (rubber around a wheel)

toast (browned bread slices)
toast (wish for good luck)

toll (sound of a bell)
toll (fee paid for a privilege)

top (highest point)
top (toy that spins)

troll (ugly dwarf)
troll (method of fishing)

The Reading Teacher's Book of Lists, Third Edition, © 1993 by Prentice Hall

unaffected (not influenced)
unaffected (innocent)

vault (storehouse for valuables)
vault (jump over)

wake (stop sleeping)
wake (trail left behind a ship)

wax (substance made by bees)
wax (grow bigger)

well (satisfactory)
well (hole dug for water)

whale (large sea mammal)
whale (whip)

will (statement of desire for distribution of
　　property after one's death)
will (is going to)
will (deliberate intention or wish)

*__wind__ (air in motion)
wind (turn)

*__wound__ (hurt)
wound (wrapped around)

yak (long-haired ox)
yak (talk endlessly)

yard (enclosed space around a house)
yard (thirty-six inches)

yen (strong desire)
yen (unit of money in Japan)

See Also List 1, Homophones, and List 3, Near Misses.

3. *Near Misses*

Near Misses are words that sound similar or have other confusing characteristics. They have different meanings, and their misuse can cause embarrassing errors.

accede (v.)—to comply with
exceed (v.)—to surpass
accent (n.)—stress in speech or writing
ascent (n.)—act of going up
assent (v., n.)—consent
accept (v.)—to agree or take what is offered
except (prep.)—leaving out or excluding
access (n.)—admittance
excess (n., adj.)—surplus
adapt (v.)—to adjust
adept (adj.)—proficient
adopt (v.)—to take by choice
adverse (adj.)—opposing
averse (adj.)—disinclined
affect (v.)—to influence
affect (n.)—feeling
effect (n.)—result of a cause
effect (v.)—to make happen
alley (n.)—narrow street
ally (n.)—supporter
allusion (n.)—indirect reference
delusion (n.)—mistaken belief
illusion (n.)—mistaken vision
all ready (adj.)—completely ready
already (adv.)—even now or by this time
all together (pron. and adj.)—everything or everyone in one place
altogether (adv.)—entirely
anecdote (n.)—short amusing story
antidote (n.)—something to counter the effect of poison
angel (n.)—heavenly body
angle (n.)—space between two lines that meet in a point
annul (v.)—to make void
annual (adj.)—yearly
ante—prefix meaning before
anti—prefix meaning against
any way (adj. and n.)—in whatever manner
anyway (adv.)—regardless
appraise (v.)—to set a value on
apprise (v.)—to inform

area (n.)—surface
aria (n.)—melody
biannual (adj.)—occurring twice per year
biennial (adj.)—occurring every other year
bibliography (n.)—list of writings on a particular topic
biography (n.)—written history of a person's life
bizarre (adj.)—odd
bazaar (n.)—market, fair
breadth (n.)—width
breath (n.)—respiration
breathe (v.)—to inhale and exhale
calendar (n.)—a chart of days and months
colander (n.)—a strainer
casual (adj.)—informal
causal (adj.)—relating to cause
cease (v.)— to stop
seize (v.)—to grasp
click (n.)—short, sharp sound
clique (n.)—small exclusive subgroup
collision (n.)—a clashing
collusion (n.)—a scheme to cheat
coma (n.)—an unconscious state
comma (n.)—a punctuation mark
command (n.,v.)—an order, to order
commend (v.)—to praise, to entrust
comprehensible (adj.)—understandable
comprehensive (adj.)—extensive
confidant (n.)—friend or advisor
confident (adj.)—sure
confidentially (adv.)—privately
confidently (adv.)—certainly
conscience (n.)—sense of right and wrong
conscious (adj.)—aware
contagious (adj.)—spread by contact
contiguous (adj.)—touching or nearby
continual (adj.)—repeated, happening again and again
continuous (adj.)—uninterrupted, without stopping

The Reading Teacher's Book of Lists, Third Edition, © 1993 by Prentice Hall

The Reading Teacher's Book of Lists, Third Edition, © 1993 by Prentice Hall

cooperation (n.)—the art of working together

corporation (n.)—a business organization

costume (n.)—special way of dressing

custom (n.)—usual practice of habit

credible (adj.)—believable

creditable (adj.)—deserving praise

deceased (adj.)—dead

diseased (adj.)—ill

decent (adj.)—proper

descent (n.)—way down

dissent (n., v.)—disagreement, to disagree

deference (n.)—respect

difference (n.)—dissimilarity

deposition (n.)—a formal written statement

disposition (n.)—temperament

depraved (adj.)—morally corrupt

deprived (adj.)—taken away from

deprecate (v.)—to disapprove

depreciate (v.)—to lessen in value

desert (n.)—arid land

desert (v.)—to abandon

dessert (n.)—course served at the end of a meal

desolate (adj.)—lonely, sad

dissolute (adj.)—loose in morals

detract (v.)—to take away from

distract (v.)—to divert attention away from

device (n.)—a contrivance

devise (v.)—to plan

disapprove (v.)—to withhold approval

disprove (v.)—to prove something to be false

disassemble (v.)—to take something apart

dissemble (v.)—to disguise

disburse (v.)—to pay out

disperse (v.)—to scatter

discomfort (n.)—distress

discomfit (v.)—to frustrate or embarrass

disinterested (adj.)—impartial

uninterested (adj.)—not interested

elapse (v.)—to pass

lapse (v.)—to become void

relapse (v.)—to fall back to previous condition

elicit (v.)—to draw out

illicit (adj.)—unlawful

elusive (adj.)—hard to catch

illusive (adj.)—misleading

eminent (adj.)—well known

imminent (adj.)—impending

emerge (v.)—rise out of

immerge (v.)—plunge into

emigrate (v.)—to leave a country and take up residence elsewhere

immigrate (v.)—to enter a country for the purpose of taking up residence

envelop (v.)—to surround

envelope (n.)—a wrapper for a letter

erasable (adj.)—capable of being erased

irascible (adj.)—easily provoked to anger

expand (v.)—to increase in size

expend (v.)—to spend

expect (v.)—to suppose; to look forward

suspect (v.)—to mistrust

extant (adj.)—still existing

extent (n.)—amount

facility (n.)—ease

felicity (n.)—happiness

farther (adj.)—more distant (refers to space)

further (adj.)—extending beyond a point (refers to time, quantity, or degree)

finale (n.)—the end

finally (adv.)—at the end

finely (adv.)—in a fine manner

fiscal (adj.)—relating to finance

physical (adj.)—relating to the body

formally (adv.)—with rigid ceremony

formerly (adv.)—previously

human (adj.)—relating to mankind

humane (adv.)—kind

hypercritical (adj.)—very critical

hypocritical (adj.)—pretending to be virtuous

imitate (v.)—to mimic

intimate (v.)—to hint or make known; familiar, close

incredible (adj.)—too extraordinary to be believed

incredulous (adj.)—unbelieving, skeptical

indigenous (adj.)—native
indigent (adj.)—needy
indignant (adj.)—angry
infer (v.)—to arrive at by reason
imply (v.)—to suggest meaning indirectly
ingenious (adj.)—clever
ingenuous (adj.)—straightforward
later (adj.)—more late
latter (adj.)—second in a series of two
lay (v.)—to set something down or place something
lie (v.)—to recline
least (adj.)—at the minimum
lest (conj.)—for fear that
lend (v.)—to give for a time
loan (n.)—received to use for a time
loose (adj.)—not tight
lose (v.)—not win; misplace
magnet (n.)—iron bar with power to attract iron
magnate (n.)—person in prominent position in large industry
message (n.)—communication
massage (v.)—rub body
moral (n.,adj.)—lesson; ethic
morale (n.)—mental condition
morality (n.)—virtue
mortality (n.)—the state of being mortal; death rate
of (prep.)—having to do with; indicating possession
off (adv.)—not on
official (adj.)—authorized
officious (adj.)—offering services where they are neither wanted nor needed
oral (adj.)—verbal
aural (adj.)—listening
pasture (n.)—grass field
pastor (n.)—minister
perfect (adj.)—without fault
prefect (n.)—an official
perpetrate (v.)—to be guilty of; to commit
perpetuate (v.)—to make perpetual

perquisite (n.)—a privilege or profit in addition to salary
prerequisite (n.)—a preliminary requirement
persecute (v.)—to harass, annoy, or injure
prosecute (v.)—to press for punishment of crime
personal (adj.)—private
personnel (n.)—a body of people, usually employed in some organization
peruse (v.)—to read
pursue (v.)—to follow in order to overtake
picture (n.)—drawing or photograph
pitcher (n.)—container for liquid; baseball player
precede (v.)—to go before
proceed (v.)—to advance
preposition (n.)—a part of speech
proposition (n.)—a proposal or suggestion
pretend (v.)—to make believe
portend (v.)—to give a sign of something that will happen
quiet (adj.)—not noisy
quit (v.)—to stop
quite (adv.)—very
recent (adj.)—not long ago
resent (v.)—to feel indignant
respectably (adv.)—in a respectable manner
respectively (adv.)—in order indicated
respectfully (adv.)—in a respectful manner
restless (adj.)—constantly moving, uneasy
restive (adj.)—contrary, resisting control
suppose (v.)—assume or imagine
supposed (adj.)—expected
than (conj.)—used in comparison
then (adv.)—at that time; next in order of time
through (prep.)—by means of; from beginning to end
thorough (adj.)—complete
use (v.)—employ something
used (adj.)—secondhand
veracious (adj.)—truthful
voracious (adj.)—greedy

See also List 1, Homophones; and List 2, Homographs and Heteronyms.

The Reading Teacher's Book of Lists, Third Edition, © 1993 by Prentice Hall

4. *Instant Words*

These are the most common words in English, ranked in frequency order. The first 25 make up about a third of all printed material. The first 100 make up about half of all written material, and the first 300 make up about 65 percent of all written material. Is it any wonder that all students must learn to recognize these words instantly and to spell them correctly also?

THE INSTANT WORDS* FIRST HUNDRED

The Reading Teacher's Book of Lists, Third Edition, © 1993 by Prentice Hall

WORDS 1–25	WORDS 26–50	WORDS 51–75	WORDS 76–100
the	or	will	number
of	one	up	no
and	had	other	way
a	by	about	could
to	word	out	people
in	but	many	my
is	not	then	than
you	what	them	first
that	all	these	water
it	were	so	been
he	we	some	call
was	when	her	who
for	your	would	oil
on	can	make	its
are	said	like	now
as	there	him	find
with	use	into	long
his	an	time	down
they	each	has	day
I	which	look	did
at	she	two	get
be	do	more	come
this	how	write	made
have	their	go	may
from	if	see	part

Common suffixes: *-s, -ing, -ed, -er, -ly, -est*

---

*For additional instant words, see *Spelling Book* by Edward Fry, Laguna Beach Educational Books, 245 Grandview, Laguna Beach, CA 92651.

SECOND HUNDRED

WORDS 101–125	WORDS 126–150	WORDS 151–175	WORDS 176–200
over	say	set	try
new	great	put	kind
sound	where	end	hand
take	help	does	picture
only	through	another	again
little	much	well	change
work	before	large	off
know	line	must	play
place	right	big	spell
year	too	even	air
live	mean	such	away
me	old	because	animal
back	any	turn	house
give	same	here	point
most	tell	why	page
very	boy	ask	letter
after	follow	went	mother
thing	came	men	answer
our	want	read	found
just	show	need	study
name	also	land	still
good	around	different	learn
sentence	form	home	should
man	three	us	America
think	small	move	world

Common suffixes: *-s, -ing, -ed, -er, -ly, -est*

The Reading Teacher's Book of Lists, Third Edition, © 1993 by Prentice Hall

THIRD HUNDRED

WORDS 201–225	WORDS 226–250	WORDS 251–275	WORDS 276–300
high	saw	important	miss
every	left	until	idea
near	don't	children	enough
add	few	side	eat
food	while	feet	face
between	along	car	watch
own	might	mile	far
below	close	night	Indian
country	something	walk	really
plant	seem	white	almost
last	next	sea	let
school	hard	began	above
father	open	grow	girl
keep	example	took	sometimes
tree	begin	river	mountain
never	life	four	cut
start	always	carry	young
city	those	state	talk
earth	both	once	soon
eye	paper	book	list
light	together	hear	song
thought	got	stop	being
head	group	without	leave
under	often	second	family
story	run	later	it's

Common suffixes: *-s, -ing, -ed, -er, -ly, -est*

The Reading Teacher's Book of Lists, Third Edition, © 1993 by Prentice Hall

FOURTH HUNDRED

WORDS 301–325	WORDS 326–350	WORDS 351–375	WORDS 376–400
body	order	listen	farm
music	red	wind	pulled
color	door	rock	draw
stand	sure	space	voice
sun	become	covered	seen
questions	top	fast	cold
fish	ship	several	cried
area	across	hold	plan
mark	today	himself	notice
dog	during	toward	south
horse	short	five	sing
birds	better	step	war
problem	best	morning	ground
complete	however	passed	fall
room	low	vowel	king
knew	hours	true	town
since	black	hundred	I'll
ever	products	against	unit
piece	happened	pattern	figure
told	whole	numeral	certain
usually	measure	table	field
didn't	remember	north	travel
friends	early	slowly	wood
easy	waves	money	fire
heard	reached	map	upon

FIFTH HUNDRED

WORDS 401–425	WORDS 426–450	WORDS 451–475	WORDS 476–500
done	decided	plane	filled
English	contain	system	heat
road	course	behind	full
halt	surface	ran	hot
ten	produce	round	check
fly	building	boat	object
gave	ocean	game	am
box	class	force	rule
finally	note	brought	among
wait	nothing	understand	noun
correct	rest	warm	power
oh	carefully	common	cannot
quickly	scientists	bring	able
person	inside	explain	six
became	wheels	dry	size
shown	stay	though	dark
minutes	green	language	ball
strong	known	shape	material
verb	island	deep	special
stars	week	thousands	heavy
front	less	yes	fine
feel	machine	clear	pair
fact	base	equation	circle
inches	ago	yet	include
street	stood	government	built

The Reading Teacher's Book of Lists, Third Edition, © 1993 by Prentice Hall

SIXTH HUNDRED

WORDS 501–525	WORDS 526–550	WORDS 551–575	WORDS 576–600
can't	picked	legs	beside
matter	simple	sat	gone
square	cells	main	sky
syllables	paint	winter	glass
perhaps	mind	wide	million
bill	love	written	west
felt	cause	length	lay
suddenly	rain	reason	weather
test	exercise	kept	root
direction	eggs	interest	instruments
center	train	arms	meet
farmers	blue	brother	third
ready	wish	race	months
anything	drop	present	paragraph
divided	developed	beautiful	raised
general	window	store	represent
energy	difference	job	soft
subject	distance	edge	whether
Europe	heart	past	clothes
moon	sit	sign	flowers
region	sum	record	shall
return	summer	finished	teacher
believe	wall	discovered	held
dance	forest	wild	describe
members	probably	happy	drive

SEVENTH HUNDRED

WORDS 601–625	WORDS 626–650	WORDS 651–675	WORDS 676–700
cross	already	hair	rolled
speak	instead	age	bear
solve	phrase	amount	wonder
appear	soil	scale	smiled
metal	bed	pounds	angle
son	copy	although	fraction
either	free	per	Africa
ice	hope	broken	killed
sleep	spring	moment	melody
village	case	tiny	bottom
factors	laughed	possible	trip
result	nation	gold	hole
jumped	quite	milk	poor
snow	type	quiet	let's
ride	themselves	natural	fight
care	temperature	lot	surprise
floor	bright	stone	French
hill	lead	act	died
pushed	everyone	build	beat
baby	method	middle	exactly
buy	section	speed	remain
century	lake	count	dress
outside	consonant	cat	iron
everything	within	someone	couldn't
tall	dictionary	sail	fingers

The Reading Teacher's Book of Lists, Third Edition, © 1993 by Prentice Hall

EIGHTH HUNDRED

WORDS 701–725	**WORDS 726–750**	**WORDS 751–775**	**WORDS 776–800**
row	president	yourself	caught
least	brown	control	fell
catch	trouble	practice	team
climbed	cool	report	God
wrote	cloud	straight	captain
shouted	lost	rise	direct
continued	sent	statement	ring
itself	symbols	stick	serve
else	wear	party	child
plains	bad	seeds	desert
gas	save	suppose	increase
England	experiment	woman	history
burning	engine	coast	cost
design	alone	bank	maybe
joined	drawing	period	business
foot	east	wire	separate
law	pay	choose	break
ears	single	clean	uncle
grass	touch	visit	hunting
you're	information	bit	flow
grew	express	whose	lady
skin	mouth	received	students
valley	yard	garden	human
cents	equal	please	art
key	decimal	strange	feeling

NINTH HUNDRED

WORDS 801–825	**WORDS 826–850**	**WORDS 851–875**	**WORDS 876–900**
supply	guess	thick	major
corner	silent	blood	observe
electric	trade	lie	tube
insects	rather	spot	necessary
crops	compare	bell	weight
tone	crowd	fun	meat
hit	poem	loud	lifted
sand	enjoy	consider	process
doctor	elements	suggested	army
provide	indicate	thin	hat
thus	except	position	property
won't	expect	entered	particular
cook	flat	fruit	swim
bones	seven	tied	terms
tail	interesting	rich	current
board	sense	dollars	park
modern	string	send	sell
compound	blow	sight	shoulder
mine	famous	chief	industry
wasn't	value	Japanese	wash
fit	wings	stream	block
addition	movement	planets	spread
belong	pole	rhythm	cattle
safe	exciting	eight	wife
soldiers	branches	science	sharp

The Reading Teacher's Book of Lists, Third Edition, © 1993 by Prentice Hall

TENTH HUNDRED

WORDS 901–925	WORDS 926–950	WORDS 951–975	WORDS 976–1000
company	sister	gun	total
radio	oxygen	similar	deal
we'll	plural	death	determine
action	various	score	evening
capital	agreed	forward	nor
factories	opposite	stretched	rope
settled	wrong	experience	cotton
yellow	chart	rose	apple
isn't	prepared	allow	details
southern	pretty	fear	entire
truck	solution	workers	corn
fair	fresh	Washington	substances
printed	shop	Greek	smell
wouldn't	suffix	women	tools
ahead	especially	bought	conditions
chance	shoes	led	cows
born	actually	march	track
level	nose	northern	arrived
triangle	afraid	create	located
molecules	dead	British	sir
France	sugar	difficult	seat
repeated	adjective	match	division
column	fig	win	effect
western	office	doesn't	underline
church	huge	steel	view

See also List 6, Work Words; List 7, Daily Living Words; List 8, Highway Travel Words; and List 5, Picture Words.

5. Picture Words

Combined with the first hundred Instant Words these picture words make a powerful beginning reading and writing vocabulary.

1. **People**
   boy
   girl
   man
   woman
   baby

2. **Toys**
   ball
   doll
   train
   game
   skateboard

3. **Numbers**
   one
   two
   three
   four
   five

4. **Clothing**
   shirt
   pants
   dress
   shoes
   hat

5. **Pets**
   cat
   dog
   rabbit
   bird
   fish

6. **Furniture**
   table
   chair
   sofa
   chest
   desk

7. **Eating Objects**
   cup
   plate
   bowl
   fork
   spoon

8. **Transportation**
   bicycle
   truck
   bus
   plane
   boat

9. **Buildings**
   store
   school
   house
   building
   garage

10. **School Workers**
    teacher
    bus driver
    secretary
    principal
    custodian

11. **Zoo Animals**
    elephant
    giraffe
    bear
    lion
    monkey

12. **School Items**
    marker
    scissors
    paste
    ruler
    chalkboard

13. **Plants**
    bush
    flower
    grass
    tomatoes
    tree

14. **Sky Things**
    sun
    moon
    star
    cloud
    rain

15. **Earth Things**
    water
    rock
    dirt
    field
    hill

16. **Farm Animals**
    horse
    cow
    pig
    chicken
    duck

17. **Workers**
    farmer
    police officer
    cook
    doctor
    nurse

18. **Entertainment**
    television
    radio
    movie
    ball game
    band

19. **Writing Tools**
    pen
    pencil
    crayon
    typewriter
    computer

20. **Reading Things**
    book
    newspaper
    magazine
    sign
    letter

See also List 4, Instant Words.

The Reading Teacher's Book of Lists, Third Edition, © 1993 by Prentice Hall

6. Work Words

These meaningful words and phrases help adults and adolescents improve their reading and writing skills so they can obtain better employment.

DANGER WORDS I

Acid
Caution
Combustible
Danger
High Voltage
Keep Out
Live Power Supply
Radioactive
Explosives
Do Not Close
Do Not Drink
Do Not Place Near Heat
Electrical Outlet
Extend Hose Completely
    Before Opening Valves
Flammable
For Fire Use Only
Fuel
Gas
Harmful if Swallowed
No Admittance
No Trespassing
Oxygen
Poison
Private Property
Stop
Walk
Warning

DANGER WORDS II

Alarm
Arrested
Aspirin
Break Glass
Close Door
Danger Below This Line
Do Not Use
Down
Emergency Exit Only
Fire Escape
Fire Hose
For Burns
Hot

No Smoking
Not for Electrical Fire
One Way
Open Door Out
Pedestrians
Proceed at Your Own Risk
Railroad (R.R.)
Smoking Prohibited
Swim at Your Own Risk
This Way Out

DANGER WORDS III

Blasting
Keep Away
Danger—Slow
Do Not Clean or Oil
    Machinery While in
    Motion
Do Not Close Switch
Do Not Get off While in
    Motion
Do Not Open Valve
Do Not Operate Without
    Guards
Do Not Stand Up
Do Not Use This Machine
Do Not Wear Loose
    Clothing or Gloves
    Around Machines
Don't Stand Above This
    Line
Equipment Must Not Be
    Taken Within 10' of
    Electric Lines
Fire Exit Only
Break Glass
Open Door
Keep Fingers out of Meat
    Grinder-Use Tamper
Keep Your Hands and Arms
    Within Sides of Car
Only Regular Machine
    Operator Allowed to
    Use Machine

Open Truck
Report Dangerous
    Conditions at Once
Stairway
Stay Clear of Moving Cars
Stop—Blow Horn
Proceed with Caution
This Is an Empty Elevator
    Shaftway
Truck Crossing
Watch Out for Persons
    Below
Your Eyes Are Priceless—
    Wear Proper Protection

ROAD SIGNS I

Children Crossing
Divided Highway Ends
Do Not Drive
Do Not Enter
Do Not Pass
Driveway Ahead
Keep Right
Left Lane Must Turn Left
Low Clearance 10 Feet
Low Shoulder
Merging Traffic
Minimum Speed
No Left Turn
Pass with Care
Railroad Crossing
Safe Speed 15 mph
School Crossing
School Zone
Shoulder Work Ahead
Slippery When Wet
Slow Ahead
Slow Traffic
Keep Right
Soft Shoulder
Two-Way Traffic Ahead
Yield

ROAD SIGNS II

Bridge May Be Slippery
Dead End
Detour Ahead
End Construction
End One Way
Express Lane
Highway Ends
Narrow Bridge
No Thoroughfare
No Trucks
No Turns
Pavement Ends
Ramp
Roadside Table
Route
Signal Ahead
Signal Set for 35 mph
Speed Zone Ahead
Speed Limit 50 mph
Through Traffic Keep Right
Traffic Ahead
Truck Crossing
Trucks Use Right Lane
Turnpike Use Next Exit

SIGNS I

Alcohol
Burns
Do Not Close
Do Not Smoke
Drinking Water
Enter
Falling Rock
First Aid
Gentlemen
Glass
Information
Keep Refrigerated
Key
Ladies
Men
Not Allowed
Not Permitted
Out of Order
Perishable
Reset Safety Switch

Shut Off Valve
Turn Bottom Up
Walk on Left Facing Traffic
Water
Women

SIGNS II

Bus
Cab
Do Not Bend
East (E.)
Elevator
Follow Signs
Fragile
Handle with Care
Keep Door Closed
Keep Flat
Lay Flat
Men Working
No Exchange
North (N.)
Passengers
Pull
Push
South (S.)
This End Up
This Side Up
Turn Off Engine
Use No Hooks
Watch for Signal
Watch Your Step
West (W.)

SIGNS III

All the Way Down
Apply Pressure
Automatic
Call
Cleaners
Cold
Cool
Delivery
Deposit a Quarter and Dime
   or Two Nickels
Deposit 10¢ in Coin
Dimes Only
Entrance Gate

Fold Back
Hospital Zone
Inch
Insert Coins
No Storage
Operator
Per Couple
Press Button
Self-Service
Straight Ahead
Use Other Door
Wash
Warm

SIGNS IV

Bath
Check Your Valuables
Cook
Customer Must Present
   Identification
Fifth Floor
Fold on Dotted Line
Free
Inside Front Cover
Lights
Lock Door
Main Door
Lobby
Next Counter
Next Exit
Notice
Not Responsible
Damaged Merchandise
Please Do Not Touch
Public Parking
Refrigerator
Reset Cycle
Take Your Seat
Tear at Perforations
Tickets
Toll
Use Key

SIGNS V

Bakery
Beauty Shop
Breakfast Being Served

The Reading Teacher's Book of Lists, Third Edition, © 1993 by Prentice Hall

Cafeteria
Cleaners
Closet
Dance
Delicatessen
Dentist
Discount Drugs
Garage
Hardware
Laundry
M.D.
Nurse
Pick Up
Purchase Price
Repair Service
Rinse
Sale
Tavern
Taxi
Telephone
Tobacco
Wash

WANT ADS I

Ability to Learn
Apply in Person
Available Immediately
Beginner
Call
Certificate
Department
Eligible
Employment
Evening (Eve.)
Inexperienced
License
Manager
Mature
Office (Off)
Over 21 Years of Age
Personnel
Phone
Post Office Box (P.O.)
Trainees

WANT ADS II

Assemblers
Assist

Attendant
Automotive Machine
Cook
Second Relief
Counterman
Driver
Factory (Facty)
Food Service Helper
Hospital
Janitor
Maid
Maintenance
Painters
Production Workers
Rotating Shift
Stock Man
Trucking
Warehouseman
Waitress

WANT ADS III

Blue Cross
Blue Shield
Bonus
Incentive Plan
Company Benefits
Compensation
Earn
Equal Opportunities
Fringe Benefits
Forty-Hour Week
Full Time
Life Insurance
Overtime
Paid Vacation
Part Time
Pension Plan
Per Hour
Positions
Sick Leave
Steady Income
Working Conditions

GROCERY AND DRUG I

Aspirin
Bayer
St. Joseph
Baby Food

Strained
Junior
Baking Powder
Bread
Butter
Cellophane
Cereal
Chocolate
Corn
Crackers
Dozen
Eggs
Flour
Gallons
Jello
Juice
Laxatives
Margarine
Net Weight
Noodles
Orange
Ounces (oz)
Pancake Mix
Peas
Pepper

GROCERY AND DRUG II

Pint
Potatoes
Pounds (lbs)
Quart (qt)
Rice
Salt
Sanitary Napkins
Sausage
Shortening
Soap
Soda
Soup
String Beans
Sugar
Tablespoon
Tablets
Teaspoon
Tincture of Iodine
Tincture of Mercury
Tissues
Turkey

Vanilla
Vegetable Oil
Vegetables
Vinegar

MENUS

Bean
Cheeseburger
Chicken Noodle
Grilled Cheese
Ham and Cheese
Hamburger
Hoagies
Meat Ball
Pork Roll
Steak
Tuna Fish
Vegetable
Beans
Chicken
Choice of Two Vegetables
Cole Slaw
Fish and Chips
French Fries
Mashed Potatoes
Peas
Pizza
Pork Chops
Roast Beef
Turkey
Coffee
Cola
Iced Tea
Milk
Milk Shake
Tea

JOB APPLICATIONS I

Address
Age
Birth
Children
City
Date
Employer
Female
Husband
Male

Miss
Mr.
Mrs.
Name (First, Last)
Print
Signature
Social Security
State
Wife
Year

JOB APPLICATIONS II

Answer All Questions
Applicant Sign Here
Citizen of U.S.A.
   (American?)
Employed
Employment
Former Employer
Home
Income
Last Year
List
Married
Do Not Use This Space
Number of Dependents
Relation
Salary
Separate
Single
Start
Write
Zip Code

JOB APPLICATIONS III

Work Experience
List in Order
Last Job
Former Employer
Employer's Address
Employed from–to—
Month—Year
Describe Type of Work
   Done
Seniority
Reason for Leaving
Education
School—Name and Location

Graduate
Kind of Job Applying for
Work Preference
First Choice
Second Choice
A.M.
P.M.
Part Time
Permanent
Salary Expected
Per Week

JOB APPLICATIONS IV

Are You Employed Now?
Maiden Name
Residence
Number of Children
Widow
Board
Own Home
Rent
Own Car
Telephone
Do You Have a Relative
   Working with the
   Company?
Relationship
In Case of Emergency
Bonded
Arrested
References
Number of Days Sick
Speech
Vision
Sex (Male–Female)
Height (Ht.)
Weight (Wt.)
Inches (In.)
Answer in Full All Items
Examination Announcement
Legal Residence
Voting Residence
Title of Examination
Lowest Rate You Will
   Accept
Temporary
Career
Christmas

The Reading Teacher's Book of Lists, Third Edition, © 1993 by Prentice Hall

INCOME TAX

If Filing Joint Return
First Names
Middle Initials
Spouse's
Check One
Married Filing Joint Return
Married Filing Separately
Enter Total Wages
Tips
Interest
Dividends
Total Income Tax from Tax
    Table
Total Federal Income Tax
    Withheld
Larger Than
Balance Due
Refund
Dependent's Support
Amount Furnished
If Filing 100% Write "All"
Sign Here
Both Must Sign
Initials—Middle
Interest
Joint Return
Larger Than
Married
Withholding Allowances
Attached Certificate
Deductions Allowed
Exemptions
Itemized Deductions

CREDIT TERMS

Badge
Bank Balance
Business Phone
Extension
Checking Account
Contract Expires
Draft Status
Driver's License
Excluding Overtime
Finance Company
Account
Furniture Value

Address of School
How Long
Insurance Coverage
Landlord
List Your Debts
Creditors
Live with My Parents
Loan Value
Mortgage Balance
Purchase Price
Registration Number
Take-Home Pay

HOSPITAL

Accident
Admissions
Aerosol
Ambulance
Cancel
Dispensary
Disposal Plastic Syringe
Drain
Glass Cans
Hospital
In Laboratory
Local
Manual
Nurse
Oxygen
Pick-up
Physician
Seamstress
Slop
Storeroom
Steam
Vinyl Plastic
Ward
Water Level
X-ray

AIRPORT

Aircraft Landing Zone
Air Express
Air Freight
Concourse
Direct Line
Do Not Use Grease or Oil
    Near Unit

Equipment Operators
Check Fuel and Engine Oil
    Before Placing Machine
    in Operation
Final Destination
Flight Leaves
Flight Number
Ground Transportation
If in Doubt Contact Your
    Supervisor
Keep Cart 4 Feet from
    Airplane
Keep Within Yellow Lines
Moving Aircraft Proceed
    with Caution
Never Use Oxygen as
    Compressed Air
No Carrying Lighted
    Materials Beyond This
    Point
This P.I.V. Controls
    Sprinklers
Warning! These are
    Instantaneous Switches—
    Do Not Hold Push Button

TRUCKING I

Bags
Barrels
Bill of Lading (B/L)
Bottles
Bundles
Cartons
Case (Cs)
Commodities Rate
Consigner
Consignor
Crate
Delivery Number
Destination
Dispatcher
Don't Tailgate
Drums
Explosives
**Class A,B,C
Fiber Drums
F.O.B. (Free on Board)
Look Before Backing

TRUCKING II

C.O.D. (Collect on Delivery)
First Class Rates
Gross Load
Gross Weight
Kegs
L/T/1 (Less Than Truckload)
Livestock
Number Pieces
Paid Insurance
Pails
Prepaid
Pro Number
Protective Signature Service
Received in Good Condition
Second Class Rates
Shipper
Storage
Tailgate
Total Due
Vehicle Number

CONSTRUCTION

Acetone
Caution—Keep Walking
   Paths Clear
Caution—Only Regular
   Operator Allowed to Use
   This Machine
Cement
Men Working Above
Riding on This Forbidden
This Means You
Employees Only Allowed
   Past This Point
Fuse
Heater Room
Kerosene
Lock
Mortar Cement
Negative
Panel
Pile All Materials Properly
Positive
Projecting Nails Cause
   Accidents—Bend Them
   Over

Replace Guards and
   Barriers Immediately
Solvent
Stop Machines Before
   Cleaning or Adjusting
This Hoist for Materials
   Only—Do Not Ride
Warning—Stop Machines
   Before Clearing Jams
   or Repairing
Wear Your Hard Hat
Wire

SALES

Bill of Lading
Cash
Charge
C.O.D. (Collect on Delivery)
Collect
Do Not Write in Above
   Space
Due
F.O.B. (Free on Board)
Invoice
Item
License Number
Price Includes Tax
Quantity (Qty)
Rate
Received by
Received in Good Condition
Sales Tax
Sold by
Sold to
Total

LUMBER I

Base
Bevel
Birch
Cedar
Colonial
Common
Crosscuts
Crown
Dowel
Drip Cap

FAS 1 (Front and
   Sideboards Clear on
   1 Side)
FAS 2 (Front and
   Sideboards Clear on
   2 Sides)
Fencing
Fir
Flat Grain
Hemlock
Jambs
Knotty Pine
Mahogany
Mldg. (Moulding)

LUMBER II

Nutmeg
Oak
Panels
PCS (Pieces)
Pine
Ply
Rail
Ranch Trim
Rips
S 2 S (Surface 2 Sides)
S 4 S (Surface 4 Sides)
Shoe
Siding
Sill
Spruce
Square Feet (Sq. Ft.)
Standard
Sterling
Vertical Grain
Walnut

TELEPHONE

Phone
Telephone
Directory
Area Code
Local Call
Long Distance
Information
Directory Assistance
Exchange
Person-to-Person

The Reading Teacher's Book of Lists, Third Edition, © 1993 by Prentice Hall

Dial
Dial Tone
Assistance
Emergency Call
Deposit 25¢
Business Office

Operator
Repair Service
White Pages
Yellow Pages
Classified Directory
Location

Day Rate
Evening Rate
Night Rate
Collect Call
Telegram
Credit Card

See also List 7, Daily Living Words and List 8, Highway Travel Words.

7. Daily Living Words

Words are all around us. The following are part of the American daily living experience. Use these words in literacy education for new and native speakers of English, students with special educational needs, and young students. Check students' comprehension of key survival words such as "flammable," "acid," and "combustible."

acid
admission
alarm
ambulance
apartment
automated teller machine
  (ATM)
bakery
bank
beauty shop
breakfast
bus
bus stop
cab
cafeteria
cancel
car
cash
caution
charge
checks
church
cigarettes
clean
cleaners
closed
cold
cold drinks
collect
combustible
coupon
credit cards
customer service
danger
delicatessen
delivery
dentist
deposit
destination
dinner
directions
do not bend

do not drink
doctor
don't walk
down
driver
drug store
drugs
due
east
electric
elevator
emergency
enter
entrance
exit
explosives
fire escape
fire exit
fire hose
first aid
first class
flammable
follow signs
food
fragile
free
fuel
garage
gas
gentlemen
glass
grocery store
handle with care
harmful if swallowed
help
help wanted
hospital
hot
hotel
information
insert coins
job

keep off
keep out
keep refrigerated
ladies
laundry
license number
lights
local
lost
lunch
M.D.
manager
map
medicine
money
money order
newspapers
no admittance
no smoking
no trespassing
north
northbound
notice
nurse
one way
open
operator
order
out
out of order
oxygen
parking
passengers
pedestrians
perishable
phone
pick-up
poison
police
post office
press
price

The Reading Teacher's Book of Lists, Third Edition, © 1993 by Prentice Hall

private
public parking
pull
push
quiet
railroad
receipt
refund
rent
repair service
reservations
reserved
rest rooms
restaurant
rinse
sale
sales tax
schedule

school
self-service
sick
size
skills
smoking prohibited
south
southbound
stairs
stairway
stop
store
straight ahead
subway
supper
tax
taxi

telephone
this way
timetable
toll
total
train
use other door
walk
warm
warning
wash
watch your step
water
weekday
west
women
work

See also List 6, Work Words and List 8, Highway Travel Words.

8. *Highway Travel Words*

Traveling the highways is part of earning a living, visiting favorite friends, exploring the world. Many students eagerly look forward to the day they will qualify for a driver's license. Mastering this list will help students pass the test and navigate the roadways.

alternate route
bike route
bridge freezes before road
bridge may be slippery
bridge out
camping
cattle Xing (crossing)
caution
children crossing
congested area ahead
construction ahead
curve
danger
dangerous curve
dangerous intersection
dead end
deer Xing (crossing)
detour ahead
dip
divided highway
do not block entrance
do not enter
do not pass
emergency parking only
end construction
entrance
exit
exit only
express lane
expressway
falling rock
farm machinery
fine for littering
food
four-way stop
freeway
gasoline
go slow
hidden driveway
highway ends
hill—trucks use lowest gear
hospital zone
information center
intersection

interstate
junction
keep right
left lane ends
left lane must turn left
left turn on signal only
local traffic only
low clearance
low shoulder
maximum speed ____
mechanic on duty
men working
merge
merge left/merge right
merging traffic
minimum speed ____
narrow bridge
next gas ____ miles
next right/next left
no dumping
no left turn
no parking this side
no passing zone
no right turn on red
no thoroughfare
no trucks
no turns
no turn on red
north
not a through street
no U turn
one way
one way—do not enter
parking ahead
parkway
pavement ends
pedestrian crossing
pedestrians prohibited
ped Xing (pedestrian crossing)
plant entrance
private road—keep out
railroad crossing

ramp speed ____
reduce speed ahead
restricted lane ahead
resume speed
right lane must turn right
right turn only
right turn on red after stop
road closed
road construction next ____ miles
roadside table
route
runaway truck ramp
school bus crossing
school zone when flashing
signal ahead
slippery when wet
slow
slower traffic keep right
soft shoulder
south
speed checked by radar
speed limit ____
speed zone ahead
steep grade
stop
stop ahead
towaway zone
trail
truck route
turnpike
two-way traffic
use low gear
walk
watch for fallen rocks
wayside park
weigh station
weight limit ____ tons
west
winding road
wrong way
yield
yield right of way

See also List 138, Traffic Signs.

40

The Reading Teacher's Book of Lists, Third Edition, © 1993 by Prentice Hall

9. Collective Nouns

Groups of nouns (persons, animals, and things) often have a special word to name the group. These special words are called collective nouns.

ACADEMY of scholars
ARRAY of numbers
ASSOCIATION of lawyers
ASSORTMENT of jewels (also tools, characters)
BALE of cotton
BAND of musicians (also robbers)
BATCH of cookies (also biscuits)
BED of flowers (also vegetables)
BEVY of ladies (also quail)
BLOCK of houses (also stamps)
BUNDLE of sticks (also clothes, money)
CHAPTER of verse (also book)
CHEST of drawers
CLUB of anything (humans)
CLUMP of grass (also earth, dirt)
CLUSTER of diamonds
COLLECTION of things (also books, stamps)
COLONY of ants (also artists, writers)
COMMITTEE of anything (humans)
COMPANY of soldiers
CONGLOMERATION of businesses
CONGREGATION of worshipers
CONGRESS of delegates
CONVENTION of professionals
CORPS of Marines (also drummers)
COUNCIL of chiefs
COVEY of doves (also partridges)
CREW of sailors (also painters)
CROWD of people
DECK of cards
FLEET of ships
FLOCK of sheep (also birds)
FLOOD of emotion (also money, complaints)
FLOTILLA of ships
GAGGLE of geese
GALAXY of stars
GANG of criminals
GROVE of trees
HEAP of dirt
HERD of cows (also reindeer, buffalo)
HORDE of enemy soldiers

LEAGUE of teams (also nations)
LINE of people
MOB of radicals
MOUND of dirt (also things)
MULTITUDE of followers
NEST of snakes (also spies, bowls)
PACK of gum (also lies, dogs)
PARTY of fishermen (also diners)
PEOPLE of a city
PILE of papers
PORTFOLIO of stocks (also pictures)
POSSE of deputies
PRIDE of lions
ROUNDUP of cattle
SCHOOL of fish
SECTION of seats (also laws)
SET of dishes
SHELF of books
SHOCK of wheat (also hair)
SQUAD of police
STACK of pancakes
SWARM of bees (also reporters)
TEAM of athletes
TRIBE of Indians
TROOP of Scouts (also baboons, State Police, soldiers)
UNION of workers (also Nations)
WAVE of insects (also water, emotion)

SECTION II
Core Subject Words

10. *Mathematics Vocabulary—Primary*

Beginning mathematics is challenging for many primary-grade students. Not only must they master mathematics concepts and rules of computation, they must learn to read, write, and comprehend numbers, and they must understand the specialized vocabulary of mathematics—no small feat for students just learning basic word recognition and comprehension skills. Use these words to review meaning, spelling, and to develop word-problem skills. Use the money, time, and measurement section as practice in reference-material use and to strengthen concept relationships.

The Reading Teacher's Book of Lists, Third Edition, © 1993 by Prentice Hall

add
addition
alike
all
amount
Arabic numeral

baker's dozen
between
billion
both

center
change
column
compare
connect
contain
corner
count
counting numbers
curve

degree (temperature)
difference
digit
distance
double
dozen

each
equal
even number

fact
family of facts
fewer
figure
fraction

graph
greater than (>)
group
grouping

half
horizontal

inside

join

least
less
less than (<)

many
match
mathematics
measure
member
middle

million
minus
missing
more
most

negative
number
number line

odd number
opposite
order

pair
pattern
pictograph
plus
positive
problem

rounded number
row

same
sample
score
sequence
set
shaded
sharing

similar
simple
single
size
solution
solve
some
space
straight
subset
subtract
sum
symbol

table
temperature
thermometer
thousand
times
total

unequal
unit
unknown

value
vertical

weight

zero

Money

1 penny	equals	1 cent	1¢	$ .01
1 nickel	equals	5 cents	5¢	$ .05
1 dime	equals	10 cents	10¢	$ .10
1 quarter	equals	25 cents	25¢	$ .25
1 dollar	equals	100 cents	100¢	$1.00

change
coin
cost
dollar sign
five dollar bill
ten dollar bill
twenty dollar bill

Time

1 minute	equals	60 seconds
1 hour	equals	60 minutes
1 day	equals	24 hours
1 week	equals	7 days
1 month	equals	4 weeks
1 year	equals	52 weeks
1 year	equals	365 days
1 year	equals	12 months

A.M.
P.M.
morning
noon
afternoon
night
midnight
calendar
clock
Roman numerals
watch

The Reading Teacher's Book of Lists, Third Edition, © 1993 by Prentice Hall

MEASUREMENT—Primary

Customary System

In the customary system, the unit used for measuring length is the **inch**. The unit used for measuring liquid is the **ounce**. We use inch rulers and yard sticks to measure length in the customary system.

Length

1 foot	equals	12 inches
1 yard	equals	36 inches
1 yard	equals	3 feet
1 mile	equals	5,280 feet

Liquid

1 cup	equals	8 ounces
1 pint	equals	2 cups
1 quart	equals	2 pints
1 gallon	equals	4 quarts

Weight

1 pound	equals	16 ounces
1 ton	equals	2,000 pounds

Metric System

In the metric system, the unit used for measuring length is the **meter**. The unit used for measuring liquid is the **liter**. We use centimeter rulers and meter sticks to measure length in the metric system.

Length

1 centimeter	equals	10 millimeters
1 meter	equals	100 centimeters
1 kilometer	equals	1,000 meters

Liquid

1 liter	equals	1,000 milliliters
1 kiloliter	equals	1,000 liters

Weight

1 gram	equals	1,000 milligrams
1 kilogram	equals	1,000 grams
1 metric ton	equals	1,000 kilograms

See also List 13, Measurement.

11. *Mathematics Vocabulary—Elementary*

Because mathematics is an essential skill, instructional focus is being placed on students' understanding of the concepts behind the computation. These words are found in primary-grade texts and should be recognized and understood by most intermediate-grade students. Share the list with your students' math instructor. Not understanding these words may cause students trouble with "word problems" and interfere with their learning math in the intermediate grades.

addend
array
array diagram
associative property
  (grouping property)
average

bar graph
base
base ten
basic fact
broken-line graph

capacity
Celsius
circle graph
combine
common denominator
common factor
common multiple
commutative property
  (order property)
compass
compatible number
composite number
coordinates
cubic centimeter
customary system of
  measurement

data
decimal
decimal point
decimeter
degree Celsius
degree Fahrenheit
denominator
distributive property
divide
dividend
divisible
divisor

elapsed time
element
empty set
equal decimals
equal fractions
equally likely
equation
equivalent
equivalent fractions
equivalent measures
estimate
expanded numeral

factor
factor tree
Fahrenheit
flow chart
fluid ounce
frequency

gram
greatest common factor (gcf)
grid
grouping property of addition
grouping property of
  multiplication

hundredth

identify
improper fraction
inequality
infinite set
integers
is divisible by

label
least common denominator
  (lcd)
least common factor (lcf)
least common multiple (lcm)
lowest terms

mass
mean
median
minuend
missing factor
mixed number
mode
model
multiple
multiplication
multiplication property of
  one
multiplication property of
  zero
multiply

natural order
net
number pair
number sentence
numerator

one hundredth
one tenth
one-to-one
operation
order property of addition

The Reading Teacher's Book of Lists, Third Edition, © 1993 by Prentice Hall

order property of
   multiplication
ordered pair
ordinal
ordinal number
organized list
outcome

parenthesis, parentheses
percent
perimeter
pint
place holder
place value
prediction
prime factor
prime number
principle
probability
procedure
product

proper fraction
property of one
property of zero

quotient

range
ratio
reciprocal
rectangular array
regroup
related facts
remainder
rename
repeating decimal

sign
simplest form
square centimeter
square feet
square inch
square mile

square number
square products
standard units of measure
statistics
subtrahend
survey

tally chart
tenth
terminating decimal
triangular numbers

union
unit fraction
unit price
unnamed

watt
whole number

zero property of addition
zero property of
   multiplication

12. *Mathematics Vocabulary—Intermediate*

The concepts behind these words build on those learned in elementary math. These words were found in popular math texts for grades four through eight. Many will also be repeated in secondary-school texts. Consider a lesson on "math verbs"—knowing **what to do** is key to carrying out mathematical operations. Here are a few examples of "math verbs": **decrease, subtract, convert, determine, reduce.**

abscissa
absolute value
acre
actual
additive
additive inverse
alternate
approximately
arithmetic mean
associative property of
    addition
associative property of
    multiplication
avoirdupois

baker's dozen
base (of a percent)
base (of an exponent)
base five
base two
billion
binary operation
binary system
box plot

calculate
cardinal
caret
cast out
centigrade
centigram
centiliter
century
certain event
clock arithmetic
closure property
combination
commutative property of
    addition
commutative property of
    multiplication
comparison

complementary events
complex
complex fraction
computation
consecutive
constant
convert
cosine
cosine ratio
cross-product
cross-section
cubed
cubic
currency

decade
decrease
dependent events
deposit
depth
derive
determine
deviation
diagram
discount
disprove (a statement)
distributive property of
    multiplication
division
dot graph
dry measure
duplicate

equal ratios
equality
equivalent ratios
error of measurement
evaluate
exact
experiment
experimental probability
exponent

exponential notation
expression
extend

face value
factorial
family of facts
favorable outcome
Fibonacci sequence
finite
fixed
foci
foot-pound
formula
frequency
frequency table
function

generalization
given
graduated scale
graph
graph of the equation
greatest possible error
greatest possible multiple
gross
gross weight

histogram

identity property of
    multiplication
imply
impossible event
include
increase
independent events
indirect measurement
inequality
inference
input
interest rate
interpret

The Reading Teacher's Book of Lists, Third Edition, © 1993 by Prentice Hall

interquartile range
interval
inverse
irrational number

koliter

like terms
line plot
linear
linear equation
lower quartile

magic square
markup
maximum
mental math
metric system
micron
midpoint
midway
minimum
mixed numeral
multiplicand
multiplication principle
multiplier
mutually exclusive events

natural number
negative correlation
negative number
negative slope
notation
numeral
numeration
numeration system

odds
open equation
open sentence
opposites
order of operations
ordered pair
origin
output
overestimate

partial
pattern
per
percent

percentage
percentiles
perfect number
perfect square
period
permutation
pi
pictograph
plot
population
positive correlation
positive numbers
positive slope
possible outcomes
power
precision
profit
progression
proportion
proportional

quadrant
quantity
quartiles

random
random sample
ranking
rate
rational number
real numbers
reduce
reflexive property

relation
relative error
repeat (probability)
restriction
reverse

sample
satisfies
scatter plot
scientific notation
sequence
short division
signed number
significant digits
simplest terms
simplify
sine
sine ratio
skip counting
slope
solution
square root
squared
standard order of operations
statistics
stem-and-leaf plot
story problem
string
subscript
substitute
successive
super set
system

tally
term
terminate
theorem
theoretical probability
topologically equivalent
topology
transformation
transitive property
translation (slide)

transversal
tree diagram
trial
trigonometry
triple
truncate

underestimate
undivided
union of sets
unit rate

universal set
unlimited
unmatched
upper limit
upper quartile

variable
variable expression
Venn diagram

word problem

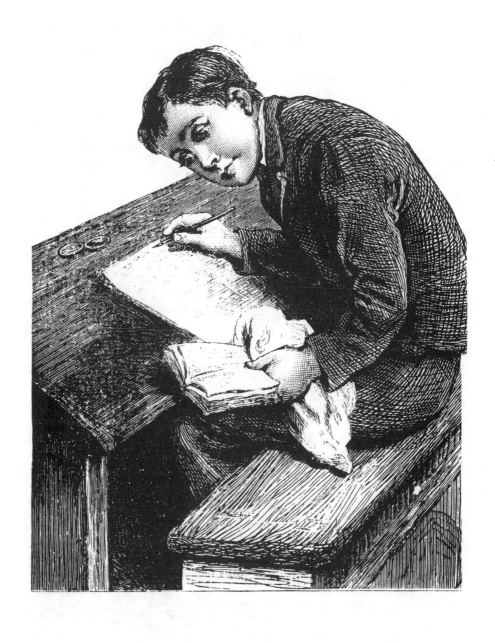

13. *Measurement*

CUSTOMARY SYSTEM

In the customary system of measurement, the reference unit used for length is the **inch**; the reference unit used for liquid capacity is the **ounce**. Inch rulers and yard sticks are used to measure length in the customary system.

Length

12 inches (12 in.)	equal	1 foot (1 ft.)
3 feet (3 ft.)	equal	1 yard (1 yd.)
220 yards (220 yds.)	equal	1 furlong (1 fur.)
8 furlongs (8 fur.)	equal	1 mile (1 mi.)

Liquid Capacity

8 fluid ounces (8 fl. oz.)	equal	1 cup (1 c.)
2 cups (2 c.)	equal	1 pint (1 pt.)
16 fluid ounces (16 fl. oz.)	equal	1 pint (1 pt.)
2 pints (2 pt.)	equal	1 quart (1 qt.)
32 fluid ounces (32 fl. oz.)	equal	1 quart (1 qt.)
4 quarts (4 qt.)	equal	1 gallon (1 gal.)
128 fluid ounces (128 fl. oz.)	equal	1 gallon (1 gal.)

Mass Weight

16 ounches (16 oz.)	equal	1 pound (1 lb.)
2,000 pounds (2,000 lb.)	equal	1 ton (1 T.)

Area

144 square inches (144 sq. in.)	equal	1 square foot (1 sq. ft.)
9 square feet (9 sq. ft.)	equal	1 square yard (1 sq. yd.)
4,840 square yards (4,840 sq. yd.)	equal	1 acre (1 A.)

Volume

1,728 cubic inches (1,728 cu. in.)	equal	1 cubic foot (1 cu. ft.)
27 cubic feet (27 cu. ft.)	equal	1 cubic yard (1 cu. yd.)

METRIC SYSTEM

In the metric system of measurement, the reference unit used for length is the **meter**; the reference unit used for capacity is the **liter**. Centimeter rulers and meter sticks are used to measure length in the metric system.

Length

10 millimeters (10 mm)	equal	1 centimeter (1 cm)
10 centimeters (10 cm)	equal	1 decimeter (1 dm)
100 millimeters (100 mm)	equal	1 decimeter (1 dm)
10 decimeters (10 dm)	equal	1 meter (1 m)
100 centimeters (100 cm)	equal	1 meter (1 m)
1,000 meters (1000 m)	equal	1 kilometer (1 km)

Liquid Capacity

10 milliliters (10 ml)	equal	1 centiliter (1 cl)
1,000 milliliters (1000 ml)	equal	1 liter (1 L)

Mass (Weight)

10 milligrams (10 mg)	equal	1 centigram (1 cg)
1,000 milligrams (1000 mg)	equal	1 gram (1 g)
1,000 grams (1000 g)	equal	1 kilogram (1 kg)
1,000 kilograms (1000 kg)	equal	1 metric ton (1 t)

Area

100 square millimeters (100 mm^2)	equal	1 square centimeter (1 cm^2)
10,000 square centimeters (10,000 cm^2)	equal	1 square meter (1 m^2)
10,000 square meters (10,000 m^2)	equal	1 hectare (1 ha)

Volume

1,000 cubic millimeters (1000 mm^3)	equal	1 cubic centimeter (1 cm^3)
1,000 cubic centimeters (1000 cm^3)	equal	1 cubic decimeter (1 dm^3)
1,000,000 cubic centimeters (1,000,000 cm^3)	equal	1 cubic meter (1 m^3)

The Reading Teacher's Book of Lists, Third Edition, © 1993 by Prentice Hall

SOME EQUIVALENT MEASURES

CUSTOMARY SYSTEM		METRIC SYSTEM
1 inch	equals	2.5 centimeters
1 foot	equals	30 centimeters
1 yard	equals	0.9 meters
1 mile	equals	1.6 kilometers
1 pound	equals	0.45 kilogram
1 quart	equals	0.95 liter
1 gallon	equals	3.8 liters

METRIC SYSTEM		CUSTOMARY SYSTEM
1 meter	equals	3.3 feet
1 hectare	equals	2.5 acres
1 centimeter	equals	0.4 inch
1 liter	equals	1.06 quarts
1 liter	equals	0.26 gallon
1 gram	equals	0.035 ounce
1 kilogram	equals	2.2 pounds

See also List 10, Mathematics Vocabulary Primary.

14. *Geometry Vocabulary*

Geometry has many practical as well as scientific and mathematical applications. We use it to calculate the size rug we need for a room, to find our location at sea, to build bridges and other structures. But geometry also has a wonderfully artistic side. Introduce your students to geometric art through computers and have them write poetry inspired by their art work.

ELEMENTARY GRADES 3–6

area
acute angle
angle

center of a circle
circle
circumference
closed figure
cone
congruent
congruent figures
cube
cylinder

degree (of an angle)
diagonal
diameter

edge
endpoint

face
flip

geometric figure
geometry

half turn
half-turn symmetry
height
hexagon

intersect
intersecting lines

length
line
line graph
line of symmetry
line plot
line segment

obtuse angle
octagon

parallel
parallel lines
parallelogram
pentacube
pentagon
pentomino
perpendicular
perpendicular lines
plane
point
polygon
polyhedron
polyomino
prism
protractor
pyramid

quadrilateral

radius
ray
rectangle
rectangular prism
regular polygon
rhombus
right angle
right triangle
round

segment
shape
side
similar figures
solid figure
sphere
square
surface
symmetric figure
symmetrical

triangle
turn
turn center
turn image

vertex (vertices)
volume

width

INTERMEDIATE GRADES 7–9

acute triangle
adjacent
adjacent angles
adjacent vertices
alternate interior (exterior) angles
altitude
arc
axis

base (of a prism)
bisect

central angle
chord
circumscribe
closed curve
complementary angles
composite solid
concave polygon
concentric
construct
convex polygon
coordinate axis
coordinate plane
corresponding
corresponding parts

dilation
dimension

equiangular triangle
equilateral triangle
exterior

45°–45°–90° triangle

The Reading Teacher's Book of Lists, Third Edition, © 1993 by Prentice Hall

half-planes
hemisphere
hexagonal prism
hypotenuse

inscribed angle
interior
intersection
irregular polygon
isosceles triangle

lateral
leg (of a triangle)
legs (of a right
    triangle)
line
line of best fit
line of symmetry
line segment

median (of a
    triangle)
mirror image

obtuse triangle
open figure

perpendicular
    bisector
plane figure
Pythagorean theorem

quadrilateral

radian
radii
reflection (flip)
regular polyhedron
rotation (turn)

scale
scale drawing
scalene triangle
sector
semicircle
skew lines
slant height
straight angle

straight edge
supplementary
    angles
surface area

tangent
tangent line
tangent ratio
tessellation
30–60–90 triangle
trapezoid
triangular pyramid
turn symmetry
two-dimensional

vertical angle
vertical axis

x-axis
x-coordinate

y-axis
y-coordinate

See also Lists 10, 11, and 12, Mathematics Vocabulary.

15. *Science Vocabulary—Elementary*

Harness a student's natural curiosity with books about dinosaurs, volcanos, and optical illusions, and create a lifelong interest in science. These terms are from elementary-grade science texts. Science words pose pronunciation and spelling challenges to many students. Be sure to review key words before independent reading assignments.

GENERAL SCIENCE

absorb
accurate
apply
astronaut
astronomer
atmosphere
atom

balance
barometer
boil

calcium
carbon dioxide
Celsius
census
centimeter
chemical
chemical change
chemical symbol
chemistry
chlorine
classify
climate
cloud
community
compass
compound
condense
constellation
continent
contract
control
convection
core
crust

decay
decompose
degree
desert

dew
dissolve

earth
eclipse
environment
equator
erosion
evaporate
evidence
expand

Fahrenheit
filament
flood
flow
fog
frost
fuel
funnel

gas
geyser
glacier

hail
heat
hemisphere
horizon
humus
hurricane

iceberg
image

jet

lava
liquid

mantle
marble
matter
melting point
mercury

meteor
meter
metric
microscope
mineral
model
moisture
molecule
moon

natural resource
nucleus

orbit
outlet
oxygen

periodic
planet
pollute
predict
preserve
property
prove
pure

radiant
rainfall
range
recycle
response
ridge

satellite
scale
season
sediment
sedimentary
series
smog
solid
solution
space

starch
stimulus
surface
system

temperature
thermometer
thunder
tides
transparent

variable
volcano

water vapor

LIFE SCIENCE

abdomen
adaptation
algae
amoeba
amphibian
ancestor

backbone
bacteria
behavior
blood vessels
breathe

capillary
carbohydrate
cartilage
cell
chlorophyll
circulation

diaphragm
digestion
dinosaur
disease

ear
eardrum

earthworm
egg
embryo
esophagus
extinct

fat
fern
fertile
fertilizer
flower
food chain
fossil
fruit

gills
grain

habitat
hatch
hibernate

incisor
infection
insect
instinct

joint

larva
leaf
lens
lungs

mammal
marine biologist

membrane
molar
mold
muscle

nerves

optical
organ
organism
ovary

paramecium
parasite
pesticide
physical
plankton
pollen
population
predator
prescribe
prey
produce
protein
protozoan
pulse
pupa
pupil

red blood cell
reproduction
reptile
retina
rib
root

saliva
seed
senses
skeleton
skin
sperm
spinal
spore
stem
stomach
survive

taste
tendon
terrarium
treatment

vein
vitamin

PHYSICAL SCIENCE

air current
air pressure

battery

circuit
concave
conductor
constant
convex
current

density
distance

echo
electricity
energy

focus
force
friction

gravity

insulate

length

magnet
mass
motion

pendulum
phase
pitch
power

rate
reflection
revolve

sound
switch

vibration

wave
weight

16. General Science Vocabulary—Intermediate

Our rapidly changing, high-tech world makes it necessary for every citizen to have an understanding of the principles of general science. These terms were selected from general science texts for grades six through eight.

air pressure
algae
alloy
amino acid
amorphous
antibiotic
asexual reproduction
astronomy
atomic mass
atomic number
aurora

bacillus
bacterium
binomial
    nomenclature
boiling
boiling point
botany
Boyle's law

canine
carnivore
cartilage
catalyst
cell membrane
cell wall
Charles's law
chemical equation
chemical formula
chemical property
chemical reaction
chromosome
cilium
class
cleavage
coastal plains
coefficient
cold-blooded
competition
compound
condensation
consumer
continental glacier
crop

crystal
crystalline solid
cytoplasm

data
density
diffusion
division of labor
DNA
ductility

ecology
ecosystem
electron
electron microscope
element
energy level
enzyme
epidermis
excretion

family
fermentation
fertilization
flammability
focus
food web
fracture
freezing
freezing point
frond
fungus

gem
genus
germination
glucose
gravity
ground water

hardness
herbaceous
herbivore
heterogeneous
heterotroph
homeostasis

homogeneous
host
hypothesis

igneous
inertia
ingestion
inland plains
inorganic
inorganic compound
insoluble
intrusive
invertebrate
ion
isotope

jet stream

kingdom

larva
leaching
lichen
life span
luster

magma
malleable
marsupial
mass
meiosis
metabolism
metamorphic
metamorphosis
microbiology
migrate
mitosis
mixture
Mohs hardness scale
mountain range
multicellular
mutualism

neutron
niche
nonmetal
nuclear membrane

nucleic acid
nucleolus

oil
order
ore
organic compound
organic rock
osmosis
ozone

permafrost
petal
phase
pheromone
photosynthesis
phylum
physical change
physical property
physics
pistil
plains landscape
plasma
plateau landscape
pollen
pollination
population
pore
precipitation
producer
proton
protoplasm
pseudopod

quark

reproduction
respiration
response
rhizoid
rhizome
ribosome
RNA

scavenger
scientific method

The Reading Teacher's Book of Lists, Third Edition, © 1993 by Prentice Hall

secondary waves
seismic
seismograph
sexual reproduction
slime mold
solubility
soluble
solute
solvent
species
spontaneous
  generation

stalk
stamen
stoma
stratosphere
streak
subatomic particle
sublimation
subscript
subsoil
suspension
symbiosis

taxonomy
tissue
topsoil
toxin

unicellular

valley glacier
vaporization
variable
venom
vertebrate

virus
volume

warm-blooded
water table
weathering

zoology

17. *Life Science Vocabulary—Intermediate*

These life science terms will be found in texts for grades four through nine. Consider a lesson or two on science-related prefixes, suffixes, and root words. They will help word recognition and comprehension. Teach word variants when vocabulary is introduced. For example, when introducing **immune**, also teach: **immunity, immunize, immunology**.

acid rain
acquired immunity
adrenal
agar
alcoholism
allele
allergy
anaphase
anatomy
antibody
antigen
aorta
artery
atrium
autonomic nervous
   system

benign
binary fission
biome
biotechnology
bronchus

calorie
cancer
carcinogen
cardiac muscle
cardiovascular
cellulose
central nervous
   system
cerebellum
cerebrum
chloroplast
cholesterol
chronic disorder
circulatory system
classification
colorblindness
communicable
   disease
coniferous forest
connective tissue

conservation
cross-pollination
cytoplasm

deciduous forest
dendrite
depletion
depressant
dermis
desert
diatom
digestive system
division of labor
dominant
drug
drug abuse

ecological succession
ecology
ecosystem
effector
embryology
endangered species
endocrine system
epiglottis
erosion
estrogen
evaporation
evolution
exhale
exocrine gland
extinction

Fallopian
feedback mechanism
fetus
formula
fossil
fossil fuel

gene
genetic engineering
genetics
genotype

geothermal energy
grassland

half-life
hallucinogen
hazardous waste
hemoglobin
hemophilia
homologous
hormone
hybrid
hypertension
hypothalamus
hypothesis

immune
immunity
inbreeding
incomplete
   dominance
incubate
infectious disease
inflammation
inhale
interferon
interphase
invertebrate

kidney

large intestine
larynx
ligament
liver
lymph

malignant
marrow
medulla
menopause
menstruation
metabolism
metamorphosis
metaphase

microorganism
monoclonal
motor neutron
multiple allele
multicellular
muscle tissue
mutation

natural immunity
natural resource
natural selection
nerve impulse
nerve tissue
nervous system
nonrenewable
   resource
nuclear energy
nuclear fission
nuclear fusion
nutrient

omnivore
opiate
order
organelle
organ system
osmosis
ossification
ovary
over-the-counter drug
ovulation

pancreas
parathyroid
pasteurization
peripheral
peristalsis
petroleum
physical dependence
pituitary
plasma
plasmid
platelet

The Reading Teacher's Book of Lists, Third Edition, © 1993 by Prentice Hall

pollution
pore
prescription drug
primate
probability
prophase
psychological
   dependence
puberty
punctuated
   equilibrium

radioactive dating
radioactive material
receptor
recessive
recombinant DNA
reflex
regeneration
renewable resource

replication
reproductive system
respiratory system
retina

savanna
sedimentary rock
self-pollination
sensory neuron
sex chromosome
sex-linked trait
sexual reproduction
skeletal muscle
small intestine
smog
smooth muscle
solar energy
species
sperm
sphygmomanometer

spinal cord
stimulant
stoma
symbiosis
symptom
synapse

taiga
telophase
temperature
   inversion
testosterone
theory
thyroid
tolerance
toxic
toxin
trachea
trait
transfusion

transpiration
tropical rain forest
tumor
tundra

urea
urethra
urinary bladder
uterus

vaccine
valve
variation
ventricle
vertebra
virus
vocal cord

white blood cell

zygote

18. Physical Science Vocabulary—Intermediate

These terms are basic to the study of energy, movement, light, and work in intermediate and high school grades. When reviewing them with students, be sure to point out tricky spellings or pronunciations.

absolute zero
acceleration
acoustics
alternating current (AC)
ampere
amplify
amplitude
angle of incidence
angle of reflection
Archimedes' principle

Bernoulli's principle
binding energy
Boyle's law
Brownian motion
buoyancy

calorie
calorimeter
centripetal acceleration
chemical bonding
chemical energy
chemical equation
circuit breaker
collision theory
combustion
compression
concave
concentrated solution
condensation
condenser coil
conduction
constant speed
constructive interference
conversion factor
convex
corrosion
covalent bonding
crest
crystal lattice

deceleration
decomposition reaction
destructive interference
diffraction

diffuse
dilute solution
dimensional analysis
diode
direct current (DC)
dissociation
distillation
Doppler effect
double-replacement reaction
drag
dry cell

efficiency
effort
electric charge
electric current
electrochemical cell
electrode
electrolyte
electromagnetic energy
electromagnetic force
electron-dot diagram
endothermic
energy conversion
evaporation
exothermic

fiber optics
fluid friction
fluorescent
focal length
focal point
force of attraction
force of repulsion
Freon
frequency
fulcrum
fuse

galvanometer
gamma ray
Geiger counter
generator
geothermal energy
grounding

half-life
halogen
heat transfer
hertz
heterogeneous
hologram
holography
homogeneous
horsepower
hydrocarbon
hydroelectric

illuminate
incandescent
incident wave
inclined plane
index of refraction
indicator
induction
inert
infrared ray
insoluble
intensity
interference
invisible spectrum
ionic bonding
ionization
isomer

joule

Kelvin scale
kinetic

laser
law of conservation of energy
law of conservation of mass
law of conservation of
     momentum
laws of motion
law of reflection
law of universal gravitation
lever
lift
lubricant

The Reading Teacher's Book of Lists, Third Edition, © 1993 by Prentice Hall

machine
magnetic field
magnetism
mechanical advantage
mechanical energy
meniscus
metallic bond
modulation
molecule
momentum

natural frequency
neon
neutralization
noble gas
node
nuclear chain reaction
nuclear energy
nuclear fission
nuclear fusion
nuclear waste

ohm
Ohm's law
opaque
orbital motion
oxidation number

parallel circuit
particle accelerator
periodic law
permanent magnet
phase change
photoelectric effect
photon
photovoltaic cell
physical change
physical property
physics

piston
polarity
polarized light
polymer
potential energy
power
precipitate
pressure
primary coil
product
projectile
proton
pulley

quality
quark

radar
radiation
radioactivity
radio wave
rarefaction
reactant
reflected wave
refraction
resistance
resonance
reverberation
rolling friction

saturated
screw
semiconductor
series circuit
single-replacement reaction
sliding friction
slope
solar energy
sonar

specific gravity
standing wave
static electricity
structural formula
subatomic particle
sublimation
supersaturated
synthesis reaction
synthetic element

temperature inversion
temporary magnet
terminal velocity
thermal expansion
thermocouple
thermostat
thrust
tidal power
transistor
translucent
transmutation
transverse wave
trough

ultrasonic
ultraviolet ray

valence electron
velocity
viscosity
visible spectrum
voltage

watt
wavelength
wedge
wet cell
wheel and axle
work

19. *Social Studies Vocabulary—Elementary*

Students in grades three through five will encounter these words. Younger students will benefit from frequent pronunciation and spelling review of the more "difficult" words.

adobe
age
American Revolution
ancestors
ancient
appointed
archaeologists
archaeology
armada
artifact
astronaut
authority

barbarian
barter
bicentennial
bill
Bill of Rights
boundary

cabinet
campaign
candidate
capital
capitol
census
century
charter
checks and balances
chronological order
citizen
city
civil
civil rights
civil war
civilization
colony
commerce
communities
compromise
Congress
conquer
conquistador
Constitution

consulate
consumer
contiguous United States
continents
convention
convert
cotton gin
country
craftsmen

Declaration of Independence
democracy
discover
discovery
document

election
expedition
explore
explorer

factory
fleet
foreign
fossil
founded
freedom
frontier

ghetto
goods
government
governor
group
growth

heritage
history
housing

illegal
immigrant
invention

knowledge

labor
law
legal
local

majority
manufacture
mayor
militia
minimum
minority
minutemen
missionary
mosque
museum

Native American
New World
nobles
northwest passage

official
opinion
opportunity
opposed
oral history
Oregon Trail
organization

Parliament
passage
patriot
peasant
peon
pilgrim
pioneer
plantation
political party
population
poverty
president
property
Puritans

religion
represent
Revolutionary War
rule
rural

satellite
Senate
settlements
shortage
slave state
slavery

The Reading Teacher's Book of Lists, Third Edition, © 1993 by Prentice Hall

slum
social scientist
society
space shuttle
Sputnik
St. Augustine
state
strike
suburbs

term
territory
time line
town meeting
trade
traditional
trails
treaty
trial

tribes
troops
truce

union
unite
United Nations
urban
urban blight
urban renewal

veteran
violence
volunteer
voyage

wages
warfare
wilderness
worship

20. *Social Studies Vocabulary—Intermediate*

The heart of any good story is the link between its characters and the events. A good idea is to focus social studies reading on people and how their lives were touched by the events of history. Details will be remembered, if the story telling was superb. This list was taken from social studies texts, grades four through eight. Many of these words are also basic in secondary school texts.

abolish
abolitionist
absolute monarchy
administration
affluent
AFL-CIO
aggressor
agribusiness
alien
alliance
Allied Powers
ally
amendment
amnesty
annex
apartheid
apprentice
aristocracy
armistice
Articles of
   Confederation
assassinate
assembly
atomic energy
autocracy
automation
Axis Powers

balance of power
Bank of the United
   States
birth rate
bloc
blockade
bonds
boom
boycott
bureaucracy

capitalism
captains of industry
carpetbaggers

caucus
Central Powers
cold war
collective bargaining
collective farm
colonialism
colonization
Committees of
   Correspondence
commodity exchange
Common Market
commonwealth
communism
competition
concentration camps
Confederate States
   of America
confederation
conflicts
conservative
consumer goods
contraband
cooperative
corporation
credit
crisis
crude oil
currency
customs
czar

death rate
debate
debt
declaration
defense
delegates
demand
demarcation
democrat
deposits
depression

desegregation
dictator
dictatorship
diplomat
disarmament
discrimination
dissent
divine right
divorce
draft
duty
dynasty

economy
elastic clause
electoral vote
emancipate
Emancipation
   Proclamation
embargo
emigration
emperor
empire
enforce
environment
equality
ethnic
excise
executive
executive branch
exile
exploration
export

Far East
fascism
favored
Federal Reserve
   System
federalism
Federalist
filibuster

foreign policy
fossil fuels
free enterprise
Free World

graduated income tax
grandfather clause
granges
gross national product

habeas corpus
homestead
hostage
House of
   Representatives
humanitarian

illiteracy
immigration
impeach
imperialism
import
inaugurate
income
indentured servant
independence
industrial
Industrial Revolution
inflation
initiative
integration
interchangeable parts
invasion
investigation
investment
Iron Curtain
Islam
isolationism

judicial branch
judiciary
jury
justice

Ku Klux Klan

labor union
laissez faire
Latin America
League of Nations
legislative branch
legislature
liberal
life expectancy
literacy
lockout
loyalist

mandate
Manifest Destiny
manufacturing
martial law
mass production
Mayflower Compact
megalopolis
mercantilism
merchant
metropolis
metropolitan area
middle class
Middle East
migrant
migratory farming
military
minority groups
missile
moderates
monarchy
monopoly
monotheism
Monroe Doctrine
Moslem
mother country
movement
muckrakers

nationalism
natural resources
Nazism
negotiate
neutral
New Deal
nobility
nominate

nonviolence
North Atlantic
    Treaty Organization
nuclear weapons
null and void

occupied
open housing laws
oppression
Orient

pacifists
patent
patriotism
Peace Corps
per capita income
persecute
petition
platform
pocket veto
policy
political process
politician
politics
poll tax
pollution
polytheism
population density
possessions
postwar
preamble
precedent
prehistoric
prejudice
primary
primary source
prime minister
proclamation
profit
progressive
prohibit
prohibition
propaganda
prospector
protectorate
protest
Protestant
province
provision

public domain
public opinion
public works

radicals
ratify
ration
raw materials
reapportionment
rebellion
rebels
recall
recession
reconstruction
recovery
referendum
reform
Reformation
refugee
regulation
relocation centers
renewable resource
repeal
representative
republic
republican

reservations
reserves
resign
resolution
resources
retreat
revenue
revolt
revolution
riots
royalist
ruins

sabotage
sanction
satellite country
scandal
secede
secession
secondary source
sectionalism
segregation
Selective Service Act
senator
seniority
separation of powers

sharecropper	stock market	terrorism	tyrant
siege	strategy	textile	
smuggling	surplus	theory	unanimous
social security	surrender	tolerance	unconstitutional
socialist	survive	totalitarian	underdeveloped
sociology	sweatshops	traitor	underground railroad
sovereignty	system	transcontinental	unskilled worker
Soviet		treason	
spoils system	tariff	trend	veto
standard of living	taxation	triangular trade	
stock	technology	tyranny	war hawks
			welfare

21. *Geography Vocabulary*

The world in which we live is a fascinating place. Computers, satellite transmission, and changing boundaries have moved us into a global village. Growing cultural, economic and political ties to countries around the world increase the importance of students' knowledge of geography. Encourage students to become pen pals, or computer network links, with others across the globe. International student-exchange programs are sources for pen-pal information. The words listed here are from recently published middle-grade geography texts. How worldwise and wordwise are your students? Can they name and locate the major cities and other key geographic sites? These skills are part of the new world literacy.

The Reading Teacher's Book of Lists, Third Edition, © 1993 by Prentice Hall

agriculture
alluvial
altitude
Antarctic Circle
arable
archipelago
Arctic Circle
arid
atmosphere
autonomy
axis

balance
barren
basin
bay
bayou
belt
blizzard
boundary
branch
broadleaf

canal
canyons
cape
capital
cartographer
cash crop
census
central
city
cliff
climate
coast
commercial
communal
community
compass

Compass Rose
condensation level
coniferous
continent
continental divide
contour
cottage industry
country
county
crater
crop rotation
crops
crust
cultivation
cultural region
culture
current
customs
cyclone

dam
data
death rate
deciduous
degree
delta
density
desert
developing nation
dew point
diversity
doldrums
domestic
drought
dust bowl
dust storm

earth
earthquake

east
eastern hemisphere
eclipse
ecology
economy
elevation
environment
equal area map
equator
equinox
erosion
estuary
ethnic
evaporation
evergreen
export

fathom
fault
fertile
fiord
flash flood
flood plain

foliage
fossil
fuel

geologist
geyser
glacier
globe
goods
grain
grasslands
gravity
great circle
Great Plains
greenhouse effect
grid
gross national
    product
growing season
gulf
Gulf Stream

harbor
harvest

hemisphere
highlands
hinterlands
horizon
humidity
hurricane
hydroelectric

ice cap
iceberg
import
income
industry
inland
inlet
International Date
  Line
international waters
irrigation
island
isolated
isthmus

jet stream
jungle

lagoon
lake
landlocked
latitude
lava
legend
levee
level
life expectancy
lines of latitude
lines of longitude
literacy
longitude
lowlands

mainland
manufacture
map
marine
marine climate

marsh
mass
meadow
megalopolis
Mercator map
meridian
mesa
metropolitan area
moderate
monsoon
moraine
mountain
mouth of a river

nation
nationalism
nationality
native
natural resources
navigable
navigation
neighborhood
neutral
nomad
nonrenewable
  resource
North Pole

oasis
occidental
ocean
ocean current
oceanography
orbit
outback
overpopulation

parallel
pasture
peak
peninsula
petroleum
physical map
plain
planet

plateau
polar
polar map
pollution
population density
port
prairie
precipice
precipitation
Prime Meridian

rain forest
rainfall
range
rapids
raw materials
reef
refinery
region
relief
relief map
religion
renewable resource
reservoir
resort
resources
river
rotation
route
rural

savannah
scale
scale of miles
sea
sea level
season
sediment
seismograph
semiarid
silt
smog
solar
South Pole
sphere

standard of living
steppe
strait
subtropical
suburb
supply
surplus
survey
swamp

tableland
technology
temperature
tidal wave
tide
tidewater
timberline
time line
topography
topsoil
trade
tributary
tropic
Tropic of Cancer
Tropic of Capricorn
tundra
typhoon

universal
urban

valley
vast
vegetation
vertical
vital statistics
volcano

water power
watershed
weather
Western Hemisphere
wharf
whirlpool
wilderness

zone

The Reading Teacher's Book of Lists, Third Edition, © 1993 by Prentice Hall

CONTINENTS

	Area in sq. mi.	Area in sq. km.
Asia	10,428,300	27,009,297
Africa	11,647,720	30,167,594
North America	8,430,730	21,835,591
South America	6,839,890	17,715,315
Europe	1,879,810	4,868,708
Antarctica	14,000,000	36,260,000
Australia	2,967,900	7,686,861

WORLD'S LARGEST URBAN AREAS IN 1990

Urban Area, Country	Population
Tokyo-Yokohama, Japan	26,952,000
Mexico City, Mexico	20,207,000
Sao Paulo, Brazil	18,052,000
Seoul, Korea	16,268,000
New York, United States	14,622,000
Osaka-Kobe-Kyoto, Japan	13,826,000
Bombay, India	11,777,000
Calcutta, India	11,663,000
Buenos Aires, Argentina	11,518,000

RELIGIONS OF THE WORLD

Christianity	1,548,500,000	32.4%
Islam	817,000,000	17.1
Hinduism	647,500,000	13.5
Buddhism	295,600,000	6.2
Judaism	17,800,000	0.4
regional/tribal	437,200,000	9.1
non-religious or atheist	1,026,400,000	21.3
	4,781,200,000	100.0

The Reading Teacher's Book of Lists, Third Edition, © 1993 by Prentice Hall

WORLD OCEANS

	Area in sq. mi.	Area in sq. km.
Pacific Ocean	63,800	165,250

Includes:

South China Sea
Sea of Okhotsk
Bering Sea
Sea of Japan
East China Sea
Yellow Sea

Atlantic Ocean	31,830	82,440

Includes:

Arctic Ocean*
Caribbean Sea
Mediterranean Sea
Norwegian Sea
Gulf of Mexico
Hudson Bay
Greenland Sea
North Sea
Black Sea
Baltic Sea

Indian Ocean	28,360	73,440

Includes:

Arabian Sea
Bay of Bengal
Red Sea

The Reading Teacher's Book of Lists, Third Edition, © 1993 by Prentice Hall

---

*Considered a marginal sea because of its small size; (5,400 sq. mi., 14,090 sq. km.).

MAJOR RIVERS OF THE WORLD

Name	Length Miles	Length km	Continent
Nile	4,145	6,673	Africa
Amazon	4,000	6,440	South America
Yangtze (Changjiang)	3,720	5,989	Asia
Yenisei-Angara	3,650	5,877	Asia
Amur-Argun	3,590	5,780	Asia
Ob-Irtysh	3,360	5,410	Asia
Plata-Parana	3,030	4,878	South America
Hyang He (Yellow)	2,903	4,674	Asia
Congo (Zaire)	2,900	4,669	Africa
Lena	2,730	4,395	Asia
MacKenzie	2,635	4,242	North America
Mekong	2,600	4,186	Asia
Niger	2,600	4,186	Africa
Missouri	2,533	4,078	North America
Mississippi	2,348	3,780	North America

LARGE U.S. CITIES 1990

U.S. Cities—Rank

1	New York, NY	26	Nashville-Davidson, TN	42	Austin, TX
2	Chicago, IL	27	St. Louis, MO	43	Oakland, CA
3	Los Angeles, CA	28	Kansas City, MO	44	Albuquerque, NM
4	Philadelphia, PA	29	El Paso, TX	45	Tucson, AZ
5	Houston, TX	30	Atlanta, GA	46	Newark, NJ
6	Detroit, MI	31	Pittsburgh, PA	47	Charlotte, NC
7	Dallas, TX	32	Oklahoma City, OK	48	Omaha, NE
8	San Diego, CA	33	Cincinnati, OH	49	Louisville, KY
9	Baltimore, MD	34	Fort Worth, TX	50	Birmingham, AL
10	San Antonio, TX	35	Minneapolis, MN	51	Wichita, KS
11	Phoenix, AZ	36	Portland, OR	52	Sacramento, CA
12	Honolulu, HI	37	Long Beach, CA	53	Tampa, FL
13	Indianapolis, IN	38	Tulsa, OK	54	St. Paul, MN
14	San Francisco, CA	39	Buffalo, NY	55	Norfolk, VA
15	Memphis, TN	40	Toledo, OH	56	Virginia Beach, VA
16	Washington, DC	41	Miami, FL	57	Rochester, NY
17	San Jose, CA				
18	Milwaukee, WI				
19	Cleveland, OH				
20	Columbus, OH				
21	Boston, MA				
22	New Orleans, LA				
23	Jacksonville, FL				
24	Seattle, WA				
25	Denver, CO				

U.S. Cities—Rank

58 Akron, OH	73 Yonkers, NY	87 Chattanooga, TN
59 St. Petersburg, FL	74 Des Moines, IA	88 Columbus, GA
60 Corpus Christi, TX	75 Knoxville, TN	89 Las Vegas, NV
61 Jersey City, NJ	76 Grand Rapids, MI	90 Salt Lake City, UT
62 Anaheim, CA	77 Montgomery, AL	91 Worcester, MA
63 Baton Rouge, LA	78 Lubbock, TX	92 Warren, MI
64 Richmond, VA	79 Anchorage, AK	93 Kansas City, MO
65 Fresno, CA	80 Fort Wayne, IN	94 Arlington, TX
66 Colorado Springs, CO	81 Lincoln, NE	95 Flint, MI
67 Shreveport, LA	82 Spokane, WA	96 Aurora, CO
68 Lexington-Fayette, KY	83 Riverside, CA	97 Tacoma, WA
69 Santa Ana, CA	84 Madison, WI	98 Little Rock, AR
70 Dayton, OH	85 Huntington Beach, CA	99 Providence, RI
71 Jackson, MS	86 Syracuse, NY	100 Greensboro, NC
72 Mobile, AL		

SECTION III
Word Groups

22. Synonyms

Synonyms are words that have similar meanings. Dictionaries often use synonyms in their definitions. There are whole books of synonyms and special reference works, such as the thesaurus, that have clusters of words or phrases, all with similar meanings. These are particularly useful in finding just the right word when writing.

able – capable – competent
abrupt – sudden – hasty
achieve – accomplish – attain
add – total – sum up
after – following – subsequent
aim – purpose – goal
all – every – entire
allow – permit – grant
anger – rage – fury
answer – response – reply
arrive – reach – get to
ask – question – interrogate
astonish – surprise – amaze

back – rear – behind
bear – endure – tolerate
before – prior to – in front of
begin – start – initiate
below – under – beneath
birth – origin – genesis
border – edge – margin
bother – annoy – pester
boy – lad – youth
brave – courageous – daring
bulge – swell – protrude
busy – occupied – engaged

call – shout – yell
calm – composed – serene
car – auto – vehicle
carry – tote – lug
careful – cautious – prudent
change – vary – alter
charm – fascinate – enchant
cheat – deceive – swindle
children – youngsters – tots
city – borough – town
close – shut – seal
consent – agree – acquiesce
continue – persevere – persist
country – nation – state
cure – heal – restore

danger – peril – hazard
decrease – lessen – diminish

defect – flaw – blemish
delay – postpone – procrastinate
different – varied – diverse
disaster – calamity – catastrophe
divide – separate – split
during – while – at the same time
dwell – live – reside

eat – consume – devour
effort – exertion – endeavor
end – finish – complete
energy – power – strength
enough – adequate – sufficient
error – mistake – fallacy
explain – expound – elucidate

faith – trust – reliance
fat – plump – stout
fetch – bring – retrieve
find – locate – discover
fix – repair – mend
flat – level – flush
food – nourishment – sustenance
form – shape – make up
fragile – delicate – breakable
freedom – independence – liberty
frequent – often – many times

gay – lively – vivacious
gift – present – donation
give – grant – hand over
glum – morose – sullen
go – leave – depart
grateful – appreciative – thankful
great – grand – large
grow – mature – develop

happy – glad – joyous
have – own – possess
hard – difficult – troublesome
hate – detest – despise
heal – mend – cure
help – aid – assist
hide – conceal – secrete
high – tall – lofty

The Reading Teacher's Book of Lists, Third Edition, © 1993 by Prentice Hall

hold – grasp – clutch
hurry – rush – accelerate

idea – thought – concept
ill – sick – indisposed
income – revenue – earnings
injure – wound – hurt

job – work – occupation
junk – rubbish – waste
just – fair – right

keep – hold – retain
key – answer – solution
kind – considerate – helpful
kill – slaughter – murder

large – big – enormous
last – endure – persist
late – tardy – delayed
learn – acquire – understand
leave – depart – go away
like – enjoy – be fond of
listen – hear – attend
little – small – petite
long – lengthy – drawn out
look – glance – see

mad – crazy – insane
make – build – construct
many – multitudinous – numerous
marvelous – wonderful – extraordinary
mean – stand for – denote
mend – repair – restore
method – way – manner
might – may – perhaps
mistake – error – blunder
move – transport – propel

name – title – designation
near – close by – in the vicinity
need – require – want
new – fresh – recent
noise – uproar – clamor
novice – beginner – learner

occur – happen – take place
often – frequently – repeatedly
omit – delete – remove
one – single – unit
old – aged – ancient
open – unlock – unseal

ornament – decoration – adornment
outlive – survive – outlast

page – sheet – leaf
pain – ache – hurt
pair – couple – duo
pardon – forgive – excuse
part – portion – piece
peak – summit – top
people – public – populace
play – frolic – romp
praise – acclaim – applaud
primary – chief – principal
prohibit – forbid – restrict
put – place – locate

raid – attack – invade
reckless – careless – rash
remote – distant – secluded
renew – restore – revive
respect – honor – revere
revise – alter – correct
right – correct – proper

say – state – remark
seem – appear – look
sell – vend – market
shame – humiliation – mortification
sorry – regretful – penitent
speed – haste – hurry
start – begin – commence
stop – halt – end
story – tale – account
show – demonstrate – display
still – unmoving – silent
strength – power – energy
supply – provide – furnish
surpass – exceed – outdo

take – grab – seize
tense – taut – rigid
terrify – frighten – alarm
thanks – gratitude – appreciation
thaw – melt – dissolve
thief – robber – crook
thin – slender – slim
think – reflect – contemplate
time – period – season
timid – fearful – cowardly
tiny – small – diminutive

The Reading Teacher's Book of Lists, Third Edition, © 1993 by Prentice Hall

trial – test – experiment
try – attempt – endeavor
turn – revolve – pivot
true – faithful – loyal

ugly – homely – plain
understand – comprehend – discern
unify – consolidate – combine
uproar – tumult – pandemonium
urge – press – exhort
use – operate – employ

vacant – empty – unoccupied
value – worth – price

vast – huge – immense
verify – confirm – substantiate
victor – winner – champion

walk – stroll – saunter
want – desire – crave
waver – fluctuate – vacillate
weak – feeble – impotent
wealth – riches – fortune
word – term – expression
work – labor – toil
world – globe – earth
write – record – draft

See also List 23, Antonyms; List 24, Analogies; List 25, Similes and List 26, Metaphors.

23. *Antonyms*

Antonyms are words that mean the opposite or nearly the opposite of each other for one meaning. Both synonyms and antonyms are often used in tests and language drills.

above – below
absent – present
accident – intent
accomplishment – failure
achieve – fail
add – subtract
adjacent – distant
admire – detest
admit – reject
adore – hate
advance – retreat
affirm – deny
afraid – confident
after – before
aid – hinder
alarm – comfort
alert – asleep
alive – dead
allow – forbid
alone – together
amateur – professional
amuse – bore
ancient – modern
annoy – soothe
answer – question
apparent – obscure
argue – agree
arrive – depart
arrogant – humble
ascend – descend
attack – defend
attract – repel
awake – asleep
awkward – graceful

back – front
bad – good
bare – covered
beautiful – ugly
before – after
bent – straight
better – worse
big – little
birth – death

bitter – sweet
black – white
blunt – sharp
body – soul
bold – timid
bottom – top
brave – cowardly
break – repair
brief – long
bright – dull
bring – remove
boy – girl
busy – idle
buy – sell

capture – release
cause – effect
cautious – careless
center – edge
change – remain
cheap – expensive
child – adult
chilly – warm
clean – dirty
close – open
cold – hot
command – obey
complex – simple
compliment – insult
constant – variable
continue – interrupt
cool – warm
copy – original
countrymen – foreigner
crazy – sane
crooked – straight
cruel – kind
cry – laugh
curse – bless

damage – improve
dark – light
dawn – sunset
day – night

deep – shallow
destroy – create
difficult – easy
dim – bright
divide – unite
doubt – trust
drunk – sober
dull – sharp
dumb – smart

earth – sky
east – west
easy – hard
elementary – advanced
end – begin
even – odd
evening – morning
evil – good
exceptional – common
expand – shrink

fail – pass
failure – success
false – true
famous – unknown
fancy – plain
fast – slow
fat – thin
fiction – fact
find – lose
finish – start
firm – flabby
fix – break
follow – lead
forgive – blame
forward – backward
free – restricted
fresh – stale
friend – enemy
funny – sad
full – empty

gain – lose
generous – stingy
gentle – harsh

get – give
give – receive
glad – sad
gloomy – cheerful
glossy – dull
go – come
gorgeous – ugly
great – small
greed – generous
grief – joy
ground – sky
guard – attack
guess – know

handsome – ugly
happy – sad
hard – soft
hate – love
he – she
head – foot
heal – infect
healthy – sick
heaven – hell
heavy – light
height – depth
help – hinder
hero – coward
high – low
hill – valley
him – her
hire – fire
his – hers
hot – cold
horrible – pleasant
huge – tiny
hurry – slow
hurt – help

idle – active
in – out
individual – group
innocent – guilty
inside – outside
intelligent – stupid

jolly – serious
joy – sadness

keep – lose
kind – cruel
knowledge – ignorance

large – small
last – first
laugh – cry
leading – following
leave – arrive
left – right
less – more
let – prevent
level – uneven
lie – truth
life – death
like – dislike
likely – unlikely
liquid – solid
little – big
lively – inactive
lonely – crowded
long – short
loose – tight
lost – found
loud – soft
love – hate

maintain – discontinue
major – minor
make – destroy
male – female
man – woman
many – few
marvelous – terrible
mature – immature
melt – freeze
mess – tidiness
miscellaneous – specific
mistake – accuracy
mix – separate
moist – dry
more – less
most – least
mother – father
move – stay

naive – sophisticated
nasty – nice
near – far
never – always
new – old
no – yes
nobody – everybody
noise – quiet

none – all
north – south
nothing – something
now – then

obese – thin
obvious – hidden
odd – even
offend – please
offer – refuse
often – seldom
old – young
on – off
one – several
ordinary – uncommon
other – same
over – under

pacify – agitate
pain – pleasure
panic – calm
part – whole
partial – complete
particular – general
pass – fail
passive – active
peace – disturbance
perceive – ignore
permanent – unstable
permit – refuse
pessimistic – optimistic
physical – spiritual
place – misplace
plain – fancy
play – work
plentiful – sparse
plump – thin
polish – dull
polite – rude
pollute – purify
poor – rich
positive – negative
powerful – weak
praise – criticism
preceding – following
present – absent
pretty – ugly
prevent – encourage
pride – modesty
private – public

problem – solution
profit – loss
prohibit – allow
pupil – teacher
push – pull

quality – inferiority
quick – slow
quiet – noisy
quit – start

raise – lower
random – specific
rapid – slow
rare – common
raw – cooked
ready – unprepared
rear – front
reduce – increase
regret – rejoice
relax – tighten
remember – forget
repair – destroy
retain – lose
revenge – forgiveness
ridiculous – sensible
right – wrong
rigid – flexible
rise – sink
rough – smooth
rude – polite

sad – happy
same – different
satisfy – displease
secluded – public
segregate – integrate
seldom – often
sell – buy
send – receive
sensational – dull
servant – master
shack – palace
shade – light
shame – honor
sharp – dull
she – he

short – long
show – hide
shy – trusting
sick – healthy
silence – sound
single – married
single – plural
sit – stand
slave – master
slender – fat
slow – fast
small – large
soak – dry
sober – drunk
some – none
something – nothing
sorrow – gladness
sour – sweet
speechless – talkative
spend – earn
stale – fresh
start – stop
started – finished
stay – leave
steal – provide
sterile – fertile
stiff – flexible
still – moving
stingy – generous
stop – go
stranger – friend
strength – weakness
student – teacher
sturdy – weak
sunrise – sunset
superb – inferior
supple – rigid
survive – die
suspect – trust

take – give
tall – short
tame – wild
teach – learn
temporary – permanent
thaw – freeze

there – here
thin – thick
thorough – incomplete
thrifty – wasteful
tidy – messy
tie – loosen
timid – bold
to – from
together – apart
told – asked
top – bottom
toward – away
tragic – comic
transform – retain
transparent – opaque
triumph – defeat
true – false
truth – lie

ultimate – primary
union – separation
unique – common
up – down
upset – stabilize
urge – deter

vacant – full
vague – definite
vanish – appear
vast – limited
vertical – horizontal
villain – hero
visitor – host/hostess

waive – require
wake – sleep
wealth – poverty
weep – laugh
well – badly
wet – dry
white – black
wild – tame
win – lose
with – without
worship – detest
worth – uselessness
wreck – create

The Reading Teacher's Book of Lists, Third Edition, © 1993 by Prentice Hall

See also List 22, Synonyms.

24. Analogies

Analogies are used for teaching and testing. The key is to determine the relationship of the first pair of words and then find a second pair of words that has the same relationship. For example, "in" is to "out" as "hot" is to "_____"? (In the notation used below, this is written: "in : out : : hot :   .") Since "out" is the opposite of "in," the answer is "cold," which is the opposite of "hot." Below are some common types of analogies and several examples for each.

Antonyms

win : lose : : stop : start
much : little : : early : late

Synonyms

small : little : : big : large
own : possess : : find : locate

Object – Action

ear : hear : : mouth : speak
dog : bark : : bird : chirp

Part – Whole

finger : hand : : page : book
room : house : : branch : tree

Use

chair : sit : : bed : sleep
kettle : soup : : griddle : pancakes

Cause and Effect

tired : sleep : : hungry : eat
work : success : : study : learn

Numerical Relationships

three : six : : four : eight
two : three : : five : six

Sequence

breakfast : lunch : : morning : afternoon
pour : drink : : cook : eat

Degree

pretty : beautiful : : warm : hot
intelligent : brilliant : : star : super star

Object – Description

silk : smooth : : sandpaper : rough
snow : cold : : sun : hot

Grammar

she : her : : he : him
eat : ate : : sleep : slept

Place

bear : den : : bee : hive
bird : sky : : fish : sea

Object – Class

blue : color : : round : shape
dog : animal : : carrot : vegetable

Member – Group

fish : school : : student : class
professor : faculty : : sister : sorority

Object – User

hammer : carpenter : : pen : writer
bat : baseball player : : whistle : referee

MORE ANALOGIES

mother : aunt : : father : uncle
car : driver : : plane : pilot
green : color : : cinnamon : spice
coffee : drink : : hamburger : eat
arrow : bow : : bullet : gun
ceiling : room : : lid : pan
page : book : : Ohio : U.S.
glove : hand : : boot : foot
swim : pool : : jog : road
meat : beef : : fruit : apple
date : calendar : : time : clock
carpenter : house : : composer : symphony
soldier : regiment : : star : constellation
duck : drake : : bull : cow
cells : skin : : bricks : wall
paw : dog : : fin : fish
moon : earth : : earth : sun
tree : lumber : : wheat : flour
library : books : : cupboard : dishes
princess : queen : : prince : king
story : read : : song : sing
length : weight : : inches : pounds
one : three : : single : triple
blind : deaf : : see : hear
wrist : hand : : ankle : foot
engine : go : : brake : stop
glass : break : : paper : tear
book : character : : recipe : ingredient
sing : pleased : : shout : angry
penny : dollar : : foot : yard
cabin : build : : well : dig
temperature : humidity : : thermometer : hygrometer
left : right : : top : bottom
easy : simple : : hard : difficult

The Reading Teacher's Book of Lists, Third Edition, © 1993 by Prentice Hall

25. *Similes*

A simile is a figure of speech that uses the word "as" or "like." Figures of speech are used like adjectives or adverbs. They modify or describe a person, place, thing, or action with a colorful and often visual term or phrase. Creative writers and poets make good use of these. The following are frequently used similes.

SIMILES USING "AS"

as bright as the noonday sun
as busy as a bee
as clear as a bell
as clear as day
as clear as the nose on your face
as cool as a cucumber
as certain as death and taxes
as cold as ice
as comfortable as an old shoe
as cute as a button
as cuddly as a baby
as dark as night
as deaf as a doorpost
as dry as a bone
as deep as the ocean
as fat as a pig
as flat as a pancake
as fresh as dew
as innocent as a newborn baby
as green as grass
as hard as rock
as hard as nails
as happy as a lark
as hungry as a bear
as loud as thunder
as light as a feather
as lovely as a rose
as meek as a lamb
as quick as a wink
as quiet as a mouse
as rough as sandpaper
as smooth as glass
as strong as an ox
as soft as old leather
as sly as a fox
as stubborn as a mule

as smart as a whip
as soft as silk
as skinny as a rail
as slow as molasses in January
as stiff as a board
as sweet as honey
as white as new fallen snow

SIMILES USING "LIKE"

acts like a bull in a china shop
eat like it's going out of style
eat like a pig
chatters like a monkey
cry like a baby
cheeks like roses
drinks like a fish
eats like a bird
eyes like stars
feel like two cents
fits like a glove
fought like cats and dogs
laugh like a hyena
moves like a snail
run around like a chicken with its head
   cut off
run like a deer
sing like a bird
slept like a log
stood out like a sore thumb
sit there like a bump on a log
spoke like an orator
sparkled like diamonds
walk like an elephant
work like a dog
waddle like a duck
works like a charm

See also List 28, Common Word Idioms; List 80, Descriptive Words; and List 26, Metaphors.

26. Metaphors

Metaphors are figures of speech that compare two things, but do not use the words "like" and "as." These colorful phrases are used like adverbs or adjectives to describe persons, places, things, or actions. Students must learn not to take them literally but to enjoy their use. This is not an exhaustive list, but it might be just enough to get a lesson or an essay started. See List 27, Idiomatic Expressions, for additional metaphors.

Ann is a walking encyclopedia.

John's head is a computer.

Jealousy is a green-eyed monster.

That car is an old dinosaur.

Her porcelain skin is flawless.

She's a regular adding machine.

He is faster than a streak of lightening.

A fossil of a man greeted us at the door.

Use kid gloves when handling this.

Skip is a clown.

Her heart is a fountain of kindness.

The mountain of paperwork seemed to grow.

His heart is an iceberg.

The army of ants attacked the fallen lollipop.

Tom is a marionette; his brother Bill works the strings.

She is the shining star in his dark, dreary life.

He is a snail when it comes to getting his work done.

Mr. Mather's bark is worse than his bite.

The toddler was a clinging vine near his mother.

His books were steamships and starships taking him to new worlds.

His new car turned out to be a lemon.

She was thunderstruck when she learned she had won.

He's top banana where he works.

The police were determined to get to the bottom of the mystery.

When her mother died, she shouldered the burden of raising the children.

I'm a real chicken when it comes to getting an injection.

At night my bedroom is a real icebox.

When my mother saw how poor my grades were, she gave me a real tongue lashing.

When I was lost in the woods, the branches of the trees became hands reaching out to grab me.

By the time she finished her first day at work, she was dead tired.

His stomach was a bottomless pit.

The night was growing old, and there was still so much to be done.

My grandmother is very broad-minded about most things.

He turned thumbs down at the idea of moving to a new town.

The Reading Teacher's Book of Lists, Third Edition, © 1993 by Prentice Hall

27. Idiomatic Expressions

Idiomatic expressions cannot be understood from the literal meanings of their words. Instead, these colorful phrases must be "translated." Idiomatic expressions are used often in conversation and informal writing; however, most are not suitable for formal writing. Students who are learning the English language find idiomatic expressions particularly troublesome. Teach the expressions just as you would teach single vocabulary words.

The Reading Teacher's Book of Lists, Third Edition, © 1993 by Prentice Hall

Kathryn *caught a cold* during vacation.

Fred put the old papers in the *circular file*.

Gloria and Camille *don't see eye to eye* on everything.

Carla has always been *afraid of her own shadow*.

David finished the project *ahead of time*.

It *cost an arm and a leg* to get the VCR fixed.

Willie was *asleep at the switch* and missed his chance.

Nobody likes a *backseat driver*.

We need to *clear the air*.

I *got cold feet* when it was my turn to speak.

The cop told the man *to come clean*.

We each *coughed up* a dollar.

Jody hardly *cracked a book* all weekend.

Samantha was still *dead to the world* at noon.

Darin was *down in the dumps* all day.

Tell Gerry to *drop me a line*.

Alicia *drove a hard bargain*.

The math quiz was *duck soup*.

The price goes up *every time I turn around*.

His *eyes popped out* when he saw the bill.

Money *burns a hole in his pocket*.

We have *a fat chance* of getting done in time.

Lilly's *head* was *in the clouds*.

Christopher was *fishing for* the answer.

It takes Romeo *forever and a day* to get ready.

The party was *for the birds*.

I'd *give my right arm* to own a plane.

Steve's such a *good egg*.

The driver always *gets up with the chickens*.

Do you have any more *half-baked ideas*?

Debbie saw the *writing on the wall*.

Jennifer's new car *hugged the road*.

She's got *music in her blood*.

We're all *in the same boat*.

Keep your *eye on the ball* and you'll succeed.

Janet *lost her marbles* after the accident.

Sue tried to *mend her fences* before leaving.

Adam kept his *nose in a book* all afternoon.

His *days were numbered*.

She's *not playing with a full deck*.

Jason *has* football *on the brain*.

Lunch was *on the house*.

Ryan *got up on the wrong side of the bed*.

That book *really opened my eyes*.

The car *came out of nowhere* and hit the pole.

We got a long *song and dance* about the rules.

Christine *stole the spotlight*.

We need *to stick together*.

Well, doesn't that *take the cake*?

Lisa *took the rap* for the others.

Do you *get the picture*?

He didn't *know the ropes*.

Keep it under your hat.

She's been *walking on air* all day.

We're not *out of the woods* yet.

She *lost her temper* for no reason.

Straighten up the house before you leave.

Don't *get hung up* on the problem.

Joey's grandmother has *a green thumb*.

He quit smoking *cold turkey*.

See also List 80, Descriptive Words; and List 28, Common Word Idioms.

28. Common Word Idioms

Many idioms are formed around common words. Use this list as a starter for exploring American idioms.

all	all along, all at once, all but, all ears, all eyes, all hours, all in all, all out, all over, all set, all systems go, all there, all thumbs, all wet
back	back down, back out, back up, back and forth, back off, back street, backseat driver, back to the salt mines
beat	beat around the bush, beats all, beat down, beat it, beat the band, beat the bushes, beat someone to the punch, beat up
blow	blow a fuse, blow hot and cold, blow your own horn, blow out, blow one's mind, blow one's lines, blow over, blow the whistle, blow up, blow the lid off
break	break down, break in, break into, break one's promise, break out, break the ice, break the news, break up, break even, break ground, break one's heart, break one's neck, break through
bring	bring about, bring around, bring down the house, bring (something) home to one, bring home the bacon, bring in, bring off, bring on, bring one to do something, bring out, bring up
burn	burn one's bridges, burn one's fingers, burn out, burn rubber, burn the candle at both ends, burn the midnight oil, burn up
call	call a halt, call a spade a spade, call attention to, call for, call forth, call in, call names, call on, call out, call up, call a strike, call it quits, call it a day, call the shots, call to order
catch	catch cold, catch fire, catch on, catch one's breath, catch one's eye, catch up
come	come about, come again, come alive, come a long way, come back, come by, come clean, come across, come around, come down on, come in for, come into, come into your own, come off, come off it, come out, come to pass, come up, come up to, come upon, come-on, come over, come to, come through, come to think of it
cut	cut across, cut corners, cut in, cut out, cut someone out, cut out for, cut up, cut into, cut off, cut the mustard
do	do away with, do justice to, do for, do in, do someone proud, do out of, do up, do well by someone, do without, do the honors, do away with
eat	eat away, eat humble pie, eat crow, eat like a bird, eat like a horse, eat dirt, eat someone out of house and home, eat your heart out, eat your words, eat your hat, eat out of your hand, eat it up
fall	fall by the wayside, fall down, fall flat, fall for, fall in with, fall out, fall over each other, fall short, fall through, fall behind, fall back on, fall over backwards
get	get along, get at, get away with, get back at, get by, get carried away by, get even with, get in with, get into, get on, get on someone's nerves, get your back up, get someone's goat, get out of, get over, get the better of, get the hang of, get up, get wind of, get across, get ahead, get around to, get cracking, get lost, get off the ground, get one's feet wet, get the ax, get the show on the road, get up and go
give	give a damn, give away, give in, give of, give out, give up, give a hand, give oneself up, give up the ship

The Reading Teacher's Book of Lists, Third Edition, © 1993 by Prentice Hall

The Reading Teacher's Book of Lists, Third Edition, © 1993 by Prentice Hall

go   go all out, go by, go down, go easy, go far, go for, go in for, go into, go off the deep end, go on, go one better, go out, go over, go to the dogs, go with, go without, go ahead, go back on a promise, go broke, go fly a kite, go haywire, go it alone, go like clockwork

hang   hang around, hang on, hang out, hang up, hang in there, hang ten

have   have it both ways, have it coming, have it in for someone, have it out with someone, have a heart, have had it, have it made

hit   hit your stride, hit the books, hit the ceiling, hit the roof, hit the hay, hit the sack, hit the headlines, hit the high points, hit the nail on the head, hit upon, hit bottom, hit and run, hit it off, hit the road, hit the jackpot, hit the spot, hit the bull's eye

hold   hold a candle to, hold forth, hold on, hold down, hold back, hold everything, hold your fire, hold out, hold up, hold the fort, hold your own

keep   keep a straight face, keep company, keep on, keep your head, keep your head above water, keep your word, keep the pot boiling, keep the wolf from the door, keep up, keep up appearances, keep up with, keep it down, keep one's chin up, keep one's nose clean, keep track, keep one's fingers crossed

lay   lay a finger on someone, lay aside, lay down one's life, lay down the law, lay hands on, lay it on, lay off, lay your hand on something, lay yourself open to, lay out, lay up, lay low, lay to rest

let   let off steam, let on, let your hair down, let sleeping dogs lie, let the cat out of the bag, let up, let down, let go of

look   look down on, look down your nose at, look for, look into, look out, look up, look up to someone, look after, look back, look over

make   make a move, make a play for, make certain, make something do, make ends meet, make fun of, make good, make haste, make heads or tails of something, make believe, make a point, make friends, make sense of, make it, make out, make over, makeshift, make sure, make the fur fly, make the grade, make up, make up for, make up your mind, make up to

play   play at something, play down, play fast and loose, play havoc with, play hooky, play into someone's hands, play on, play second fiddle, play the devil, play the fool, play the game, play by ear, play along with, play off, play possum, play the field, play up to, play with fire

pull   pull a fast one, pull off, pull your weight, pull strings, pull through, pull to pieces, pull together, pull up, pull the wool over your eyes, pull up stakes, pull rank, pull the plug, pull the rug out from under

put   put away, put an end to, put in one's place, put one's foot down, put it on the map, put someone on, put to bed, put to use, put down, put forward, put in for, put off, put on, put your cards on the table, put out, put right, put two and two together, put up, put up with

run   run across, run into, run away, run down, run afoul of, run in, run out of, run over, run ragged, run rings around, run through, run the risk of, run away with, run short, run wild

see   see about, see eye to eye, see into, see through, see to, see daylight, see off, see red, see to it

sit sit on, sit on the fence, sit out, sit pretty, sit tight, sit up, sit back, sit-in, sit tight

take take aim, take after, take a bath, take advantage of, take in, take by surprise, take by storm, take effect, take a back seat, take a powder, take care, take it easy, take someone for, take for granted, take heart, take ill, take in, take issue, take it from me, take it hard, take it into your head, take it out on someone, take something lying down, take note of, take off, take on, take your time, take out, take over, take the cake, take to heart, take the trouble, take it upon yourself

throw throw a curve, throw one's hat in the ring, throw the book at, throw cold water on, throw a fit, throw a party, throw in the sponge, throw light on, throw off, throw one's weight around, throw out, throw up

turn turn a cold shoulder to, turn color, turn off, turn one's stomach, turn the clock back, turn the tide, turn thumbs down, turn over a new leaf, turn a deaf ear, turn down, turn in, turn loose, turn on, turn your head, turn out, turn over, turn the tables on someone, turn to, turn turtle, turn up

The Reading Teacher's Book of Lists, Third Edition, © 1993 by Prentice Hall

See also List 27, Idiomatic Expressions; and List 80, Descriptive Words.

29. Proverbs

Proverbs are common, wise, or thoughtful sayings that are short and often applicable to different situations. Every culture and language has its own, from the ancient Chinese Confucius "A picture is worth a thousand words" to the American "A stitch in time saves nine." Here are just a few: you and your students might enjoy adding to the collection. These can also be suggestions for student-written stories or their own fables.

Animals

Birds of a feather flock together.
When the cat's away the mice will play.
He who lies down with dogs gets up with fleas.
Don't count your chickens until they're hatched.
A bird in the hand is worth two in the bush.
You can lead a horse to water, but you can't make it drink.
The early bird catches the worm.
Curiosity killed the cat.
You can't teach an old dog new tricks.
Don't change horses in midstream.
Let sleeping dogs lie.

Food

Don't cry over spilt milk.
The proof of the pudding is in the eating.
Too many cooks spoil the broth.
You can't have your cake and eat it too.
An apple a day keeps the doctor away.
Half a loaf is better than none.

Money

A penny saved is a penny earned.
Time is money.
Lend your money and lose your friend.
Money burns a hole in your pocket.
All that glitters is not gold.
A fool and his money are soon parted.
Early to bed, early to rise makes a man healthy, wealthy, and wise.

Nature

It never rains but it pours.
A rolling stone gathers no moss.
Make hay while the sun shines.
Every cloud has a silver lining.
Leave no stone unturned.
The grass always looks greener on the other side.
One tree doesn't make a forest.
Still waters run deep.

Relationships

Marry in haste, repent at leisure.
If you can't beat them, join them.
Familiarity breeds contempt.
Short visits make long friends.
A faint heart never won a fair lady.
Like father, like son.
Absence makes the heart grow fonder.
Good fences make good neighbors.
A friend in need is a friend indeed.
Do unto others as you would have them do unto you.

Miscellaneous

If the shoe fits wear it.
People who live in glass houses shouldn't throw stones.
Two wrongs don't make a right.
The pen is mightier than the sword.
Necessity is the mother of invention.
Actions speak louder than words.
Haste makes waste.
He who hesitates is lost.

Look before you leap.

Beggars can't be choosers.

A stitch in time saves nine.

Two heads are better than one.

Many hands make light work.

Fool me once, shame on you. Fool me twice, shame on me.

Strike while the iron is hot.

Where there's smoke there's fire.

Out of the frying pan and into the fire.

A watched pot never boils.

Sometimes you have to turn as fast as you can just to stay in the same place.

The reason for doing it right today is tomorrow.

This is the first day of the rest of your life.

Now is a great experience.

Do not blame a man until you have walked a mile in his moccasins.

One hand for the ship and one hand for yourself.

The palest ink is better than the most retentive memory.

Waste not, want not.

A quitter never wins and a winner never quits.

In the land of the blind, the one-eyed man is king.

Sticks and stones can break my bones, but names can never hurt me.

A picture is worth a thousand words.

See also List 30, Murphy's Law and Others.

30. *Murphy's Law And Others*

Murphy's Law and other principles might amuse or bemuse you. Some have a little jab of truth in them. Society is governed by certain immutable laws and principles. Murphy's Law, though, of somewhat doubtful authorship, is nonetheless real. Ask any engineer, mechanic, office manager, or computer programmer.

Both the Peter Principle and Parkinson's Law were developed by very real college professors, and both are explained somewhat seriously in full books.

The other principles given here are sometimes original and sometimes borrowed from the common folklore. Use them and amuse with them as needed. Both you and your students might like to add to this important list of real-life observations for fun and profitable insight.

Murphy's Law: If anything can go wrong, it will, and at the worst possible moment.

Corollaries

The other line always moves faster.
The race isn't always to the swift or the battle to the strong, but that's the way to bet.
When in doubt, use a bigger hammer.
A Smith & Wesson beats four aces.
If you play with anything long enough, you'll break it.
If everything seems to be going fine, you've probably overlooked something.
Nature always sides with the hidden flaw.

Peter Principle

In a hierarchy every employee tends to rise to his or her level of incompetence.

Corollaries

All useful work is done by those who have not yet reached their levels of incompetence.
Cream rises until it sours.

Parkinson's Law

Work expands to fill time available for its completion.

Corollaries

An administrator wants to multiply subordinates, not rivals.
Administrators make work for each other.

Fry's Observation

The more obnoxious the kid, the less he or she will be absent.

The Reading Teacher's Book of Lists, Third Edition, © 1993 by Prentice Hall

Kling's Axiom

Any simple idea can be worded in a complicated way.

Miscellaneous

No matter how hard you teach a thing, some student is certain not to learn it.
Trouble never comes at a convenient time.
Everything takes longer than you think.
The greater the hurry, the slower the traffic.
No amount of careful planning will ever beat dumb luck.
A good theory might be worth a thousand words, but that won't make it any more practical.
School budgets are always cut in a manner so as to create the most disruption.
There are three kinds of lies: white lies, damned lies, and statistics.
Extracurricular activities sometimes are neither extra nor curricular.
One person's exuberance is the next person's annoyance.
Principals may come and principals may go, but the secretary will run the school regardless.
You can plan anything you like; just don't expect it to happen that way.
Things don't get lost, but they sometimes are carefully put away in some strange places.
People who ask for just a minute of your time don't have very accurate watches.
There's got to be a way to eliminate the last few days of school.
Just when you are sure kids are no good, one of them will do something nice for you.
Maybe a school could exist without heat, light, and water, but take away the duplicating machine and it would have to close down.
If Saint Peter uses multiple-choice tests, we are all in for trouble.
Whoever said the worst students aren't creative? Look at their excuses.
Don't fix it if it is not baroque.
These are the good old days of the next generation.
Kids are the only future the human race has.
You can't have everything; where would you put it?
Nobody notices big errors.
Any change looks terrible at first.
Everybody who does not work has a scheme that does.

31. *Euphemisms*

These euphemisms might stand you in good stead at report-card time or for parent interviews. They might also take some of the puffery out of some reports you may have to read. Students enjoy euphemisms; share some of these with your class and have them add to the list.

BLUNT TRUTH	EUPHEMISM
Lies	Shows difficulty in distinguishing between imaginary and factual material.
Is a klutz	Has difficulty with motor control and coordination.
Needs nagging	Accomplishes task when interest is constantly prodded.
Fights	Resorts to physical means of winning his or her point or attracting attention.
Smells bad	Needs guidance in development of good habits of hygiene.
Cheats	Needs help in learning to adhere to rules and standards of fair play.
Steals	Needs help in learning to respect the property rights of others.
Is a wise guy or gal	Needs guidance in learning to express himself or herself respectfully.
Is lazy	Requires ongoing supervision in order to work well.
Is rude	Lacks a respectful attitude toward others.
Is selfish	Needs help in learning to enjoy sharing with others.
Is gross	Needs guidance in developing the social graces.
Has big mouth	Needs to develop quieter habits of communication.
Eats like a pig	Needs to develop more refined table manners.
Bullies others	Has qualities of leadership, but needs to use them more constructively.
Is babyish	Shows lack of maturity in relationships with others.
Hangs out	Seems to feel secure only in group situations; needs to develop sense of identity and independence.
Is disliked by others	Needs help in developing meaningful peer relationships.
Is often late	Needs guidance in developing habits of responsibility and punctuality.
Is truant	Needs to develop a sense of responsibility in regard to attendance.

Also see List 59, Comprehension Thesaurus and List 105, Doublespeak.

SECTION IV
Word Origins

32. Clipped Words—Words Shortened by Common Usage

These are words that have been shortened or clipped by common use, as in *sub* for *submarine*. This shortening is called Zipf's Principle and is well known in the study of languages.

ad	advertisement	memo	memorandum
auto	automobile	miss	mistress
bike	bicycle	mod	modern
burger	hamburger	movie	moving picture
bus	omnibus	mum	chrysanthemum
bust	burst	pants	pantaloons
cab	cabriolet	pen	penitentiary
canter	Canterbury gallop	pep	pepper
cent	centum	perk	percolate
champ	champion	perk	perquisite
chemist	alchemist	phone	telephone
clerk	cleric	photo	photograph
coed	coeducational student	pike	turnpike
con	convict	plane	airplane
copter	helicopter	pop	popular
cuke	cucumber	prof	professor
curio	curiosity	prom	promenade
deb	debutante	ref	referee
doc	doctor	scram	scramble
dorm	dormitory	specs	spectacles
drape	drapery	sport	disport
exam	examination	stat	statistics
fan	fanatic	stereo	stereophonic
flu	influenza	still	distill
fridge	refrigerator	sub	submarine
gab	gabble	tails	coattails
gas	gasoline	taxi	taxicab
grad	graduate	teen	teenager
gym	gymnasium	tie	necktie
hack	hackney	trig	trigonometry
iron	flatiron	trump	triumph
lab	laboratory	tux	tuxedo
limo	limousine	typo	typographical error
lube	lubricate	van	caravan
lunch	luncheon	varsity	university
margarine	oleomargarine	vet	veteran
mart	market	vet	veterinarian
math	mathematics	wig	periwig
mend	amend	zoo	zoological garden

See also List 33, Portmanteau Words; and List 34, Compound Words.

33. *Portmanteau Words—Words That Have Been Blended Together*

Alice, in *Alice in Wonderland*, asks Humpty Dumpty what "slithy" (from the Jabberwocky) means. He tells her that it means "lithe" and "slimy." "You see there are two meanings packed into one word."

autobus	automobile + bus	modem	modulator + demodulator
bit	binary + digit	moped	motor + pedal
blimp	B + limp	motel	motor + hotel
blotch	blot + botch	motocross	motor + cross country
bleep	blankout + beep	motorcade	motor + cavalcade
brunch	breakfast + lunch	napalm	naphthene + palmitate
because	by + cause	o'clock	of (the) + clock
chortle	chuckle + snort	paratroops	parachute + troops
clash	clap + crash	pixel	picture + element
clump	chunk + lump	skylab	sky + laboratory
con man	confidence + man	slosh	slop + slush
daisy	day's + eye	smash	smack + mash
farewell	fare + ye + well	smog	smoke + fog
flare	flame + glare	sparcity	sparceness + scarcity
flurry	flutter + hurry	splatter	splash + spatter
flush	flash + gush	squiggle	squirm + wriggle
fortnight	fourteen + nights	taxicab	taximeter + cabriolet
gerrymander	Gerry + salamander	telethon	television + marathon
glimmer	gleam + shimmer	travelogue	travel + monologue
goodbye	God + be (with) + ye	twinight	twin + night
hi-fi	high + fidelity	twirl	twist + whirl

See also List 32, Clipped Words—Words Shortened by Common Usage; and List 45, Greek and Latin Roots.

The Reading Teacher's Book of Lists, Third Edition, © 1993 by Prentice Hall

34. Compound Words—Words Glued Together to Form New Words

Compound words do not always join the meanings of the two words used. For example, *brainstorm*. These words are great fun to illustrate the silliness of literal translations.

The Reading Teacher's Book of Lists, Third Edition, © 1993 by Prentice Hall

afternoon	cutout	holdup	playpen	sweetheart
airline	daydream	homemade	ponytail	teacup
airmail	daytime	jellyfish	popcorn	textbook
airport	dishpan	landlady	postcard	Thanksgiving
anchorman	doorknob	landlord	postman	thumbtack
anchorwoman	doorway	leftover	pushover	thunderstorm
another	downpour	lifeboat	quicksand	timetable
applesauce	downstairs	lifeguard	railroad	tiptoe
ashtray	downtown	lipstick	railway	toenail
backyard	dragonfly	lookout	rainbow	toothbrush
bareback	drawbridge	loudspeaker	rattlesnake	toothpick
barefoot	drive-in	midnight	rawhide	touchdown
baseball	driveway	moonship	redwood	tugboat
basketball	dropout	moonwalk	ripoff	turntable
bathroom	drugstore	motorcycle	rowboat	turtleneck
bedspread	earring	newsboy	runway	undercover
billfold	earthquake	newscast	sailboat	underground
birthday	eyeball	newspaper	sandpaper	understand
blackbird	ferryboat	newsprint	scarecrow	undertake
blackboard	filmstrip	nightgown	screwball	uproot
blackout	fireplace	notebook	screwdriver	uptown
bloodhound	flashback	nutcracker	shipwreck	vineyard
blueprint	flashcube	oatmeal	shoelace	volleyball
bookkeeper	flashlight	offbeat	shortstop	washcloth
breakfast	folklore	outboard	sidewalk	wastebasket
broadcast	football	outcome	silverware	watchman
bulldog	frogman	outfield	skateboard	watercolor
buttercup	frostbite	outfit	skyscraper	waterfall
buttermilk	fruitcake	outlaws	slipcover	waterfront
campfire	gentleman	outstanding	snowdrift	watermelon
carpool	goldenrod	overalls	snowfall	weatherman
cattail	goldfish	overcoat	softball	weekend
classmate	grasshopper	overlook	splashdown	whirlpool
clipboard	haircut	overpass	spotlight	wholesale
clothesline	handcuff	pancake	starfish	wildcat
clothespin	handlebar	paperback	streetcar	windmill
copout	hangup	payoff	suitcase	windpipe
copperhead	hardware	peanut	sunbeam	windshield
copyright	haystack	peppermint	sunflower	wiretapping
cowboy	headache	pigtail	sunrise	woodland
crosswalk	headlight	pinball	sunset	woodpecker
cupboard	headquarters	pinpoint	sunshine	wristwatch
cupcake	highway	playmate	sweatshirt	

35. *Contractions*

Contractions substitute an apostrophe for a letter or letters. You will find the grouping of contractions a good teaching strategy.

am	is, has	would, had	have	will	not
I'm	he's	I'd	I've	I'll	can't
	she's	you'd	you've	you'll	don't
are	it's	he'd	we've	she'll	isn't
you're	what's	she'd	they've	he'll	won't
we're	that's	we'd	could've	it'll	shouldn't
they're	who's	they'd	would've	we'll	couldn't
who're	there's	it'd	should've	they'll	wouldn't
	here's	there'd	might've	that'll	aren't
	one's	what'd	who've	these'll	doesn't
		who'd	there've	those'll	wasn't
		that'd		there'll	weren't
			let	this'll	hasn't
			let's	what'll	haven't
				who'll	hadn't
					mustn't
					didn't
					mightn't
					needn't

The Reading Teacher's Book of Lists, Third Edition, © 1993 by Prentice Hall

See also List 32, Clipped Words—Words Shortened By Common Usage.

36. Acronyms and Initializations

Everyone knows about TGIF, but what about MMB (Monday Morning Blues)? Acronyms and initializations are used frequently in media and everyday communication. This reference should keep you and your students well informed.

ABC	American Broadcasting Company
ACTION	American Council to Improve Our Neighborhoods
AID	Agency for International Development
AIDS	Acquired Immune Deficiency Syndrome
APO	Army Post Office
ASAP	As soon as possible
AWOL	Absent without leave
BASIC	Beginners All-Purpose Symbolic Instruction Code (See List 145, Computer Terms)
BASIC	British-American Scientific International Commercial English
BBC	British Broadcasting Corporation
BLT	Bacon, lettuce, and tomato
BMOC	Big man on campus
BTO	Big-time operator
CARE	Cooperative for American Relief Everywhere
CB	Citizen's Band
CBS	Columbia Broadcasting System
CETA	Comprehensive Employment and Training Act
CLASS	Computer-based Laboratory for Automated School Systems
CLASSMATE	Computer Language to Aid and Stimulate Scientific, Mathematical, and Technical Education
COBOL	Common Business-Oriented Language (see List 145, Computer Terms)
COD	Cash on delivery
CORE	Congress of Racial Equality
CPA	Certified Public Accountant
CPO	Chief petty officer
DA	District attorney
DDT	Dichlorodiphenyltrichloroethane
DEW	Distant Early Warning
DEWLINE	Distant Early Warning Line
DJ	Disc jockey
DOA	Dead on arrival
EDP	Electronic data processing
EEG	Electroencephalogram
EKG, ECG	Electrocardiogram
ERA	Equal Rights Amendment
EURAILPASS	European railway passenger
FIAT	Fabbrica Italiana Automobili Torino
FORTRAN	Formula Translation (see List 145, Computer Terms)
GASP	Group Against Smoking in Public
GESTAPO	Geheime Staats Polizei
GI	Government issue
HEW	Health, Education & Welfare

HQ	Headquarters
HUD	Housing and Urban Development
ICBM	Intercontinental ballistic missile
IQ	Intelligence quotient
IRA	Irish Republican Army, International Reading Association
IRS	Internal Revenue Service
JAYCEES	U.S. Junior Chamber of Commerce
JEEP	General Purpose (vehicle)
JOBS	Job Opportunities for Better Skills
KKK	Ku Klux Klan
LASER	Light amplification by stimulated emission of radiation
LEM	Lunar Excursion Module
LIFO	Last in, first out
LP	Long playing (phonograph record)
LSD	Lysergic acid diethylamide
MIA	Missing in action
MO	Modus operandi
MYOB	Mind your own business
NAACP	National Association for the Advancement of Colored People
NABISCO	National Biscuit Company
NASA	National Aeronautics and Space Administration
NATO	North Atlantic Treaty Organization
NAZI	National Socialist German Workers' Party
NBC	National Broadcasting Company
NOW	National Organization for Women
OPEC	Organization of Petroleum Exporting Countries
PA	Public address
PAC	Pacific Athletic Conference, Political Action Committee
PBS	Public Broadcasting System
PDQ	Pretty darn quick
POW	Prisoner of war
PS	Postscript
PUSH	People United to Save Humanity
RADAR	Radio detecting and ranging
RAM	Random Access Memory (see List 145, Computer Terms)
RIP	Rest in peace
ROM	Read Only Memory (see List 145, Computer Terms)
ROTC	Reserve Officer Training Corps
RR	Railroad
RSVP	Répondez s'il vous plaît
RV	Recreational vehicle
SALT	Strategic Arms Limitation Talks
SCUBA	Self-contained underwater breathing apparatus
SNAFU	Situation normal, all fouled up
SNCC	Student Nonviolent Coordinating Committee
SONAR	Sound navigation ranging
SOS	Save our ship
SWAK	Sealed with a kiss

The Reading Teacher's Book of Lists, Third Edition, © 1993 by Prentice Hall

The Reading Teacher's Book of Lists, Third Edition, © 1993 by Prentice Hall

SWAT	Special weapons action team
TEFLON	Tetrafloroethylene resin
TELEX	Teletypewriter Exchange Service
TGIF	Thank God It's Friday
TLC	Tender loving care
TNT	Trinitrotoluene
TV	Television
UFO	Unidentified flying object
UNESCO	United Nations Educational, Scientific, and Cultural Organization
UNICEF	United Nations International Children's Education Fund
VEEP	Vice-president
VIP	Very important person
VISTA	Volunteers in Service to America
WAC	Women's Army Corps
WASP	White Anglo-Saxon Protestant
WAVES	Women Accepted for Volunteer Emergency Service
WHO	World Health Organization
ZIP	Zone Improvement Plan

See also List 124, State Abbreviations and Capitols; List 125, Common Abbreviations; and List 13, Measurement.

37. Words Borrowed From Names

Did you know that the popular *cardigan* sweater was named after the Earl of Cardigan? Or that the word *maverick* came into use after Samuel Maverick, a Texan, refused to brand his cattle? These and other eponyms, words borrowed from names, can be used to stimulate an interest in word origins.

WORDS COINED FROM PEOPLE'S NAMES

Adam's apple	Adam, the first man, who tradition says ate the forbidden fruit, an apple, in the Garden of Eden
America	Amerigo Vespucci, an Italian merchant-explorer who came to the New World shortly after Columbus
baud	Jean Baudot, a French inventor who worked on telegraphic communications
Beaufort scale	Sir Francis Beaufort, an English naval officer, who developed it to describe wind speed
bloomers	Amelia Bloomer, a pioneer feminist who made them popular
bowie knife	James Bowie, an American frontiersman who made this type of knife famous
boycott	Charles Boycott, a British army officer and first victim
braille	Louis Braille, a French teacher of the blind
cardigan	Earl of Cardigan, a British officer whose soldiers wore the knitted sweaters during the Crimean War
chauvinist	Nicholas Chauvin, a soldier who worshipped France and Napoleon uncritically
diesel	Rudolf Diesel, a German automotive engineer
dunce	Johannes Duns Scotus, a theologian whose followers were called Dunsmen
ferris wheel	G. M. Ferris, an American engineer
frisbee	William Frisbie, a pie company owner in Connecticut in 1871. Yale students played catch with the pie tins.
fudge	Supposedly named after Captain Fudge, a seventeenth-century seaman who had a reputation for not telling the truth
gerrymander	Elbridge Gerry, a Massachusetts governor in 1810
graham crackers	Sylvester Graham, an American reformer in dietetics and a vegetarian
guillotine	Joseph Guillotin, a French physician who urged its use
leotard	Jules Leotard, a French acrobat who designed it as a costume for his trapeze act
macadam	John Loudon McAdam, a Scottish engineer who invented this road-building material
maverick	Samuel Maverick, a Texan who didn't brand his cattle
mesmerize	Fredrich Mesmer, an Austrian physician who practiced hypnotism
nicotine	Jean Nicot, a French diplomat who introduced the tobacco plant to France about 1561
pasteurize	Louis Pasteur, a French bacteriologist
sandwich	John Montagu, fourth Earl of Sandwich, who invented it so he could gamble without stopping for a regular meal

The Reading Teacher's Book of Lists, Third Edition, © 1993 by Prentice Hall

saxophone	Anton Sax, Belgian instrument maker who combined a clarinet's reed with oboe fingering
sequoia	A Cherokee Indian chief who invented an alphabet. The trees were named for him by a Hungarian botanist
sideburns	Ambrose Burnside, a civil war general and governor of Rhode Island who had thick side whiskers
silhouette	Etienne de Silhouette, a French finance minister of Louis XV whose fiscal policies and amateurish portraits (by him) were regarded as inept
stetson	John Stetson, an American who owned a hat factory in Philadelphia that featured western styles
valentine	St. Valentine, a Christian martyr whose feast day is February 14—the same date, according to Roman tradition, that birds pair off to nest
tawdry	St. Audrey, queen of Northumbria; used to describe lace sold at her fair
teddy bear	Teddy Roosevelt, president of the United States who spared the life of a bear cub on a hunting trip in Mississippi
vandal	Vandals, the Germanic tribe that sacked Rome

SCIENCE WORDS COINED FROM PEOPLE'S NAMES

ampere	Andre Ampere, a French physicist
celsius	Anders Celsius, a Swedish astronomer and inventor
decibel	Alexander Bell, a Scottish-American inventor of the telephone
fahrenheit	Gabriel Fahrenheit, a German physicist
mach number	Named for Ernst Mach, an Austrian philosopher and physicist
ohm	Georg Simon Ohm, a German physicist
Richter scale	Charles Richter, an American seismologist
volt	Alessandro Volata, an Italian physicist
watt	James Watt, a Scottish engineer and inventor

FLOWER NAMES COINED FROM PEOPLE'S NAMES

begonia	Michel Begon, French governor of Santo Domingo and a patron of science
camellia	George Kamel, European Jesuit missionary to the Far East
dahlia	Andreas Dahl, a Swedish botanist
gardenia	Alexander Garden, a Scottish-American botanist
magnolia	Pierre Magnol, a French botanist
poinsettia	Joel Poinsettia, U.S. ambassador to Mexico
wisteria	Caspar Wistar, an American anatomist
zinnia	J. G. Zinn, a German botanist

WORDS COINED FROM PLACE NAMES

academy	Academeia, a garden where Plato taught his students
cashmere	Kashmir, India
cologne	Cologne, Germany

The Reading Teacher's Book of Lists, Third Edition, © 1993 by Prentice Hall

denim	Nimes, France—serge de Nimes (fabric of Nimes)
frankfurter	Frankfurt, Germany
hamburger	Hamburg, Germany
manila paper	Manila, the Philippines
rhinestone	Rhine, river that flows from Switzerland through Germany and the Netherlands
Tabasco sauce	Tabasco, Mexico
tangerine	Tangier, Morocco

BORROWED CALENDAR WORDS

Sunday	The sun's day
Monday	The moon's day
Tuesday	Tiw's day; Tiw was the Teutonic god of war
Wednesday	Woden's day; Woden was the Norse god of the hunt
Thursday	Thor's day; Thor was the Norse god of the sky
Friday	Fria's day; Fria, the wife of Thor, was the Norse goddess of love and beauty
Saturday	Saturn's day; Saturn was the Roman god of agriculture
January	In honor of Janus, the Roman god with two faces, one looking forward and one looking backward
February	In honor of *februa*, the Roman feast of purification
March	In honor of Mars, the Roman god of war
April	A reference to spring, *aprilis*, the Latin word for opening
May	In honor of Maia, a Roman goddess and mother of Mercury
June	In honor of Juno, the Roman goddess of marriage
July	In honor of the Roman general and statesman Julius Caesar
August	In honor of the Roman emperor Augustus Caesar
September	In reference to *septem*, the Latin word for seven; September was the seventh month of the Roman calendar
October	In reference to *octo*, the Latin word for eight; October was the eighth Roman month
November	In reference to *novem*, the Latin word for nine; November was the ninth Roman month
December	In reference to *decem*, the Latin word for ten; December was the tenth Roman month

WORDS FROM ROMAN AND GREEK MYTHOLOGY

Achilles heel	Greek warrior and leader in the Trojan War whose only vulnerable spot was his heel
amazon	Amazons, in Greek mythology, were a tribe of female warriors
aphrodisiac	Aphrodite, Greek goddess of love and beauty
atlas	Atlas, in Greek mythology, was forced to hold the heavens on his shoulders
cereal	Ceres, a Roman goddess of agriculture
echo	Echo, in Greek mythology, was a wood nymph cursed with repeating the last words anyone said to her

The Reading Teacher's Book of Lists, Third Edition, © 1993 by Prentice Hall

erotic	Eros, Greek god of love and son of Aphrodite
hygiene	Hygeia, the Greek goddess of health
mentor	Mentor, in Greek mythology, was a loyal friend and advisor to Odysseus and teacher to his son, Telemachus
morphine	Morpheus, the Greek god of dreams
oedipus complex	King Oedipus, in Greek mythology, unwittingly murdered his father and married his mother
ogre	Orcus, the Roman god of the underworld
panacea	Panacea, the Roman goddess of health
volcano	Volcan, Roman god of fire

See also List 45, Greek and Latin Roots.

38. *Foreign Words and Phrases*

Foreign words and phrases are used in many novels, magazines, and newspapers, and in some academic writing. Your students might enjoy learning some of the more common ones. Some will demonstrate a *penchant* for picking up foreign phrases *tout de suite* and using them to impress their friends. *N'est-ce pas?*

addenda—list of additions (Latin)

ad hoc—with respect to this condition (Latin)

ad infinitum—to infinity (Latin)

ad nauseam—to the point of disgust (Latin)

à la carte—according to the menu (French)

à la mode—in fashion (French)

aloha—hello or goodbye (Hawaiian)

alfresco—outdoors (Italian)

au contraire—on the contrary (French)

au courant—well informed (French)

au revoir—until we meet again (French)

à votre santé—to your health (French)

bona fide—in good faith (Latin)

bon jour—good day (French)

bon soir—good evening (French)

bon vivant—lover of good living (French)

bon voyage—have a good voyage (French)

carte blanche—full authority (French)

caveat emptor—let the buyer beware (Latin)

circa—about (Latin)

cogito ergo sum—I think, therefore I am (Latin)

coup d'etat—quick political change (French)

cul-de-sac—dead end (French)

de rigueur—required (French)

double entendre—double meaning (French)

emeritus—retired after long service (Latin)

en masse—in a large group (French)

en route—on the way (French)

entourage—those closely associated with a person (French)

e pluribus unum—one from many (Latin)

errata—list of errors (Latin)

esprit de corps—group spirit (French)

et cetera—and others (Latin)

eureka—I have found it (Greek)

faux pas—mistake or mistakes (French)

fiancé—man to whom one is engaged (French)

fiancée—woman to whom one is engaged (French)

hors d'oeuvre—appetizer (French)

in memoriam—in memory of (Latin)

in re—regarding (Latin)

in toto—totally (Latin)

je ne sais quoi—I don't know what (French)

khaki—olive tan color (Hindi)

laissez faire—noninterference (French)

maître d'hôtel—head waiter (French)

malapropos—out of place (French)

mañana—tomorrow (Spanish)

mardi gras—Shrove Tuesday (French)

mea culpa—my fault (Latin)

modus operandi—manner of working (Latin)

née—born (French)

n'est-ce pas?—isn't that so? (French)

noblesse oblige—rank imposes obligations (French)

Noel—Christmas (Latin)

nom de plume—pen name (French)

non sequitur—it does not follow (Latin)

nota bene—note well (Latin)

nuance—subtle distinction (French)

pardonnez-moi—excuse me (French)

penchant—strong liking or inclination (French)

The Reading Teacher's Book of Lists, Third Edition, © 1993 by Prentice Hall

persona non grata—person not accepted (Latin)

per—for (Latin)

pièce de resistance—the irresistible part (French)

prima donna—first lady (Italian)

pro forma—done as a matter of formality (Latin)

pro rata—according to a rate or proportion (Latin)

protégé—one under the guidance of another (French)

quid pro quo—one thing for another (Latin)

raconteur—story teller (French)

raison d'être—reason for existence (French)

résumé—summary (French)

savoir faire—social know-how (French)

shampoo—hair wash (Hindi)

sine qua non—indispensable (Latin)

status quo—the way things are (Latin)

stet—leave as is (Latin)

sub rosa—secret or confidential (Latin)

tempus fugit—time flies (Latin)

tortilla—round, flat unleavened bread (Spanish)

tout de suite—immediately (French)

veranda—large porch (Hindi)

vice versa—conversely (Latin)

vis-à-vis—in relation to (French)

voilà—there it is (French)

wanderlust—passion for traveling (German)

See also List 37, Words Borrowed from Names; List 45, Greek and Latin Roots.

39. Onomatopoeia—Words Borrowed from Sounds

Onomatopoeic words, borrowed from sounds, resemble the real sound that they refer to. For example, a cow *moos*. These words are favorites with poets and comic-strip writers. Entertainers love them, and children's authors use them regularly. Your students will enjoy them and probably add some to this list.

arf arf	cock a doodle do	honk	slurp
	cuckoo	hop	smack
bang	crack	howl	smash
bark	crackle	hum	smooth
beep	crash		snap
blink	creak	kerchoo	spank
blip	crinkle		splash
boom	crunch	meow	splat
bong		moan	sputter
bow wow	ding a ling	moo	squeak
bump	ding dong	murmur	squeal
burp	drip		squish
buzz	drop	oink oink	swish
		ping	
chirp	fizz	plop	tap
choo choo	flap	pop	ticktock
chug	flip flop		thump
clang		quack	twang
clank	giggle		
clatter	grate	rip	whack
click	grind	roar	woof woof
clink	groan	rush	
clip clop	growl	rustle	zap
clomp			zip
cluck	hee haw	screech	zoom
	hiss	sigh	zonk
		slop	

The Reading Teacher's Book of Lists, Third Edition, © 1993 by Prentice Hall

40. *Phobia and Cide Word Families*

The Greek word *phobos*, meaning "fear," is combined with a variety of roots to form an interesting group of phobias. Some of these, such as claustrophobia (fear of closed spaces) or acrophobia (fear of high places), are quite common; others may be new to you. Use the root words of List 45 to coin a few of your own. How about "bibliophobia"? The root cide means killing.

PHOBIA WORDS

Acrophobia	fear of heights (edges)
aerophobia	fear of flying
agoraphobia	fear of open spaces
ailurophobia	fear of cats
amaxophobia	fear of vehicles, driving
androphobia	fear of men
anthophobia	fear of flowers
anthropophobia	fear of people
arachnophobia	fear of spiders
aquaphobia	fear of water
arachibutyrophobia	fear of peanut butter sticking to the roof of your mouth
astraphobia	fear of lightning
brontophobia	fear of thunder
claustrophobia	fear of closed spaces
chromophobia	fear of color
cynophobia	fear of dogs
dementophobia	fear of insanity
gephyrophobia	fear of bridges
gerontophobia	fear of old age
hemophobia	fear of blood
herpetophobia	fear of reptiles
ideophobia	fear of ideas
mikrophobia	fear of germs
murophobia	fear of mice
nebulaphobia	fear of clouds
necrophobia	fear of death
numerophobia	fear of numbers
nyctophobia	fear of darkness
ochlophobia	fear of crowds
ophidiophobia	fear of snakes
optophobia	fear of opening your eyes
ornithophobia	fear of birds
phonophobia	fear of speaking aloud
pyrophobia	fear of fire
thaasophobia	fear of being bored
trichophobia	fear of hair
triskaidekaphobia	fear of the number thirteen
xenophobia	fear of strangers

CIDE WORDS

bactericide	killing of bacteria
fratricide	killing of a brother
genocide	killing of people of one race
herbicide	killing of plants
homicide	killing of a person
infanticide	killing of a baby
insecticide	killing of insects
pesticide	killing of pests
regicide	killing of a king, ruler
sororicide	killing of a sister
suicide	killing of self
uxoricide	killing of one's wife

See also List 41, -Ology Word Family; List 45, Greek and Latin Roots.

41. -Ology Word Family

Many subjects that are studied in schools and colleges have -ology in their names. The suffix -ology means "the science of" or "the study of." For example, since *cardia* means "heart," *cardiology* means "the science of the heart." Moreoover, since the suffix -ist means "one who practices" (see Suffix List 44), a *cardiologist* is "one who practices the science of the heart."

anthropology	man (culture)	**ideology**	doctrine of a group
archaeology	antiquities (ancient people)	**meteorology**	weather
		microbiology	microbes
astrology	stars (divination by stars—the study of stars is referred to as astronomy)	**mineralogy**	minerals
		morphology	structure of animals and plants
		musicology	music
audiology	hearing	**neurology**	nerves
bacteriology	bacteria	**ornithology**	birds
biology	life	**paleontology**	fossils
cardiology	heart	**pathology**	diseases
cosmetology	cosmetics	**pharmacology**	drugs
cosmology	universe	**physiology**	life processes
criminology	crime	**pomology**	fruit
cryptology	codes and cyphers	**psychology**	mind
cytology	cells	**radiology**	radiation
dermatology	skin	**seismology**	earthquakes
ecology	relationship of organisms with their environment	**sociology**	society
		technology	applied science
embryology	embryo	**theology**	God
entomology	insects	**toxicology**	poisons
epistemology	knowledge	**typology**	classification based on type
ethnology	historical development of cultures	**zoology**	animals
etymology	word origins		
genealogy	ancestors		
geology	earth		
gerontology	old age		
gynecology	women		
herpetology	reptiles		
histology	living tissue		
hydrology	water		

See also List 40, Phobia and Cide Word Families; and List 45, Greek and Latin Roots.

The Reading Teacher's Book of Lists, Third Edition, © 1993 by Prentice Hall

42. Prefixes—Alphabetical Order

Prefixes—small but meaningful letter groups added before a base word or root—change the meaning of a word. Knowing the meaning of these prefixes, together with the meaning of common base words and Greek and Latin roots, will give students the tools for unlocking the meanings of hundreds of words. In addition to teaching these prefixes directly, it is also a good idea to explain prefixes and their meanings when students encounter them in new vocabulary words throughout the year.

ALPHABETICAL ORDER

PREFIX	MEANING	EXAMPLES
a-	on	aboard, afire, afoot, ashore, atop
a-	not	apathy, atheist, atrophy, atypical
ab-	from	abnormal, abhor, abolish, abstain, abstract
ac-	to	accent, accept, access, acquire
ad-	to	adapt, add, addict, adhere, admit
af-	to	affair, affect, affiliate, affirm, afflict
after-	after	afterglow, afternoon, aftertaste, afterward
ag-	to	agglomeration, aggrandize, aggravate, aggregate, aggressive
ambi-	both, around	ambidextrous, ambience, ambiguous, ambivalent
amphi-	both, around	amphibian, amphitheater, amphora
an-	not	anemia, anarchy, anesthesia, anorexia, anonymous
an-	to	annex, annihilate, annotate, announce, annul
ante-	before	antebellum, antecedent, antedate, antediluvian, anterior
anti-	against	antiwar, antisocial, antislavery
as-	to	ascend, ascertain, aspect, aspire, assert
atto-	quintillionth	attosecond
auto-	self	automobile, automatic, autograph, autobiography
be-	make	becalm, befriend, beguile, bewitch
bene-	good	benediction, benefactor, beneficial, benefit, benign
bi-, bin-	two	bicycle, binocular, biceps, bifocal
by-	near, aside	bypass, byplay, bystander, byway
cent-	hundred	centigrade, century, cent, centimeter
circu-	around	circulate, circumference, circumspect, circumstance, circus
co-	together	co-author, cognate, coincide, cooperate, coordinate
col-	with	collaborate, collateral, colleague, collect
com-	with	combat, combine, comfort, commune, complain
con-	with	concede, concur, concert, confident, connect
counter-	opposite	counteract, countermand, counteroffensive, counterproposal
contra	against	contraband, contraception, contradict, contrary, contraindicated
de-	from, down	debate, decay, deceive, decide, deform

PREFIX	MEANING	EXAMPLES
de-	opposite	deactivate, deform, degrade, deplete, descend
dec-	ten	decade, decathlon, December, decagram
deci-	ten	decimal, decimeter, decimate, decile
demi-	half	demigod, demitasse
di-	two	digraph, dioxide, diploma, diphthong
dia-	through, across	diagnose, diagonal, dialogue, diameter
dis-	opposite	disagree, disarm, discontinue, disgust, dishonest
du-	two	dual, duet, duo, duplex, duplicate
dys-	bad	dysentery, dysfunction, dyspepsia, dysphasia
e-	out, away	effect, effort, eject, emigrate, erupt
em-	in	embalm, embed, embezzle, embrace, embroider
en-	in	enchant, enclose, encounter, encourage, envelop
ennea-	nine	enneagon, enneahedron, ennead
enter-	among, between	enterprise, entertain
epi-	after	epilogue, epitaph
epi-	upon	epicenter, epidemic, epidermis, epithet
equi-	equal	equal, equilibrium, equidistant, equator, equation
eu-	good	Eucharist, eugenic, euphoria, eulogy
ex-	out	excel, exalt, exceed, exhaust, exit
exa-	quintillion	exameter
extra-	outside	extracurricular, extraordinary, extravagant
femto-	quadrillionth	femtosecond
for-	not	forbid, forget, forgo, forswear
giga-	billion	gigameter, gigawatt, gigahertz
hect-	hundred	hectogram, hectare, hectometer
hemi-	half	hemisphere, hemicycle
hept-	seven	heptagon, heptameter
hetero-	different	heterodox, heteronym, heterosexual
hex-	six	hexagon, hexameter, hexagram
homo-	same	homogeneous, homogenize, homograph, homophone, homosexual
hyper-	excessive	hyperactive, hyperbole, hypercritical, hypertension, hyperglycemia
hypo-	under, too little	hypochondria, hypodermis, hypothesis
il-	not	illegal, illegible, illegitimate, illiterate, illogical
im-	into	immediate, immerse, immigrate, implant, import
im-	not	imbalance, immaculate, immature, immobilize, impossible
in-	into	incision, include, induce, inhale, infect
in-	not	inaccurate, inactive, inadvertent, incognito, indecisive

The Reading Teacher's Book of Lists, Third Edition, © 1993 by Prentice Hall

PREFIX	MEANING	EXAMPLES
inter-	among, between	interrupt, intermission, international, interpret, intervene
intra-	within	intramural, intrastate, intravenous
intro-	inside	introduce, introspect, introject, introvert
ir-	not	irregular, irreconcilable, irredeemable, irregular, irresponsible
is-	equal	isometric, isomorph, isosceles, isotope
kilo-	thousand	kilometer, kilogram, kilowatt, kiloliter
macro-	large, long	macrocosm, macron, macroscope, macrobiotic
magni-	great	magnify, magnitude, magnificent, magnanimous, magnum
mal-	bad	maladjusted, malaise, malevolent, malfunction, malice
mega-	large	megacycle, megalith, megalomania, megaphone, megaton
mega-	million	megawatt, megaton, megabyte, megabuck
meta-	change	metabolism, metamorphosis, metaphor, metastasis
micro-	small, short	microphone, microscope, microbe, microfilm
micro-	millionth	microsecond
mid-	middle	midnight, midshipman, midsummer, midway, midyear
milli-	thousand	millibar, milligram, millimeter, million
mis-	bad	misanthrope, misbehave, miscarriage, misconduct, misfortune
mon-, mono-	one	monk, monarch, monocular, monogamy, monorail
multi-	many, much	multicolored, multifarious, multimillionaire, multiply, multitude
myria-	ten thousand	myriad, myriameter
nano-	billionth	nanosecond, nanowatt, nanometer
ne-	not	nefarious, never
neg-	not	negative, neglect, negotiate
neo-	new	neoclassic, neologism, neon, neonatal, neophyte
non-	not	nonchalant, nonconformist, nondescript, nonpartisan, nonsense
non-	nine	nonagenarian
nove-	nine	November, novena
oct-	eight	October, octet, octane, octopus
off-	from	offset, offshoot, offshore, offspring, offstage
olig-	few	oligarchy, oligopoly, oligophagous
omni-	all	omnibus, omnificent, omnipotent, omnivorous
on-	on	oncoming, ongoing, onrush, onshore, onward
out-	surpassing	outbid, outclass, outdo, outlive, outnumber
over-	too much	overactive, overbearing, overblown, overdo, overprice

PREFIX	**MEANING**	**EXAMPLES**
pan-	all	panacea, pandemonium, Pandora, panorama, panegyric
para-	beside	paradigm, paragraph, parallel, paraphrase
para-	almost	paralegal, paramedic
pen(e)-	almost	peninsula, penultimate, peneplain, penumbra
pent-	five	pentagon, pentathlon, Pentecost
per-	throughout	perceive, percolate, perfect, perform, pervade
peri-	all around	perimeter, periscope, peripatetic, periphery
peta-	quadrillion	petameter
pico-	trillionth	picosecond, picometer
poly-	many	polyandry, polyester, polygamy, polyglot, polysyllabic
post-	after	postdate, postdoctoral, posterior, postpone, postscript
pre-	before	preamble, precaution, prefix, prejudice
pro-	before	prognosis, progeny, program, prologue, prophet
pro-	forward	proceed, produce, proficient, progress, project
pro-	favor	prowar, pro-American, pro-education
prot-	first	protagonist, protein, proton, prototype
pseudo-	false	pseudoclassic, pseudonym, pseudopod
quadr-	four	quadrangle, quadrant, quart, quarter
quint-	five	quintuplet, quintessential, quintet
re-	again	redo, rewrite, reappear, repaint, relive
re-	back	recall, recede, reflect, repay, retract
retro-	back	retroactive, retrogress, retrospect
self-	self	self-denial, self-respect, selfish, self-support, self-taught
semi-	half	semiannual, semicircle, semiconscious
sept-	seven	September, septuagenarian
sex-	six	sextet, sextant, sextuple
sub-	under	subcontract, subject, submerge, subordinate, subterranean
super-	over	superimpose, superscript, supersede, supervisor
super-	more than	superfine, superhuman, supernatural, superpower, supernova
syl-	together	syllable, syllogism
sym-	together	symbiosis, symbol, symmetry, sympathy, symphony
syn-	together	synchronize, syndrome, synergy, synonym, synthesis
tele-	distant	telephone, telescope, telegram, television
tera-	trillion	terameter, teracycle
tetra-	four	tetrahedron, tetrameter
trans-	across	transatlantic, transcend, transcribe, transfer, translate
tri-	three	triangle, tricycle, trillion, triplet
ultra-	beyond	ultraconservative, ultramodern, ultranationalism

The Reading Teacher's Book of Lists, Third Edition, © 1993 by Prentice Hall

PREFIX	MEANING	EXAMPLES
un-	not	unhappy, unable, uncomfortable, uncertain, unbeaten
under-	below	underneath, undercover, underground, underpass
under-	less than	underage, underdone, underripe, undervalue, underweight
uni-	one	unicorn, uniform, unify, universe
with-	back, away	withdraw, withhold, within, without, withstand

GROUPED BY MEANING

Prefixes Expressing Number

demi-	half	demigod, demitasse
hemi-	half	hemisphere, hemicycle
semi-	half	semiannual, semicircle, semiclassic
prot-	first	protagonist, protein, proton, prototype
mon-, mono-	one	monk, monarch, monocular, monogamy
uni-	one	unicorn, uniform, unify, unite, universe
di-	two	digraph, dioxide, diploma, diphthong
bi-, bin-	two	bicycle, binocular, biceps, bifocal, biplane
du-	two	dual, duet, duo, duplex, duplicate
tri-	three	triangle, tricycle, trillion, triplet
tetra-	four	tetrahedron, tetrameter
quadr-	four	quadrangle, quadrant, quart, quarter
pent-	five	pentagon, pentathlon, Pentecost
quint-	five	quintuplet, quintessential, quintet
hex-	six	hexagon, hexameter, hexagram
sex-	six	sextet, sextant, sextuple
hept-	seven	heptagon, heptameter
sept-	seven	September, septuagenarian
oct-	eight	octet, October, octane, octopus
ennea-	nine	enneagon, enneahedron, ennead
non-	nine	nonagenarian
nove-	nine	November, novena
dec-	ten	decade, decathalon, decagram, December, decameter
deci-	ten	decimal, decimeter, decigram, decile
cent-	hundred	centigrade, century, cent, centigram
hect-	hundred	hectogram, hectometer, hectare
milli-	thousand	millibar, milligram, millimeter, million
kilo-	thousand	kilometer, kilogram, kilowatt, kiloliter
myria-	ten thousand	myriameter, myriad

Prefixes for Super-Large Numbers

PREFIX	MEANING	EXAMPLE
kilo-	thousand, 10^3	kilometer
mega-	million, 10^6	megameter
giga-	billion, 10^9	gigameter
tera-	trillion, 10^{12}	terameter
peta-	quadrillion, 10^{15}	petameter
exa-	quintillion, 10^{18}	exameter

Prefixes for Super-Small Numbers

deci-	tenth, 10^{-1}	decimeter
centi-	hundredth, 10^{-2}	centimeter
milli-	thousandth, 10^{-3}	millimeter
micro-	millionth, 10^{-6}	micrometer (micron)
nano-	billionth, 10^{-9}	nanometer (10^{-10} = angstrom)
pico-	trillionth, 10^{-12}	picometer
femto-	quadrillionth, 10^{-15}	femtometer (fermi)
atto-	quintillionth, 10^{-18}	attometer

Prefixes that Describe Size

macro-	large, long	macrocosm, macron, macroscopic
magni-	great	magnify, magnitude, magnificent
mega-	large	megacycle, megalith, megalomania
micro-	small, short	microbe, microphone, microcosm

Prefixes that Describe When

after-	after	afterglow, afternoon, aftertaste
ante-	before	antebellum, antecedent, antedate
epi-	after	epilogue, epitaph
post-	after	postdate, postdoctoral, posterior, postpone, postscript
pre-	before	preamble, precaution, prefix, prejudice
pro-	before	prognosis, progeny, program, prologue

Prefixes that Describe Where

a-	on	aboard, afire, afoot, ashore, atop
ab-	from	abnormal, abhor, abolish, abstain
ac-	to	accent, accept, access, accident, acquire
ad-	to	adapt, add, addict, adhere, admit
af-	to	affair, affect, affiliate, affirm, afflict
ag-	to	agglomeration, aggrandize, aggravate
an-	to	annex, annihilate, annotate, announce
as-	to	ascend, ascertain, aspect, aspire, assert
by-	near, aside	bypass, byplay, bystander, byway

PREFIX	MEANING	EXAMPLES
circu-	around	circulate, circumference, circumspect
de-	from, down	debate, decay, deceive, decide, deform
dia-	through, across	diagnose, diagonal, dialogue, diameter
e-	out, away	effect, effort, eject, emigrate, erupt
em-	in	embalm, embed, embezzle, embrace
en-	in	enchant, enclose, encounter, encourage
enter-	among, between	enterprise, entertain
epi-	upon	epicenter, epidemic, epidermis, epithet
ex-	out	excel, exalt, exceed, exhaust, exit
extra-	outside	extracurricular, extraordinary
hypo-	under	hypochondria, hypodermic, hypothesis
im-	into	immediate, immerse, immigrate, implant
in-	into	incision, include, induce, inhale, infect
inter-	among, between	intercede, interpret, interrupt
intra-	within	intramural, intrastate, intravenous
intro-	inside	introduce, introspect, introject, introvert
mid-	middle	midriff, midshipman, midsummer
off-	from	offset, offshoot, offshore, offspring
on-	on	oncoming, ongoing, onrush, onshore
para-	beside	paradigm, paragraph, parallel, paraphrase
per-	throughout	perceive, percolate, perfect, perform
peri-	all around	perimeter, periscope, peripatetic
pro-	forward	proceed, produce, proficient, progress
pro-	in front of	proclaim, profane, profess
re-	back	recall, recede, reflect, repay, retract
retro-	back	retroactive, retrogress, retro-rocket
sub-	under	subcontract, subject, submerge
super-	over	superimpose, superscript, supersede
tele-	distant	telegram, telekinesis, telephone
thorough-	through	thoroughbred, thoroughfare
trans-	across	transatlantic, transcend, transcribe
under-	below	undercover, underground, underneath
with-	back, away	withdraw, withhold, within, without

Prefixes that Describe Amount or Extent of

equi-	equal	equal, equilibrium, equidistant, equator
extra-	beyond	extraordinary, extravagant
hyper-	excessive	hyperactive, hyperbole, hypercritical
hypo-	too little	hypoactive, hypoglycemic
is-	equal	isometric, isomorph, isosceles, isotope
multi-	many, much	multicolored, multifarious, multiply
olig-	few	oligarchy, oligopoly, oligophagous
omni-	all	omnibus, omnificent, omnipotent
out-	surpassing	outbid, outclass, outdo, outlive
over-	too much	overactive, overbearing, overblown
pan-	all	panacea, Pandemonium, Pandora

PREFIX	MEANING	EXAMPLES
pene-	almost	peneplain, peninsula, penultimate
poly-	many	polyandry, polyester, polygamy, polyglot
super-	more than	superfine, superhuman, supernatural
ultra-	beyond	ultraconservative, ultramodern
under-	less than	underage, underdone, underripe

Prefixes that Express Togetherness and Separateness

ab-	away from	abdicate, abduct, aberrant, absent
co-	together	coauthor, cognate, coincide, cooperate
col-	with	collaborate, collateral, colleague, collect
com-	with	combat, combine, comfort, commune
con-	with	concede, concur, concert, confident
syl-	together	syllable, syllogism
sym-	together	symbiosis, symbol, symmetry, sympathy
syn-	together	synchronize, syndrome, synergy

Prefixes Expressing Negation

a-	not	apathy, atheist, atropy, atypical
an-	not	anemia, anarchy, anesthesia, anorexia
counter-	opposite	counteract, countermand
de-	opposite	deactivate, deform, degrade, deplete
dis-	opposite	disagree, disarm, discontinue, disgust
il-	not	illegal, illegible, illegitimate, illiterate
im-	not	imbalance, immaculate, immature
in-	not	inaccurate, inactive, inadvertent
ir-	not	irrational, irreconcilable, irredeemable
for-	prohibit	forbid, forget, forgo, forsake, forswear
ne-	not	nefarious, never
neg-	not	negative, neglect, negotiate
non-	not	nonchalant, nonconformist, nondescript
un-	opposite	unable, undo, unbeaten, uncertain

Prefixes that Make a Judgment

anti-	against	antinuclear, antisocial, antislavery
bene-	good	benediction, benefactor, beneficial
contra-	against	contraband, contraception, contradict
dys-	bad	dysentery, dysfunction, dyspepsia
eu-	good	Eucharist, eugenic, euphoria, eulogy
mal-	bad	maladjusted, malaise, malevolent
mis-	bad	misanthrope, misbehave, miscarriage
pro-	for	pro-American, pro-education

The Reading Teacher's Book of Lists, Third Edition, © 1993 by Prentice Hall

Miscellaneous Prefixes

PREFIX	MEANING	EXAMPLES
ambi-	both, around	ambidextrous, ambience, ambiguous
amphi-	both, around	amphibian, amphitheater, amphora
auto-	self	autobiography, autocratic, autograph
be-	make	becalm, befriend, beguile, bewitch
hetero-	different	heterodox, heteronym, heterosexual
homo-	same	homogeneous, homogenize, homograph
meta-	change	metabolism, metamorphosis, metaphor
neo-	new	neoclassic, neologism, neon, neonatal
para-	almost	paralegal, paramedic
pseudo-	false	pseudoclassic, pseudonym, pseudopod
re-	again	reappear, reclassify, recopy, redo, repaint
self-	self	self-denial, self-respect, selfish

The Reading Teacher's Book of Lists, Third Edition, © 1993 by Prentice Hall

See also List 41, -Ology Word Family; List 40, Phobia and Cide Word Families; List 45, Greek and Latin Roots; and List 43, Suffixes.

43. Suffixes

Suffixes are letter groups that are added to the end of a base word or root. Suffixes frequently signify the part of speech and sometimes add meaning. In this list, suffixes are grouped by part of speech.

Some suffixes are best understood, not as having a particular meaning but as expressing grammar or syntax. These suffixes enable you to express an idea in many different ways by using the variation of the key word that best fits the sentence structure.

For example, in the sentences:

1. The boy is *quiet*.
2. The boy played *quietly*.
3. The boy's *quietness* was undisturbed.

the word *quiet* was altered to fit the sentence structure. In (1) it is used as an adjective; in (2) the suffix -*ly* was added so that it could be used as an adverb; in (3) the suffix -*ness* was added so that it could be used as a noun.

NOUN SUFFIXES

SUFFIX	MEANING	EXAMPLES
-a	plural	data, criteria, memoranda
-ade	action or process	blockage, escapade, parade, promenade
-ade	product or thing	lemonade, marmalade
-ae	plural (feminine)	alumnae, formulae, larvae, algae
-age	action or process	marriage, voyage, pilgrimage
-ance	state or quality of	repentance, annoyance, resistance
-ancy	state or quality of	buoyancy, truancy, vacancy, vagrancy
-ant	one who	servant, immigrant, assistant, merchant
-ar	one who	beggar, liar
-ard	one who	drunkard, steward, coward, wizard
-arian	one who	librarian, humanitarian, libertarian
-arium	place for	aquarium, planetarium, solarium
-ary	place for	library, mortuary, sanctuary, infirmary
-ation	state or quality of	desperation, starvation, inspiration
-ation	action or process	emancipation, narration, computation
-cle	small	corpuscle, particle, icicle, cubicle
-cule	small	minuscule, molecule
-cy	state or quality of	accuracy, bankruptcy, ecstacy, conspiracy
-cy	action or process	truancy, diplomacy, vagrancy, piracy
-dom	state or quality of	freedom, boredom, martyrdom, wisdom
-ectomy	surgical removal of	tonsillectomy, appendectomy, mastectomy
-ee	object of action	payee, lessee, employee
-ence	state or quality of	violence, absence, reticence
-ency	state or quality of	frequency, clemency, expediency, consistency
-enne	female	commedienne, equestrienne, tragedienne

126

The Reading Teacher's Book of Lists, Third Edition, © 1993 by Prentice Hall

SUFFIX	MEANING	EXAMPLES
-ent	one who	superintendent, resident, regent
-er	one who	teacher, painter, seller, shipper
-er	action or process	murder, thunder, plunder, waiver
-ery, -ry	trade or occupation	surgery, archery, sorcery, dentistry
-ery	establishment	bakery, grocery, fishery, nunnery
-ery, -ry	goods or products	pottery, jewelry, cutlery
-ery, -ry	state or quality of	bravery, savagery, forgery, butchery
-ess	one who (female)	waitress, actress, countess, hostess
-et	small	midget, sonnet, bassinet, cygnet
-ette	small (female)	dinette, cigarette, majorette
-eur	one who	chauffeur, connoisseur, masseur
-eur	state or quality of	hauteur, grandeur
-hood	state or quality of	childhood, adulthood, falsehood
-i	plural	alumni, foci
-ics	scientific or social system	physics, economics, politics, statistics
-ier, -yer	one who	cashier, financier, gondolier, lawyer
-ide	chemical compound	fluoride, bromide, peroxide
-ina	female	czarina, Wilhelmina, ballerina
-ine	chemical or basic substance	iodine, chlorine, caffeine, quinine
-ine	female	heroine, Josephine, Pauline
-ing	material	bedding, roofing, frosting, stuffing
-ion	state or quality of	champion, companion, ambition, suspicion
-ism	state or quality of	baptism, heroism, racism, despotism
-ism	doctrine of	capitalism, socialism, hedonism
-ist	one who practices	biologist, capitalist, communist
-ite	mineral or rock	granite, anthracite, bauxite
-itis	inflammation of	laryngitis, arthritis, bronchitis
-ity	state or quality of	necessity, felicity, civility, parity
-ization	state or quality of	civilization, standardization, organization
-kin	small	lambkin, napkin, manikin, Munchkin
-let	small	owlet, rivulet, starlet, leaflet, islet
-ling	small	duckling, yearling, suckling, fledgling
-man	one who works with	cameraman, mailman, doorman
-ment	action or process	embezzlement, development, government
-ment	state or quality of	amusement, predicament, amazement
-ment	product or thing	instrument, ornament, fragment
-mony	product or thing	testimony, matrimony, ceremony, alimony
-ness	state or quality of	happiness, kindness, goodness, darkness
-ol	alcohols	methanol, ethanol, glycol

SUFFIX	**MEANING**	**EXAMPLES**
-ology	study or science of	biology, psychology (see List 41, -ology Word Family)
-or	one who	actor, doctor, donor, auditor
-or	state or quality of	error, stupor, candor, fervor, pallor
-orium	place for	auditorium, emporium
-ory	place for	laboratory, conservatory, purgatory
-ose	sugars	glucose, sucrose, fructose, dextrose
-phobia	fear of	claustrophobia, acrophobia (see List 40, -phobia Word Family)
-s, -es	plural	pens, books, boxes, parentheses
-ship	skill or art of	penmanship, showmanship, horsemanship
-ship	state or quality of	friendship, hardship, citizenship
-sion	state or quality of	tension, compulsion
-th	state or quality of	strength, warmth, filth, depth, length
-tion	state or quality of	attention, caution, fascination
-trix	female	aviatrix, executrix
-tude	state or quality of	gratitude, fortitude, beatitude
-ty	state or quality of	loyalty, honesty, amnesty, unity
-ure	action or process	censure, failure, enclosure, exposure
-wright	one who works with	playwright, shipwright, wheelwright

ADJECTIVE SUFFIXES

-acious	inclined to	loquacious, mendacious, audacious, fallacious
-al	relating to	natural, royal, maternal, suicidal
-an	relating to	urban, American, Alaskan, veteran
-ant	inclined to	vigilant, pleasant, defiant, buoyant
-ary	relating to	honorary, military, literary, ordinary
-ate	state or quality of	fortunate, desperate, passionate
-ative	inclined to	demonstrative, pejorative, talkative
-ble	inclined to	gullible, perishable, voluble, durable
-en	relating to	golden, ashen, wooden, earthen
-ent	inclined to	competent, different, excellent
-er	more (comparative)	fatter, smaller, crazier, smarter
-ern	direction	eastern, western, northern, postern
-ese	state or quality of	Japanese, Portuguese, Chinese, Siamese
-esque	relating to	statuesque, picturesque, Romanesque
-est	most (comparative)	fattest, smallest, smartest, fastest
-etic	relating to	alphabetic, dietetic, frenetic
-ful	full of	thoughtful, joyful, careful, fearful
-ial	relating to	filial, commercial, remedial
-ian	relating to	barbarian, physician, Christian
-ic	relating to	comic, historic, poetic, public

The Reading Teacher's Book of Lists, Third Edition, © 1993 by Prentice Hall

SUFFIX	MEANING	EXAMPLES
-ical	relating to	comical, rhetorical, economical
-ide	state or quality of	candid, sordid, lucid, splendid, rigid
-ile	state or quality of	virile, agile, volatile, docile, fragile
-ine	relating to	feminine, bovine, feline, marine
-ious	state or quality of	gracious, ambitious, religious
-ish	relating to	childish, whitish, fiftyish, Scottish
-ive	inclined to	active, passive, negative, affirmative
-less	without	thoughtless, tireless, ageless, careless
-like	resembling	childlike, homelike, lifelike, boylike
-ly	resembling	fatherly, motherly, scholarly
-ly	every	daily, weekly, monthly, yearly
-most	most	utmost, westernmost, innermost
-oid	resembling	humanoid, asteroid, paranoid, planetoid
-ose	full of	verbose, morose, bellicose, comatose
-ous	full of	joyous, virtuous, nervous, wondrous
-some	inclined to	meddlesome, awesome, tiresome
-th, -eth	numbers	fifth, twelfth, twentieth, fiftieth
-ulent	full of	turbulent, corpulent, fraudulent
-ular	relating to	granular, cellular, circular, popular
-und	state or quality of	rotund, fecund, moribund, jocund
-uous	state or quality of	contemptuous, tempestuous, sensuous
-ward	direction	forward, backward, eastward, upward
-y	state or quality of	fruity, sunny, rainy, funny, gooey

ADVERB SUFFIXES

-ly	forms adverb from adjective	slowly, beautifully, happily, largely
-ways	manner	sideways, always, longways, crossways
-wise	manner, direction	clockwise, lengthwise
-wise	reference	schoolwise, marketwise, timewise

VERB SUFFIXES

SUFFIX	MEANING	EXAMPLES
-ade	action or process	blockade, promenade, parade
-age	action or process	ravage, pillage
-ate	to make	activate, fascinate, annihilate, liberate
-ble	repeated action	stumble, squabble, mumble, tumble, fumble
-ed, -d	past tense	talked, walked, baked, raised
-en	past completed action	taken, eaten, proven, stolen
-en	to make	strengthen, fasten, lengthen, frighten, weaken
-er	action or process	discover, murder, conquer, deliver
-fy	to make	satisfy, terrify, falsify, beautify
-ing	continuous action	singing, talking, jumping, eating
-ish	action or process	finish, flourish, nourish, punish
-ize	to make	standardize, computerize, popularize
-ure	action or process	censure, procure, endure, inure

The Reading Teacher's Book of Lists, Third Edition, © 1993 by Prentice Hall

See also List 42, Prefixes; List 45, Greek and Latin Roots; and List 82, Parts of Speech.

44. *Spelling Rules for Adding Suffixes*

ADDING SUFFIXES

Basic Rule: Just Add the Suffix.

Examples: want—wanted, wanting, wants

Exceptions:

For Words Ending in "e"

    a. Drop the final "e" if the suffix begins with a vowel. Example: rose - rosy; name - naming, named

    b. Keep the final "e" if the suffix begins with a consonant. Example: safe - safely

    c. Keep the final "e" if a vowel precedes it. Example: see - seeing

    d. Drop the final "le" if the suffix is "ly" (no double "l"). Example: able - ably

For Words Ending in "y"

    e. Change the "y" to "i" if "y" is preceded by a consonant. Example: carry - carried (suffix here is "-ed")

    f. Don't change the "y" to "i" if the "y" is preceded by a vowel. Example: joy - joyful

    g. Don't change the "y" to "i" if the suffix begins with an "i." Example: carry - carrying (suffix here is "-ing")

For Words Ending in "c"

    h. Add a "k" before any suffix beginning with an "e," "i," or "y." Example: picnic - picnicking; panic - panicky

Doubling the Final Letter

    i. Double the final consonant before adding the suffix if:
        (1) the word has one syllable (or the final syllable is accented)
        (2) the word ends in a single consonant (not "x")
        (3) the word has a single vowel letter
        (4) the suffix begins with a vowel
    Examples: brag - bragged; (not "x," box - boxing)

    j. You do not double the final consonant (Basic Rule applies) if:
        (1) the suffix begins with a consonant. Example: bag - bagful
        (2) the vowel has two letters. Example: rain - rained
        (3) the word has two final consonants. Example: hard - harder

The Reading Teacher's Book of Lists, Third Edition, © 1993 by Prentice Hall

131

(4) the suffix begins with a consonant. Example: bag - bags

(5) the final syllable is not accented. Example: benefit - benefited

k. If the word has two syllables and is accented on the last syllable, treat it as a one-syllable word. (See h. and j. above.) Example: admit – admittance

l. If the word has two syllables and is accented on the first syllable, do not double the last letter (back to the Basic Rule). Example: equal - equaled

m. The final "l" is kept when adding "ly." (This really restates the Basic Rule and rule j., but it looks funny when you see two "l's.") Example: cool - coolly

Note: Prefixes are much more regular; just add the prefix in front of the root word—no spelling change or letter doubling.

See also List 92, Plurals.

45. *Greek and Latin Roots*

Most modern English words originated in other languages. The study of word origins, or etymology, is a fascinating subject. The Greek and Latin roots in this list can form the basis for a vocabulary-building course. Roots are taught successfully in families such as *microscope, telescope, periscope,* to illustrate that *scope* means "see." In the following list, Greek roots are indicated with "g" and Latin roots with "l." Roots that are easy are marked with an asterisk (*).

ROOT	MEANING	EXAMPLES
*act (l)	do	action, actor, react, transact, enact
aero(g)	air	aerobics, aerodynamics, aeronautics, aerate, aeronautics
aesthet (g)	sense, perception	aesthetic, aesthete (see also esth)
agri (l)	field	agriculture, agrarian, agronomy
alt (l)	high	altitude, altimeter, alto, altocumulus
alter (l)	other	alternate, alternative, altercation
ambul (l)	walk, go	ambulance, amble, preamble, circumambulate, somnambulant
amo, ami (l)	love	amiable, amorous, amateur, amity
andr (g)	man	androgynous, philander, polyandry
ang (l)	bend	angle, triangle, quadrangle, angular
anim (l)	life, spirit	animate, animosity, animal, inanimate
ann, enn (l)	year	annual, biennial, anniversary, annuity
anthr (g)	man	anthropology, philanthropist, anthropoid, misanthrope
apt, ept (l)	suitable	aptitude, inept, adept, apt
aqua (l)	water	aquarium, aquatic, aqueous, aquamarine
arch (g)	chief	monarch, archbishop, archenemy, oligarchy
arch (g)	primitive, ancient	archaeology, archaic, archetype, archive
art (l)	skill	artisan, artist, artificial, artifact
*ast (g)	star	astronaut, astronomy, disaster, asterisk
*aud (l)	hear	audience, auditorium, audiovisual, audible, audition
baro (g)	weight	barometer, barograph, isobar
belli (l)	war	bellicose, antebellum, belligerent, rebellion
biblio (g)	book	bibliography, Bible, bibliophile
bio (g)	life	biology, biography, biochemistry, biopsy
brev (l)	short	abbreviation, brevity, breve
cad, cas (l)	fall, perish	cadence, cascade, decadence, cadaver
cal (l)	hot	calorie, caldron, scald
cam (l)	field	camp, campus, encamp, campaign
cand (l)	glow, white	candle, candidate, incandescent
cap (l)	head	cap, captain, capital, decapitate, caput
cardi (g)	heart	cardiac, cardiology, cardiogram
cede, ceed (l)	go, yield	proceed, exceed, succeed, concede
ceive, cept (l)	take, receive	receive, reception, accept, conception
centr (l)	center	central, centrifugal, egocentric, eccentric

ROOT	MEANING	EXAMPLES
cert (l)	sure	certain, certify, ascertain, certificate
cess (l)	go, yield	process, recess, access, cessation
chron (g)	time	chronological, synchronize, anachronism, chronicle, chronic
cide, cise (l)	cut, kill	suicide, scissor, incision, insecticide
cip (l)	take, receive	recipient, incipient, participate, recipe
claim, clam (l)	shout	proclaim, exclaim, acclaim, clamor
clar (l)	clear	clarity, declare, clarify, declaration
cline (l)	lean	incline, recline, decline, inclination
clud (l)	shut	include, conclude, exclude, preclude, seclude
cogn (l)	know	recognize, cognition, cognizant, incognito
commum (l)	common	community, communicate, communism, communal
cord (l)	heart	cordial, accord, concord, discord
corp (l)	body	corporation, corpus, corpse, corps
cosm (g)	universe	cosmonaut, cosmos, cosmopolitan, microcosm
crat (g)	rule	democrat, aristocrat, bureaucracy, theocracy, autocratic
*cred (l)	believe	credit, discredit, incredible, credulous
cum (l)	heap	cumulative, accumulate, cumulus
cur (l)	care	cure, manicure, pedicure, curable
cur (l)	run	current, occur, excursion, concur, recur
*cycl (g)	circle, ring	bicycle, cyclone, cycle, encyclopedia
dem (g)	people	democrat, demography, demagogy, epidemic
dent (l)	tooth	dentist, trident, dentifrice, indent
*dic (l)	speak	dictate, predict, contradict, verdict, diction
div (l)	divide	divide, divorce, division, dividend
doc (l)	teach	doctrine, document, doctor, docile
domin (l)	master	dominate, predominate, dominion, A.D. (*Anno Domini*)
don, donat (l)	give	donation, donor, pardon, donate
dont (g)	tooth	orthodontist
dogma (g)	opinion	dogma, dogmatic, dogmatism
dox (g)	belief	orthodox, unorthodox, heterodox
*duc (l)	lead	duct, conduct, educate, induct, aquaduct
esth (g)	feeling	anesthetic, anesthetist, esthetic (see also aesthet)
*fac (l)	make, do	factory, manufacture, benefactor, facsimile
fer (l)	bear, carry	transfer, ferry, conifer, infer, refer
fic (l)	make, do	efficient, proficient, sufficient
fid (l)	faith	fidelity, confidence, infidel, bona fide
fig (l)	form	figure, figment, configuration, disfigure, effigy
firm (l)	securely fixed	confirm, infirm, affirm, firmament
flect (l)	bend	reflect, deflect, reflection, inflection
flex (l)	bend	reflex, flexible, flexor

The Reading Teacher's Book of Lists, Third Edition, © 1993 by Prentice Hall

ROOT	MEANING	EXAMPLES
form (l)	shape	form, uniform, transform, reform
fract (l)	break	fracture, fraction
frag (l)	break	fragment, fragile
frater (l)	brother	fraternal, fraternity, fratricide
fric (l)	rub	friction, dentifrice, fricative
fug (l)	flee	fugitive, refugee, centrifugal, refuge
funct (l)	perform	function, malfunction, dysfunctional
gam (g)	marriage	polygamy, monogamy, bigamy
gen (g)	birth, race	generation, genocide, progeny, genealogy, generate
geo (g)	earth	geography, geometry, geology, geophysical
gnos (g)	know	gnostic, agnostic, diagnostic, prognosis
gon (g)	angle	pentagon, octagon, diagonal, trigonometry
grad (l)	step, stage	grade, gradual, graduation
gress (l)	step, stage	progress, egress, regress
*gram (g)	letter, written	telegram, diagram, grammar, epigram, monogram
*graph (g)	write	telegraph, photograph, phonograph, autograph
grat (l)	pleasing	gratify, gratitude, congratulate, ungrateful
greg (l)	gather	gregarious, congregation, segregation, aggregate
gyn (g)	woman	gynecologist, misogynist, monogyny, androgyny
hab, hib (l)	hold	habit, habitual, habitat, prohibit, exhibit
homo (l)	man	homicide, *Homo sapiens*, hombre, homage
hosp, host (l)	host	host, hostess, hospital, hospitality, hospice
hydr (g)	water	hydroelectric, hydrogen, hydrant, dehydrant
iatr (g)	medical care	psychiatry, podiatry, pediatrician, geriatrics
imag (l)	likeness	image, imagine, imaginative, imagery
init (l)	beginning	initial, initiate, initiative
integ (l)	whole	integrate, integral, integrity, integer
ject (l)	throw	project, inject
junct (l)	join	juncture, conjunction, adjunct, injunction
jud (l)	law	judge, judicial, judicate, judicious
jur (l)	law	jurisdiction, jurisprudence, jury
jus (l)	law	justice, just, justify
kine, cine (g)	movement	kinetic, hyperkinesia, cinema
lab (l)	work	labor, laboratory, collaborate, elaborate
laps (l)	slip	elapse, collapse, relapse, prolapse
lat (l)	carry	translate, relate, collate, prelate
lat (l)	side	lateral, bilateral, unilateral, quadrilateral
liber (l)	free	liberty, libertine, liberal, liberate
lith (g)	stone	lithograph, monolith, paleolithic, neolithic
*loc (l)	place	location, locate, dislocate, allocate
log (g)	word	prologue, apology, dialogue, eulogy, monologue
luc (l)	light	lucid, elucidate, translucent

ROOT	MEANING	EXAMPLES
lud (l)	play	ludicrous, interlude, elude
lum (l)	light	luminous, illuminate, luminescent
luna (l)	moon	lunar, lunatic
lus (l)	play	illusion, illusive
lust (l)	shine	luster, illustrate, lackluster, illustrious
lys (g)	break down	analysis, paralysis, electrolysis, catalyst
*man (l)	hand	manual, manufacture, manuscript, manipulate
mand (l)	order	command, demand, mandate, remand
mania (g)	madness	maniac, pyromania, cleptomania, megalomania
mar (l)	sea	marine, maritime, submarine, mariner
mater (l)	mother	maternal, maternity
matr (l)	mother	matricide, matrimony, matron, matrix
max (l)	greatest	maximum, maxim, maximize
mech (g)	machine	mechanic, mechanism, mechanize
mem (l)	mindful of	memory, remember, memorial, commemorate
ment (l)	mind	mental, mention, demented, menticide
merge (l)	dip	submerge, emerge, merge, merger
mers (l)	dip	submerse, immerse
*meter (g)	measure	thermometer, centimeter, diameter, barometer
*migr (l)	change, move	migrate, immigrant, emigrate, migratory
mim (l)	same	mime, mimic, pantomime, mimeograph
min (l)	small, less	minute, mini, minor, minus, minimize
minist (l)	serve	minister, administer, administration
*miss (l)	send	missile, dismiss, mission, remiss
mit (l)	send	submit, remit, admit, transmit
*mob (l)	move	automobile, mobile, mobilize, mobility
mon (l)	advise	admonish, premonition, admonition, monitor
morph (g)	shape	amorphous, metamorphosis, morphology, polymorphous, anthropomorphic
mort (l)	death	mortician, mortuary, mortal, immortal
*mot (l)	move	motion, motor, promote, demote, motile
mov (l)	move	remove, movement, unmoved
mut (l)	change, interchange	mutation, immutable, mutual, commute
narr (l)	tell	narrate, narrative, narrator
nat (l)	born	natal, native, nation, nativity, innate
nav (l)	ship	navy, naval, navigate, circumnavigate
neg (l)	no	negation, abnegation, negative, renege
neo (g)	new	neophyte, neoclassic, neologism, neon, neonatal
not (l)	mark	notation, notable, denote, notice
nun, noun (l)	declare	announce, pronounce, denounce, enunciate
nov (l)	new	novel, novelty, novice, innovate, nova
numer (l)	number	numeral, enumerate, numerous, enumerable
ocu (l)	eye	oculist, binocular, monocular
onym (g)	name	synonym, antonym, pseudonym
opt (g)	eye	optician, optometrist, optic, optical

The Reading Teacher's Book of Lists, Third Edition, © 1993 by Prentice Hall

The Reading Teacher's Book of Lists, Third Edition, © 1993 by Prentice Hall

ROOT	MEANING	EXAMPLES
opt (l)	best	optimum, optimist, optimal, optimize
ord (l)	row	order, ordinary, ordinal, extraordinary, ordinance
orig (l)	beginning	origin, original, originate, aborigine
ortho (g)	straight, right	orthodontist, orthodox, orthopedist
paleo (g)	old	paleontology, paleolithic
pater (l)	father	paternity, paternal, patriarch, patricide
path (g)	feeling, suffer	pathology, sympathy, empathy, antipathy, pathos
ped (g)	child	encyclopedia, pediatrician, pedagogical
*ped (l)	foot	pedal, pedestrian, biped, pedestal
pel (l)	drive	compel, propel, expel, repel
pend (l)	hang	pendulum, suspend, append, appendix
pens (l)	weigh	pensive, pension, compensate
phil (g)	love	philosophy, philanthropist, philharmonic, Anglophile, philately
phob (g)	fear	claustrophobia, xenophobia, acrophobia
*phon (g)	sound	phonograph, symphony, telephone, microphone, phonics
*photo (g)	light	photograph, telephoto, photosynthesis
phys (g)	nature	physical, physique, metaphysical, physician
plex (l)	fold	complex, duplex, plexiglass, perplex
plic (l)	fold	complicated, multiplication, duplicate, implicate, explicate
plur (l)	more	plural, plurality, pluralism
pod (g)	foot	podiatrist, podium, tripod
poli (g)	city	metropolis, cosmopolitan, police, political
pon (l)	place	opponent, exponent, proponent, postpone
*pop (l)	people	population, popular, pop, populace
*port (l)	carry	portable, transport, import, porter
pos (l)	place	position, compose, deposit, composite
psych (g)	mind, soul	psychology, psyche, psychopath, psychiatrist
pug (l)	fight	pugnacious, pugilist, repugnant, impugn
pul (l)	urge	compulsory, expulsion, compulsion, repulse
put (l)	think	computer, reputation, deputy, disrepute
quer, quir (l)	ask, seek	query, inquiry
ques (l)	ask, seek	question, inquest, request, quest
rad (l)	ray, spoke	radius, radio, radiology, radium
ras (l)	scrape	erase, abrasive, rasp, razor
rect (l)	straight	erect, rectangle, rectify, direction, correct
reg (l)	guide, rule	regal, reign, regulate, regime, regent
rid (l)	laugh	ridiculous, deride, ridicule, derisive
*rupt (l)	break	erupt, interrupt, abrupt, rupture, bankrupt
san (l)	health	sanitary, sanitarium, sane, insanity

ROOT	MEANING	EXAMPLES
scend (l)	climb	ascend, descend, descendent, transcend
sci (l)	know	science, conscience, conscious, omniscient, scientific
*scop (g)	see	microscope, telescope, periscope, stethoscope
scribe (l)	write	scribe, inscribe, describe, prescribe
script (l)	write	script, transcript, scripture
sect (l)	cut	section, dissect, intersect, sect
sed (l)	settle	sedative, sediment, sedentary, sedate
sens (l)	feel	sensation, sense, sensitive, sensible, sensory
sent (l)	feel	consent, sentimental, dissent, assent
serv (l)	save, keep	conserve, preserve, reserve, reservoir
serv (l)	serve	serve, servant, service, servile
*sign (l)	mark	signature, signal, significant, insignia
sim (l)	like	similar, simultaneous, simulate, simile
sist (l)	stand	consist, resist, subsist, assist
sol (l)	alone	solo, solitary, desolate, soliloquy
solv (l)	loosen	dissolve, solve, solvent, resolve
son (l)	sound	sonar, sonata, sonnet, unison, sonorous
soph (g)	wise	philosopher, sophomore, sophisticated, sophist
*spec (l)	see	inspect, suspect, respect, spectator, spectacle
spir (l)	breathe	respiration, inspire, spirit, perspire, conspirator
sta (l)	stand	station, status, stabile, stagnant, statue, stationary
stell (l)	star	stellar, constellation
stimu (l)	goad	stimulate, stimulus, stimulant
strict (l)	draw tight	strict, restrict, constrict, stricture
struct (l)	build	structure, construct, instruct, destruction
sum (l)	highest	summit, summary, sum, summons
surg (l)	rise	surge, insurgent, resurgent
surr (l)	rise	resurrect, insurrection, resurrection
tact (l)	touch	tactile, intact, contact, tact
tain (l)	hold	retain, contain, detain, attain
tang (l)	touch	tangible, tangent, intangible
ten (l)	hold	tenacious, tenure, tenant, retentive, tenable
ten (l)	stretch	tendon, tendency, tension, tent, tense
term (l)	end	terminal, determine, exterminate
terr (l)	land	territory, terrain, terrestrial, terrace
tex (l)	weave	text, texture, textile, context
the (g)	god	theology, atheism, monotheism, polytheism, pantheism
*therm (g)	heat	thermometer, thermal, thermostat, thermos
tort (l)	twist	torture, contort, retort, tort
*tract (l)	pull, drag	tractor, attract, subtract, traction
trib (l)	give	contribute, tribute, tributary, attribute
trud (l)	push	intrude, protrude, intruder
trus (l)	push	abstruse, intrusive, obtrusive

The Reading Teacher's Book of Lists, Third Edition, © 1993 by Prentice Hall

ROOT	MEANING	EXAMPLES
turb (l)	confusion	disturb, turbulent, perturb, turbine, turbid
*urb (l)	city	urban, suburb, urbane, suburban
*vac (l)	empty	vacant, vacation, vacuum, evacuate, vacate
vag (l)	wander	vagrant, vague, vagabond, vagary
var (l)	different	vary, invariable, variant, variety
ven (l)	come	convene, convention, advent, invent, venue
ver (l)	truth	verdict, verify, verity, aver, veracity
ver (l)	turn	convert, reverse, versatile, introvert
vict (l)	conquer	victory, victim, conviction
*vid (l)	see	video, evidence, provide, providence
vinc (l)	conquer	convince, invincible
voc (l)	voice	vocal, advocate, evocation, convocation
void (l)	empty	devoid, avoid, void, voided
vol (l)	wish, will	volition, volunteer, voluntary, benevolent, malevolent
*volv (l)	roll	revolve, involve, evolve, revolver, revolution
vor (l)	eat	carnivorous, voracious, herbivorous, omnivorous

See also List 40, Phobia and Cide Word Families; List 41, -Ology Word Family; Lists 42 and 43, Prefixes; and List 44, Suffixes.

SECTION V
Phonics

46. *Initial Consonant Sounds*

The following are all the beginning consonant sounds for either words or syllables. They constitute what some linguists call the "onset" for the syllable. The rest of the syllable must have a vowel or a vowel plus a consonant (a vowel plus a consonant is called a phonogram or rime, see List 47). For words that use these initial consonant sounds see List 48, Phonics Example Words.

SINGLE CONSONANTS

b	h	n	v
c	j	p	w
d	k	r	y
f	l	s	z
g	m	t	

CONSONANT DIGRAPHS

ch
sh
th (voiced)
th (voiceless)
wh (hw blend)

CONSONANT BLENDS

(r family)	(l family)	(s family)	(3 letter)	(no family)
br	bl	sc	scr	tw
cr	cl	sk	squ	
dr	fl	sm	str	
fr	gl	sn	thr	
gr	pl	sp	spr	
pr	sl	st	spl	
tr		sw	shr	
wr			sch	

IMPORTANT EXCEPTIONS

qu = /kw/ blend as in "quick"
   (the letter "q"
   never used without "u")
ph = /f/ sound as in "phone"
c = /s/ before i, e or y,
   as in "city"
c = /k/ before a, o, or u, as in "cat"

g = /j/ before i, e, or y, as in "gem"
g = /g/ before a, o, or u, as in "good"
x = /ks/ blend as in "fox"
s = /z/ sound at the end
   of some words − "is"

RARE EXCEPTIONS

ch = /k/ as in "character"
ch = /s/ as in "chef"
ti = /sh/ as in "attention"
s = /sh/ as in "sure"
x = /gz/ as in "exact"

SILENT CONSONANTS

gn = /n/ as in "gnat"
kn = /n/ as in "knife"
wr = /r/ as in "write"

See also List 47, Phonograms, and List 48, Phonics Example Words.

The Reading Teacher's Book of Lists, Third Edition, © 1993 by Prentice Hall

47. Phonograms

As teachers, we found it hard to get a good list of phonograms, so we decided to build our own using many teacher lists and a rhyming dictionary. We think this is the most complete one in existence. A phonogram is usually a vowel sound plus a consonant sound, but it is often less than a syllable, hence less than a word—it needs an initial consonant or blend to make it a word. These are useful for all kinds of games and drills in reading and spelling. Phonograms, or "rimes" as some linguists call them, have been used in teaching reading since Colonial times and are currently used in regular classrooms, remedial reading, ESL, and adult literacy instruction. Since syllable rimes also include just vowel endings like -ay in "say" or -ea in "tea," we have included some of them in this list. The phonograms in this list are all in one-syllable words; however, the same phonograms appear in many polysyllable words.*

-ab (ă)	-ack (ă)	-ad (ă)	spade	wag	-ail (ā)	drain
cab	back	bad	trade	brag	bail	grain
dab	hack	cad		crag	fail	plain
gab	Jack	dad	**-aff (ă)**	drag	Gail	slain
jab	lack	fad	gaff	flag	hail	Spain
lab	Mack	gad	chaff	shag	jail	sprain
nab	pack	had	quaff	slag	mail	stain
tab	quack	lad	staff	snag	nail	strain
blab	rack	mad		stag	pail	train
crab	sack	pad	**-aft (ă)**	swag	quail	
drab	tack	sad	daft		rail	
flab	black	tad	raft	**-age (ā)**	sail	**-aint (ā)**
grab	clack	Brad	waft	cage	tail	faint
scab	crack	Chad	craft	gage	wail	paint
slab	knack	clad	draft	page	flail	saint
stab	shack	glad	graft	rage	frail	taint
	slack	shad	shaft	sage	snail	quaint
-ace (ā)	smack			wage	trail	
face	snack	**-ade (ā)**	**-ag (ă)**	stage		
lace	stack	bade	bag		**-ain (ā)**	**-air (ā)**
mace	track	fade	gag		lain	
pace	whack	jade	hag	**-aid (ā)**	main	fair
race		made	jag	laid	pain	hair
brace	**-act (ă)**	wade	lag	maid	rain	lair
grace	fact	blade	nag	paid	vain	pair
place	pact	glade	rag	raid	wain	chair
space	tact	grade	sag	braid	brain	flair
trace	tract	shade	tag	staid	chain	stair

---

*Technical note: Some people might argue that combinations like "-aw" as in "saw" or "-ay" as in "say" are technically not phonograms because they end in a vowel sound and don't have a consonant sound at the end. We have included them, however, because they have a consonant letter and they might be useful to teachers in teaching reading or spelling. Vowel combinations like "aw" without consonants are "rimes." The criteria for selecting these phonograms is that they appear in three or more not-obscure single-syllable words. Most of these phonograms (rimes) appear in many more polysyllable words.

The Reading Teacher's Book of Lists, Third Edition, © 1993 by Prentice Hall

-aise (ā)

raise
braise
chaise
praise

-ait (ā)

bait
gait
wait
strait
trait

-ake (ā)

bake
cake
fake
Jake
lake
make
quake
rake
take
wake
brake
drake
flake
shake
snake
stake

-ale (ā)

bale
dale
gale
hale
male
pale
sale
tale
scale
shale
stale
whale

-alk (ô)

balk

calk
talk
walk
chalk
stalk

-all (ô)

ball
call
fall
gall
hall
mall
pall
tall
wall
small
squall
stall

-alt (ô)

halt
malt
salt

-am (ă)

cam
dam
ham
jam
Pam
ram
Sam
tam
yam
clam
cram
dram
gram
scam
scram
sham
slam
swam
tram

-ame (ā)

came
dame
fame
game
lame
name
same
tame
blame
flame
frame
shame

-amp (ă)

camp
damp
lamp
ramp
tamp
vamp
champ
clamp
cramp
scamp
stamp
tramp

-an (ă)

ban
can
Dan
fan
man
pan
ran
tan
van
bran
clan
flan
plan
scan
span
than

-ance (ă)

dance
lance
chance
France
glance
prance
stance
trance

-anch (ă)

ranch
blanch
branch
stanch

-and (ă)

band
hand
land
sand
bland
brand
gland
stand
strand

-ane (ā)

bane
cane
Jane
lane
mane
pane
sane
vane
wane
crane
plane

-ang (ă)

bang
fang
gang
hang
pang
rang

sang
tang
clang
slang
sprang
twang

-ank (ă)

bank
dank
hank
lank
rank
sank
tank
yank
blank
clank
crank
drank
flank
Frank
plank
prank
shank
spank
stank
thank

-ant (ă)

can't
pant
rant
chant
grant
plant
scant
slant

-ap (ă)

cap
gap
lap
map
nap
pap
rap

sap
tap
yap
chap
clap
flap
scrap
slap
snap
strap
trap
wrap

-ape (ā)

cape
gape
nape
rape
tape
drape
grape
scrape
shape

-ar (ä)

bar
car
far
jar
mar
par
tar
char
scar
spar
star

-ard (ä)

bard
card
guard
hard
lard
yard
shard

-are (ār)

bare
care
dare
fare
hare
mare
pare
rare
ware
blare
flare
glare
scare
share
snare
spare
square
stare

-arge (ä)

barge
large
charge

-ark (ä)

bark
dark
hark
lark
mark
park
Clark
shark
spark
stark

-arm (ä)

farm
harm
charm

-arn (ä)

barn
darn
yarn

-arp (ä)

carp
harp
tarp
sharp

-art (ä)

cart
dart
mart
part
tart
chart
smart
start

-ase (ā)

base
case
vase
chase

-ash (ă)

bash
cash
dash
gash
hash
lash
mash
rash
sash
brash
clash
flash
slash
smash
stash
thrash
trash

-ask (ă)

ask
cask
mask
task
flask

-asm (ă)

chasm
plasm
spasm

-asp (ă)

gasp
hasp
rasp
clasp
grasp

-ast (ă)

cast
fast
last
mast
past
vast
blast

-aste (ā)

baste
haste
paste
taste
waste
chaste

-ass (ă)

bass
lass
mass
pass
brass
class
glass
grass

-at (ă)

bat
cat
fat
gnat
hat
mat
pat

rat
sat
tat
vat
brat
chat
drat
flat
scat
slat
spat
that

-atch (ă)

batch
catch
hatch
latch
match
patch
scratch
thatch

-ate (ā)

date
fate
gate
hate
Kate
late
mate
rate
crate
grate
plate
skate
state

-ath (ă)

bath
lath
math
path
wrath

-aught (ô)

caught

naught
taught
fraught

-aunch (ô)

haunch
launch
paunch

-aunt (ô)

daunt
gaunt
haunt
jaunt
taunt
flaunt

-ave (ā)

cave
Dave
gave
pave
rave
save
wave
brave
crave
grave
shave
slave
stave

-aw (ô)

caw
gnaw
jaw
law
paw
raw
saw
claw
draw
flaw
slaw
squaw
straw

-awl (ô)

bawl
brawl
crawl
drawl
shawl
scrawl
trawl

-awn (ô)

dawn
fawn
lawn
pawn
yawn
brawn
drawn
prawn
spawn

-ax (ă)

lax
Max
tax
wax
flax

-ay (ā)

bay
day
gay
hay
jay
lay
may
nay
pay
quay
ray
say
way
bray
clay
cray
fray
gray
play

pray
slay
spray
stay
stray
sway
tray

-aze (ā)

daze
faze
gaze
haze
maze
raze
blaze
craze
glaze
graze

-ea (ē)

pea
sea
tea
flea
plea

-each (ē)

beach
leach
peach
reach
teach
bleach
breach
preach
screech

-ead (ĕ)

dead
head
lead
read
bread
dread
spread

thread
tread

-ead (ē)

bead
lead
read
knead
plead

-eak (ē)

beak
leak
peak
teak
weak
bleak
creak
freak
sneak
speak
squeak
streak
tweak

-eal (ē)

deal
heal
meal
peal
real
seal
teal
veal
zeal
squeal
steal

-ealth (ĕ)

health
wealth
stealth

-eam (ē)

beam
ream
seam

cream
dream
gleam
scream
steam
stream
team

-ean (ē)

bean
dean
Jean
lean
mean
wean
clean
glean

-eap (ē)

heap
leap
reap
cheap

-ear (ē)

dear
fear
gear
hear
near
rear
sear
tear
year
clear
shear
smear
spear

-ear (ĕ)

bear
pear
wear
swear

-east (ē)

beast

feast
least
yeast

-eat (ē)

beat
feat
heat
meat
neat
peat
seat
bleat
cheat
cleat
pleat
treat
wheat

-eave (ē)

heave
leave
weave
cleave
sheave

-eck (ĕ)

deck
heck
neck
peck
check
fleck
speck
wreck

-ed (ĕ)

bed
fed
led
Ned
red
Ted
wed
bled
bred
fled

Fred
shed
shred
sled
sped

-edge (ĕ)

hedge
ledge
wedge
dredge
pledge
sledge

-ee (ē)

bee
fee
knee
lee
see
tee
wee
flee
free
glee
tree

-eech (ē)

beech
leech
breech
screech
speech

-eed (ē)

deed
feed
heed
kneed
need
reed
seed
weed
bleed
breed
creed
freed

greed
speed
steed
treed
tweed

-eek (ē)

leek
meek
peek
reek
seek
week
cheek
creek
Greek
sleek

-eel (ē)

feel
heel
keel
kneel
peel
reel
creel
steel
wheel

-eem (ē)

deem
seem
teem

-een (ē)

keen
queen
seen
teen
green
preen
screen
sheen

-eep (ē)

beep
deep

jeep
keep
peep
seep
weep
cheep
creep
sheep
sleep
steep
sweep

-eer (ē)

beer
deer
jeer
leer
peer
queer
seer
sneer
steer

-eet (ē)

beet
feet
meet
fleet
greet
sheet
skeet
sleet
street
sweet
tweet

-eeze (ē)

breeze
freeze
sneeze
squeeze
tweeze
wheeze

-eft (ĕ)

deft

heft
left
cleft
theft

-eg (ĕ)

beg
keg
leg
meg
peg

-eigh (ā)

neigh
weigh
sleigh

-eld (ĕ)

held
meld
weld

-ell (ĕ)

bell
cell
dell
fell
hell
jell
knell
Nell
sell
tell
well
yell
dwell
quell
shell
smell
spell
swell

-elp (ĕ)

help
kelp
yelp

-elt (ĕ)

belt
felt
knelt
melt
pelt
welt
dwelt
smelt

-em (ĕ)

gem
hem
stem
them

-en (ĕ)

Ben
den
hen
Ken
men
pen
ten
yen
glen
then
when
wren

-ence (ĕ)

fence
hence
whence

-ench (ĕ)

bench
wench
clench
drench
French
quench
stench
trench
wrench

-end (ĕ)	-erge (ŭ)	guest	brew	kick	-ie (ī)	knife
bend	merge	jest	chew	lick	die	life
end	serge	lest		Nick	fie	rife
fend	verge	nest	-ex (ĕ)	pick	lie	wife
lend		pest		quick	pie	strife
mend		rest	hex	Rick	tie	
rend	-erk (ŭ)	test	sex	sick	vie	-iff (i)
send	jerk	vest	vex	tick		miff
tend	clerk	west	flex	wick	-ied (ī)	tiff
vend		zest		brick	died	cliff
wend	-erm (ŭ)	blest	-ey (ā)	chick	lied	skiff
blend	berm	chest	hey	click	dried	sniff
spend	germ	crest	gray	flick	fried	whiff
trend	term	quest	prey	slick	tried	
	sperm	wrest	they	stick		-ift (i)
-ense (ĕ)			whey	thick	-ief (ē)	gift
dense	-ern (ŭ)	-et (ĕ)		trick	brief	lift
sense	fern	bet	-ib (i)		chief	rift
tense	tern	get	bib		grief	sift
	stern	jet	fib	-id (i)	thief	drift
-ent (ĕ)		let	jib	bid		shift
bent	-erve (ŭ)	met	rib	did	-ield (ē)	swift
cent	nerve	net	crib	hid	field	thrift
dent	serve	pet	glib	kid	yield	
gent	verve	set		lid	shield	-ig (i)
Kent	swerve	wet	-ibe (i)	mid		big
lent		yet	jibe	quid	-ier (i)	dig
rent		Chet	bribe	rid	brier	fig
sent	-esh (ĕ)	fret	scribe	grid	crier	gig
tent	mesh	whet	tribe	skid	drier	jig
vent	flesh			slid	flier	pig
went	fresh		-ice (i)			rig
scent		-etch (ĕ)	dice			wig
spent	-ess (ĕ)	fetch	lice	-ide (i)	-ies (i)	brig
	Bess	retch	mice	bide	dies	sprig
-ep (ĕ)	guess	sketch	nice	hide	lies	swig
pep	less	wretch	rice	ride	pies	twig
rep	mess		vice	side	ties	
prep	bless		price	tide	cries	-igh (i)
step	chess	-ew (ü)	slice	wide	dries	high
	dress	dew	splice	bride	flies	nigh
-ept (ĕ)	press	few	thrice	chide	fries	sigh
kept	stress	hew	twice	glide	skies	thigh
wept	tress	Jew		pride	tries	
crept		knew	-ick (i)	slide		-ight (i)
slept	-est (ĕ)	new	Dick	snide	-ife (i)	knight
swept	best	pew	hick	stride	fife	light

The Reading Teacher's Book of Lists, Third Edition, © 1993 by Prentice Hall

might	fill	trim	**-inch (i)**	fling	**-ip (i)**	hire
night	gill	whim		sling		tire
right	hill		cinch	spring	dip	wire
sight	ill	**-ime (i)**	finch	sting	hip	spire
tight	Jill		pinch	string	lip	
blight	kill	dime	winch	swing	nip	**-irk (er)**
bright	mill	lime	clinch	thing	quip	
flight	pill	mime	flinch	wring	rip	quirk
fright	quill	time			sip	shirk
plight	rill	chime	**-ind (i)**	**-inge (i)**	tip	smirk
slight	sill	clime			zip	
	till	crime	bind	binge	blip	**-irt (er)**
-ike (i)	will	grime	find	hinge	chip	
	chill	prime	hind	singe	clip	dirt
bike	drill	slime	kind	tinge	drip	flirt
dike	frill		mind	cringe	flip	shirt
hike	grill	**-imp (i)**	rind	fringe	grip	skirt
like	skill		wind	twinge	ship	squirt
Mike	spill	limp	blind		skip	
pike	still	chimp	grind	**-ink (i)**	slip	**-irth (er)**
spike	swill	crimp			snip	
strike	thrill	primp	**-ine (i)**	kink	strip	birth
	trill	skimp		link	trip	firth
-ild (i)	twill	blimp	dine	mink	whip	girth
			fine	pink		mirth
mild	**-ilt (i)**	**-in (i)**	line	rink	**-ipe (i)**	
wild			mine	sink		**-ise (i)**
child	gilt	bin	nine	wink	pipe	
	jilt	din	pine	blink	ripe	guise
-ile (i)	hilt	fin	tine	brink	wipe	rise
	kilt	gin	vine	chink	gripe	wise
bile	tilt	kin	wine	clink	snipe	
file	wilt	pin	brine	drink	stripe	**-ish (i)**
mile	quilt	sin	shine	shrink	swipe	
Nile	stilt	tin	shrine	slink	tripe	dish
pile		win	spine	stink		fish
tile	**-im (i)**	chin	swine	think	**-ir (er)**	wish
vile		grin	whine			swish
smile	dim	shin		**-int (i)**	fir	
stile	him	skin	**-ing (i)**		sir	**-isk (i)**
while	Jim	spin		hint	stir	
	Kim	thin	bing	lint	whir	disk
-ilk (i)	rim	twin	ding	mint		risk
	Tim		king	tint	**-ird (er)**	brisk
bilk	vim	**-ince (i)**	ping	glint		frisk
milk	brim		ring	print	bird	whisk
silk	grim	mince	sing	splint	gird	
	prim	since	wing	sprint	third	**-isp (i)**
-ill (i)	slim	wince	zing	squint		
	swim	prince	bring	stint	**-ire (i)**	lisp
bill			cling			wisp
dill					fire	crisp

-iss (i)

hiss
kiss
miss
bliss
Swiss

-ist (i)

fist
list
mist
wrist
grist
twist

-it (i)

bit
fit
hit
kit
knit
lit
pit
quit
sit
wit
flit
grit
skit
slit
spit
split
twit

-itch (i)

bitch
ditch
hitch
pitch
witch
switch

-ite (i)

bite
kite
mite
quite

rite
site
white
write
sprite

-ive (i)

dive
five
hive
jive
live
chive
drive
strive
thrive

-ix (i)

fix
mix
six

-o (ü)

do
to
who

-o (ō)

go
no
so
pro

-oach (ō)

coach
poach
roach
broach

-oad (ō)

goad
load
road
toad

-oak (ō)

soak
cloak
croak

-oal (ō)

coal
foal
goal
shoal

-oam (ō)

foam
loam
roam

-oan (ō)

Joan
loan
moan
groan

-oar (ô)

boar
roar
soar

-oast (ō)

boast
coast
roast
toast

-oat (ō)

boat
coat
goat
moat
bloat
gloat
float
throat

-ob (ŏ)

Bob
cob

fob
gob
job
knob
lob
mob
rob
sob
blob
glob
slob
snob

-obe (ō)

lobe
robe
globe
probe

-ock (ŏ)

dock
hock
knock
lock
mock
rock
sock
tock
block
clock
crock
flock
frock
shock
smock
stock

-od (ŏ)

cod
God
mod
nod
pod
rod
sod
Tod
clod

plod
prod
shod
trod

-ode (ō)

code
lode
mode
node
rode
strode

-oe (ō)

doe
foe
hoe
Joe
toe
woe

-og (ŏ)

bog
cog
dog
fog
hog
jog
log
tog
clog
flog
frog
grog
slog
smog

-ogue (ō)

brogue
rogue
vogue

-oil (oy)

boil
coil
foil
soil

toil
spoil
broil

-oin (oy)

coin
join
loin
groin

-oist (oy)

foist
hoist
joist
moist

-oke (ō)

coke
joke
poke
woke
yoke
broke
choke
smoke
spoke
stoke
stroke

-old (ō)

bold
cold
fold
gold
hold
mold
old
sold
told
scold

-ole (ō)

dole
hole
mole
pole
role

stole
whole

-oll (ō)

poll
roll
toll
droll
knoll
scroll
stroll
troll

-olt (ŏ)

doll
loll
moll

-olt (ō)

bolt
colt
jolt
molt
volt

-ome (ō)

dome
home
Nome
Rome
tome
gnome
chrome

-ome (ŭ)

come
some

-omp (ŭ)

pomp
romp
chomp
stomp

The Reading Teacher's Book of Lists, Third Edition, © 1993 by Prentice Hall

-on (ŭ)

son
ton
won

-ond (ŏ)

bond
fond
pond
blond
frond

-one (ō)

bone
cone
hone
lone
tone
zone
clone
crone
drone
phone
prone
shone
stone

-ong (ô)

bong
dong
gong
long
song
tong
prong
strong
thong
wrong

-oo (ü)

boo
coo
goo
moo
poo
too
woo

zoo
shoo

-ood (u̇)

good
hood
wood
stood

-ood (ü)

food
mood
brood

-oof (o͞o)

goof
roof
proof
spoof

-ook (u̇)

book
cook
hook
look
nook
took
brook
crook
shook

-ool (ü)

cool
fool
pool
tool
drool
school
spool
stool

-oom (ü)

boom
doom
loom
room
zoom

bloom
broom
gloom
groom

-oon (ü)

coon
loon
moon
noon
soon
croon
spoon
swoon

-oop (ü)

coop
hoop
loop
droop
scoop
sloop
snoop
stoop
swoop
troop

-oor (oo)

poor
boor
moor
spoor

-oose (ü)

goose
loose
moose
noose

-oot (ü)

boot
hoot
loot
moot
root
toot

scoot
shoot

-op (ŏ)

bop
cop
hop
mop
pop
sop
top
chop
crop
drop
flop
plop
prop
shop
slop
stop

-ope (ō)

cope
dope
hope
lope
mope
nope
pope
rope
grope
scope
slope

-orch (ô)

porch
torch
scorch

-ord (ô)

cord
ford
lord
chord
sword

-ore (ô)

bore
core
fore
gore
more
pore
sore
tore
wore
chore
score
shore
snore
spore
store
swore

-ork (ô)

cork
fork
pork
York
stork

-orm (ô)

dorm
form
norm
storm

-orn (ô)

born
corn
horn
morn
torn
worn
scorn
shorn
sworn
thorn

-ort (ô)

fort
Mort
port

sort
short
snort
sport

-ose (ō)

hose
nose
pose
rose
chose
close
prose
those

-oss (ô)

boss
loss
moss
toss
cross
floss
gloss

-ost (ô)

cost
lost
frost

-ost (ō)

host
most
post
ghost

-ot (ŏ)

cot
dot
got
hot
jot
knot
lot
not
pot
rot
tot

blot
clot
plot
shot
slot
spot
trot

-otch (ŏ)

botch
notch
blotch
crotch
Scotch

-ote (ō)

note
quote
rote
vote
wrote

-oth (ô)

moth
broth
cloth
froth
sloth

-ouch (ou)

couch
pouch
vouch
crouch
grouch
slouch

-oud (ou)

loud
cloud
proud

-ough (ŭ)

rough
tough
slough

-ought (ô)

bought
fought
ought
sought
brought
thought

-ould (u̇)

could
would
should

-ounce (ou)

bounce
pounce
flounce
trounce

-ound (ou)

bound
found
hound
mound
pound
round
sound
wound
ground

-oup (o͞o)

soup
croup
group
stoup

-our (ou)

hour
sour
flour
scour

-ouse (ou)

douse
house
louse

mouse
rouse
souse
blouse
grouse
spouse

-out (ou)

bout
gout
lout
pout
rout
tout
clout
flout
grout
scout
shout
snout
spout
sprout
stout
trout

-outh (ou)

mouth
south

-ove (ō)

cove
wove
clove
drove
grove
stove
trove

-ove (ŭ)

dove
love
glove
shove

-ow (ō)

bow

know
low
mow
row
sow
tow
blow
crow
flow
glow
grow
show
slow
snow
stow

-ow (ou)

bow
cow
how
now
row
sow
vow
brow
chow
plow
prow
scow

-owl (ou)

fowl
howl
jowl
growl
prowl
scowl

-own (ou)

down
gown
town
brown
clown
crown
drown
frown

-own (ō)

known
mown
sown
blown
flown
grown
shown
thrown

-owse (ou)

dowse
browse
drowse

-ox (ŏ)

box
fox
lox
pox

-oy (oi)

boy
coy
joy
Roy
soy
toy
ploy

-ub (ŭ)

cub
dub
hub
nub
pub
rub
sub
tub
club
drub
flub
grub
scrub
shrub
snub
stub

-ube (o͞o)

cube
rube
tube

-uck (ŭ)

buck
duck
luck
muck
puck
suck
tuck
Chuck
cluck
pluck
shuck
stuck
struck
truck

-ud (ŭ)

bud
cud
dud
mud
spud
stud
thud

-ude (ü)

dude
nude
rude
crude
prude

-udge (ŭ)

budge
fudge
judge
nudge
drudge
grudge
sludge
smudge
trudge

-ue (ü)

cue
due
hue
Sue
blue
clue
flue
glue
true

-uff (ŭ)

buff
cuff
huff
muff
puff
ruff
bluff
fluff
gruff
scuff
sluff
snuff
stuff

-ug (ŭ)

bug
dug
hug
jug
lug
mug
pug
rug
tug
chug
drug
plug
shrug
slug
smug
snug
thug

-uke (oo)

duke

nuke
puke
fluke

-ule (o͞o)

mule
pule
rule
yule

-ulk (ŭ)

bulk
hulk
sulk

-ull (ŭ)

cull
dull
gull
hull
lull
mull
skull

-ull (u̇)

bull
full
pull

-um (ŭ)

bum
gum
hum
mum
rum
sum
chum
drum
glum
plum
scum
slum
strum
swum

-umb (ŭ)

dumb

numb
crumb
plumb
thumb

-ume (o͞o)

fume
flume
plume
spume

-ump (ŭ)

bump
dump
hump
jump
lump
pump
rump
chump
clump
frump
grump
plump
slump
stump
thump
trump

-un (ŭ)

bun
fun
gun
nun
pun
run
sun
shun
spun
stun

-unch (ŭ)

bunch
hunch
lunch
munch
punch
brunch
crunch

-une (ü)

June
tune
prune

-ung (ŭ)

dung
hung
lung
rung
sung
clung
flung
slung
sprung
stung
strung
swung
wrung

-unk (ŭ)

bunk
dunk
funk
hunk
junk
punk
sunk
chunk
drunk

flunk
plunk
shrunk
skunk
slunk
spunk
stunk
trunk

-unt (ŭ)

bunt
hunt
punt
runt
blunt
grunt
shunt
stunt

-up (ŭ)

cup
pup
sup

-ur (er)

cur
fur
blur
slur
spur

-ure (o͞o)

cure
lure
pure
sure

-url (er)

burl

curl
furl
hurl
purl
churl
knurl

-urn (er)

burn
turn
churn
spurn

-urse (er)

curse
nurse
purse

-urt (er)

curt
hurt
blurt
spurt

-us (ŭ)

bus
pus
plus
thus

-use (o͞o)

fuse
muse
ruse

-ush (ŭ)

gush
hush

lush
mush
rush
blush
brush
crush
flush
plush
slush
thrush

-uss (ŭ)

buss
cuss
fuss
muss
truss

-ust (ŭ)

bust
dust
gust
just
lust
must
rust
crust
thrust
trust

-ut (ŭ)

but
cut
gut
hut
jut
nut
rut
Tut
glut

shut
slut
smut
strut

-utch (ŭ)

Dutch
hutch
clutch
crutch

-ute (ü)

cute
jute
lute
mute
brute
chute
flute

-utt (ŭ)

butt
mutt
putt

-y (ī)

by
my
cry
dry
fly
fry
ply
pry
shy
sky
sly
spy
spry
try
why

-ye (ī)

aye
dye
eye
lye
rye

See also List 46, Initial Consonant Sounds; and List 48, Phonics Example Words.

48. *Phonics Example Words*

This is an important list at the heart of phonics instruction. It alphabetically lists 99 single phonemes (speech sounds) and consonant blends (usually two phonemes), and it gives example words for each of these, often for their use in the beginning, middle, and end of words. These example words are also common English words, many taken from the list of Instant Words. This list solves the problem of coming up with a good common word to illustrate a phonics principle for lessons and worksheets.

A VOWEL SOUND: SHORT A

INITIAL			MEDIAL		
and	add	am	that	has	began
at	act	animal	can	than	stand
as	adjective	ant	had	man	black
after	answer	ax	back	hand	happen
an	ask	Africa	last	plant	fast

apple

A VOWEL SOUND: LONG A—OPEN SYLLABLE RULE

INITIAL	MEDIAL				
able	paper	lazy	label	vibration	
acre	lady	flavor	equator	basis	
agent	baby	tomato	relation	hazy	
apron	radio	navy	vapor	potato	
Asia	crazy	station	enable	ladle	
apex	labor	basic	volcano	vacation	
April					

table

A–E VOWEL SOUND: LONG A—FINAL E RULE

INITIAL		MEDIAL			
ate	ape	make	late	table	baseball
able	ace	made	tale	gave	spaceship
acre		face	place	base	tablecloth
age		same	name	plane	racetrack
ache		came	wave	game	shapeless
ale		state	space	shape	

cake

The Reading Teacher's Book of Lists, Third Edition, © 1993 by Prentice Hall

AI VOWEL SOUND: LONG A

INITIAL   **MEDIAL**

aim	rain	mail	claim	obtain	faint
aid	train	pain	detail	paid	grain
ailment	wait	sail	explain	remain	rail
ail	tail	strait	fail	wait	
	chain	afraid	gain	plain	
	jail	brain	main	laid	

nail

AY VOWEL SOUND: LONG A

MEDIAL   **FINAL**

always	gayly	jaywalk	day	pay	repay
mayor	haystack	player	say	gray	anyway
layer	wayside	daylight	away	bay	way
crayon	payment		play	stay	pray
maybe	rayon		may	birthday	lay
			today	highway	gay

hay

A VOWEL SOUND: SCHWA

INITIAL   **MEDIAL**   **FINAL**

about	appear	several	canvass	antenna	china
above	away	national	familiar	algebra	comma
ago	again	senator	career	alfalfa	idea
alone	ahead	thousand	purchase	banana	
America	another	magazine	compass		
alike	agree	breakfast	diagram		

announce

AL VOWEL SOUND: BROAD O

INITIAL   **MEDIAL**   **FINAL**

all	altogether	talk	scald	call	baseball
always	alternate	walk	walnut	tall	wall
also	altar	chalk	fallen	fall	stall
already	albeit	salt		overall	recall
almost	almanac	false		hall	
although	almighty	falter		small	

ball

AU VOWEL SOUND: BROAD O

INITIAL

August	Australia	audible
author	autoharp	authentic
autumn	auction	auditor
auditorium	auburn	
autograph	auxilliary	
audience	automatic	

MEDIAL

because	cause	
caught	dinosaur	
laundry	sauce	launch
haul	caution	faucet
daughter	exhaust	sausage
fault	fraud	overhaul

 auto

AW VOWEL SOUND: BROAD O

INITIAL

awful
awkward
awning
awe
awl
awfully

MEDIAL

lawn	yawn
drawn	tawny
lawyer	drawer
hawk	shawl
lawful	bawl

crawl
squawk
scrawl

FINAL

law	paw
jaw	claw
draw	flaw
straw	gnaw
thaw	caw
taw	

saw

AR VOWEL SOUND: AIR SOUND

INITIAL

area

MEDIAL

January	February
dictionary	tiara
vary	parent
primary	wary
secretary	careful
canary	scare
daring	scarcely

declare
beware
flare

FINAL

care	fare
rare	stare
aware	glare
share	welfare
spare	hare
bare	square
dare	

library

AR VOWEL SOUND: AR SOUND

INITIAL

are	argument
arm	article
army	arch
art	armor
artist	ark
arctic	arbor

MEDIAL

card	garden
March	start
farm	dark
hard	yard
part	party
large	

FINAL

car	mar
far	par
bar	scar
jar	
tar	

star

The Reading Teacher's Book of Lists, Third Edition, © 1993 by Prentice Hall

B CONSONANT SOUND: REGULAR

INITIAL		MEDIAL		FINAL	
be	back	number	subject	tub	job
by	but	problem	baby	cab	club
boy	because	remember		rob	rub
been	below	object		cub	grab
box	before	probably		rib	adverb
big	better			verb	bulb

book

BL CONSONANT SOUND: BL BLEND

INITIAL				MEDIAL	
black	blame	blank	blink	oblige	obliterate
blue	bloom	blast	blur	emblem	grumbling
bleed	blossom	blend	blow	tumbler	oblivious
blood	blond	blue	blanket	nosebleed	gambler
blind	blade	blot	bleach	ablaze	rambling
				nimbly	

block

BR CONSONANT SOUND: BR BLEND

INITIAL				MEDIAL	
bread	bring	brush	library	daybreak	algebra
break	breath	breeze	umbrella	cobra	embrace
brick	branch	bridge	celebrate	membrane	lubricate
broad	bright	brain	vibrate	outbreak	
brother	broken	brass	abroad	zebra	
brown	brave	breakfast			

broom

C CONSONANT SOUND: REGULAR (K SOUND)

INITIAL		MEDIAL		FINAL	
can	call	because	across	back	check
come	country	picture	become	rock	stick
came	cut	American	quickly	sick	black
camp	car	second		lock	pick
color	cold			kick	thick
could	carry			music	electric

cat

The Reading Teacher's Book of Lists, Third Edition, © 1993 by Prentice Hall

C CONSONANT SOUND: S SOUND

INITIAL

cent	certain	cigar
circle	civil	cyclone
cycle	ceiling	cellar
circus	celebrate	cease
center	cereal	
cell	cinder	

MEDIAL

face	decide	acid
since	Pacific	dancing
pencil	percent	peaceful
fancy	precise	
ice	process	
concert	sincere	

city

CH CONSONANT SOUND: CH DIGRAPH

INITIAL

children	chief
church	chart
change	chin
chance	chest
cheer	chain
check	chase

MEDIAL

pitcher	searching
attached	stretched
purchase	exchange
merchant	

FINAL

which	catch
each	branch
much	touch
such	inch
teach	reach
rich	watch

chair

CL CONSONANT SOUND: CL BLEND

INITIAL

clean	clear	clever	climb
cloth	class	cliff	click
clay	clap	close	
claim	claws	cloud	
club	clerk	clues	

MEDIAL

enclose	eclipse	
include	acclaim	disclose
cyclone	conclude	decline
exclaim	reclaim	proclaim
exclude	declare	incline

clock

CR CONSONANT SOUND: CR BLEND

INITIAL

cry	crew	cried	cruel
crack	crazy	crops	credit
crowd	cross	crayon	
crash	crow	creek	
cream	create	crown	

MEDIAL

across	aircraft	recruit
secret	sacred	scarecrow
increase	concrete	screen
microscope	disease	
democrat	decree	

crab

The Reading Teacher's Book of Lists, Third Edition, © 1993 by Prentice Hall

D CONSONANT SOUND: REGULAR

INITIAL		MEDIAL		FINAL	
do	does	study	order	and	find
day	door	under	Indians	good	need
did	done	idea	didn't	had	did
dear	different	body		said	old
down	during			red	around
deep	don't			would	end

 dog

DR CONSONANT SOUND: DR BLEND

INITIAL			MEDIAL		
dry	dream	drift	address	undress	hydrogen
draw	dragon	drama	hundred	withdraw	laundress
drug	drill	drain	children	daydream	redress
drove	drink	drip	dandruff	eardrum	dewdrop
drop	drive	drench	cathedral	laundry	
dress	drew	droop			

drum

E VOWEL SOUND: SHORT E

elephant

INITIAL			MEDIAL			
end	empty	ever	when	let	set	men
egg	energy	edge	then	them	went	spell
every	explain	enter	get	very	help	next
extra	enjoy	elf	left	tell	well	red
enemy	engine	else				

E VOWEL SOUND: LONG E—OPEN SYLLABLE RULE

INITIAL	MEDIAL			FINAL	
even	cedar	meter	being	me	we
equal	demon	prefix	recent	he	be
ether	secret	react	legal	she	maybe
evil	Negro	area	really		
ecology	zebra	female	depot		

Egypt

The Reading Teacher's Book of Lists, Third Edition, © 1993 by Prentice Hall

EE VOWEL SOUND: LONG E

INITIAL	MEDIAL		FINAL		
eel	sleep	seem	see	bee	fee
eerie	green	teeth	three	degree	spree
	keep	sweet	tree	flee	referee
	street	week	free	knee	
	feet	screen	agree	glee	
	wheel	fifteen			
	feel				

deer

EA VOWEL SOUND: LONG E

INITIAL			MEDIAL		FINAL
eat	eager	ease	neat	leaf	sea
each	easel	eaves	read	feast	tea
east	Easter	easily	least	peach	flea
easy	eaten		beat	meat	plea
eagle	eastern		clean	weak	pea
			deal	peanut	

peach

EA VOWEL SOUND: SHORT E SOUND

bread

MEDIAL					
head	breath	feather	meadow	threaten	heaven
heavy	dear	death	pleasant	treasure	dread
ready	ahead	measure	spread	weapon	pleasure
thread	breakfast	instead	heading	weather	widespread
steady	already	leather	sweat	overhead	gingerbread
dead					

E VOWEL SOUND: SCHWA

INITIAL		MEDIAL			
efface	effective	happen	scientist	fuel	label
effect	efficient	problem	item	given	absent
efficiency		hundred	united	level	agent
erratic		arithmetic	quiet	heaven	hundred
essential		children	diet	even	often
erroneous		calendar	different	happen	

 eleven

The Reading Teacher's Book of Lists, Third Edition, © 1993 by Prentice Hall

The Reading Teacher's Book of Lists, Third Edition, © 1993 by Prentice Hall

E VOWEL SOUND: SILENT

MEDIAL		FINAL			
sometimes	homework	are	were	make	because
careful	lifetime	one	before	time	write
statement	something	there	here	more	home
safety	evening	come	came	people	
movement		little	these	place	
moreover		like	some	sentence	

whale

ER VOWEL SOUND: R SOUND

MEDIAL		FINAL			
camera	afternoon	her	better	another	river
allergy	liberty	mother	sister	baker	winter
bakery	operate	over	under	wonder	liver
wonderful	federal	other	after	ever	shower
dangerous	battery	were	water	offer	lower

letter

F CONSONANT SOUND: REGULAR

INITIAL		MEDIAL		FINAL	
for	father	after	different	if	chief
first	face	before	Africa	half	stuff
find	family	often	beautiful	myself	brief
four	follow	careful		off	cliff
funny	far			leaf	itself
food	few			himself	wolf

fish

FL CONSONANT SOUND: FL BLEND

INITIAL				MEDIAL	
flower	floor	fleet	flea	afflict	inflame
flat	flavor	flow	fluffy	inflict	afloat
flight	flood	flap		conflict	reflect
flew	flute	flock		influence	inflate
fly	flame	fling		aflame	inflexible
float	flash	flip		snowflake	

flag

FR CONSONANT SOUND: FR BLEND

INITIAL

				MEDIAL	
free	frost	fruit	frisky	afraid	defraud
from	frank	freedom		affront	infringe
front	freshman	frozen		befriend	leapfrog
friend	frame	France		bullfrog	refrain
Friday	fresh	freighter		carefree	refresh
fry	fraction	fragile		confront	infrequent

frog

G CONSONANT SOUND: REGULAR

INITIAL

		MEDIAL		**FINAL**	
go	gun	again	segment	dog	frog
good	game	ago	regular	big	pig
got	gas	began	figure	egg	log
gave	gift	sugar		leg	bag
girl	gone	wagon		fig	
get	garden	signal		flag	

gate

G CONSONANT SOUND: J SOUND

INITIAL

		MEDIAL	**FINAL**	
gem	gym	gesture	danger	change	page
giraffe	gypsy	genius	energy	large	village
gentlemen	ginger	genuine	region	bridge	huge
geography	gelatin	generate	engine	age	strange
generous	germ		original		
gently	general		vegetable		
			oxygen		

giant

GL CONSONANT SOUND: GL BLEND

INITIAL

				MEDIAL	
glad	glisten	glare	glider	eyeglass	hourglass
globe	gloom	glass	glimpse	jingling	bugler
glow	glue	glade	glitter	spyglass	angler
glory	glum	gleam	glance	smuggling	mangling
glove	glamour	glee	glaze	wiggling	singly

glass

The Reading Teacher's Book of Lists, Third Edition, © 1993 by Prentice Hall

GR CONSONANT SOUND: BLEND

INITIAL

grade	grand	grant
great	green	grin
grow	ground	gradual
grew	group	grandfather
grass	grab	gravity
gray	grain	

MEDIAL

hungry	Negro	disgrace
angry	program	fragrant
congress	regret	outgrow
agree	degrade	engross
degree	engrave	

grapes

GH: SILENT CONSONANTS

MEDIAL

daughter	eighth	delight	thought
might	night	light	fought
brighter	neighbors	right	bought
throughout	fight	sight	caught
highway	thoroughly	tight	taught

FINAL

high	sleigh
sigh	although
bough	plough
through	dough
weigh	neigh
though	

eight

H CONSONANT SOUND: REGULAR

INITIAL

he	help	half	high
had	here	his	hit
have	happy	hen	house
her	home	hero	
him	hard	hide	
how	has	hill	

MEDIAL

behind	rehearse
ahead	behold
unhappy	unhook
behave	ahoy
overhead	
autoharp	

hand

I VOWEL SOUND: SHORT I

INITIAL

in	it	ill
is	invent	include
if	important	India
into	insect	isn't
inch	instead	inside

MEDIAL

with	will	different
did	big	until
this	still	miss
little	give	begin
which	his	city
him		

Indian

The Reading Teacher's Book of Lists, Third Edition, © 1993 by Prentice Hall

I VOWEL SOUND: LONG I—OPEN SYLLABLE RULE

INITIAL   **MEDIAL**

I	icy	bicycle	pilot	variety	title	
idea	Irish	tiny	quiet	dinosaur	spider	
I'll	iodine	silent	triangle	giant	diagram	
iris	Iowa	rifle	climate	lion	China	
I'm	ivory					
item						

iron

I—E VOWEL SOUND: LONG I—FINAL E RULE

INITIAL   **MEDIAL**

idle	five	fire	nine	mile	drive
ire	white	write	bite	size	wire
isle	ride	life	like	wide	mine
I've	time	side	line	describe	wife

ice

IR VOWEL SOUND: R SOUND

MEDIAL   **FINAL**

girl	skirt	thirteen	shirk	circuit	fir
first	birthday	girth	mirth	girdle	sir
third	thirsty	birth	confirm	stirrup	stir
shirt	affirm	circus	Virginia	dirty	tapir
dirt	circle	thirty	firm		whir
					astir

girl

J CONSONANT SOUND: REGULAR

INITIAL   **MEDIAL**

just	jet	June	object	project	unjust
jump	job	jungle	enjoy	adjust	majesty
January	joke	junior	subject	dejected	majority
jaw	joy	jacket	major	overjoyed	rejoice
July	juice	join	banjo	adjoin	
			adjective	reject	

jar

The Reading Teacher's Book of Lists, Third Edition, © 1993 by Prentice Hall

K CONSONANT SOUND: REGULAR

INITIAL		MEDIAL		FINAL	
kind	kiss	monkey	market	like	work
key	kitten	broken	packing	make	mark
kill	kid	turkey	stroking	book	speak
king	kettle	worker		look	milk
keep	kick			cake	bank
kin	keen			cook	break

kite

KN CONSONANT SOUND: N

knife

INITIAL					MEDIAL
knee	knelt	knack	knockout	knell	unknown
knew	knit	kneel	knickers	kneecap	doorknob
know	knock	knapsack	knothole	knives	penknife
knowledge	knight	knob	knoll	knotty	acknowledge
knot	knuckle	knead	knave	known	knick knack
					knock-kneed

L CONSONANT SOUND: REGULAR

INITIAL		MEDIAL		FINAL	
little	large	only	really	will	oil
like	last	below	follow	all	tell
long	line	along	family	girl	until
look	learn	children		school	spell
live	left			shall	well
land	light			small	vowel

letter

M CONSONANT SOUND: REGULAR

INITIAL		MEDIAL		FINAL	
me	more	number	important	from	farm
my	mother	American	example	them	room
make	move	something	family	am	arm
much	must	complete		seem	team
many	made			warm	form
may	men			him	bottom

man

N CONSONANT SOUND: REGULAR

INITIAL		MEDIAL		FINAL	
not	name	many	until	in	man
no	number	under	any	on	even
new	need	answer	animal	can	own
night	never	country		when	open
next	near			an	been
now	next			then	than

nut

NG CONSONANT SOUND: NG

MEDIAL		FINAL			
slingshot	gangster	sing	long	bang	spring
lengthen	singer	bring	song	lung	strong
longing	hanger	thing	gang	wing	fang
kingdom	gangplank	going	hang	ring	hung
youngster	gangway	swing	young	fling	string
					wrong

king

O VOWEL SOUND: SHORT O

INITIAL		MEDIAL			
odd	opera	not	fox	follow	rock
olive	oxygen	box	drop	got	bottom
opposite	operate	hot	pop	problem	copy
oxen	on	stop	pot	top	job
October	occupy	body	clock	product	cannot
opportunity					

box

O VOWEL SOUND: LONG O—OPEN SYLLABLE RULE

INITIAL		MEDIAL	FINAL		
open	odor	October	go	zero	echo
over	omit	program	no	cargo	volcano
obey	oboe	Roman	so	piano	
ocean	okra	moment	hello	Negro	
Ohio		poem	ago	potato	
		total	also	hero	
		broken	auto		

radio

The Reading Teacher's Book of Lists, Third Edition, © 1993 by Prentice Hall

O–E VOWEL SOUND: LONG O—FINAL E RULE

INITIAL **MEDIAL**

owe	home	rode	whole	rose	stove
	those	nose	slope	spoke	awoke
	hope	stone	bone	smoke	phone
	note	joke	tone	drove	
	alone	globe	pole	vote	

rope

OA VOWEL SOUND: LONG O

INITIAL **MEDIAL**

oak	coat	toast	approach	croak	coal
oat	soap	goat	loaf	soak	toad
oath	road	goal	groan	cloak	moan
oatmeal	coast	loan	foam	roach	throat
oaf	load	float	roast	boast	coach

boat

OW VOWEL SOUND: LONG O

INITIAL **MEDIAL** **FINAL**

own	bowl	crowbar	show	follow	mow
owe	stowaway	bowling	low	tomorrow	glow
owing	snowball	mower	slow	throw	know
owner	towboat		snow	blow	crow
			row	grow	arrow
			yellow	flow	borrow

window

OW VOWEL SOUND: OU DIPHTHONG

MEDIAL **FINAL**

down	crown	towel	how	somehow	endow
town	cowboy	powder	now	eyebrow	vow
brown	power	tower	cow	bow	prow
flower	vowel	chowder	plow	scow	avow
crowd	downward	shower	allow	sow	snowplow

owl

OY VOWEL SOUND: OI DIPHTHONG

INITIAL	MEDIAL		FINAL		
oyster	royal	joyous	toy	decoy	convoy
	voyage	disloyal	joy	newsboy	envoy
	loyal	loyalty	enjoy	annoy	corduroy
	boycott	enjoyment	employ	soy	
	annoying	joyful	destroy	viceroy	
	employer	boyish	coy	Troy	
	boyhood		cowboy	alloy	

boy

O VOWEL SOUND: SCHWA

INITIAL		MEDIAL		FINAL
other	oblige	mother	action	kimono
original	obstruct	money	canyon	
official	oppose	atom	weapon	
observe	occasion	second	period	
opinion	oppress	nation	mission	
objection	opossum	method	riot	

violin

OI VOWEL SOUND: OI DIPHTHONG

INITIAL		MEDIAL			
oilcloth	join	broil	coil	sirloin	joint
oilwell	point	spoil	moisture	disappoint	embroider
oily	voice	avoid	exploit	toil	typhoid
ointment	coin	poison	doily	void	
	choice	boil	soil	broiler	
	noise	turmoil	rejoice		

oil

OU VOWEL SOUND: OU DIPHTHONG

INITIAL		MEDIAL			FINAL
out	outer	hour	aloud	doubt	thou
our	outline	sound	found	count	
ounce	outside	about	council	boundary	
oust	outlook	around	ground		
ourselves	outcry	round	loud		
outdoors	outfield	scout	cloud		
ouch		amount	mountain		

house

The Reading Teacher's Book of Lists, Third Edition, © 1993 by Prentice Hall

O VOWEL SOUND: BROAD O

INITIAL

			MEDIAL		
off	onto	offhand	soft	wrong	moth
office	offset	offshore	log	cloth	frost
officer	offspring	ostrich	long	toss	cross
often	onward		along	coffee	belong
on	onset		cost	strong	
offer	oncoming		across	song	

dog

OR VOWEL SOUND: OR SOUND

INITIAL		**MEDIAL**			**FINAL**
or	Oregon	short	score	corner	for
order	organ	horn	form	store	more
ore	ordinary	fork	before	north	nor
orbit	oral	forget	horse	force	
orchestra	orchard	born	story		
ordinary	orchid	cord	important		

fork

OO VOWEL SOUND: 1-DOT U, OR SHORT OO

book

MEDIAL

look	took	foot	shook	brook	cook
good	wood	stood	goodbye	wool	dogwood
hook	rook	soot	lookout	notebook	rookie
afoot	hoof	cookie	football	understood	handbook
hood	crook	nook	wooden	neighborhood	overlook
motherhood					

OO VOWEL SOUND: 2-DOT U, OR LONG OO

INITIAL	**MEDIAL**			**FINAL**	
ooze	soon	tooth	mood	too	bamboo
	school	cool	roof	zoo	cuckoo
	room	goose	loose	shampoo	boo
	food	troop	balloon	woo	igloo
	shoot	fool	noon	coo	
	smooth	boot		tattoo	
	pool	tool		kangaroo	

moon

P CONSONANT SOUND: REGULAR

INITIAL		MEDIAL		FINAL	
put	point	open	perhaps	up	ship
people	piece	example	happy	sleep	top
page	pass	paper		jump	step
pair	person	important		help	map
part	paper	upon		stop	deep
picture	pull			group	drop

pencil

PH CONSONANT SOUND: F

INITIAL

photo	phase
phonics	phantom
phrase	phonetic
physical	pharmacy
physician	phoenix
pheasant	phenomenon

MEDIAL

alphabet	cellophane
orphan	emphasis
nephew	gopher
sulphur	graphic
geography	trophy
	sophomore

telephone

FINAL

photograph	telegraph
phonograph	graph
autograph	triumph
paragraph	

PL CONSONANT SOUND: PL BLEND

INITIAL

play	place
plant	plan
plain	plane
please	planets
plow	plastic
plus	platform

MEDIAL

player	supply	display	airplane
pleasant	multiply	explain	applaud
plot	employ	supplying	apply
plank	reply	surplus	complain
plug	perplex		
	imply		

plate

PR CONSONANT SOUND: PR BLEND

INITIAL

pretty	president	present	probably
price	prince	problem	prove
press	program	produce	pray
prize	practice	property	products
print	prepare	provide	

MEDIAL

surprise	approach
April	approximate
improve	appropriate
apron	impression
express	

propeller

Q CONSONANT SOUND: KW SOUND

INITIAL

			MEDIAL		
quart	quiet	quote	square	liquid	squirm
quite	quack	quill	equal	equipment	sequence
question	quail	quality	squirrel	equator	squeak
quick	quake		frequent	equivalent	inquire
quit	quilt		require	squash	
queer	quiz		equation	earthquake	

queen

R CONSONANT SOUND: REGULAR

INITIAL		**MEDIAL**		**FINAL**	
run	rest	very	large	our	other
red	ride	part	story	their	over
right	road	word	form	for	water
ran	rock	around		year	her
read	room			dear	after
rat	rod			your	near

ring

S CONSONANT SOUND: REGULAR

INITIAL		**MEDIAL**		**FINAL**	
some	sound	also	question	this	less
so	say	person	inside	us	across
see	sentence	answer	system	likes	its
said	side	himself		makes	gas
soon	same			yes	bus
set	sea			miss	perhaps

saw

S CONSONANT SOUND: Z SOUND

MEDIAL		**FINAL**			
music	observe	please	is	odds	news
easy	museum	cheese	as	says	hers
busy	present	wise	was	suds	does
those	result	these	his	yours	
because	season		has	tongs	
desert	poison		ours	days	

eyes

The Reading Teacher's Book of Lists, Third Edition, © 1993 by Prentice Hall

SC CONSONANT SOUND: SC BLEND

INITIAL

				MEDIAL	
score	scatter	scream	scoop	describe	inscribe
school	scholar	scallop	scrub	telescope	unscramble
screen	scout	screw		description	microscopic
scratch	scare	scared		microscope	unscrupulous
scarf	scramble	scab		nondescript	telescoping
scar	scrape			unscrew	descriptive

scale

SH CONSONANT SOUND: DIGRAPH

INITIAL **MEDIAL** **FINAL**

she	shot	dashed	ashes	wish	rush
shall	shirt	splashing	friendship	wash	dish
show	shell	sunshine		fish	crash
ship	sheet	worship		push	bush
short	shop	fisherman		finish	flash
shape	shut			fresh	establish

shoe

SK CONSONANT SOUND: SK BLEND

INITIAL **MEDIAL** **FINAL**

sky	skeleton	skillet	outskirts	desk	mask
skin	skull	skirmish	askew	task	husk
skill	skid	skinny	muskrat	ask	dusk
skunk	sketch	skylark	numskull	brisk	
skirt	ski	skeptic	rollerskate		
skip	skim		muskmelon		
			masked		

skate

SL CONSONANT SOUND: SL BLEND

INITIAL **MEDIAL**

slow	sled	slope	sly	asleep	oversleep
sleep	slave	slam	slash	landslide	snowslide
slept	sleeve	slate	slab	onslaught	grandslam
slip	slant	slipper	sleek	enslave	nonslip
slid	slice	sleet	slimy	bobsled	
slap	slight	slim		manslaughter	

slide

The Reading Teacher's Book of Lists, Third Edition, © 1993 by Prentice Hall

SM CONSONANT SOUND: SM BLEND

INITIAL

smile	smash	smock	smote	smuggler
smooth	smear	smoky	smokestack	smattering
smell	smith	smudge	smelt	smorgasbord
small	smolder	smuggle	smite	
smart	smack	smug	smithy	
smother	smog	smitten	smoker	

MEDIAL

blacksmith
gunsmith
silversmith
locksmith

smoke

SN CONSONANT SOUND: SN BLEND

INITIAL

snow	snuggle	snapshot	sniff	snooze	snuff
snowball	snip	sneak	sniffle	snorkel	snowman
snare	snarl	snatch	snipe	snort	sniper
sneeze	snap	sneakers	snob	snout	snowy
snore	snack	sneer	snoop	snub	
snug	snail				

snake

SP CONSONANT SOUND: SP BLEND

INITIAL

sports	speed
space	spell
speak	spot
spring	spin
spread	spoke
special	spare

spider
spend
spark

MEDIAL

inspect	despair
respect	inspire
respond	despite
despise	
unspeakable	
respectful	

FINAL

clasp
crisp
gasp
grasp
wasp
lisp
wisp

spoon

ST CONSONANT SOUND: ST BLEND

INITIAL

stop	story
step	street
stay	stand
state	star
still	study
store	strong

stick
stone
stood

MEDIAL

instead	restless
destroy	poster
restore	tasty
westward	
haystack	
destruction	

FINAL

best
cast
dust
fast
least
past
west

stamp

The Reading Teacher's Book of Lists, Third Edition, © 1993 by Prentice Hall

SW CONSONANT SOUND: SW BLEND

INITIAL

swim	switch	sweet	swollen	swampy	swarthy
swell	swallow	swift	sway	swirl	swat
swept	swung	swan	swine	swarm	swerve
sweat	swam	swagger	swoop	swear	sworn
sweater	swamp	swap	swindle	swelter	swish
sweep					

swing

T CONSONANT SOUND: REGULAR

INITIAL	MEDIAL		FINAL	
to	took	city	later	not	what
two	table	into	sentence	at	set
take	ten	water	until	it	part
tell	talk	after		out	got
too	today			get	put
time	told			but	want

top

TH CONSONANT SOUND: TH DIGRAPH VOICELESS

INITIAL	MEDIAL		FINAL	
thank	thought	something	toothbrush	with	truth
think	thread	author	python	both	death
thing	threw	nothing		ninth	south
third	thumb	athlete		worth	fifth
thirty	thunder	faithful		cloth	bath
thick	threat	bathtub		teeth	

three

TH CONSONANT SOUND: TH DIGRAPH VOICED

INITIAL	MEDIAL		FINAL
the	though	mother	weather	smooth
that	thus	other	gather	
them	thy	brother	breathing	
they	thence	father	rhythm	
this	their	although	farther	
there	then	bother	leather	
than	thou	clothing	northern	
these		either		

feather

The Reading Teacher's Book of Lists, Third Edition, © 1993 by Prentice Hall

TR CONSONANT SOUND: TR BLEND

INITIAL

			MEDIAL		
track	trick	trouble	extra	control	country
tractor	travel	trap	electric	sentry	patrol
train	tree	trail	central	waitress	
trade	trim	triangle	attract	contract	
truly	trip	traffic	entry	patron	
try	true		subtract	contrast	

truck

TW CONSONANT SOUND: TW BLEND

INITIAL

					MEDIAL
twelve	twirl	twinkle	twinge	twelfth	between
twenty	twine	twist	twang	twill	entwine
twice	tweed	twitter	twentieth	twiddle	untwist
twig	twilight	twitch	tweet		intertwine

twins

U VOWEL SOUND: SHORT U

INITIAL

			MEDIAL		
up	unhappy	unless	but	number	such
us	upon	umpire	run	must	hunt
under	usher		much	study	summer
until	unusual		just	hundred	jump
ugly	uproar		cut	sudden	gun
uncle	upset		funny	sun	

umbrella

U VOWEL SOUND: LONG U—OPEN SYLLABLE RULE

INITIAL	**MEDIAL**			**FINAL**
unit	unify	future	humid	fugitive
united	unique	human	museum	funeral
Utah	utilize	valuable	continuous	beautiful
uniform		humor	fuel	unusual
universe		January	bugle	musician
usual		pupil	cubic	puny
university		community	communicate	menu

music

U VOWEL SOUND: 1-DOT U

MEDIAL

bullet	bush	cushion	bull's-eye	pulpit	bulldog
full	bushel	ambush	bushy	fully	armful
pull	sugar	bulletin	pullet	bullfrog	bully
push	pudding	handful	pushcart	fulfill	bullfight
put	butcher	pulley	bulldozer	bulwark	output

bull

U VOWEL SOUND: 2-DOT U

ruler

MEDIAL

June	flute	tune	punctuation	revolution	tuna
July	prune	conclusion	constitution	ruby	influence
truth	parachute	tube	duty	prudent	solution
junior	cruel	February	nutrition	situation	rhubarb
rule	numeral	aluminum	reduce	ruin	truly
crude					

UR VOWEL SOUND: R SOUND

INITIAL	MEDIAL			FINAL	
urn	turn	purple	further	fur	spur
urban	burn	hurt	purpose	sulfur	cur
urchin	hurry	turkey	burst	murmur	bur
urge	curl	curb	surf	concur	
urgent	Thursday	nurse	turtle	occur	
	purse	surface		slur	

church

V CONSONANT SOUND: REGULAR

INITIAL		MEDIAL		FINAL	
very	vowel	over	however	give	live
visit	van	even	cover	five	move
voice	verb	never	several	love	above
vote	vase	river		gave	leave
view	violin			twelve	wave
vest	valley			have	believe

Valentine

The Reading Teacher's Book of Lists, Third Edition, © 1993 by Prentice Hall

W CONSONANT SOUND: REGULAR

INITIAL			MEDIAL			
we	water	would	away	awake	halfway	
with	way	wave	reward	aware	sidewalk	window
will	were	win	forward	unwind	upward	
was	word	woman	want	highway	midway	
work	week	wait	sandwich	backyard	tapeworm	

WH CONSONANT SOUND: WH DIGRAPH (HW BLEND)

INITIAL				MEDIAL		
when	white	whip	whiskey	awhile	buckwheat	
what	while	whisper	whack	bobwhite	cartwheel	
which	why	whistle	whiff	overwhelm	somewhere	
whether	wheat	wheeze	whimper	somewhat	anywhere	
where	whale	wharf	whiz	everywhere	nowhere	wheel
				meanwhile		

WR CONSONANT SOUND: R SOUND

INITIAL				MEDIAL		
write	wrestle	wretch	wrung	awry	typewriter	
writing	wrist	wrinkle	wry	rewrite	monkeywrench	
written	wreath	wrapper	wrangle	handwriting	typewritten	
wrote	wring	wrathful		unwrap		
wrong	wreck	wreckage		playwright		wrench
wrap	wren	wriggle		shipwreck		

X CONSONANT SOUND: KS SOUND

MEDIAL		FINAL				
Mexico	explain	fox	fix	complex	vex	
Texas	axis	ax	relax	index	wax	box
mixture	oxen	six	next	lax	sex	
extremely	extra	tax	mix	hex	perplex	
sixty	excuse	ox	prefix	lox		
expert	exclaim					

Y CONSONANT SOUND: REGULAR

INITIAL

				MEDIAL	
you	youth	yam	yew	lawyer	vineyard
year	yawn	yank	yeast	canyon	papaya
yellow	yard	yak	yen	beyond	dooryard
yes	yet	yodel	yolk	courtyard	stockyard
yell	your	yacht	yonder	barnyard	backyard
young					

yarn

Y VOWEL SOUND: LONG E

MEDIAL	**FINAL**			
anything	very	happy	country	early
babysit	any	lady	city	money
everyone	many	story	really	quickly
ladybug	pretty	family	body	heavy
bodyguard	only	study	usually	ready
copying	funny	every	easy	energy
everything				

baby

Y VOWEL SOUND: LONG I SOUND

MEDIAL		**FINAL**			
myself	type	my	sky	shy	reply
nylon	lying	by	July	defy	sly
cycle	rhyme	why	fry	dry	deny
dying	python	buy	apply	ally	
style	hyena	cry	pry	spy	

fly

Z CONSONANT SOUND: REGULAR

INITIAL		**MEDIAL**			**FINAL**
zero	zipper	lazy	citizen	size	quiz
zoo	zoom	crazy	frozen	freeze	whiz
zone		puzzle	breeze	prize	buzz
zest		dozen	grazing		fizz
zenith		magazine	organize		fuzz
zigzag		realize	seize		jazz
zinc					adz

zebra

See also List 46, Initial Consonant Sounds; List 47, Phonograms; and List 49, Phonically Irregular Words.

The Reading Teacher's Book of Lists, Third Edition, © 1993 by Prentice Hall

49. *Phonically Irregular Words*

As every reading teacher knows, there are many words that do not follow regular phonics rules. Here are two such groups of common words. The first group contains common words with silent consonants. The second group contains common words with other types of phonic irregularities. Clearly, these are words that students need to be taught to recognize as sight words.

WORDS WITH SILENT CONSONANTS

The following words with silent consonants were taken from List 4, Instant Words. The words are listed in order of frequency, with those that are most frequent listed first. Two types of consonants that could be considered silent were *not* included in this list: (1) double consonants, where the second consonant adds nothing to the sound of the first (example, *all*); and (2) consonant digraphs (example, *ch, th, ph*, and *gh* pronounced as "*f*").

would	light	listen	window	design
write	thought	quickly	edge	straight
could	might	scientists	sign	stick
know	often	known	snow	caught
back	night	island	bright	sight
through	walk	brought	although	eight
right	enough	though	couldn't	science
answer	watch	check	catch	adjective
should	talk	picked	climbed	stretched
high	knew		wrote	bought
				track

WORDS WITH OTHER PHONIC IRREGULARITIES

a	earth	have	off	something	water
again	enough	heard	old	sure	were
any	example	kind	on	the	what
are	eyes	learn	once	their	where
become	father	live	one	there	who
been	few	many	only	they	women
both	find	measure	other	to	words
color	four	most	people	today	work
come	friends	mother	picture	two	world
country	from	mountain	piece	usually	you
do	give	move	said	want	young
does	great	of	some	was	your
door	group				

See also List 94, Spelling Demons—Elementary.

The Reading Teacher's Book of Lists, Third Edition, © 1993 by Prentice Hall

50. *Sound Awareness Books*

Here are some books that are particularly useful for encouraging sound recognition and production. For example, what sound do you hear at the beginning of "cat"? What sound do you hear at the end of "cat"? In any event, these books that play with sounds in language can be a lot of fun.

Allen, Pamela. (1983) *Bertie and the Bear*. New York: Putnam.

Barrett, Judy. (1980) *Animals Should Definitely Not Act Like People* and (1974) *Animals Should Definitely Not Wear Clothing*. New York: Macmillan.

Degen, Bruce. (1983) *Jamberry*. New York: Harper.

Hoberman, Mary A. (1982) *A House Is a House for Me*. New York: Penguin.

Hutchins, Pat. (1982) *Don't Forget the Bacon!* New York: Penguin and (1977) *Follow That Bus!* New York: Knopf.

Leedy, Loreen. (1989) *Pingo the Plaid Panda*. New York: Holiday House.

Peet, Bill. (1983) *No Such Things* and *Zella, Zack, and Zodiac*. Boston: Houghton Mifflin.

Pomerantz, Charlotte. (1987) *How Many Trucks Can a Tow Truck Tow?* New York: Random House.

Seuss, Dr. (1987) *I Am Not Going to Get Up Today!* and (1972) *Marvin K. Mooney, Will You Please Go Now!* New York: Random House.

Shaw, Nancy. (1986) *Sheep in a Jeep* and (1989) *Sheep on a Ship*. Boston: Houghton Mifflin.

Terban, Marvin. (1984) *I Think I Thought*. Boston: Houghton Mifflin.

Wadsworth, Olive A. (1986) *Over in the Meadow*. New York: Penguin.

The Reading Teacher's Book of Lists, Third Edition, © 1993 by Prentice Hall

51. Speech Sound Development

Oral speech sounds (phonemes) develop slowly over five or six years. Here is a chart showing the age at which 75 percent of children had mastered each spoken phoneme.

CONSONANTS

IPA*	Conventional	INITIAL Age	MEDIAL Age	FINAL Age
m		2	2	3
n		2	2	3
ŋ	(ng) sing	—	3	nt**
p		2	2	4
b		2	2	3
t		2	5	3
d		2	3	4
k		3	3	4
g		3	3	4
r		5	4	4
l		4	4	4
f		3	3	3
v		5	5	4
θ	(th voiceless) thin	5	nt	nt
ɣ	(th voiced) this	5	5	nt
s		5	5	5
z		5	3	3
ʃ	(sh) shoe	5	5	5
ʒ	(zh) measure	nt	5	nt
h		2	nt	—
w		2	2	—
j	(y) yes	4	4	—
tʃ	(ch) chief	5	5	4
dʒ	(j) just	4	4	6

VOWELS AND DIPHTHONGS

IPA	Conventional		Age
i	Long E	Me	2
I	Short I	Is	4
ε	Short E	Met	3
æ	Short A	At	4
ʌ	Short U	Up	2
ə	Schwa	Alone	2
ɑ	Broad A	Father	2
ɔ	Broad O	Off	3
ʊ	Short OO	Look	4
u	Long OO	Moon	2
ju	Long U	Use	3
ou	Long O	Go	2
au	Ou	Out	3
eI	Long A	May	4
aI	Long I	Ice	3
ɔI	OI	Boy	3

CONSONANT BLENDS

Blend	Age	Blend	Age
pr-	5		
br-	5		
tr-	5		
dr-	5	sl-	6
kr-	5	sw-	5
gr-	5	tw-	5
fr-	5	kw-	5
θr-	6	-ŋk	4
pl-	5	-ŋg	5
bl-	5	-mp	3
kl-	5	-nt	4
gl-	5	-nd	6
fl-	5	spr-	5
-ld	6	spl-	6
-lk	5	str-	5
-lf	5	skr-	5
-lv	5	skw-	5
-lz	5	-ns	5
sm-	5	-ps	5
sn-	5	-ts	5
sp-	5	-mz	5
st-	5	-nz	5
-st	6	-ŋz	6
sk-	5	-dz	5
-ks	5	-gz	5

*IPA stands for International Phonetic Alphabet. **Not tested.

52. *English Sounds Not Used In Other Languages*

Some sounds are used in English, but are not parts of other languages. Students whose primary language is not English may have difficulty pronouncing words that use these sounds. To master them, students will need to practice recognizing the sounds in words they hear, then pronouncing the sounds.

LANGUAGE	ENGLISH SOUNDS NOT USED IN THE LANGUAGE						
Spanish	dg	j	sh	th	z		
Chinese	b	ch	d	dg	g	oa	sh
	s̲	th	t̲h̲	v	z		
French	ch	ee	j	ng	oo	th	t̲h̲
Greek	aw	ee	i	oo	schwa		
Italian	a	ar	dg	h	i	ng	th
	t̲h̲	schwa					
Japanese	dg	f	i	th	t̲h̲	oo	v
	schwa						

53. *Problem English Sounds For ESL Students*

Some English sounds are difficult for students whose primary language is not English. It will help to practice pronouncing these sounds in initial, final, and medial positions in English words. Use the Phonics Example Words, Major Phonograms, and Minor Phonograms for practice.

LANGUAGE	PROBLEM SOUNDS									
Spanish	b	d	dg	h	j	m	n	ng	r	sh
	t	th	v	w	y	z	s-clusters			
	end clusters									
Chinese	b	ch	d	dg	f	g	j	l	m	n	ng
	ō	sh	s̲	th	t̲h̲	v	z	l-clusters		
	r-clusters									
French	ā	ch	ē	h	j	ng	oo	oy	s	th
	t̲h̲	s̲	schwa							
Italian	a	ar	dg	h	i	ng	th	t̲h̲	v	schwa
	l-clusters	end clusters								
Japanese	dg	f	h	i	l	th	t̲h̲	oo	r	sh
	s̲	v	w	schwa	l-clusters	r-clusters				
Korean	b	l	ō	ow	p	r	sh	t	t̲h̲	
	l-clusters	r-clusters								

For further information, consult *The ESL Teacher's Book of Lists* (Prentice Hall, 1993) by Jacqueline Kress.

The Reading Teacher's Book of Lists, Third Edition, © 1993 by Prentice Hall

SECTION VI
Comprehension

54. *Signal Words*

These are words that the author uses to tell us how to read. Signal words help us to understand how information is organized and provide clues about what is important. Teach signal words one group at a time. Give your students a few examples from a category and have them add others as they run across them in their reading. In terms of schema theory, signal words tell the reader about the enabling schema, story grammar, or structure. Note that signal words are independent of the content; they can be used with any kind of article or story.

1. Continuation Signals *(Warning—there are more ideas to come.)*

and	also	another
again	and finally	first of all
a final reason	furthermore	in addition
last of all	likewise	more
moreover	next	one reason
other	secondly	similarly
too	with	

2. Change-of-Direction Signals *(Watch out—we're doubling back.)*

although	but	conversely
despite	different from	even though
however	in contrast	instead of
in spite of	nevertheless	otherwise
the opposite	on the contrary	on the other hand
rather	still	yet
while	though	

3. Sequence Signals *(There is an order to these ideas.)*

first, second, third	A, B, C
in the first place	for one thing
then	next
before	now
after	while
into *(far into the night)*	until
last	during
since	always
o'clock	on time
later	earlier

4. Time Signals *(When is it happening?)*

when	immediately	now
lately	already	little by little
at the same time	final	after awhile
once	during	

5. Illustration Signals *(Here's what that principle means in reality.)*

for example	specifically
for instance	to illustrate
such as	much like
in the same way as	similar to

6. Emphasis Signals *(This is important.)*

a major development	it all boils down to
a significant factor	most of all
a primary concern	most noteworthy
a key feature	more than anything else
a major event	of course
a vital force	pay particular attention to
a central issue	remember that
a distinctive quality	should be noted
above all	the most substantial issue
by the way	the main value
especially important	the basic concept
especially relevant	the crux of the matter
especially valuable	the chief outcome
important to note	the principal item

7. Cause, Condition, or Result Signals *(Condition or modification is coming up.)*

because	if	of
for	from	so
while	then	but
that	until	since
as	whether	in order that
so that	therefore	unless
yet	thus	due to
resulting from	consequently	without

8. Spatial Signals *(This answers the "where" question.)*

between	below	about	left	alongside
here	outside	around	close to	far
right	over	away	side	near
near	in	into	beside	
middle	next to	beyond	north	
east	on	opposite	over	
south	there	inside	in front of	
under	these	out	behind	
across	this	adjacent	above	
toward	west	by	upon	

The Reading Teacher's Book of Lists, Third Edition, © 1993 by Prentice Hall

The Reading Teacher's Book of Lists, Third Edition, © 1993 by Prentice Hall

9. Comparison-Contrast Signals *(We will now compare idea A with idea B.)*

and	or	also
too	best	most
either	less	less than
more than	same	better
even	then	half
much as	like	analogous to
but	different from	still
yet	however	although
opposite	rather	while
though		

10. Conclusion Signals *(This ends the discussion and may have special importance.)*

as a result	consequently	finally
from this we see	in conclusion	in summary
hence	last of all	therefore

11. Fuzz Signals *(Idea is not exact, or author is not positive and wishes to qualify a statement.)*

almost	if	looks like
maybe	could	some
except	should	alleged
nearly	might	reputed
seems like	was reported	purported
sort of	probably	

12. Nonword Emphasis Signals

exclamation point (!)
<u>underline</u>
italics
bold type
subheads, like *The Conclusion*
    indentation of paragraph
graphic illustrations
numbered points (1, 2, 3)
very short sentence: *Stop war.*
"quotation marks"

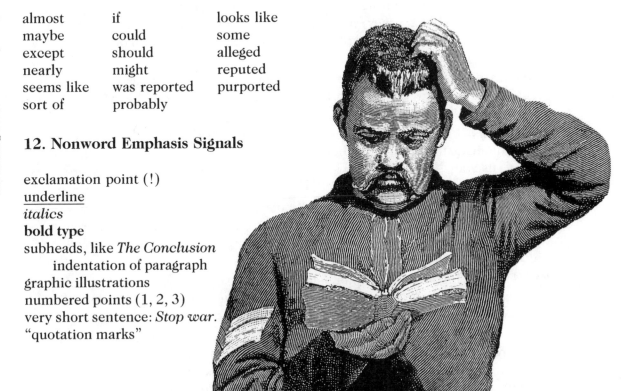

See also List 75, Test and Workbook Words; and List 77, Important Modifiers.

55. *Propaganda Techniques*

These persuasion devices are often used in advertising and political campaigning. Teach your students to be critical readers and listeners by being alert to these attempts to mold their choices and viewpoints.

Bandwagon. Using the argument that because everyone is doing it, you should, too. *Last year 30 million winners switched to AIR-POPS athletic shoes. Isn't it time you did, too?*

Card Stacking. Telling only one side of the story as though there is no opposing view. *This tape is specially designed to give the best audio playback money can buy.* (No mention is made that the tape wears out very quickly and is expensive.)

Exigency. Creating the impression that your action is required immediately or your opportunity will be lost forever. *Saturday and Sunday only! It's your last chance to get a really great deal on Camp jeans.*

Flag Waving. Connecting the person, product, or cause with patriotism. *Me drink foreign beer? Never! I drink Bot Beer—American all the way.*

Glittering Generality. Using positive or idealistic words based on a detail or minor attribute to create an association in the reader's mind between the person or object and something that is good, valued, and desired. *Ron's been on the varsity team for all four years—you couldn't find a better team player or a more sportsmanlike young man.*

Innuendo. Causing the audience to become wary or suspicious of the product, person, or cause by hinting that negative information may be being kept secret. *Other products claim they can handle the big, grimy, once-a-year cleaning jobs like a garage floor. Think what they will do to the no-wax finish on your kitchen floor where your baby plays.*

Name Calling. Using negative or derogatory words to create an association in the reader's mind between the person or object and something that is bad, feared, or distasteful. *Do you really want a mob-linked mayor?*

Plain Folks. Using a person who represents the "typical" target of the ad to communicate to the target audience the message that because we are alike and I would use/buy/believe this, you should, too. *If you're a sinus sufferer like me, take extra-strength Azap. It helps me. It'll help you, too.*

Prestige Identification. Showing a well-known person with the object, person, or cause in order to increase the audience's impression of the importance or prestige of the object, person, or cause. *We treat our hotel guests like stars (the ad shows a celebrity walking into the hotel).*

Red Herring. Highlighting a minor detail as a way to draw attention away from more important details or issues. *The XT399—the only sports car available in 32 eye-catching colors.*

Snob Appeal. Associating the product, person, or cause with successful, wealthy, admired people to give the audience the idea that if they buy or support the same things, they will also be one of the "in-crowd." *There really isn't a better racket (man in tennis clothes holding a racket in front of a very elegant country club building).*

The Reading Teacher's Book of Lists, Third Edition, © 1993 by Prentice Hall

Testimonial. Using the testimony or statement of someone to persuade you to think or act as he or she does. *I'm a doctor, and this is what I take when I have a headache.*

Transfer. Linking a known personal goal or ideal with a product or cause in order to transfer the audience's positive feelings to the product or cause. *Buy Pino in the biodegradable box and help end water pollution.*

See also List 58, Comprehension Skills.

56. *Comprehension Questions*

Here are some question types to help you add variety to your questioning. These questions can be adapted for use with any prose. Examples of each question type are based on the story of Cinderella.

Vocabulary

1. Questions to help students understand the meaning of a particular word. For example: *What does the word **jealous** mean? What did the stepsisters do that shows that they were jealous?*

2. Questions to help students understand words used in the text in terms of their own lives. For example: *Have you ever known someone who was jealous? Have you ever been jealous? Why?*

3. Questions to help students understand multiple meanings of words. For example: *What does **ball** mean in this story? Can you think of any other meaning of the word **ball**?*

Pronoun Referents

4. Questions to help students understand what or who some pronouns refer to and how to figure them out. For example: *In the second sentence of the third paragraph, who does **she** refer to? How do you know?*

Causal Relations

5. Questions to help students recognize causal relations stated directly in the text. For example: *Why were Cinderella's stepsisters jealous of Cinderella?*

6. Questions to help students recognize causal relations not directly stated in the text. For example: *Why did the stepmother give Cinderella extra work to do on the day of the ball?*

Sequence

7. Questions to help students understand that the sequence of some things is unchangeable. For example: *What steps did the Fairy Godmother follow in order to make a coach for Cinderella? Could the order of these steps be changed? Why or why not?*

8. Questions to help students understand that the sequence of some things is changeable. For example: *What chores did Cinderella do on the day of the ball? Could she have done some of them in a different order? Why or why not?*

Comparison

9. Questions to encourage the students to compare things within the text. For example: *How did the behavior of the stepsisters differ from the behavior of Cinderella?*

The Reading Teacher's Book of Lists, Third Edition, © 1993 by Prentice Hall

10. Questions to encourage students to compare elements of the story with elements of other stories. For example: *In what ways are the stories of Cinderella and Snow White similar? In what ways are they different?*

11. Questions to encourage students to compare elements of the story with their own experiences. For example: *If you were in Cinderella's place how would you have acted toward your stepsisters? Is this similar or different from the way Cinderella acted?*

Generalizing

12. Questions to encourage students to generalize from one story to another. For example: *Are most heroines of fairy tales as kind as Cinderella? Give some examples to support your answer.*

13. Questions to encourage students to generalize from what they read to their own experiences. For example: *Can we say that most stepmothers are mean to their stepchildren? Why or why not?*

Predicting Outcomes

14. Questions to encourage students to think ahead to what may happen in the future. For example: *After Cinderella's beautiful dress changes back to rags what do you think happens?*

Detecting Author's Point of View

15. Questions to help students detect the author's point of view. For example: *What is the author's opinion of the stepsisters and what makes you think this? Support your answer with examples from the story.*

See also List 58, Comprehension Skills; List 59, Comprehension Thesaurus; and Section VII, Learning and Study Skills.

57. Sentence Tunes

If you have any doubt that changing the way you say something can change the meaning, this example should convince you. Your students will enjoy playing with this sentence and should be able to create their own multituned sentences.

Directions: Emphasize italicized word to change meaning.

I did not say you stole my red bandana.   *(Someone else said it)*
I *did* not say you stole my red bandana.   *(Disputatious denial)*
I did *not* say you stole my red bandana.   *(Disputatious denial)*
I did not *say* you stole my red bandana.   *(I implied or suspected)*
I did not say *you* stole my red bandana.   *(Someone else stole it)*
I did not say you *stole* my red bandana.   *(You did something else with it)*
I did not say you stole *my* red bandana.   *(You stole someone else's)*
I did not say you stole my *red* bandana.   *(You stole one of another color)*
I did not say you stole my red *bandana*.   *(You stole something else red)*

Now try shifting emphasis on these sentences:

You are not invited to his birthday lunch today.

You are a friend of mine.

Give me more money from Sam.

The Reading Teacher's Book of Lists, Third Edition, © 1993 by Prentice Hall

58. *Comprehension Skills*

This is a traditional list of comprehension skills such as might be found in any textbook about reading or on the scope and sequence chart of a basal reader.

VERY TRADITIONAL COMPREHENSION SKILLS

Author's intent, purpose, and bias
Cause and effect
Classification, categories
Comparison
Conclusion
Detail recognition
Empathy and emotional reaction
Evaluation, subjective, and by external criteria, judgment
Exaggeration and hyperbole recognition
Extending interpretation, extrapolation
Factual recall
Following directions
Generalization

Inference
Literary style
Main idea
Mental imagery
Mood
Organization
Plot, story problem
Propaganda detection
Restatement
Sequence, time relationships
Separation of fact from opinion (figurative from literal)
Summarizing
Whole-part recognition

MORE MODERN APPROACH TO COMPREHENSION SKILLS

STUDENT OBSERVABLE ACTION	COGNITIVE ACTION
Output	*Thinking*

STUDENT OBSERVABLE ACTION — *Output*

Recognizing

Examples: Multiple-choice items, Underlining, Matching
True-false
Selecting correct answer in context, or from choices given

Recalling

Examples: Write short answer, Completion (cloze), Remembering, not selecting

Paraphrasing

Examples: Summarizing, Restating in own words

Classifying

Examples: Clustering ideas in article, Putting facts or ideas into some class (columns), Outline, make table

Following Directions

Examples: Assemble toy, Pencil activities, Point to area on screen

Graphing

Examples: Draw a map, picture, time line, curve, graph, flow chart

Oral Reading

Intonation, Phrasing, Accuracy of pronunciation, fluency

COGNITIVE ACTION — *Thinking*

Directly Stated Facts

Little or no interpretation, Most common items, Literal comprehension

Main Idea

Very common but complicated and subjective concept; involves conclusion, purpose, and/or summary

Facts to Support Main Idea

Common and sometimes useful concepts, similar to relationship

Sequence

Time order, Flashbacks, May be partly inferred

Extrapolation

Going beyond stated facts, Predicting, Inference, Trends, Traits, Unstated conclusions, Use of previous learning

Appreciation

Value, Judgments, Worth, Pleasing to reader, Is it good? Would others think it good? Emotional response

Evaluation

Validity, Truthfulness
Usefulness, Reality, Opinion, Fact

Author's Intent

Persuasion, Goals, Propaganda, Mood, Style

Schema

Plot, Script, Plan, Proposition, Organization, Units, Networks

Vocabulary

Word or phrase meaning in context, Figurative language, Other meanings of word

Relationships

Cause and effect, comparisons, Relate one part or character to another, Anaphora referents

The Reading Teacher's Book of Lists, Third Edition, © 1993 by Prentice Hall

OTHER COMPREHENSION FACTORS

THE READER

Age, IQ,
Education,
Background, SES,
Out-of-school experiences
Fatigue, Health

READERS PURPOSE

Find out content, Learn,
Study for test,
Get general idea quickly,
Recreation,
Goals, Rewards

TIME

Delay, Need to remember,
Immediate post test, Action

ENVIRONMENT

Classroom, Home,
Distractions,
Light, Noise, Chair

TYPE OF MATERIAL

Fiction, Stories,
Expository articles, Textbooks,
Advertisements,
Forms, Poetry
Different subjects (for example, history,
    science)

READABILITY

Difficulty level,
Clear writing,
Personal words,
Legibility, Imagery

LENGTH

Sentence, Paragraph,
Chapter, Book

GRAPHS

Comprehend illustrations,
bar charts, maps, tables

See also List 56, Comprehension Questions; List 59, Comprehension Thesaurus;
and List 63, Study Skills List.

59. *Comprehension Thesaurus*

Here is a Comprehension Thesaurus with which you can generate an impressive ten thousand and eighty-seven (that's 10,087) different comprehension terms. Impress your principal by using a new one every day for the next 56 years.

   Directions: Select any term from Part A and link it with any term in Part B to form a Reading Comprehension Skill. (For those who don't recognize it, this list is largely "tongue in cheek," but it does make a point about the confusing multiplicity of comprehension terminology.)

PART A: THE ACTION

Getting
Identifying
Understanding
Classifying
Recalling
Selecting
Finding
Recognizing
Summarizing
Grasping
Drawing
Evaluating
Relating
Paraphrasing
Comparing
Transforming
Clarifying
Specifying
Matching
Criticizing
Analyzing
Noting
Perceiving
Extending
Restating
Reacting (to)

Organizing
Outlining
Using
Locating
Retelling
Reasoning (about)
Interpreting
Comprehending
Demonstrating
Applying
Obtaining
Predicting
Contrasting
Proving
Anticipating
Internalizing
Sifting
Inferring
Referring (to)
Drawing
Making
Concluding
Forecasting
Extrapolating
Foreshadowing
Producing (from memory)

Providing
Reading (for)
Following
Previewing
Apprehending
Determining
Working (with)
Visualizing
Thinking (about)
Thinking critically
Getting excited (about)
Dealing (with)
Judging
Translating
Synthesizing
Checking
Deriving
Integrating
Actively responding (to)
Describing
Questioning
Verbalizing
Processing
Encoding
Learning

PART B: THE CONCEPT

Main ideas
Central thoughts
Author's purpose
Author's intent
Point of view
Thought units
Story content

Ambiguous statements
Mood
Tone
Inference
Inference about author
Conjecture
Information

Climax
Outcome
Objective ideas
Subjective ideas
Events
Interactions
Relevancies

The Reading Teacher's Book of Lists, Third Edition, © 1993 by Prentice Hall

Details
Supporting details
Essential details
Specifics
Specific facts
Inferences
Wholes and parts
Conclusions
Propositions
Propositional relationships
Schema
Schemata
Constructs
Meanings
Scenarios
Scripts
Sense
Classifications
Categories
Multiple meanings
Connotations
Denotations
Causal relations
Sequence
Sequence of events
Sequence of ideas
Chronological sequence
Trends
Seriation
Anaphora
Associations
Facts
Deep structure
Analogies
Figurative language
Metaphors
Similes

Text information
Important things
Humor
Directions
Trends
Goals
Aims
Principles
Generalizations
Universals
Abstractions
Abstract ideas
Structures
Judgments
Literary style
Elements of style
Elements
Imagery
Mental imagery
Cause and effect
Organization
Story line
Story problem
Plot
Plot structure
Time of action
Types of literature
Context
Affective content
Answers
General idea
Facts
Concepts
Relationships
Lexical relationships
Textual relationships
Written works

Semantic constraints
Linguistic constraints
Convictions
Inclinations
Characterization
Personal reaction
Effects
Comparisons
Time
Event-to-time relationship
Tense
Propaganda
Flashbacks
Repetitive refrain
Personification
Answers to questions
Directly stated answers
Indirectly stated answers
Extended answers
Various purposes
Validity
Antecedents
References
Experiences
Vicarious experiences
Concrete experiences
Concepts
Familiar concepts
Unfamiliar concepts
Vocabulary
Vocabulary in context
Word meaning
Terminology
Descriptions
Criteria
Attributes
Content

See also List 58, Comprehension Skills.

60. *Story Graphs*

You can often improve a student's comprehension of a story by having the student draw a graphical representation. This list of story graphs contains only suggestions; most of them can be made larger and more complex. These story graphs can also be used in many other subjects, such as science or history. They can also be used by writers in planning stories or expository articles.

Spider Map

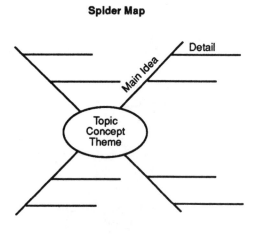

Used to describe a central idea: a thing (a geographic region), process (meiosis), concept (altruism), or proposition with support (experimental drugs should be available to AIDS victims). Key frame questions: What is the central idea? What are its attributes? What are its functions?

(how to neutralize an acid); a sequence of events (how feudalism led to the formation of nation states); or the goals, actions, and outcomes of a historical figure or character in a novel (the rise and fall of Napoleon). Key frame questions: What is the object, procedure, or initiating event? What are the stages or steps? How do they lead to one another? What is the final outcome?

Continuum Scale

1950	1960	1970	1980	1990
Born		Moved to N.Y.		Wrote book

Low   High

Used for time lines showing historical events or ages (grade levels in school), degrees of something (weight), shades of meaning (Likert scales), or ratings scales (achievement in school). Key frame questions: What is being scaled? What are the endpoints?

Series of Events Chain

Initiating Event

Event 1 Bomb exploded

↓

Event 2 Fire Dept. came

↓

Final Outcome

Event 3 Many saved

Used to describe the stages of something (the life cycle of a primate); the steps in a linear procedure

Compare/Contrast Matrix

	Maria	Sally
Attribute 1 Friendliness	Liked everybody	Liked only a few people
Attribute 2 Dependability	Always on time	Missed school often
Attribute 3		

Used to show similarities and differences between two things (people, places, events, ideas, etc.). Key frame questions: What things are being compared? How are they similar? How are they different?

The Reading Teacher's Book of Lists, Third Edition, © 1993 by Prentice Hall

Problem/Solution Outline

Who	Germany

Problem

What	Started World War II
Why	Gain territory

Solution

Attempted Solutions	Results
1. Attack France	1. Won
2. Attack Russia	2. Lost

Lost war

End Result

Used to represent a problem, attempted solutions, and results (the national debt). Key frame questions: What was the problem? Who had the problem? Why was it a problem? What attempts were made to solve the problem? Did those attempts succeed?

Human Interaction Outline

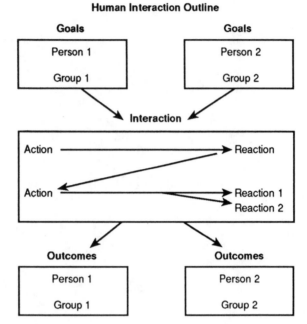

Used to show the nature of an interaction between persons or groups (European settlers and American Indians). Key frame questions: Who are the persons or groups? What were their goals? Did they conflict or cooperate? What was the outcome for person or group?

Network Tree

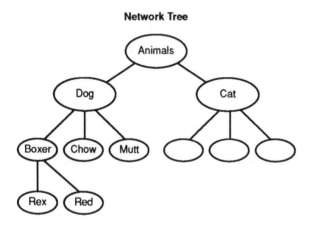

Used to show causal information (causes of poverty), a hierarchy (types of insects), or branching procedures (the circulatory system). Key frame questions: What is the superordinate category? What are the subordinate categories? How are they related? How many levels are there?

Fishbone Map

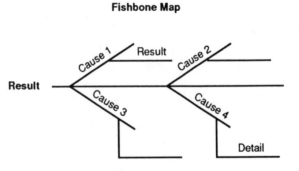

Used to show the causal interaction of a complex event (an election, a nuclear explosion) or complex phenomenon (juvenile delinquency, learning disabilities). Key frame questions: What are the factors that cause X? How do they interrelate? Are the factors that cause X the same as those that cause X to persist?

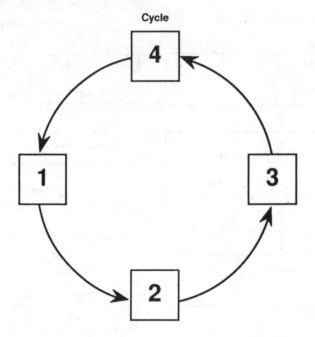

Used to show how a series of events interact to produce a set of results again and again (weather phenomena, cycles of achievement and failure, the life cycle). Key frame questions: What are the critical events in the cycle? How are they related? In what ways are they self-reinforcing?

SECTION VII
Learning and Study Skills

61. *Story Guide*

The Reading Teacher's Book of Lists, Third Edition, © 1993 by Prentice Hall

Name _____ Date _____

Title: _____

Author: _____

Story Setting:
    Time:

    Place:

Main Characters: (name and description)
    1.

    2.

    3.

    4.

Problem or Conflict:

Action Sequence:

Solution:

Theme:

See also List 60, Story Graphs; and List 62, Reading Guide.

62. *Reading Guide (SQ3R)*

Name _____ Date _____

Title: _____

SQ3R stands for Survey, Question, Read, Recite, Review.

Survey (Clues from the title, headings, pictures, graphs, charts, tables, captions, and words in bold or italic print)

This will be about:

I will probably learn:

My questions (based on headings or at end of each page).

1.
2.
3.
4.

Read and Recite (These are the answers I found.)

1.
2.
3.
4.
5.

Review (Looking at the headings or my questions, I will think about what I read. I will answer my questions silently without rereading.)

See also List 60, Story Graphs; and List 61, Study Guide.

The Reading Teacher's Book of Lists, Third Edition, © 1993 by Prentice Hall

63. *Study Skills List*

Mastering these study skills will enable students to succeed at any grade level, in any subject. Integrate instruction in these skills during subject-matter classes, applying each skill to the texts, resources, and needs of the class. Remember, skills develop through practice.

Preparing to Study

- ☐ Keeping track of assignments
- ☐ Planning your time
- ☐ Creating a study space
- ☐ Gathering your tools
- ☐ Knowing your study style

Reading with a purpose

- ☐ Knowing your purpose for reading
- ☐ Fitting your approach to the purpose
- ☐ Fitting your reading speed to the purpose
- ☐ Monitoring your understanding as you read
- ☐ Recognizing facts and opinions
- ☐ Recognizing author's bias
- ☐ Judging author's credentials
- ☐ Judging relevance of material to your assignment
- ☐ Recognizing the use of propaganda techniques

Using Your Textbooks and Other Resources

- ☐ Using the parts of your book:
  Table of contents; Introduction; Headings and subheadings; Chapter summary; Chapter/unit review questions; Chapter/unit vocabulary lists; Glossary; Appendices; Index
- ☐ Determining organizational patterns in your texts: Chronological order; Thematic; Simple/complex; Cause/Effect; Comparison/contrast
- ☐ Understanding tables, graphs, and charts
- ☐ Using a map, diagram, timeline

Learning New Vocabulary

- ☐ Using context
- ☐ Using the glossary, standard and special dictionaries
- ☐ Noting special or new meanings for familiar words
- ☐ Recognizing author's techniques to highlight key words
- ☐ Using roots and affixes
- ☐ Using signs and symbols

The Reading Teacher's Book of Lists, Third Edition, © 1993 by Prentice Hall

Gathering and Organizing Information

- ☐ Underlining key ideas
- ☐ Taking notes from text
- ☐ Outlining text
- ☐ Summarizing text
- ☐ Categorizing information
- ☐ Organizing your information
- ☐ Making a table, chart, timeline, or graph
- ☐ Listening skills
- ☐ Taking notes from lectures, audio/video presentations
- ☐ Using the library: card catalogs; on-line catalogs; library classification systems
- ☐ Using nonprint media and reference technology fiche viewers, microfilm readers, computers, projectors, VCRs, etc.
- ☐ Identifying your sources (quoting, writing footnotes, listing bibliographic information)

Learning from Texts and Other Resources

- ☐ Using SQ3R
- ☐ Using a study guide
- ☐ Creating a story map
- ☐ Using mnemonic devices

Preparing Written Assignments

- ☐ Developing an outline
- ☐ Answering the questions asked
- ☐ Writing a first draft
- ☐ Using tables, charts, graphs, timelines, and other visual displays to support your narrative
- ☐ Editing/proofreading your work

Preparing for and Taking Tests

- ☐ Reviewing your text and notes
- ☐ Making up test questions
- ☐ Knowing key test words
- ☐ Becoming testwise
- ☐ Pacing yourself during a test
- ☐ Knowing you know

See also List 62, Reading Guide;
and List 65, Memory Aids List.

64. *Time-Planning Chart*

A time-planning chart is a standard study skills tool. This is a practical one, just in case you don't have one readily available for your students. Use it to encourage leisure reading and studying.

STUDY, READING, WORK, RECREATION SCHEDULE

	Mon.	Tues.	Wed.	Thurs.	Fri.	Sat.	Sun.
Study Period During School Day						a.m.	
After School Afternoon						p.m.	
Early Evening							
Late Evening							

Directions: Fill in every square with one or two of the following activities:

1. STUDY: Homework assignments, activity related to courses you are taking.
2. READING: Reading primarily books for your pleasure, or, at most, supplemental or extra-interest material for course you are taking.
3. WORK: Work that you do outside of school for pay, or at home.
4. RECREATION: Talking to friends, watching TV, sports, goofing around.

See also List 63, Study Skills; and List 149, Taxonomy of Graphs.

65. *Memory Aids*

Here are some techniques that are useful in memorizing. Show your students how to use these techniques when they study for your tests.

1. **Study actively.** You are more likely to remember material if you write it down or say it out loud than if you merely read it or hear it.

2. **Make sure you understand.** If you understand what you're trying to learn, you'll find that you can remember it better and for a longer period of time.

3. **Associate new information with old.** When learning something new, try to compare it with something similar that you are already familiar with.

4. **Make up examples.** When learning general principles, try to make up examples of your own. In addition to helping you remember the principle better, this will also help you check your understanding. If you're not sure that your example is correct, check it with your teacher.

5. **Visualize what you're trying to learn.** This can involve creating a mental image or drawing a graph (a time line to help with time sequences, a hierarchical chart for organizations or family trees, etc.). (See List 149, Taxonomy of Graphs, for other ideas.)

6. **Group items into categories.** If you have to learn a long list of things, try to group similar items together. For example, to memorize a shopping list you would want to group vegetables together, meats together, dairy products, and so on.

7. **Be selective.** Most of the time you will not be able to memorize every detail, and if you try you may end up learning almost nothing. Concentrate on general concepts and a few examples to go with each. Pay particular attention to information the teacher indicates is important. Teachers frequently send signals to help you identify what is most important (information written on the chalk board, or repeated several times orally, or prefaced by statements such as "You should know this."). (See List 54, Signal Words.)

8. **Space your study sessions.** You are more apt to remember material if you study over several days rather than in one crash session.

9. **Use key words.** For example, to learn this list of suggestions for improving your memory, pick out a key word for each suggestion and then learn just the key words. To learn items 1 through 9, you might choose the following key words: active, understand, associate, examples, visualize, group, selective, space, key words.

10. **Learn how many items are on the list.** When learning lists, make sure you learn the number of items on the list. For example, in item 9, it is not enough to learn the key words. You also should learn that there are nine items. This will aid you in recalling all the items.

The Reading Teacher's Book of Lists, Third Edition, © 1993 by Prentice Hall

The Reading Teacher's Book of Lists, Third Edition, © 1993 by Prentice Hall

11. **Rhymes and sayings can be helpful.** For example, how many of us can remember the number of days in the months without:

> Thirty days has September,
> April, June, and November;
> All the rest have thirty-one,
> Excepting February alone,
> Which has just four and twenty-four,
> And every leap year one day more.

12. **Use alliteration.** Repeating initial sounds can be helpful in remembering information. For example, to remind sailors entering a harbor to keep the red harbor light on their right, they learn:

> Red to right returning

13. **Try acrostics.** Sometimes you can use the first letter of a list of words to form another word or sentence. These are referred to as acrostics and are similar to acronyms (see List 36, Acronyms and Initializations). For example, "ROY G. BIV" can help us remember the colors of the spectrum: Red, Orange, Yellow, Green, Blue, Indigo, and Violet.

14. **Exaggerate.** This is especially helpful when you are using visualization. Try to make your images big, colorful, and with lots of details. This will make them interesting and easier to remember.

15. **Have confidence.** Don't go around saying, "I can't remember names." You can if you try.

16. **Use a mnemonic device.** This is very useful when memorizing a list of anything.

See also List 63, Study Skills; and List 66, Mnemonic Device.

66. Mnemonic Device

This mnemonic device has actually been known for centuries. It is still impressive as a study technique. Done with a bit of showmanship, it will also provide great entertainment. Your students can impress their parents by memorizing a list of twenty objects in just a few minutes (after they study and learn the mnemonic device).

The following is (1) an interesting trick with which the students can interest and amuse their friends, (2) a serious experiment in psychology that clearly demonstrates the power of associative learning, and (3) a useful skill that can sometimes help the student to remember a long and not necessarily related list of facts (useful in passing some examinations and in going to the grocery shop).

First, let us give an example of how the trick might be done in school. The student asks his or her friends to call out slowly a list of objects—any objects. The friends call out "clock-chair-hammer," and so on. Often a friend will write them down on the blackboard so that the others will not forget them: "1. clock; 2. chair; 3. hammer." The student does not look at the blackboard. After twenty objects, or however many the students decide, someone calls a halt and immediately announces that he or she has memorized all the objects and can call them out in any order—forwards, backwards, every other way—in fact, he or she can tell them the number of any object (without looking at the board). The friends say that they do not believe the student; one of them asks, "What is number three?" The student immediately replies, "Hammer." Then after a few such questions, the student demonstrates complete mastery by calling off the whole list either forwards or backwards.

Now, almost anyone can do this trick, once he or she knows how. The secret lies in memorizing a set of "key objects." You must first take a little time to memorize (make mental associations between) a "key object" and the number. For example, the key object for number one is "sun" and the key object for number two is "shoe," and so on (see list on the following page). You must learn the association between the key object and the number so well that whenever you say "one" to yourself you visualize "sun." You should easily be able to learn the first ten key objects and their numbers in a short learning session on the first day, ten more the next day, and so on. After you have learned the key objects well, you are ready to do the trick. When the first friend calls out the word "clock" as the first item for you to memorize, you must mentally picture a "clock" next to a "sun," which is your key object for number 1. After you have made a clear mental picture of a clock next to a sun, you then allow the next friend to call out a second item to be memorized, such as "chair"; you then mentally picture a chair with your key object, a shoe, sitting on it. You control the rate at which your friends can call out names of objects; at first, you will go rather slowly, but after you have done the trick a few times you can go more rapidly.

The Reading Teacher's Book of Lists, Third Edition, © 1993 by Prentice Hall

KEY OBJECTS

1. Sun	**11.** Elephant
2. Shoe	**12.** Twig
3. Tree	**13.** Throne
4. Door	**14.** Fort
5. Hive	**15.** Fire
6. Sticks	**16.** Silver coin
7. Heaven (an angel)	**17.** Sea
8. Gate	**18.** Apron
9. Sign	**19.** Knife
10. Pen	**20.** Baby

There are several important learning principles involved in this trick that also apply to other learning. One is the "mental visualization"—it is a powerful factor in memory and can be developed with relatively little practice. Another important factor is self-confidence; if you say beforehand "I can't do it" you probably won't be able to. Self-confidence is also important during the trick, for you must concentrate only on the object to be remembered; you cannot worry about "Did I learn the first three things?" Exaggeration of mental pictures, making them large, brightly colored, or even purposefully distorted, will often aid memory.

This type of memorizing is not a new discovery. It was well known by the ancient people of both Greece and India.

The key objects have been chosen to take advantage of another learning principle—that of rhyming. The first ten objects all have an end-rhyme with the name of the number. The second ten objects all begin with the same sound as the name of the number, except for 20, where a rough rhyme is used to avoid confusion with 12. If you wish to extend the list of objects to 50 or 100, or to change any of the suggested list, you can choose any key objects that you wish. The important thing is that they be easily visualized and never change.

See also List 65, Memory Aids; List 74, Test-taking Strategies; and List 149, Taxonomy of Graphs.

67. *Skimming Illustration*

This illustration gives a good picture of skimming. In order for students to become proficient at skimming, they need lots of practice. Twice a week for half a year isn't too much.

Usually the first paragraph will be read at average speed all the way through. It often contains an introduction or overview of what will be talked about.

Sometimes, however, the second paragraph contains the introduction or overview. In the first paragraph, the author might just be "warming up" or saying something clever to attract attention.

Reading a third paragraph completely might be unnecessary but ··· ···
··· ··· ··· ··· ··· ··· ··· ···
··· ··· ··· ··· ··· ··· ··· ···
··· ··· ··· ··· ··· ··· ··· ···
the main idea is usually contained in the opening sentence
··· ··· ··· ··· ··· ··· ···
··· ··· ··· ··· ··· topic sentence ··· ··· ··· ··· ···
··· ··· ··· ··· ··· ··· ···
··· ··· ··· ··· ··· ··· ···

Besides the first sentence, the reader should get some but not all the detail from the rest of the paragraph··· ···
··· ··· ··· ··· ··· ··· ···
··· ··· ··· ··· ··· ··· ···
··· ··· ··· ··· ··· ··· ···
··· ··· ··· ··· names ···
··· ··· ··· ··· ··· ··· ···
··· ··· ··· date ··· ··· ···
··· ··· ··· ··· ··· ··· ···
··· ··· ··· ··· ··· ··· ···
This tells you nothing ··· ···
··· ··· ··· ··· ··· ··· ···
··· ··· ··· ··· ··· ··· ···
hence, sometimes the main idea is in the middle or at the end of the paragraph.

Some paragraphs merely repeat ideas ··· ··· ··· ··· ··· ···
··· ··· ··· ··· ··· ··· ···
··· ··· ··· ··· ··· ··· ···

Occasionally the main idea can't be found in the opening sentence. The whole paragraph must then be read.

Then leave out a lot of the next paragraph ··· ··· ··· ··· ···
··· ··· ··· ··· ··· ···
··· ··· ··· ··· ··· ···
··· ··· to make up time
··· ··· ··· ··· ··· ···
··· ··· ··· ··· ··· ···

Remember to keep up a very fast rate
··· ··· ··· ··· ··· ···
··· ··· ··· ··· ··· ···
··· ··· ··· ··· 800 w.p.m.
··· ··· ··· ··· ··· ···
··· ··· ··· ··· ··· ···

Don't be afraid to leave out half or more of each paragraph ··· ··· ···
··· ··· ··· ··· ··· ···
··· ··· ··· ··· ··· ···

Don't get interested and start to read everything ··· ··· ··· ··· ···
··· ··· ··· ··· ··· ···
··· ··· ··· ··· ··· ···
skimming is work ··· ··· ··· ···
··· ··· ··· ··· ··· ···

Lowered comprehension is expected
··· ··· ··· ··· ··· ···
··· ··· 50% ··· ···
··· ··· ··· ··· not too low
··· ··· ··· ··· ··· ···
··· ··· ··· ··· ··· ···

Skimming practice makes it easier
··· ··· ··· ··· ··· ··· ···
··· ··· ··· ··· ··· ··· ···
··· ··· ··· ··· ··· ··· ···
··· ··· gain confidence ··· ···
··· ··· ··· ··· ··· ··· ···
··· ··· ··· ··· ··· ··· ···
··· ··· ··· ··· ··· ··· ···

Perhaps you won't get anything at all from a few paragraphs ··· ··· ···
··· ··· ··· ··· ··· ··· ···
··· ··· ··· ··· dont' worry
··· ··· ··· ··· ··· ··· ···
··· ··· ··· ··· ···

Skimming has many uses ··· ···
··· ··· ··· ··· ··· ··· ···
··· ··· ··· reports
··· ··· newspapers ··· ···
··· ··· ··· ··· supplementary
··· ··· text ··· ··· ···

The ending paragraphs might be read more fully as often they contain a summary.

Remember that the importance of skimming is to get only the author's main ideas at a very fast speed.

The Reading Teacher's Book of Lists, Third Edition, © 1993 by Prentice Hall

See also list 58, Comprehension Skills; and List 63, Study Skills List.

68. *Working in Teams*

A person can do and understand many things, but no one person has enough knowledge and skill to understand and do everything. Working in teams will help you learn more and solve complex problems in school and out. Before starting to work, decide who will have each of the jobs described below. Change jobs every time you start a new team project so that everyone has an opportunity to try each job.

Team Manager

- Describes the task or problem to the team, including what product or result is required;
- Explains the outcome that the teacher will use to judge whether the team is successful and keeps track of the team's progress toward the goal;
- Monitors the team's work to be sure it stays on target;

Organizer

- Schedules meetings, if they are not during class;
- Gets materials the group will need;
- Returns materials after use;
- Organizes and is responsible for clean-up;
- Arranges for computer time, AV equipment, etc.;

Researcher

- Checks facts, computations, and other information;
- Locates library and other reference materials;
- Skims background materials and makes brief summary presentations to the team;
- Keeps log of sources and bibliographic information;

Member

- Suggests ideas in brainstorming and problem solving;
- Shares knowledge and skills related to the task;
- Criticizes ideas, not people;
- Stays on task;
- Does a fair share of the work;

Charter

- Creates flowcharts, diagrams, timelines, and other visual presentations of the problem and the solution;

Scribe

- Writes down brainstorming ideas, checking that the written statements match the team members' ideas;
- Records steps in the team's process or activities;
- Records the team's discoveries and answers;
- Drafts the report of the team's work;

Editor

- Checks the draft report for accuracy and completeness;
- Does final report and gives copies to team members and the teacher;

Presenter

- Gives an oral presentation of the team's work;
- Prepares video and/or audiotape presentation, if used.

See also List 69, Teamwork Rules; and List 72, Group Project Guide.

The Reading Teacher's Book of Lists, Third Edition, © 1993 by Prentice Hall

69. *Teamwork Rules*

Teamwork means working together to achieve a shared goal. These rules will help your teamwork work:

- Respect all teammates.
- Disagree without being disagreeable.
- Take turns speaking; don't interrupt.
- Be on time and prepared for meetings.
- Offer to share your special skills, for example, artistic talent, computer skills, typing.
- Share ideas; if you find or know something that will help a teammate, pass it on.
- Speak loudly enough to be heard by your group, but not so loudly that you disturb other teams.
- Don't give up or go off on your own project.
- Ask for help if you are stuck or forgot something.
- Don't decide by voting; figure out the right answer.

See also List 68, Working in Teams; and List 70, Problem–Solving Guide.

70. Problem-Solving Guide

Use this three-step guide to solve problems when working alone or in problem-solving teams.

1. Understand the problem by:
   - Stating the problem in your own words.
   - Visualizing the problem.
   - Acting out the problem.
   - Drawing a diagram, flowchart, or picture of the problem.
   - Making a table, Venn diagram, or graph of the problem.
   - Looking for patterns in the problem.
   - Comparing it to another problem you have solved.
   - Listing everything you know about it.
   - Thinking about its parts, one at a time.

2. Propose and try solutions:
   - Using logical reasoning.
   - Brainstorming alternatives.
   - Writing an equation.
   - Choosing an operation and working it through.
   - Estimating and checking the results.
   - Working backward from the product or result.
   - Linking a solution to each part of the problem.
   - Solving problems within the problem.
   - Evaluating and sorting the information you have.
   - Organizing the information in a grid or matrix.
   - Eliminating solutions that don't work.
   - Solving a simpler version of the problem first.

3. Check the results by:
   - Filling in an information matrix.
   - Redoing the computation with a calculator.
   - Creating a flowchart or visual of the answer.
   - Dramatizing the result.
   - Comparing the results with the estimates made earlier.
   - Using the results on a trial basis.
   - Monitoring the effects of the results over time.
   - Checking the answer with a reference source.
   - Having another team or the teacher critique the result.

The Reading Teacher's Book of Lists, Third Edition, © 1993 by Prentice Hall

71. *Student Project Guide*

Name: _____ Today's Date: _____

Project: _____ Date due: _____

My topic: _____

Related topics & words: _____

_____

_____

Information sources I can use:

____ almanac	____ microscopic slides
____ art	____ museum exhibits
____ biographical dictionary	____ newspapers
____ biographies	____ nonfiction books
____ dictionary	____ photographs
____ encyclopedia	____ posters
____ filmstrips	____ records, CDs or tapes
____ gazateer/atlas	____ slides
____ history books	____ special reference books
____ interviews	____ television programs
____ magazines	____ thesaurus
____ maps	____ videos, video disks

Some ways I will organize my information:

TEXT	**GRAPHIC**
____ order of events	____ timeline
____ sequence	____ flow chart
____ category/subcategories	____ tables
____ comparison/contrast	____ graphs
____ cause & effect	____ cause/effect diagram
____ questions and answers	____ story map/word webs
____ logical order	
____ outline	

My project presentation will include:

____ audiotape w/poster	____ photocollage
____ demonstration	____ picture essay
____ diorama	____ press release
____ exhibit	____ speech
____ library display	____ travel brochure
____ model	____ video
____ pantomime	____ play
____ photo essay	____ poetry

Project schedule and checklist: **DATE**

____ I have planned my project.   _____

____ I have discussed my project with my teacher and we agree.   _____

____ I have located the information/materials I need.   _____

____ I have reviewed the information, and I have selected the best   _____
sources.

____ I have enough information to complete the project I planned.   _____

____ I have read and organized my information in notes and other   _____
ways as planned.

____ I have made a first draft of my report or other presentation   _____
materials.

____ I have edited the first draft.   _____

____ I have completed the project.   _____

See also List 70, Problem–Solving Guide.

The Reading Teacher's Book of Lists, Third Edition, © 1993 by Prentice Hall

72. Group Project Guide

Names: _____

Project title: _____

Related topics & words: _____

_____

_____

Information sources we can use:

_____ almanac	_____ microscopic slides
_____ art	_____ museum exhibits
_____ biographical dictionary	_____ newspapers
_____ biographies	_____ nonfiction books
_____ dictionary	_____ photographs
_____ encyclopedia	_____ posters
_____ filmstrips	_____ records, CDs or tapes
_____ gazateer/atlas	_____ slides
_____ history books	_____ special reference books
_____ interviews	_____ television programs
_____ magazines	_____ thesaurus
_____ maps	_____ videos, video disks

Some ways we will organize our information:

TEXT	**GRAPHIC**
_____ order of events	_____ timeline
_____ sequence	_____ flow chart
_____ category/subcategories	_____ tables
_____ comparison/contrast	_____ graphs
_____ cause & effect	_____ cause/effect diagram
_____ questions and answers	_____ story map/word webs
_____ logical order	
_____ outline	

The Reading Teacher's Book of Lists, Third Edition, © 1993 by Prentice Hall

Our project presentation will include:

____	audiotape w/poster	____	photocollage
____	demonstration	____	picture essay
____	diorama	____	press release
____	exhibit	____	speech
____	library display	____	travel brochure
____	model	____	video
____	pantomime	____	play
____	photo essay	____	poetry

Project schedule and checklist:

PROJECT DUE:	**DATE**
____ We have planned our project.	_____
____ We have discussed the project with our teacher and it is approved.	_____
____ We have decided how to divide the work.	_____
____ We have located the information/materials we need.	_____
____ We have reviewed the information, and we have selected the best sources.	_____
____ We have enough information to complete the project we planned.	_____
____ We have read and organized the information in notes and other ways as planned.	_____
____ We have written the first draft of the report and other presentation materials.	_____
____ We have discussed and edited the first draft.	_____
____ We have made all necessary revisions.	_____
____ We have reviewed the completed project.	_____

See also List 68, Working in Teams.

The Reading Teacher's Book of Lists, Third Edition, © 1993 by Prentice Hall

73. *Alternative Assessment Techniques*

Standardized tests, criterion-referenced tests, diagnostic tests, cloze exercises, unit tests, worksheets—these are some of the assessment tools frequently used in evaluating reading proficiency. Four alternative assessment techniques that build on classroom activities to provide insight to student learning follow:

1. Retellings

After students read a story or have one read to them, ask them to retell it as if they were telling it to a friend who never heard it before. It is important to let students know in advance that they will be asked to do this. To analyze the retelling quantitatively, use a checklist of important elements in the story (setting, plot, resolution, etc.) and assign a score for each. Qualitative evaluation focuses on students' deeper understanding of the story and ability to generalize and interpret its meaning. This type of evaluation can be noted in the form of comments at the bottom of the checklist. Retellings can be done individually or in groups. Teacher prompts may be required to help lead some students through the story.

2. Portfolios

Portfolios are systematic collections of student work over time. These collections help students and teachers assess student growth and development. It is essential that students develop a sense of ownership about their portfolios so they can understand where they have made progress and where more work is needed.

Portfolio Content. The content of portfolios will vary with the level of the student and will depend on the types of assignments they are given in class. In addition to completed reports, poems, letters, and so forth, portfolios often contain first and second drafts. Reading logs and audiotape recordings can also be included. As portfolios are assembled, it is important that students keep them in a place where they have easy access to them. Students should be encouraged to browse through their portfolios and share them with classmates.

Criteria for Selecting Items for Portfolios. Although almost all work may initially be included, portfolios can quickly become unmanageable if they are too large. Portfolios that will form the basis for assessment can be assembled at the end of each term and at the end of the school year. A specific number of items for inclusion (often five or six) and criteria for selecting them should be agreed to by the teacher and students. Some examples of criteria are: stories/reports that were favorites; papers that represent best work; work that shows progress; assignments that were the most difficult. In making selections, students should be encouraged to consult with classmates.

Evaluation of Portfolios. Portfolio evaluation often occurs at three levels: the student, the student's peers, and the teacher. For each piece selected, students may be asked to describe briefly why they chose it, what they learned, and what their future goals are. Students can also be asked to prepare an overall evaluation of their portfolio.

The Reading Teacher's Book of Lists, Third Edition, © 1993 by Prentice Hall

Classmates are frequently enlisted in portfolio evaluation. Their evaluation can focus on what they see as the special strengths of the portfolio, their personal response to some item in the portfolio, and a suggestion of one thing their classmate could work on next.

Portfolio evaluation by the teacher should build on that of the student and peers. Although the teacher evaluation may result in a grade, it is important that an opportunity be found for discussion with the student. This discussion should culminate in agreement on future goals.

Although not a part of the formal evaluation process, it is helpful, particularly for elementary-school children, for parents to review the portfolios. Portfolios can be sent home or they can be reviewed at the time of parent-teacher conferences. It is essential that teachers take steps to help parents understand that their role should be to provide encouragement and that they should focus on the positive and not be critical.

3. Reading Logs

Have students keep a log of all their independent reading at school and at home. The log should include works completed and works started but not completed. In addition to the name of the book (article, etc.) and author, the log should include personal reactions to the selection. Periodic discussions of these logs will provide insight on how the student is developing as an independent reader and suggest ways in which the teacher can give added encouragement. These logs can be placed in students' portfolios.

4. Checklists

Checklists can be completed by both teachers and students. For example, a checklist can be used by a teacher to assess word and letter knowledge. The first step is to develop a list of the concepts to be tested. The student is then asked to demonstrate understanding of these concepts using a real book. The teacher uses the checklist to identify those concepts that have been mastered and those that need further work.

Students can use checklists to review their own work. Teachers and students can prepare a list of specific skills that need to be worked on (for example, a capital letter at the beginning of each sentence), and students can then use this list to check their own work.

The Reading Teacher's Book of Lists, Third Edition, © 1993 by Prentice Hall

74. *Test-Taking Strategies*

Teaching these strategies should help make your students "test wise" and improve their performance on essay and objective tests. Although a few students may use these strategies on their own, most will need instruction and encouragement.

General

- If you have a choice of seats, try to sit in a place where you will be least disturbed (e.g., not by a door).
- When you first receive the test, glance over it, noting the types of questions and the numbers of points to be awarded for them.
- Budget your time, making sure you allow sufficient time for the questions that are worth the most points.
- Read directions carefully. Underline important direction words, such as *choose one, briefly*, and so on.
- Start with the questions that are easiest.
- Be alert for information in some questions that may provide help with other more difficult questions. If you find such information, be sure to note it before you forget.

Objective Tests

- Before you start, find out if there is a penalty for guessing and if you can choose more than one answer.
- Read the questions and all possible answers carefully.
- Be especially careful about questions with the choices *all of the above* and *none of the above*.
- Underline key words and qualifiers such as *never, always*, and so on.
- Answer all of the questions you know first.
- Make a mark next to those you can't answer so you can go back to them later.
- After you complete the questions you know, go back and reread the ones you didn't answer the first time.
- If you still can't answer a question the second time through, here are some strategies to try:

    1. For a multiple-choice item, read the question; then stop and try to think of an answer. Look to see if one of the choices is similar to your answer.
    2. Start by eliminating those answers that you know are not correct and then choose among the remaining alternatives.
    3. Read through all the answers very carefully and then go back to the question. Sometimes you can pick up clues just by thinking about the different answers you have been given to choose from.
    4. Try paraphrasing the question and then recalling some examples.

5. For a multiple-choice item, try reading the question separately with each alternative answer.

- If there is no penalty for guessing, make sure you answer all questions, even if you have to guess blindly.
- If there is a penalty for guessing, you usually should guess if you can eliminate one of the choices.
- If you have time, check over the exam. Change an answer only if you can think of a good reason to do so. Generally, you're better off if you stick with your first choice.

Essay Tests

- Read through all the questions carefully.
- Mark the important direction words that tell you what you're to do: *compare, trace, list*, and so on.
- Number the parts of the question so you don't forget to answer all of them.
- Take time to try to understand what the question is asking. Don't jump to conclusions on the basis of a familiar word or two.
- As you read through the questions, briefly jot down ideas that come into your mind.
- Briefly outline your answers before you begin to write. Refer back to the question to be sure your answer is focused on the question.
- As you write, be careful to stick to your outline.
- If possible, allow generous margins so you can add information later if you need to.
- Don't spend so much time on one question that you don't have time for other questions.
- If you have time, proofread what you have written. This is a good time to double-check to make sure you have answered all the parts of the questions.
- If you run short of time, quickly outline answers to the questions that remain. List the information without worrying about complete sentences.

Quantitative Tests

- Read the questions carefully to make sure you understand what is being asked.
- Do the questions you are sure of first.
- Budget your time to allow for questions worth the most points.
- Don't just write answers. Make sure to show your work.
- As you work out answers, try to do it neatly and to write down each step. This helps you avoid careless mistakes and makes it possible for the tester to follow your work. It may make the difference between partial credit and no credit for a wrong answer.

The Reading Teacher's Book of Lists, Third Edition, © 1993 by Prentice Hall

- Check your answer when you finish to make sure it makes sense. If it doesn't seem logical, check again.
- If you are missing information needed to calculate an answer, check to see if it was given in a previous problem or if you can compute it in some way.
- Check to see if you have used all the information provided. You may not always need to, but you should double-check to be sure.
- If you have time, go back and check your calculations.

See also List 54, Signal Words; List 56, Comprehension Questions; List 64, Time-Planning Chart; List 65, Memory Aids; List 66, Mnemonic Device; List 76, Essay Test Words; List 77, Important Modifiers; and List 78, Cloze Variations.

75. Test and Workbook Words

These words are found in directions in workbook exercises and in tests. It is absolutely essential that students understand and pay close attention to them. These key words are perhaps most effectively taught in context. Each time you give students a test or a written exercise, point them out and review their meaning.

answer sheet	definition	name	reason
best	directions	next	rhyming
blank	does not belong	none of these	right
booklet	end	not true	row
check your work	error	opposite	same as
choose	example	pairs	sample
circle	finish	paragraph	section
column	following	passage	second
compare	go on to next page	print	stop
complete	item	probably	true
contrast	mark	put an X	underline
correct	match	question	wait for directions
crossout	missing	read	

76. Essay Test Words

These words occur in essay test questions. In order for students to perform well on essay tests, they must understand the types of answers that these words require. When you give essay tests, try to use a variety of these words and take the opportunity to instruct the students on their meaning.

analyze	develop	interpret	relate
apply	diagram	justify	relationship
argue	differentiate	list	select
assess	discuss	mention	show how
categorize	distinguish	organize	significance
cause	draw conclusions	outline	solve
cite evidence	effect	paraphrase	specify
classify	enumerate	point out	state
compare	estimate	predict	suggest
construct	evaluate	propose	summarize
contrast	explain	prove	support
convince	formulate	provide	survey
create	general	rank	tell
criticize	generalize	react	trace
define	give an example of	reason	utilize
demonstrate	identify	recall	why
describe	illustrate	recommend	

The Reading Teacher's Book of Lists, Third Edition, © 1993 by Prentice Hall

77. *Important Modifiers*

These are easy words, but ones sometimes skipped over by careless readers. Failure to pay attention to these modifiers can result in a wrong answer, even though the student actually knows the right answer. One way to help avoid this is to teach your students to underline these words as they take tests.

all	good	none
always	invariably	often
bad	less	seldom
best	many	some
every	more	sometimes
equal	most	usually
few	never	worst

See also List 54, Signal Words.

78. Cloze Variations

Cloze is a sentence-completion technique in which a word (or part of a word or several words) is omitted and the student fills in the missing part. Cloze can be used as a test or drill of reading comprehension or language ability, as a research tool, or as a measure to estimate readability or passage difficulty.

To estimate the readability or difficulty level appropriate for instruction, one suggested criterion is that a student be able to fill in 35 to 44 percent of the exact missing words when every fifth word is deleted from a 250-word passage.

Cloze passages can be made easily by the teacher on any subject or any type of material. All you need to do is omit parts of the passage and ask the students to fill in the missing parts. Here is a list of some possible variations:

1. **Passage Variations** (different kinds of passage to start with)
   a. Content of Passage
      (1) Science
      (2) History
      (3) Literature, etc.
   b. Difficulty of Passage
      (1) Readability level
      (2) Imageability
      (3) Legibility
   c. Length of Passage
      (1) Sentence
      (2) Paragraph
      (3) 500 words, etc.

2. **Deletion Variations** (different kinds of deletions or blanks)
   a. Mechanical—automatic or no judgment used in deletions
      (1) Delete every nth word (5th, 10th, etc.).
      (2) Randomized deletion but average every nth word.
   b. Selective—judgment used in selecting deletions.
      (1) Delete structure words or content words only.
      (2) Delete only one part of speech. (For example, nouns omitted.)
      (3) Delete particular letters (blends, bound morphemes, prefixes, vowels, consonants, etc.).
      (4) Delete only words or letters that best fit a particular skill objective.
   c. Size of Deletion
      (1) One word, two words, etc.
      (2) One letter, two letters, etc.

3. **Cueing Variation**—different prompts or hints
   a. No cues.
   b. Multiple choice (sometimes referred to as "Maze"). If this is used, distractor words (wrong choices) can be varied as follows:
      (1) Similar to correct answer in length or different.
      (2) Similar or different in phonemes.
      (3) Similar or different in meaning.
   c. One or more letters, depending on how many letters have been deleted.

The Reading Teacher's Book of Lists, Third Edition, © 1993 by Prentice Hall

4. Administration Variations

   a. Preparation

      (1) Student reads complete passage (no blanks) before answering.

      (2) Student listens to complete passage before answering.

      (3) Student is given a brief introduction to passage.

      (4) No preparation.

   b. Answering

      (1) Student reads passage and writes answers.

      (2) Teacher reads passage orally and student writes answers.

      (3) Teacher reads passage orally and student gives answers orally.

      (4) Student told to guess or not to guess.

5. Scoring Variations

   a. Score as correct only exact word, or score synonym as correct.

   b. Correct spelling required or not required.

   c. Self-correction, teacher correction, other-student correction.

   d. Discuss answers or no discussion.

6. Uses of Cloze.

   a. *Test student's ability.* All students take the same cloze passage; students are ranked by number correct. Cloze scores can be assigned norms or grade levels.

   b. *Measure readability of a passage.* A group of students takes two different cloze passages. The passage with the highest mean score is most readable. Some research indicates that a cloze score of 35 to 45 percent correct on a fifth-word random deletion indicates Independent Reading Level for that student (or group).

   c. *Research.* Cloze is used in many types of language research. For example, ESL ability, knowledge of pronoun use, generating wrong answers for Maze, spelling, memory.

   d. *Teaching.* Cloze passages are used for reading comprehension drills, subject content knowledge, language use, discussion starters, and much more.

See also List 56, Comprehension Questions; and List 84, Basic Sentence Patterns.

SECTION VIII
Writing

79. Story Starters

Writer's block happens to even the best writers. If some students are sluggish starters, these may help.

1. "This will show them," Kara thought as she hammered the last nail into place.
2. We watched in horror as Ben came running out of the boys' bathroom and bumped right into the two men carrying the . . .
3. It all started on Monday morning when several citizens of Tumbler City noticed that the sky didn't look quite right.
4. When she reached for the light switch, Christie thought she heard someone say, "Stop right where you are, or I'll eat all your potatoes!"
5. It seemed as if it was going to be the perfect day to spend at the beach. But not long after Ted and Josh put their surfboards in the water . . .
6. There weren't many foods that my brother Alex liked to eat, so we experimented. That's how we discovered the prize-winning recipe for chocolate-covered . . .
7. Maria hungrily opened her lunchbox and, next to the apple, found . . .
8. Gus had always wanted a puppy.
9. Every season has its good and bad points. The best thing about winter is . . .
10. All the way back to the bike shop, Carlos thought about what his uncle had told him.
11. My life changed the day I discovered . . .
12. The family decided they would move to the new place in March.
13. It was a very rainy day—too rainy to go outside to play. So Adam and Christopher decided to . . .
14. I remember it all started in the middle of the week—Wednesday. That morning, I didn't feel quite well enough to go to school.
15. The steel-and-glass building looked enormous next to the little brick houses that lined the street.
16. "Get this thing away from me!" the queen shrieked.
17. The airplane landed gently, and Lee breathed a sigh of relief.
18. No one but Ayanna and I knows about the little door in the big oak tree by the pond in the park.
19. "What do you think it is?" the small purple woman asked her lavender friend as she nudged me awake with her boot.
20. Have you ever noticed that some days seem to last longer than others?
21. Anna hated her new school shoes. But she hated her . . . even more.
22. Alice gritted her teeth and began to climb to the top of . . .
23. If I didn't have my roller skates with me that day, I don't know what I would have done.
24. Our dog Tiki sometimes is too smart for her own good. Take last Sunday . . .

25. Max was lucky to get the summer job as a computer operator at the small company. It paid pretty well and he was saving up for . . .

26. Scott thought he knew Andy very well until he caught him . . .

27. It was so dark that Vicky couldn't tell the difference when she closed her eyes. "How did I ever get in a mess like this?" she thought.

28. The huge room, which had been bustling and noisy only an hour before, was silent.

29. Mark met us at the bus stop and announced that he was going to run for president.

30. Craig was excited as he boarded the plane to visit his mother in California.

31. Sometimes a cat can be a person's best friend.

32. Jenn couldn't wait for math class to be over.

33. There seemed to be no way out of the big old house. Every door opened into another room . . .

34. It's always frustrating to have to sit and wait for . . .

35. The field behind the school was Ethan's favorite place to go after school.

36. I looked around the room and noticed there was a new student in the class.

37. All of the girl's friends had very ordinary hobbies, except for . . .

38. I'd give anything in the world to see . . .

39. As she held the leaking pipe in place, Monica thought, "What is keeping Selene?"

40. I never thought it would be possible, but there I was . . .

41. Marty's mother's eyes opened wide as she exclaimed, "Where on earth did you get those . . .?"

42. Jesse couldn't pass up any opportunity to enter a contest.

43. Kathy began her routine slowly, aware that everyone was watching her every move.

44. A truck rattled down the empty street and pulled into the parking lot behind the sign that read, "Fred's Parts and Service . . . A Division of NetWork Human Industries."

45. There once was a very old, unmarried prince of moderate wealth who lived in a small castle at the edge of town.

46. By the time Darryl had walked halfway home from school, he realized that he had left his house key on the kitchen table that morning.

47. There is nothing better than the feeling you get when you . . .

48. They were at the supermarket, in the freezer section, when it happened.

49. Not long after I'd knocked, the narrow green door squeaked open to reveal . . .

50. It was the third day of the camping trip, and Jonathan knew that he would go crazy if he got one more mosquito bite.

Note Interest Inventory items, Lists 98 and 99, can also be used as story starters.

The Reading Teacher's Book of Lists, Third Edition, © 1993 by Prentice Hall

80. Descriptive Words

What do telling tales and writing poetry or reports have in common? They depend on descriptive words to create vivid and accurate images in the reader's mind. A good stock of descriptive words will bolster the quality of your students' writing exercises. Use these lists of adjectives and adverbs to nudge reluctant writers into developing characters and setting, or to help students "retire" overused words.

The Reading Teacher's Book of Lists, Third Edition, © 1993 by Prentice Hall

ABILITY—CONDITION

able	confident	gentle	lucky	smooth
adequate	courageous	hardy	manly	spirited
alive	curious	healthy	mighty	stable
assured	daring	heavy	modern	steady
authoritative	determined	heroic	open	stouthearted
bold	durable	important	outstanding	strong
brainy	dynamic	influential	powerful	super
brave	eager	innocent	real	sure
busy	easy	intense	relaxed	tame
careful	effective	inquisitive	rich	tough
capable	energetic	jerky	robust	victorious
cautious	fearless	knotted	secure	virile
clever	firm	light	sharp	zealous
competent	forceful	lively	shy	
concerned	gallant	loose	skillful	

ANGER—HOSTILITY

agitated	combative	evil	irritated	rude
aggravated	contrary	fierce	mad	savage
aggressive	cool	furious	mean	severe
angry	cranky	hard	nasty	spiteful
annoyed	creepy	harsh	obnoxious	tense
arrogant	cross	hateful	obstinate	terse
belligerent	cruel	hostile	outraged	vicious
biting	defiant	impatient	perturbed	vindictive
blunt	disagreeable	inconsiderate	repulsive	violent
bullying	enraged	insensitive	resentful	wicked
callous	envious	intolerant	rough	wrathful

DEPRESSION—SADNESS—GLOOM

abandoned	depressed	forsaken	low	ruined
alien	desolate	gloomy	miserable	rundown
alienated	despairing	glum	mishandled	sad
alone	despised	grim	mistreated	scornful
awful	despondent	hated	moody	sore
battered	destroyed	homeless	mournful	stranded
blue	discarded	hopeless	obsolete	tearful
bored	discouraged	horrible	ostracized	terrible
burned	dismal	humiliated	overlooked	tired
cheapened	downcast	hurt	pathetic	unhappy

DEPRESSION—SADNESS—GLOOM

crushed	downhearted	jilted	pitiful	unloved
debased	downtrodden	kaput	rebuked	whipped
defeated	dreadful	loathed	regretful	worthless
degraded	estranged	lonely	rejected	wrecked
dejected	excluded	lonesome	reprimanded	
demolished	forlorn	lousy	rotten	

DISTRESS

afflicted	displeased	hindered	puzzled	tormented
anguished	dissatisfied	impaired	ridiculous	touchy
awkward	distrustful	impatient	sickened	troubled
baffled	disturbed	imprisoned	silly	ungainly
bewildered	doubtful	lost	skeptical	unlucky
clumsy	foolish	nauseated	speechless	unpopular
confused	futile	offended	strained	unsatisfied
constrained	grief	pained	suspicious	unsure
disgusted	helpless	perplexed	swamped	weary
disliked				

FEAR—ANXIETY

afraid	dreading	insecure	overwhelmed	tense
agitated	eerie	intimidated	panicky	terrified
alarmed	embarrassed	jealous	restless	timid
anxious	fearful	jittery	scared	uncomfortable
apprehensive	frantic	jumpy	shaky	uneasy
bashful	frightened	nervous	shy	upset
dangerous	hesitant	on edge	strained	worrying
desperate	horrified			

INABILITY—INADEQUACY

anemic	disabled	incapable	powerless	unable
ashamed	exhausted	incompetent	puny	uncertain
broken	exposed	ineffective	shaken	unfit
catatonic	fragile	inept	shaky	unimportant
cowardly	frail	inferior	shivering	unqualified
crippled	harmless	insecure	sickly	unsound
defeated	helpless	meek	small	useless
defective	impotent	mummified	strengthless	vulnerable
deficient	inadequate	naughty	trivial	weak
demoralized				

The Reading Teacher's Book of Lists, Third Edition, © 1993 by Prentice Hall

JOY—ELATION

amused	enchanted	glorious	joyful	smiling
blissful	enthusiastic	good	jubilant	splendid
brilliant	exalted	grand	magnificent	superb
calm	excellent	gratified	majestic	terrific
cheerful	excited	great	marvelous	thrilled
comical	exuberant	happy	overjoyed	tremendous
contented	fantastic	hilarious	pleasant	triumphant
delighted	fit	humorous	pleased	vivacious
ecstatic	funny	inspired	proud	witty
elated	gay	jolly	relieved	wonderful
elevated	glad	jovial	satisfied	

LOVE—AFFECTION—CONCERN

admired	conscientious	giving	mellow	reliable
adorable	considerate	good	mild	respectful
affectionate	cooperative	helpful	moral	sensitive
agreeable	cordial	honest	neighborly	sweet
altruistic	courteous	honorable	nice	sympathetic
amiable	dedicated	hospitable	obliging	tender
benevolent	devoted	humane	open	thoughtful
benign	empathetic	interested	optimistic	tolerant
brotherly	fair	just	patient	trustworthy
caring	faithful	kind	peaceful	truthful
charming	forgiving	kindly	pleasant	understanding
charitable	friendly	lenient	polite	unselfish
comforting	generous	lovable	reasonable	warm
congenial	genuine	loving	receptive	worthy

QUANTITY

ample	few	lots	paucity	scarcity
abundant	heavy	many	plentiful	skimpy
chock-full	lavish	meager	plenty	sparing
copious	liberal	much	profuse	sparse
dearth	light	numerous	scads	sufficient
empty	loads	oodles	scant	well-stocked

SIGHT—APPEARANCE

adorable	crinkled	foggy	motionless	skinny
alert	crooked	fuzzy	muddy	smoggy
beautiful	crowded	glamorous	murky	sparkling
blinding	crystalline	gleaming	nappy	spotless
bright	curved	glistening	narrow	square
brilliant	cute	glowing	obtuse	steep
broad	dark	graceful	round	stormy
blonde	deep	grotesque	rotund	straight
bloody	dim	hazy	pale	strange
blushing	distinct	high	poised	ugly
chubby	dull	hollow	quaint	unsightly
clean	elegant	homely	shadowy	unusual
clear	fancy	light	shady	weird
cloudy	filthy	lithe	sheer	wide
colorful	flat	low	shiny	wizened
contoured	fluffy	misty	shallow	

SIZE

ample	elfin	immense	miniature	stupendous
average	enormous	large	minute	tall
behemoth	fat	little	petite	tiny
big	giant	long	portly	towering
bulky	gigantic	mammoth	prodigious	vast
colossal	great	massive	puny	voluminous
diminutive	huge	microscopic	short	wee
dwarfed	hulking	middle-sized	small	

SMELL—TASTE

acrid	fragrant	putrid	sour	sweet
antiseptic	fresh	ripe	spicy	tangy
bitter	juicy	rotten	stale	tart
choking	medicinal	salty	sticky	tasty
clean	nutty	savory	strong	tasteless
delicious	peppery	smoky	stuffy	

SOUND

bang	groan	melodic	screech	thud
booming	growl	moan	shrill	thump
buzz	harsh	mute	silent	thunderous
clatter	high-pitched	noisy	snarl	tinkle
cooing	hiss	purring	snort	voiceless
crash	hoarse	quiet	soft	wail
crying	hushed	raspy	splash	whine
deafening	husky	resonant	squeak	whispered
faint	loud	screaming	squeal	

The Reading Teacher's Book of Lists, Third Edition, © 1993 by Prentice Hall

TIME

ancient	daylight	late	outdated	sunrise
annual	decade	lengthy	periodic	sunset
brief	dusk	long	punctual	swift
brisk	early	modern	quick	tardy
centuries	eons	moments	rapid	twilight
continual	evening	noon	short	whirlwind
crawling	fast	noonday	slowly	years
dawn	flash	old	speedy	yearly
daybreak	intermittent	old-fashioned	sporadic	young

TOUCH

boiling	dirty	grubby	shaggy	stinging
breezy	dry	hard	sharp	tender
bumpy	dusty	hot	silky	tight
chilly	filthy	icy	slick	uneven
cold	fluffy	loose	slimy	waxen
cool	flaky	melted	slippery	wet
creepy	fluttering	plastic	slushy	wooden
crisp	frosty	prickly	smooth	yielding
cuddly	fuzzy	rainy	soft	
curly	gooey	rough	solid	
damp	greasy	sandpapery	sticky	

See also List 25, Similes; List 26, Metaphors; List 27, Idiomatic Expressions; and List 28, Common Word Idioms.

81. *He Said/She Said*

Dialogue can bring a story to life, or it can put the reader to sleep. Here are lively alternatives to ho-hum "he said/she said" exchanges. Use these vocal verbs in place of "said" or use the vocal adverbs to describe just how "he said/she said." Working with dialogue is a simple but very effective way to improve your storytelling.

VOCAL VERBS

added
admitted
advised
agreed
announced
answered
argued
asked
asserted
began
bellowed
blurted
called
cautioned
claimed
commented
complained
conceded
concluded
confessed
continued
cried
demanded
exclaimed
explained
gasped
groaned
insisted
interrupted
joked
lied
mentioned
moaned
mumbled
muttered
noted
objected
observed
ordered
quipped
remarked

replied
reported
responded
said
screamed
shouted
snapped
sobbed
stated
swore
taunted
teased
told
vowed
warned
whined
whispered
yelled

VOCAL ADVERBS

adamantly
admiringly
adoringly
angrily
anxiously
arrogantly
bashfully
brazenly
casually
cautiously
cheerfully
clearly
cowardly
coyly
curiously
cynically
decisively
defensively
defiantly
dramatically
eerily
energetically

fiendishly
flatly
formally
gaily
gleefully
gloomily
happily
harshly
hysterically
jealously
joyfully
joyously
loudly
lovingly
meanly
meekly
mysteriously
nervously
off-handedly
offensively
pensively
proudly

questioningly
quickly
quizzically
rapidly
sadly
sarcastically
selfishly
serenely
seriously
sheepishly
shyly
sleepily
softly
sternly
stoically
stubbornly
sullenly
tauntingly
teasingly
tenderly
thankfully
thoughtfully
unexpectedly
unhappily
wisely

82. *Parts of Speech*

Over the centuries that English has been spoken and written, patterns of word usage have developed. These patterns form the grammar or syntax for the language and govern the use of the eight parts of speech.

Noun. A word names a person, place, thing, or idea. It can act or be acted upon. *Examples:*

Roger, Father McGovern, bowlers, cousins, neighborhood, Baltimore, attic, Asia, Newark Airport, Golden Gate Bridge, glove, class, triangle, goodness, strength, stupidity, joy, perfection.

Pronoun. A word that is used in place of a noun. *Examples:*

he, you, they, them, it, her, our, your, its, their, anybody, both, nobody, someone, several, himself, ourselves, themselves, yourself, itself, who, whom, which, what, whose.

Adjective. A word that is used to describe a noun or pronoun, telling what kind, how many, or which one. *Examples:*

green, enormous, slinky, original, Italian, some, few, eleven, all, none, that, this, these, those, third.

Verb. A word that shows physical or mental action, being, or state of being. *Examples:*

swayed, cowered, dance, study, hold, think, imagine, love, approve, considered, am, is, was, were, has been, seems, appears, looks, feels, remains.

Adverb. A word that is used to describe a verb, telling where, how, or when. *Examples:*

quietly, lovingly, skillfully, slyly, honestly, very, quite, extremely, too, moderately, seldom, never, often, periodically, forever.

Conjunction. A word that is used to join words or groups of words. *Examples:*

and, or, either, neither, but, because, while, however, since, for.

Preposition. A word used to show the relationship of a noun or pronoun to another word. *Examples:*

across, below, toward, within, over, above, before, until, of, beyond, from, during, after, at, against.

Interjection. A word that is used alone to express strong emotion. *Examples:*
Heavens! Cheers! Oh! Aha! Darn!

The Reading Teacher's Book of Lists, Third Edition, © 1993 by Prentice Hall

See also List 43, Suffixes; and List 83, Irregular Verb Forms.

83. *Irregular Verb Forms*

Most rules have exceptions, and exceptions can cause problems. Here is an extensive list of verbs and their principal parts that do not follow the regular pattern. (Regular verbs form the past or past participle by simply adding *d* or an *ed*. For example *call*, *called, has called*).

PRESENT	PAST	PAST PARTICIPLE*
am	was	been
are (pl.)	were	been
beat	beat	beaten
begin	began	begun
bend	bent or bended	bent or bended
bet	bet	bet
bite	bit	bitten
bleed	bled	bled
blow	blew	blown
break	broke	broken
bring	brought	brought
build	built	built
burst	burst	burst
catch	caught	caught
choose	chose	chosen
come	came	come
cost	cost	cost
creep	crept	crept
cut	cut	cut
dig	dug	dug
dive	dived or dove	dived
do	did	done
draw	drew	drawn
dream	dreamed or dreamt	dreamed or dreamt
drink	drank	drunk
drive	drove	driven
eat	ate	eaten
fall	fell	fallen
feed	fed	fed
feel	felt	felt
fight	fought	fought
fly	flew	flown
forbid	forbade	forbidden
forget	forgot	forgotten
forgive	forgave	forgiven
freeze	froze	frozen
get	got	got or gotten
give	gave	given

*Note: The past participle also needs one of the following verbs: was, has, had, or is.

The Reading Teacher's Book of Lists, Third Edition, © 1993 by Prentice Hall

The Reading Teacher's Book of Lists, Third Edition, © 1993 by Prentice Hall

PRESENT	PAST	PAST PARTICIPLE
go	went	gone
grow	grew	grown
grind	ground	ground
hang	hung or hanged	hung
has	had	had
hear	heard	heard
hide	hid	hidden
hold	held	held
hurt	hurt	hurt
is	was	has been
keep	kept	kept
kneel	kneeled or knelt	kneeled or knelt
know	knew	known
lay	laid	laid
leap	leaped or leapt	leaped or leapt
leave	left	left
lend	lent	lent
let	let	let
lie	lay	lain
light	lit	lit
lose	lost	lost
make	made	made
mean	meant	meant
mow	mowed	mowed or mown
put	put	put
read	read	read
ride	rode	ridden
ring	rang	rung
rise	rose	risen
run	ran	run
say	said	said
saw	sawed	sawed or sawn
see	saw	seen
sell	sold	sold
sew	sewed	sewed or sewn
set	set	set
shake	shook	shaken
shed	shed	shed
shine	shined or shone	shined or shone
shoot	shot	shot
show	showed	shown or showed
shrink	shrank or shrunk	shrunk
shut	shut	shut
sing	sang	sung
sink	sank	sunk
sit	sat	sat
sleep	slept	slept

PRESENT	PAST	PAST PARTICIPLE
slide	slid	slid
sow	sowed	sowed or sown
speak	spoke	spoken
spend	spent	spent
spin	spun	spun
split	split	split
spread	spread	spread
spring	sprang or sprung	sprung
stand	stood	stood
steal	stole	stolen
stick	stuck	stuck
sting	stung	stung
strike	struck	struck
string	strung	strung
spit	spit	spit
sweat	sweat or sweated	sweat or sweated
sweep	swept	swept
swear	swore	sworn
swim	swam or swum	swum
swing	swung or swang	swung
take	took	taken
teach	taught	taught
tear	tore	torn
tell	told	told
think	thought	thought
throw	threw	thrown
understand	understood	understood
wake	woke or waked	woken or waked
wear	wore	worn
weave	wove	woven
weep	wept	wept
wet	wet	wet
win	won	won
wind	wound	wound
write	wrote	written

The Reading Teacher's Book of Lists, Third Edition, © 1993 by Prentice Hall

See also List 43, Suffixes; and List 82, Parts of Speech.

84. *Basic Sentence Patterns*

Parts of speech are put together to form sentences. The list of basic sentence patterns and variations shows the most common arrangements of words. Remember that every sentence must have at minimum a noun (or pronoun) and a verb. This is sometimes called a subject and a predicate.

N/V	noun/verb	*Children sang.*
N/V/N	noun/verb/noun	*Bill paid the worker.*
N/V/ADV	noun/verb/adverb	*Ann sewed quickly.*
N/LV/N	noun/linking verb/noun	*Arthur is President.*
N/LV/ADJ	noun/linking verb/adjective	*Chris looks sleepy.*
N/V/N/N	noun/verb/noun/noun	*Chuck gave Marie flowers.*

VARIATIONS OF BASIC SENTENCE PATTERNS

Negative—*It is raining./It is not raining.*

Question—*The bottle is empty./Is the bottle empty?*

Use of there—*A man is at the door./There is a man at the door.*

Request—*You mow the grass./Mow the grass.*

Passive—*The dog chased the fox./The fox was chased by the dog.*

Possessive—*Robert owns this car./This is Robert's car.*

Prepositional phrase added—*This is Robert's car in the garage.*

Adverbial Phrase Added—*Birds fly quietly together.*

See also List 85, Punctuation Guidelines; and List 86, Capitalization Guidelines.

The Reading Teacher's Book of Lists, Third Edition, © 1993 by Prentice Hall

85. *Punctuation Guidelines*

Review these guidelines with your students regularly. Have students refer to them when proofreading their writing.

• PERIOD

   1. At end of sentence. *Example: Birds fly.*
   2. After some abbreviations. *Example: Mr., U.S.A.*

? QUESTION MARK

   1. At the end of question. *Example: Who is he?*
   2. To express doubt. *Example: He weighs 250 (?) pounds.*

' APOSTROPHE

   1. To form possessive. *Example: Bill's bike*
   2. Omitted letters. *Example: isn't*
   3. Plurals of symbols. *Example: 1960's, two A's*

( ) PARENTHESIS

   1. Supplementary material. *Example: The map (see illustration) is good.*
   2. Stronger than commas. *Example: Joe (the bad guy) is dead.*
   3. Enclose numbers. *Example: Her car is (1) a Ford, (2) too slow.*

: COLON

   1. Introduce a series. *Example: He has three things: money, brains, charm.*
   2. Separate subtitles. *Example: The Book: How To Read It.*
   3. Set off a clause. *Example: The rule is this: Keep it simple.*
   4. Business letter salutation. *Example: Dear Sir:*
   5. Times and ratios. *Example: 7:45 A.M., Mix it 3:1.*

; SEMICOLON

   1. Stronger than a comma. *Example: Peace is difficult; war is hell.*
   2. Separate clauses containing commas. *Example: He was tired; therefore, he quit.*

The Reading Teacher's Book of Lists, Third Edition, © 1993 by Prentice Hall

From *Spelling Book* by Edward Fry, Laguna Beach Educational Books.

99 **QUOTATION MARKS**

1. Direct quote. *Example: She said, "Hello."*
2. Titles. *Example: He read "Shane."*
3. Special words or slang. *Example: He is "nuts."*

9 **COMMA**

1. Independent clauses. *Example: I like him, and he is tall.*
2. Dependent clause that precedes a main clause. *Example: After the game, we went home.*
3. Semi-parenthetical clause. *Example: Bill, the tall one, is here.*
4. Series. *Example: He likes candy, ice cream, and diamonds.*
5. Multiple adjectives. *Example: The big, bad, ugly wolf.*
6. In dialogue. *Example: She said, "Hello."*
7. Dates. *Example: July 4, 1776*
8. Titles. *Example: Joe Smith, Ph.D.*
9. Informal letter salutation. *Example: Dear Mary,*
10. Letter closing. *Example: Yours truly,*
11. Inverted names. *Example: Smith, Joe*
12. Separate city and state. *Example: Los Angeles, California*

! **EXCLAMATION POINT**

1. Show strong emotion. *Example: She is the best!*

— **DASH**

1. Show duration. *Example: 1949–50, Rome–London*
2. Parenthetical material. *Example: The girl—the pretty one—is here.*
3. To show omissions. *Example: She called him a - - - .*

See also List 84, Basic Sentence Patterns; and List 86, Capitalization Guidelines.

86. *Capitalization Guidelines*

Review these guidelines with your students and provide practice exercises for problem areas. Give "proofreading" assignments to help students become sensitive to the proper use of upper case letters.

Capitalize the pronoun I.

I often sleep late on weekends.

Capitalize the first word of any sentence.

Kittens are playful.

Capitalize the first word and all important words in titles of books, magazines, newspapers, stories, etc.

The Lion, the Witch, and the Wardrobe.

Capitalize names of specific people, places, events, date, and documents.

Eunice Jones, Toronto, Fourth of July, Thanksgiving, September, the Constitution

Capitalize the names of organizations and trade names.

Ford Motor Company, Tide detergent

Capitalize titles of respect.

Mr. Cox, Ms. Blake, Judge Rand

Capitalize names of races, languages, religions, and deity.

Negro, German, Catholic, the Almighty, Jehovah

Capitalize the first word in a direct quotation.

Ann inquired, "Where is the suntan lotion?"

Capitalize abbreviations and acronyms, all or part.

U.S., UNESCO, CA, St., Mr.

The Reading Teacher's Book of Lists, Third Edition, © 1993 by Prentice Hall

See also List 84, Basic Sentence Patterns; and List 85, Punctuation Guidelines.

87. *Syllabication Rules*

The teaching of syllabication rules is somewhat controversial. Some say you should, and some say it is not worth the effort. Syllables sometimes are part of phonics lessons because syllabication affects vowel sounds (for example, an open vowel rule), and sometimes they are part of spelling or English lessons. There is no close agreement on various lists of syllabication rules, and some of the rules have plenty of exceptions. We are not urging you to teach them, but neither are we urging you to refrain from doing so.

SYLLABICATION RULES*

Rule 1. VCV†	A consonant between two vowels tends to go with the second vowel unless the first vowel is accented and short. Example: *bro'-ken, wag'-on,* **e-vent'**
Rule 2. VCCV	Divide two consonants between vowels unless they are a blend or digraph. (See List 46.) Example: *pic-ture, ush-er*
Rule 3. VCCCV	When there are three consonants between two vowels, divide between the blend or the digraph and the other consonant. Example: *an-gler*
Rule 4. Affixes	Prefixes always form separate syllables (*un-hap-py*), and suffixes form separate syllables if they contain a vowel and in the following cases: a. The suffix -*y* tends to pick up the preceding consonant to form a separate syllable. Example: *fligh-ty* b. The suffix -*ed* tends to form a separate syllable only when it follows a root that ends in *d* or *t*. Example: *plant-ed* (not in stopped) c. The suffix -*s* never forms a syllable except sometimes when it follows an *e*. Example: *at-oms, cours-es*
Rule 5. Compounds	Always divide compound words. Example: *black-bird*

*Source: P. Costigan, *A Validation of the Fry Syllabification Generalization*. Unpublished master's thesis. Rutgers University, New Brunswick, NJ, 1977. Available from ERIC.

†V = vowel: C = consonant.

NOTE: These rules tend to give phonetic (sound) division of syllables that is in harmony with phonics instruction. Dictionaries tend to favor morphemic (meaning) division for main entries. Often, this does not conflict with the phonetic (pronunciation) division but sometimes it does, for example, "skat-er" morphemic versus "ska-ter" phonetic. The "er" is a morphemic (meaning) unit meaning "one who."

Rule 6. Final *le* Final *le* picks up the preceding consonant to form a syllable.
Example: *ta-ble*

Rule 7. Vowel Clusters Do not split common vowel clusters, such as:
a. *R*-controlled vowels *(ar, er, ir, or,* and *ur).*
Example: *ar-ti-cle*
b. Long vowel digraphs *(ea, ee, ai, oa,* and *ow).*
Example: *fea-ture*
c. Broad *o* clusters *(au, aw,* and *al).*
Example: *au-di-ence*
d. Diphthongs *(oi, oy, ou,* and *ow).*
Example: *thou-sand*
e. Double *o* like *oo.*
Example: *moon, look*

Rule 8. Vowel Problems Every syllable must have one and only one vowel sound.
a. The letter *e* at the end of a word is silent.
Example: *come*
b. The letter *y* at the end or in the middle of a word operates as a vowel.
Example: *ver-y, cy-cle*
c. Two vowels together with separate sounds form separate syllables.
Example: *po-li-o*

The Reading Teacher's Book of Lists, Third Edition, © 1993 by Prentice Hall

See also Lists 42, Prefixes; and List 43, Suffixes.

88. Build-a-Sentence

Select one from each column

Who? (subject)	What? (verb)	Why? (prepositional phrase)	When? (adverb)	Where? (object)
A boy	climbed into an airplane	for a vacation	last summer	in New York
The shark	looked everywhere	to find his mother	in 2020	on the moon
A big dump truck	slid		during the game	outside my house
The monster	laughed	to get a million dollars	next year	in a cave
	swam			on a farm
My dad	dove	for fun	today	under a rock
A rattlesnake	swung on a rope	because he was on fire	at midnight	next to a lion
Maria	fell	to fall in love	forever	100 feet beneath the ocean
Mickey Mouse	yelled loudly		before breakfast	in bed
A tiny ant	flew	for an ice cream cone	always	on top of a tree
			500 years ago	at the circus
The train	ran fast	to build a house	right now	in front of the city hall
Iron John	jumped	to fight the enemy	in a month	in a corn field
A beautiful princess	kicked		after school	behind the stove
	couldn't stop	to get to school	in an hour	in space
			yesterday	downtown
A large bird	slithered	to be kissed	during the war	inside an egg
My good friend	crawled			in Africa
	hopped on one foot	for a coat of paint	at dawn	out West
A teacher		because it was mad		on a tropical island

Feel free to add more words to make your sentence read better or add interest. You can leave out anything except a subject and a verb. Make your own Build-A-Sentence chart using a theme like a monster, earthquake or family theme.

89. *Proofreading Checklist—Elementary*

The Reading Teacher's Book of Lists, Third Edition, © 1993 by Prentice Hall

CHECK

It says what I wanted it to say. ☐

Every sentence is a complete thought. (Contains a subject and a verb.) ☐

No words are missing. ☐

Every sentence begins with a capital letter. ☐

Every sentence has an end mark. ☐

Every word is spelled correctly. ☐

I checked the verb forms I used. ☐

I checked the pronouns I used. ☐

I checked all punctuation marks. ☐

I indented the first line of every paragraph. ☐

My writing is neat and can be read. ☐

I used interesting words instead of the most common ones. ☐

If it is a letter, it has the correct format. ☐

If it is a story, it has an interesting title. ☐

90. *Proofreading Checklist—Intermediate*

CONTENT

Did I:

- [ ] Stick to my topic?
- [ ] Use good sources for information?
- [ ] Use enough sources for information?
- [ ] Organize my information carefully? (sequence, logical order, Q/A, main idea/supporting details, thesis statement/arguments, etc.)
- [ ] Check my facts?
- [ ] Consider/use graphs, tables, charts for data?
- [ ] Consider my readers and select words to catch their interest? to help them understand? to create images in their minds? to help them follow the sequence?
- [ ] Use sufficient detail and description?

FORMAT

Did I:

- [ ] Choose an appropriate title?
- [ ] Use quotations correctly?
- [ ] Use headings and subheadings?
- [ ] Label graphs, charts, and tables?
- [ ] Include a list of resources or bibliography?
- [ ] Number the pages?
- [ ] Include my name, class, and date?

MECHANICS

Did I:

- [ ] Check sentences for completeness and sense?
- [ ] Check for consistent verb tense?
- [ ] Check for consistent point of view?
- [ ] Check for subject-verb agreement?
- [ ] Check for proper use of pronouns?
- [ ] Check all spelling?
- [ ] Check for end marks and other punctuation?
- [ ] Check for capital letters and underlining?
- [ ] Check paragraph indentations?
- [ ] Check legibility?

91. *Proofreading Marks*

Helping students develop essays, short stories, term papers, or other writing goes more smoothly when you use proofreading symbols. Introduce these early in the school year and use them throughout. The time and space saved may be devoted to comments on content and encouragement.

Notation in Margin	How Indicated in Copy	Explanation
¶	true. The best rule to follow	New paragraph
⊂	living room	Close up
#	Mary hada	Insert space
⌐⌐	Mary had a lamb little	Transpose
sp	There were ⑤ children	Spell out
cap	mary had a little lamb.	Capitalize
lc	Mary had a little Lamb.	Lower case
Ꭷ	The correct procedure	Delete or take out
stet	Mary had a little lamb.	Restore crossed-out word(s) (leave stand as before corrected)
little	Mary had a lamb.	Insert word(s) in margin
⊙	Birds fly	Insert a period
⋀	Next the main	Insert a comma

See also Lists 89 and 90, Proofreading Checklists.

The Reading Teacher's Book of Lists, Third Edition, © 1993 by Prentice Hall

92. *Plurals*

Mastery of these rules will help students in any grade. The irregular spellings must be memorized. Try a fast-paced plural spelling bee for practice.

Rules for forming plurals:

1. The plural form of most nouns is made by adding -s to the end of the word.

chair	chairs	floor	floors
president	presidents	desk	desks
face	faces	drill	drills

2. If the word ends in -s, -sh, -ch, -x, or -z, the plural is formed by adding -es.

boss	bosses	dish	dishes
bench	benches	fox	foxes
waltz	waltzes	tax	taxes

3. If the word ends in a consonant followed by -y, the plural is formed by changing the -y to -i and adding -es.

city	cities	country	countries
variety	varieties	candy	candies
family	families	cherry	cherries

4. If the word ends in a vowel followed by -y, the plural is formed by adding -s.

valley	valleys	turkey	turkeys
key	keys	play	plays
journey	journeys	boy	boys

5. The plurals of most nouns ending with -f or -fe are formed by adding -s.

gulf	gulfs	belief	beliefs
cuff	cuffs	roof	roofs
cliff	cliffs	dwarf	dwarfs

6. Some words that end in -f or -fe are formed by changing the -f to -v and adding -es.

knife	knives	wife	wives
leaf	leaves	elf	elves
thief	thieves	life	lives
loaf	loaves	wolf	wolves
half	halves	self	selves
calf	calves		

7. If the word ends in a consonant followed by -o, form the plural by adding -es.

hero	heroes	potato	potatoes
tomato	tomatoes	echo	echoes
zero	zeroes	cargo	cargoes

8. If the word ends in a vowel followed by -o, form the plural by adding -s.

video	videos	radio	radios
studio	studios	patio	patios

9. To form the plural of a compound word, make the base noun, or second noun, plural.

brother-in-law	brothers-in-law	bucketseat	bucketseats
sandbox	sandboxes	passer-by	passers-by

10. Some words have irregular plural forms:

child	children	foot	feet
ox	oxen	mouse	mice
louse	lice	radius	radii
piano	pianos	Eskimo	Eskimos
sheep	sheep	tooth	teeth
trout	trout	deer	deer
salmon	salmon	woman	women
man	men	goose	geese
series	series	species	species
basis	bases	stimulus	stimuli
crisis	crises	medium	media
index	indices	criterion	criteria
solo	solos	auto	autos
axis	axes	focus	foci
oasis	oases	parenthesis	parentheses

11. Some words are used for both singular and plural meanings:

cod	deer	trout	sheep
moose	bass	corps	wheat
barley	mackerel	rye	series
traffic	dozen	fish	gross

See also List 43, Suffixes.

The Reading Teacher's Book of Lists, Third Edition, © 1993 by Prentice Hall

93. *Writeability Checklist*

The following is a list of suggestions for writing materials that are on an easy readability level. You can also use this as a readability checklist.

Vocabulary

☐ Avoid large and/or infrequent words. (submit-send)

☐ For high-frequency words use lists such as the Carroll, Davies, Richman word list or 3000 Instant Words. (See List 4, Instant Words.)

☐ For meaning lists, use *Living Word Vocabulary*.

☐ Avoid words with Latin and Greek prefixes. (See Lists 42 and 43, Prefixes.) (implement-carry out)

☐ Avoid jargon. (terms known in only one field)

☐ Okay to use technical words but make sure to define them and, if possible, give an example when you use them for the first time.

Sentences

☐ Keep sentences short on the average. For adults, keep average sentence below fifteen words.

☐ Avoid splitting sentence kernel (embedding).

☐ Keep verb active (avoid nominalizations).

☐ Watch out for too many commas. (See List 85, Punctuation Guidelines.)

☐ Semicolons and colons may indicate need for new sentence.

Paragraphs

☐ Keep paragraphs short on the average.

☐ One-sentence paragraphs are permissible at times.

☐ Indent and line up lists. (Keep lists out of paragraph)

Organization

☐ Suit organization plan to topic and your purpose.

☐ Try to use SER—Statement, Example, Restatement.

☐ Use subheads.

☐ Use signal words. (See List 54, Signal Words.)

☐ Use summaries.

☐ Watch cohesion and use signal words (See List 54.)

For further information see the chapter "Writeability: The principles of writing for increased comprehension" in *Readability, Its Past, Present, and Future*. Published by the International Reading Assn., Newark, DE.

Personal Words

- ☐ Use personal pronouns, but not too many. (*Example:* I and you)
- ☐ Use personal sentences. (*Example:* 1. Sentences directed at reader, "You should . . ." 2. Dialogue sentences, "Dick said, 'Hello.' ")

Imageability

- ☐ Use more concrete or high imagery words.
- ☐ Avoid abstract or low imagery words.
- ☐ Use vivid examples.
- ☐ Use metaphors and similes (See List 25, Similes; and List 26, Metaphors.)
- ☐ Use graphs whenever appropriate. (See List 149, Taxonomy of Graphs.)

Referents

- ☐ Avoid too many referents (*Example:* it, them, they) Replace some referents with nouns or verbs.
- ☐ Avoid too much distance between noun and referent.
- ☐ Don't use referent that could refer to two or more nouns or verbs.

Motivation

- ☐ Select interesting topics.
- ☐ Select interesting examples.
- ☐ Write at level that is a little below your audience. (See List 142, Readability Graph.)

The Reading Teacher's Book of Lists, Third Edition, © 1993 by Prentice Hall

94. *Spelling Demons—Elementary*

Those who study children's spelling errors and writing difficulties have repeatedly found that a relatively small number of words make up a large percentage of all spelling errors. Many commonly misspelled words are presented in this Spelling Demons list. Other lists in this book, such as Homophones, Instant Words, and Subject Matter Words, can also be used as spelling lists.

about	could	Halloween	off	shoes	tomorrow
address	couldn't	handkerchief	often	since	tonight
advise	country	haven't	once	skiing	too
again	cousin	having	outside	skis	toys
all right	cupboard	hear	party	some	train
along	dairy	heard	peace	something	traveling
already	dear	height	people	sometime	trouble
although	decorate	hello	piece	soon	truly
always	didn't	here	played	store	Tuesday
among	doctor	hospital	plays	straight	two
April	does	hour	please	studying	until
arithmetic	early	house	poison	sugar	used
aunt	Easter	instead	practice	summer	vacation
awhile	easy	knew	pretty	Sunday	very
balloon	enough	know	principal	suppose	wear
because	every	laid	quarter	sure	weather
been	everybody	latter	quit	surely	weigh
before	favorite	lessons	quite	surprise	were
birthday	February	letter	raise	surrounded	we're
blue	fierce	little	read	swimming	when
bought	first	loose	receive	teacher	where
built	football	loving	received	tear	which
busy	forty	making	remember	terrible	white
buy	fourth	many	right	Thanksgiving	whole
children	Friday	maybe	rough	their	women
chocolate	friend	minute	route	there	would
choose	fuel	morning	said	they	write
Christmas	getting	mother	Santa Claus	though	writing
close	goes	name	Saturday	thought	wrote
color	grade	neither	says	through	you
come	guard	nice	school	tired	your
coming	guess	none	schoolhouse	together	you're
cough	half	o'clock	several		

See also List 95, Spelling Demons—Secondary.

For all the words in a complete elementary spelling program, see *Spelling Book: Words Most Needed Plus Phonics for Grades 1–6* by Edward Fry, Laguna Beach Educational Books, 245 Grandview, Laguna Beach, CA 92651.

95. *Spelling Demons—Secondary*

Secondary students may misspell words on the elementary list of Demons, and since their writing is more advanced than the younger students they may also have trouble with these Demons. If you use these for spelling lessons, don't assign too many at once—pick and choose some you know they need.

absence	approach	category	descend
absolutely	approximately	ceiling	describe
acceptable	arctic	celebrate	description
accidentally	argue	cemetery	desert
accommodate	arguing	certainly	despair
accompany	argument	character	develop
accurate	around	chief	difference
accustom	arrangement	cite	different
ache	assistance	college	dilemma
achieve	athlete	comfortable	diligence
acknowledgment	attempt	coming	dining
acquaintance	attendance	committed	disagreeable
acquire	author	committee	disappear
across	awful	comparative	disappoint
actually	awkward	complete	disastrous
address	balloon	concede	discipline
adolescent	banquet	conceive	discover
advantageous	bargain	condemn	discussion
advertisement	beautiful	conquer	disease
advice	before	conscience	dissatisfied
again	beginning	conscientious	divided
against	belief	conscious	doubt
aisle	believe	consider	dropped
all right	beneficial	continually	drowned
almost	benefited	control	effect
although	bicycle	controversial	eighth
always	biggest	controversy	eleventh
amateur	boundary	council	eligible
ambition	breathe	courageous	embarrass
among	brilliant	courteous	emigrate
amusing	Britain	criticism	endeavor
analyze	built	criticize	enough
ancient	bulletin	crowd	environment
announces	buried	dangerous	equipment
annually	bury	deceive	equipped
answered	business	decided	especially
anticipated	busy	decision	eventually
anxious	cafeteria	defense	evidently
apology	calendar	definitely	exaggerate
apparent	captain	definition	exceed
appearance	career	democracy	excellent
appreciate	carrying	dependent	except

260

The Reading Teacher's Book of Lists, Third Edition, © 1993 by Prentice Hall

excitement	hurrying	muscle	prescription
exercise	hypocrite	mysterious	prestige
exhausted	ignorant	naturally	prevalent
exhibit	imaginary	necessary	principal
existence	immediately	neither	principle
expense	importance	niece	privilege
experience	impossible	nonsense	probably
explanation	incredible	noticeable	procedure
extraordinary	independent	numerous	proceed
extremely	Indian	obedience	profession
familiar	individual	occasion	professor
fascinate	innocent	occasionally	prominent
fascinating	intelligence	occur	pursue
favorite	interest	occurred	quantity
fierce	interrupt	occurrence	quiet
finally	irrelevant	occurring	realize
flies	its	often	really
foreign	jealousy	omitted	receipt
formerly	judgment	opinion	receive
fortunately	knife	opportunity	recognize
forty	knowledge	ordinary	recommend
forward	laboratory	paid	referred
fourth	led	parallel	referring
friend	leisure	paralyzed	relief
gaiety	library	particular	remember
gauge	license	performance	renowned
generally	lieutenant	perhaps	repetition
genuine	lightning	permanent	representative
government	likely	permitted	responsibility
grammar	listener	personal	responsible
grateful	literature	personnel	restaurant
grieve	lose	persuade	rhythm
guarantee	losing	physical	running
guard	luxury	picnicking	sacrifice
guessed	magnificent	planned	safety
guidance	making	pleasant	salary
guilty	maneuver	pledge	sandwich
handkerchief	marriage	politician	satisfactory
happened	mathematics	portrayed	saucer
having	meant	possess	scene
heard	medicine	possible	schedule
height	mere	practical	scheme
heroes	million	precede	science
hesitate	miniature	prefer	seize
hindrance	miscellaneous	preferred	sense
honorable	mischief	prejudice	sensible
hoping	mischievous	preparation	separate
humorous	moral	prepare	sergeant

serious	studying	thief	vacuum
shining	substantial	thorough	valuable
shriek	subtle	tired	vegetable
siege	succeed	together	vengeance
similar	success	toward	victim
sincerely	sufficient	tragedy	villain
skiing	suggestion	transferred	visible
soldier	summary	tremendous	waive
sophomore	supersede	tries	weigh
source	suppose	truly	weird
speak	surprise	twelfth	woman
special	susceptible	unnecessary	wrench
speech	swimming	until	write
stationary	system	unusual	writing
stopped	technique	using	written
straight	temperature	usually	yacht
strength	terrible	vacant	yield
stubborn	therefore		

The Reading Teacher's Book of Lists, Third Edition, © 1993 by Prentice Hall

See also List 94, Spelling Demons—Elementary; and List 96, National Spelling Bee List.

96. Spelling Demons—National Spelling Bee List

Every May, Scripps Howard sponsors the National Spelling Bee in Washington, DC. The 227 contestants in 1992 were sponsored by 221 newspapers from all over the nation, as well as Guam, Mexico, Puerto Rico, and the Virgin Islands. Spellers must be under 16 and not have progressed in school beyond the eighth grade.

For 54 finalists in the 1992 National Spelling Bee, a chance for the championship was lost by misspelling one of the following words. These are obviously the very hardest words. If you want a booklet, "Words of the Champions," of beginning, intermediate, and advanced words, you can write to Scripps Howard, National Spelling Bee, P.O. Box 5380, Cincinnati, Ohio 45202.

alpestrine	effaceable	knurl	obloquy	synod
anathema	emolument	lilliputian	opsimath	tendresse
beleaguer	epistrophe	linguipotence	ossuary	tralatitious
burgherly	exscind	lorgnette	paroxysm	trattoria
cabochon	famulus	loupe	pellagra	trousseau
cappuccino	gentian	lycanthrope	pylorus	usurpation
catechism	grogram	mademoiselle	requital	venireman
condign	habiliment	marquee	rescissory	vitiate
crinoline	immolate	nacelle	serigraph	wainwright
diptych	ingenue	nefarious	sinecure	zwieback
doughty	jodhpur	nonpareil	sorbefacient	

These 24 words were the last words given in each of the years from 1969 to 1992 at the Scripps Howard National Spelling Bee. They were all spelled correctly, thereby determining the national championship.

1969—interlocutory	1977—cambist	1985—milieu
1970—croissant	1978—deification	1986—odontalgia
1971—shalloon	1979—maculature	1987—staphylococci
1972—macerate	1980—elucubrate	1988—elegiacal
1973—vouchsafe	1981—sarcophagus	1989—spoliator
1974—hydrophyte	1982—psoriasis	1990—fibranne
1975—incisor	1983—purim	1991—antipyretic
1976—narcolepsy	1984—luge	1992—lyceum

97. Spelling Demons—Wise Guys

Try using these as examples of the utility of syllabication for pronouncing new words.

Antidisestablishmentarianism: State support of the church.

Supercalifragilisticexpialidocious: Mary Poppins says it means "good."

Pneumonoultramicroscopicsilicovolcanoconiosis: Lung disease caused by inhaling silica dust.

Floccinaucinihilipilification: Action of estimating as worthless.

The Reading Teacher's Book of Lists, Third Edition, © 1993 by Prentice Hall

SECTION IX
Enrichment and Discovery Activities

98. *Interest Inventory—Primary*

Use the interest inventory to get to know your students. You will find special talents, hobbies, and needs that will help you help your students.

1. In school the thing I like to do best is _____

2. Outside of school the thing I like to do best is _____

3. If I had a million dollars I would _____

4. When I grow up I will _____

5. I hate _____

6. My favorite animal is _____

7. The best sport is _____

8. When nobody is around I like to _____

9. The person I like best is _____

10. Next summer I hope to _____

11. I like to collect _____

12. My favorite place to be is _____

13. The things I like to make are _____

14. The best book I ever read was _____

15. The best TV show is _____

16. What I think is funny is _____

See also List 79, Story Starters; and List 99, Interest Inventory—Intermediate.

99. Interest Inventory—Intermediate

Assigning a topic for a report, suggesting a good book, and selecting meaningful examples can be helped by knowing students' preferences and interests. Use the interest inventory during the first week of school.

1. Outside of school my favorite activity is _____

2. I work at _____ . My job is _____

3. The sport(s) I like to watch best is (are) _____

4. The sport(s) I like to play best is (are) _____

5. After high school I plan to _____

6. The job I want to be doing as an adult is _____

7. In school my favorite subject(s) is (are) _____

8. The subject(s) in which I get the best grade(s) is (are) _____

9. I would like to learn more about _____

10. My main hobbies or leisure time activity is (are) _____

11. For pleasure I read _____

12. I spend about _____ hours or _____ minutes a week reading for fun.

13. The best book I have ever read was (title) _____

14. The book I am reading now is (title) _____

15. My favorite magazine(s) is (are) _____

16. The part of the world that interests me the most is _____

17. When I am finished with school, I hope to live in _____

18. The kinds of books or stories I like to read are _____

19. My favorite TV show is _____

20. What makes me mad is _____

21. What makes me laugh is _____

22. My favorite person is _____

23. Next summer I plan to _____

See also List 79, Story Starters; and List 98, Interest Inventory—Primary.

The Reading Teacher's Book of Lists, Third Edition, © 1993 by Prentice Hall

100. *Activities for Language Development*

Many children love acting. With these activities they can have some fun and learn a few words at the same time.

1. In One Place—Make Your Body:

wiggle	collapse	expand	hang
wriggle	shake	contract	slouch
squirm	rock	curl	droop
stretch	sway	uncurl	sink
bend	bounce	rise	tumble
twist	bob	lurch	totter
turn	spin	lean	swing
flop	whirl	sag	

2. From Place to Place—Make Your Body:

creep	hop	meander	stalk
crawl	tramp	limp	race
roll	hustle	hobbie	plod
walk	stride	stagger	amble
skip	prance	scramble	sprint
run	strut	march	slink
gallop	stroll	scurry	dodge
leap	saunter	trudge	

3. Make Your Legs and Feet:

kick	stamp	trample	mince
shuffle	tap	tip-toe	stumble
skuff	drag	slip	

4. Make Your Face:

smile	wink	yawn	wince
frown	gape	chew	grimace
sneer	scowl	stare	squint
pout	grin	glare	blink
leer	smile		

5. Make Your Hands:

open	grasp	snatch	pinch
close	clap	pluck	poke
clench	scratch	beckon	point
grab	squeeze	pick	tap
stroke	wring	slap	clasp
poke	knead	pat	rub

6. Make Your Arms and Hands:

pound	reach	thrust	throw
strike	wave	lift	fling
grind	slice	stir	catch
sweep	chop	weave	whip
cut	push	clutch	grope
beat	pull	dig	punch

7. Pantomime or Dramatize:

yawning	speaking	hiccupping	twittering
sighing	cooing	wheezing	crowing
groaning	calling	murmuring	lowing
moaning	chuckling	muttering	squalling
grunting	rustling	sputtering	neighing
growling	snoring	whistling	shinnying
howling	whimpering	hissing	rattling
roaring	wailing	cackling	clanging
bellowing	shouting	trilling	ringing
screeching	laughing	hooting	honking
screaming	sneezing	creaking	popping
crying	snickering	braying	clicking
sobbing	tittering	whispering	buzzing
gasping	giggling	singing	purring
shrieking	sniffing	humming	ticking
whining	panting	croaking	chirping
mumbling	coughing	barking	squeaking
			sizzling

8. Dramatize These Moods:

fear	boredom	despair	contempt
pain	wonder	hope	reluctance
rage	generosity	pity	admiration
joy	reverence	hate	delight
sorrow	jealousy	love	anticipation
loneliness	envy	compassion	impatience
satisfaction	resentment	horror	happiness
frustration	pride	disgust	doubt
contentment	shame	surprise	greed
discontentment	repentence	gratitude	
anxiety	resignation	gaiety	

9. Dramatize These Activities:

work	study
play	fight
worship	build
destroy	celebrate
harvest	plant

10. Represent:

cat	bee
dog	seagull
caterpillar	mosquito
apple tree	any living thing

See also List 101, Games & Methods for Teaching.

The Reading Teacher's Book of Lists, Third Edition, © 1993 by Prentice Hall

101. *Games and Methods for Teaching*

The games and methods for instruction listed here are suggestions for class activities that will help students learn many of the lists or words presented in this book.

   1. Pairs. A card game for two to five players. Five cards are dealt to each player, and the remainder of the deck is placed in the center of the table. The object of the game is to get as many pairs as possible. There are only two cards alike in each deck. To play, the player to the right of the dealer may ask any other player if he or she has a specific card, for example, "Do you have *and*?" The player asking must hold the mate in his or her hand. The player who is asked must give up the card if he or she holds it. If the first player does not get the card asked for, he or she draws one card from the pile. Then the next player has a turn at asking for a card. If a player can't read his or her own card, the player may show the card and ask any other player how to read it.

   If the player succeeds in getting the card asked for, either from another player or from the pile, he or she gets another turn. As soon as the player gets a pair, he or she puts the pair down in front of him or her. The player with the most pairs at the end of the game wins. *Note:* A deck of 50 cards (25 pairs) is good for two to five players. This game works well with an Instant Word list of 25 words with each word on two cards (see List 4). It can also work well with homophones (List 1) or any association in this section.

   2. Bingo. Played like regular Bingo except that the players' boards have 25 words in place of numbers. Children can use bits of paper for markers, and the caller can randomly call off words from a list. Be certain when making the boards that the words are arranged in a different order on each card. Use with 25 Instant Words or any 25 words. Caller can write each word called on the board to help players learn to read the words.

the	of	it	with	at
a	can	on	are	this
is	will	you	to	and
your	that	we	as	but
be	in	not	for	have

3. Board Games. Trace a path on posterboard. Mark off one-inch spaces. Write a word in each space. Students advance from start by tossing dice until one reaches the finish line. Students must correctly pronounce (or give the meaning or sample use) of the word in the square. Use three pennies if you don't have dice; shake and advance number of squares for heads up.

4. Contests. Students, individually or as teams, try to get more words in a category than anyone else. For example, the teacher may start the contest by giving three homographs. The students try to amass the longest list of homographs. There may be a time limit.

5. Spelling. Use the list words in spelling lessons or have an old-fashioned spelling bee. See List 94, Spelling Demons—Elementary, and List 95, Spelling Demons—Secondary, or Instant Words.

6. Use Words in a Sentence. Either orally or written. Award points for the longest, funniest, saddest, or most believable sentence.

7. Word Wheels. To make a word wheel, attach an inner circle to a larger circle with a paper fastener. Turn the inner wheel to match outer parts. This is great for compound words, phonograms, or matching a word to a picture clue. Sliding strips do the same thing.

8. Matching. Make worksheets with two columns of words or word parts. Students draw a line from an item in column A to the item in column B that matches (*prefix* and *root*, *word* and *meaning*, two synonyms, etc.). Matching also can be done by matching two halves of a card that has been cut to form puzzle pieces. See Association Pairs on page 275 for suitable lists of paired words.

9. Flash Cards. The word or word part is written on one side of a card. The teacher or tutor flashes the cards for the student to read instantly. Cards also can be shuffled and read by the student. Cards also can be used in sentence building, finding synonyms and antonyms, and the Concentration Game.

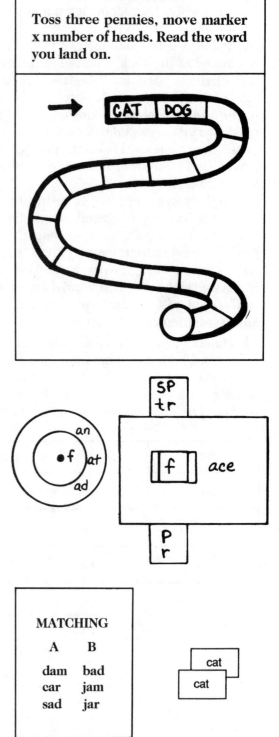

The Reading Teacher's Book of Lists, Third Edition, © 1993 by Prentice Hall

10. Hidden Words (or Word Search Puzzle). To make a word search puzzle, write words horizontally, vertically, or diagonally on a grid (graph paper is fine), one letter per box. Fill in all the other boxes with letters at random. Students try to locate all of the target words. When they find a word they circle it.

11. Concentration. To play Concentration, use one-sided flashcards or any card with a word or symbol written on one side. Cards must be in pairs (duplicate) such as two identical cards or an association pair. Shuffle four or more pairs (more for older or brighter students) and place cards face down, spread out randomly over a table surface. The player may pick up any two cards and look at them. If they are a pair, he or she keeps them; if they are not, the cards must be put back in exactly the same place from which they came. The trick is to remember where different cards are located while they are sitting on the table face down so that when you pick up one card you remember where its pair is located. Players take turns, and the object is to accumulate the most cards. Learning is needed to know what cards are pairs, for example, which definition matches which card or any association pair.

12. Association Cards. For students who don't want to fool around with games, a useful learning device is to develop a set of association pair cards with the word on one side and its definition on the other side. The student first studies both sides of a set of cards; then the student goes through a stack of cards reading the words and attempting to recall the definition. If correct, he or she puts the card into the "know pile"; if incorrect or the student can't remember, the card is studied and put into the "don't-know pile." Next, the "don't-know pile" is sorted once more into "know" and "don't-know." This process is complete when all cards are in the "know pile"; unfortunately, there is, also something called forgetting, so the stack of cards should be reviewed at later intervals, such as a few days later and a few weeks later. Students should not attempt to learn (associate) too many new (unknown) cards at one time, or learning will become boring. But as long as motivation is high

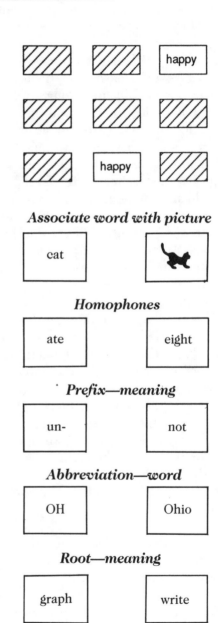

Associate word with picture

| cat | 🐈 |

Homophones

| ate | eight |

Prefix—meaning

| un- | not |

Abbreviation—word

| OH | Ohio |

Root—meaning

| graph | write |

and learning is occurring, this is an excellent learning and study technique. Primary students can use picture nouns and older students Greek Roots—See Association Pair list.

13. Tutoring. A teacher and a student, or a tutor and a student, or even two students can use these double-sided association pair cards in many ways. The tutor holds up one card, and the student calls off the associated definition. Students can take turns, have contests, win prizes, and so on.

14. Testing. Although it is often overused, testing is also a powerful learning motivator and teaching device. Done kindly and thoughtfully, testing can cause a lot of learning to occur in a classroom or tutoring situation. A technique of testing is to assign a set of association pairs to be learned (using any game or technique) and then test the results. Some teachers assign short daily tests that accumulate points or cause movement on a big chart. Other teachers give weekly tests and assign numeral or percent grades; these are shown to parents, or the five best papers are posted on a bulletin board. Part of the learning occurs because the students are motivated to study and because the students get feedback or knowledge of the results as to whether they know or don't know something. Hence, the corrected papers should be returned, or the students should trade papers and correct for more immediate and sometimes better knowledge of results.

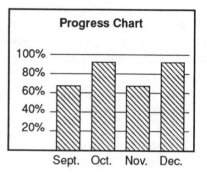

Testing also gives feedback to the teacher or tutor so that the teacher can regulate the amount of new learning (number of words) to be learned next or the amount needing review. It also can help the student to individualize and to give some students more and other students less to be learned.

15. Computer-Aided Instruction (CAI). One of the newer methods of teaching is to use computers to provide instruction, drills, and tests. CAI programs teach vocabulary both in and out of context, different types of comprehension, and subject content reading. CAI uses many elements of programmed instruction, such as small steps (limited from content), clear objectives, careful se-

The Reading Teacher's Book of Lists, Third Edition, © 1993 by Prentice Hall

quencing, active student response, immediate feedback on correctness, and often branching and recordkeeping. Most teachers buy programs already made, but it is possible to develop your own on a CAI program with the aid of a utility program in which the teacher inserts only desired content. The *Reading Teachers' Book of Lists* has much excellent content for CAI programs.

16. Association Pairs. This is a table of items to be associated or learned together. We are calling them association pairs because they are often taught by association learning. The following association pairs can be used in developing games such as Concentration and Association, and in creating programs for computer-aided instruction.

USE THESE PAIRS FOR GAMES AND LESSONS

LIST NUMBER	ASSOCIATION PAIR
1	Word—Homophone (bare - bear)
2	Homograph—Definition (stoop - bend down; stoop - porch)
3	Word-look-alike or sound-alike word (coma - comma)
13	Measurement term—Abbreviation (mm - millimeter)
13	Measurement term—Numerical relation (kilometer - 1000 meters)
13	Measurement term—Conversion (1 meter = 3.3 feet)
22	Word—Synonym (see - look)
23	Word—Antonym (back - front)
24	First three words in analogy—Last word (story:read::song:sing)
28	Idiom root word—three or four usages (do - do away, do out of, do well)
32	Clipped word—Full word (pop - popular)
33	Portmanteau word—Full words (brunch - breakfast + lunch)
35	Contraction—Full words (she'd - she would)
36	Acronym—Full words (CB - citizens band)
37	Borrowed word—Origin (pasteurize - Louis Pasteur)
38	Foreign word—Translation (origin) (bonjour - good day, French)
41	-Ology word—Definition (cryptology - codes)
5	Picture nouns (- cat)
145	Computer term—Definition (bug - error)
40	Phobia word—Definition (agoraphobia - open places)
45	Greek root—Meaning (graph - write)
45	Latin root—Meaning (duct - lead)
43	Prefix—Meaning (anti - against)
44	Suffix—Meaning (-ee - one who, ex. payee)
44	Suffix—Grammar (-s - plural)
48	Illustrating word or example word—Phoneme (at - short A)

LIST NUMBER	ASSOCIATION PAIR
55	Propaganda technique (See List 55)
149	Graph term—Example (bar graph)
66	Key object—Number (five - 15)
82	Part of speech—Definition (example: noun - name of person, place)
83	Irregular verb present—Past (am - was)
83	Irregular verb present—Past participle (am - been)
144	Literary term—Definition (ballad - long narrative poem)
124	State abbreviation - Full name (CA - California)
125	Common abbreviation - Full term (Aug. - August)
128	Latin alphabet—Hebrew or Greek or Russian alphabet (B - Dbeth)
129, 132	Alphabet—Manual alphabet or Morse Code (B - . . .)
134	Symbol—Verbal equivalent (+ - plus)
91	Proofreading symbol—Explanation (¶ - New paragraph)
137	Roman number—Arabic numeral (12 - XII)
120	Library classification symbol—Area description (D - General History)
9	Collective Nouns—Animal (gaggle - geese)
135	Native American symbol—Meaning (sun symbols - happiness; see List 135.)

17. Humor. Don't overlook the good effects of humor on learning. Both children and adults love word games and jokes. Many jokes use homophones and homographs. For example, "What is an outspoken hot dog? A frank frank." See List of Jokes and Hink Pinks, List 104. Children also like to draw humorous pictures of idiomatic expressions such as "It's raining cats and dogs" or "She's a ball of fire." Try a few Wacky Wordies (List 103).

18. Semantic Mapping. There are a number of ways to make some of the ideas in stories or expository text graphically visible. These are sometimes called Semantic Maps or Cognitive Maps, Webbing, or a number of other terms. They are also excellent for developing or enriching vocabulary.

A simple **Semantic Map** might have a term, title, or vocabulary word in the middle and four clusters or areas of related terms.

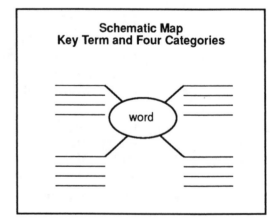

Schematic Map
Key Term and Four Categories

word

The Reading Teacher's Book of Lists, Third Edition, © 1993 by Prentice Hall

A **Semantic Feature Analysis** or grid can also be used to show which features or classes have things in common with a plus sign or not in common with a minus sign.

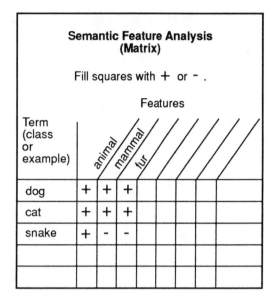

A **Structured Overview** is another type of map similar to the first simple Semantic Map that shows clusters of ideas, terms, or features.

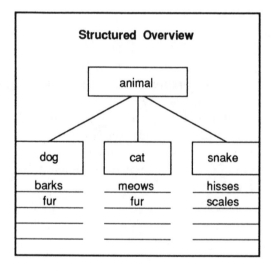

A **Venn Diagram** is often used in mathematics, but can easily be used with words and ideas to show features in common between two different concepts.

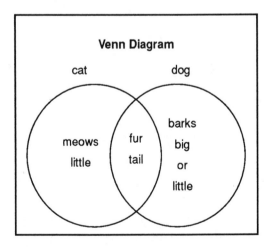

Another more formal **Class/Example Map** can show hierarchy relationship plus related features or properties.

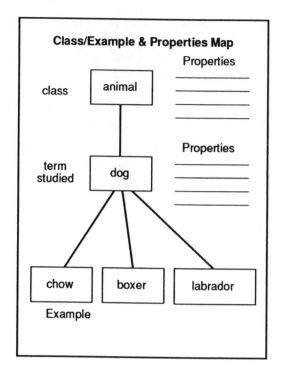

A **Coordinate Class Example Map** not only shows a hierarchy relationship, but contrasts two similar or different terms, both of which belong to the same class and have some features or properties in common and some features that are different. Both contrasted terms have different examples.

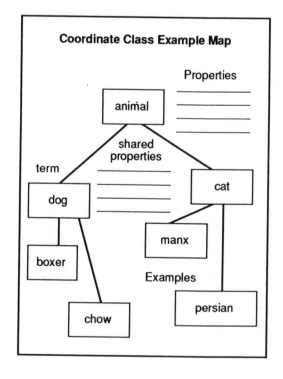

See also List 60, Story Graphs; List 102, Oral Reading Alternatives; List 110, Ten Great Ideas for Reading Teachers.

102. *Oral Reading Alternatives to Round Robin*

Choral Reading. Group oral reading. It allows strong to lead and weak to follow. Also excellent for poetry.

Glossing. The teacher reads aloud slowly and accurately with good sentence tunes. Teacher "glosses" by stopping occasionally to explain a word, phrase, or idea. Students just listen or listen and follow along in their books.

Official Announcer. Appoint a student each day to read announcements, bulletins, student writings, short selections, continuing story, and so forth. Announcer may prepare and seek help from teacher or another student.

Radio Program. Small group takes parts and reads play or radio script into tape recorder for class or parent presentation.

Overviewer Student reads aloud subheads, key words, and/or key sentences in a text before class studies it. Excellent in science or social studies.

Flash Cards. Students try to read word or phrase on flash cards the fastest, most accurate, or in turn.

Play Reading. Like radio program except students read play parts for live performance.

Singing. Read lyrics while learning new song. This is also great for E.S.L. or learning foreign language. Good for stutterers.

Games. A number of board games and other games like Trivial Pursuit™ require players to read a word, set of directions, or questions aloud.

Formal Speech. Student writes a speech for an occasion or learning unit and reads it to a group. May be part of a speech contest.

Find the Answer. Teacher asks a question, student reads aloud just the part of the text that answers the question. This activity aids comprehension improvement and generates good discussions.

Joke of the Day. Read aloud a joke or numerous selection (See List 104).

See also List 101, Games and Methods for Teaching.

The Reading Teacher's Book of Lists, Third Edition, © 1993 by Prentice Hall

103. Wacky Wordies

A. The object in solving is to discern a familiar phrase, saying, cliché, or name from each arrangement of letters and/or symbols. For example, box 1a depicts the phrase "Just Between You and Me." Box 1b shows "Hitting Below the Belt." The puzzles get more diabolical as you go.

	a	b	c	d	e	f
1	you just me	belt hitting	lo head heels ve	V I O L E T s	A B E DUMR	agb
2	cry m i l k	⊢c ℥ᴨ⊣	Symphon	ǝlddɐǝuıd cake	arrest you're	timing tim ing
3	O TV	night fly	S T I N K	injury + insult	r o rail d	my own heart a person
4	at the · of on	dothepe	wear long	strich grround	lu cky	the market
5	worl	the x way	word YYY	search and	go off coc	no ways it ways
6	oholene	t o e a r t h	ooo circus	1 at 3:46	late never	get a word in
7	let gone gone be gone gone	a chance n	O MD BA PhD	wheather	world world world world	lo ose
8	lines reading lines	chicken	y fireworks	L D S Bridge	pace k	danc t e s c etno

The Reading Teacher's Book of Lists, Third Edition, © 1993 by Prentice Hall

Reprinted from *Games* magazine (19 West 21st St., New York, NY 10010). Copyright © 1979, 1981 Playboy Enterprises, Inc.

B. The object in solving is to discern a familiar phrase, saying, cliché, or name from each arrangement of letters and/or symbols. For example, box 1a depicts "Sleeping on the Job." Box 1b shows a "cornerstone." Sounds easy, but wait until you see the others.

	a	b	c	d	e	f
1	sleeping job	s t one	jink jink jink	g n i t t e g da wn	Roger	escape
2	right=right	house prairie	goodbye	milk	c c garage r r	c o m i c
3	e L u c i l l i	clou	ieieceiie	neegr geren ngree regen	t i o n a i n l f	pölkä
4	MIRROR	momanon	clams she	ma√il	1.D 2.R 3.A 4.C 5.U 6.L 7.A	ca se case
5	TRN	ping willow	animation	sugar Please	hair_	L v o R E E A T
6	bus	age a g e age	TU↗LOIP↗S	m ce m ce m ce	eyebrows	ri poorch
7	morning	socket	TORTILLA	12safety345		s d r k i n house

C. The object in solving is to discern a familiar phrase, saying, cliché, or name from each arrangement of letters and/or symbols. For example, box 1a depicts the phrase "Eggs over easy." Box 1b shows "Trafalgar Square."

	a	b	c	d	e	f
1	eggs easy	T R A F A L G A R	told told tales	e t t r i k c i t p	new leaf	sᴛ ky
2	price	L +O ‾SS	swear bible bible bible bible	league	bridge wa t e r	school
3	–attitude	hoppin	century	E RC T O N U	orseman	D UC K
4 (set one's teeth)		or O or O	bet one's —— dollar	tpmerhao	what must	way yield
5	t o 2 par n	dictnry	rifle rifle rifle rifle	PAINS	everything pizza	L Y I N G JOB
6	tr ial	prosperity	monkey O	busines	writers	moon sonata
7	power	mesnackal	Wilson	pit	wheel wheel wheel wheel drive	✓✓ ✓ counter

black

The Reading Teacher's Book of Lists, Third Edition, © 1993 by Prentice Hall

D. The object in solving is to discern a familiar phrase, saying, cliché, or name from each arrangement of letters and/or symbols. For example, box 1a depicts "once over lightly." Box 1b shows "gossip column."

	a	b	c	d	e	f
1	once lightly	g o s s i p	~wave~ radio	c a p t$_{ai}$ n	noon good	bathing suit
2	ee ch sp	God nation ✖	✓ yearly	ses ame	d deer e r	hold second
3	r−i×s+k	pox	strokes *strokes* **strokes**	n^{p}y^{o}^{c}$_{m}$$_{a}$	law of return	e ^{a} p s $_{ua l}$ p
4	hou$_{se}$	age beauty	harm on y	encounters encounters encounters	breth	hearted
5	p a r t i c i p l e	**MAN** campus	momanon	ᴜld block	"Duty!" and beyond	day day
6	sigh	qonpſ	skating ice	inflat10n	g o s p e l	enemy enemy
7	to^{ngue}$_{ngue}$	gettingitall	e a v e s	c ^{m}‹^{e}$_{a}$r ban ana	e e q u a l s m c	aluminum

WACKIE WORDIES—ANSWERS

A

1a	Just between you and me
1b	Hitting below the belt
1c	Head over heels in love
1d	Shrinking violets
1e	Bermuda Triangle
1f	A mixed bag
2a	Cry over spilt milk
2b	Lying in wait
2c	*Unfinished Symphony*
2d	Pineapple upside-down cake
2e	You're under arrest
2f	Split-second timing
3a	Nothing on TV
3b	Fly-by-night
3c	Raise a big stink
3d	Add insult to injury
3e	Railroad crossing
3f	A person after my own heart
4a	At the point of no return
4b	The inside dope
4c	Long underwear
4d	Ostrich with its head in the ground
4e	Lucky break
4f	Corner the market
5a	World without end
5b	Way behind the times
5c	Word to the wise
5d	Search high and low
5e	Go off half-cocked
5f	No two ways about it
6a	Hole-in-one
6b	Down-to-earth
6c	Three-ring circus
6d	One at a time
6e	Better late than never
6f	Get a word in edgewise
7a	Let bygones be bygones
7b	An outside chance
7c	Three degrees below zero
7d	A terrible spell of weather
7e	World Series
7f	Cut loose
8a	Reading between the lines
8b	Chicken Little
8c	Fourth of July fireworks
8d	London Bridge
8e	Change of pace
8f	Square dance contest

B

1a	Sleeping on the job
1b	Cornerstone
1c	High jinks
1d	Getting up before the crack of dawn
1e	"Roger, over and out"
1f	Narrow escape
2a	Equal rights
2b	*Little House on the Prairie*
2c	Waving goodbye

2d	Condensed milk
2e	Two-car garage
2f	Stand-up comic
3a	Lucille Ball
3b	Partly cloudy
3c	"I before E except after C"
3d	Mixed greens
3e	Spiraling inflation
3f	Polka-dotted
4a	Full-length mirror
4b	Man in the moon
4c	Clams on the half-shell
4d	"The check is in the mail"
4e	Count Dracula
4f	Open-and-shut case
5a	No U-Turn
5b	Weeping willow
5c	Suspended animation
5d	"Pretty please with sugar on top?"
5e	Receding hairline
5f	Elevator out of order
6a	Double-decker bus
6b	Middle-age spread
6c	"Tiptoe Through the Tulips"
6d	"Three Blind Mice" (without their i's)
6e	Raised eyebrows
6f	Steal from the rich and give to the poor
7b	Top of the morning
7c	Light socket
7d	*Tortilla Flat*
7e	Safety in numbers
7f	Round of drinks on the house

C

1a	Eggs over easy
1b	Trafalgar Square
1c	*Twice-Told Tales*
1d	Round-trip ticket
1e	Turn over a new leaf
1f	Pie in the sky
2a	*The Price is Right*
2b	Total loss
2c	Swear on a stack of Bibles
2d	Little League
2e	Bridge over troubled water
2f	High school
3a	Negative attitude
3b	Shopping center
3c	Turn-of-the-Century
3d	Counterclockwise
3e	Headless Horseman
3f	Sitting duck
4a	Set one's teeth on edge
4b	Double or nothing
4c	Bet one's bottom dollar
4d	Mixed metaphor
4e	What goes up must come down
4f	Yield right of way
5a	Not up to par
5b	Abridged dictionary
5c	Repeating rifle

5d	Growing pains
5e	Pizza with everything on it
5f	Lying down on the job
6a	Trial separation
6b	Prosperity is just around the corner
6c	Monkey around
6d	Unfinished business
6e	Writer's cramp
6f	*Moonlight Sonata*
7a	Power blackout
7b	Between-meal snack
7c	Flip Wilson
7d	Bottomless pit
7e	Four-wheel drive
7f	Checkout counter

D

1a	Once over lightly
1b	Gossip column
1c	Short-wave radio
1d	Captain Hook
1e	Good afternoon
1f	Topless bathing suit
2a	Parts of speech
2b	One nation, under God, indivisible
2c	Yearly checkup
2d	Open sesame
2e	Deer crossing
2f	Hold on a second
3a	Calculated risk
3b	Smallpox
3c	Different strokes
3d	Mixed company
3e	Law of diminishing returns
3f	Round of applause
4a	Split-level house
4b	Age before beauty
4c	Three-part harmony
4d	*Close Encounters of the Third Kind*
4e	A little out of breath
4f	Light-hearted
5a	Dangling participle
5b	Big man on campus
5c	Man in the moon
5d	Chip off the old block
5e	Above and beyond the call of duty
5f	Day in and day out
6a	No end in sight
6b	Shadow of a doubt
6c	Skating on thin ice
6d	Double-digit inflation
6e	Spread the gospel
6f	Archenemies
7a	Forked tongue
7b	Getting it all together
7c	Eavesdropping
7d	Banana split with whipped cream topping
7e	$E = mc^2$
7f	Aluminum siding

104. *Hink Pinks*

Word games and jokes help to increase vocabulary and verbal fluency. Some word games such as Hink Pinks also help to increase phoneme awareness. Besides that they are fun. Use a few of these for starters, then make up some of your own. Hint: The list of phonogram example words (List 48) will help you.

What is a single speech machine?	lone phone
What is an uncovered seat?	bare chair
What is a library burglar?	book crook
What is a strong beautiful plant?	power flower
What is an entrance to a shop?	store door
What is a boring singing?	long song
What is a skyway to heaven?	air stair
What is a weak bird?	frail quail
What is a container for wood fasteners?	nail pail
What is a resting place for ducks?	quack rack
What is an unhappy father?	sad dad
What is an old marine mammal?	stale whale
What is a chicken enclosure?	hen pen
What is a beach party giver?	coast host
What is a hip place of learning?	cool school
What is a journey by boat?	ship trip
What is bad air in a swamp?	bog smog
What is a fat behind?	plump rump
What is a closed-up shack?	shut hut
What is a beginning prophet?	new guru
What is a house mortgage?	home loan
What is a skinny hotel?	thin inn
What is a cheap medieval soldier?	tight knight

JOKES

Why is 10 afraid of 7?
Because 7, 8, 9.

What kind of bird goes "Bang Bang"?
A fire quacker.

What goes tick-tick, woof-woof?
A watch dog.

Where do cows go on vacation?
Moo York.

What do you get if you cross a cat and a lemon?
A sour puss.

What do you get if you cross a centipede and a parrot?
A walkie-talkie.

What year do frogs like best?
Leap year.

Knock knock.
Who's there?
Doris.
Doris who?
Doris locked, that's why I knocked.

Knock knock.
Who's there?
Olive.
Olive who?
Olive across the street.

Knock knock.
Who's there?
Police.
Police who?
Police stop telling these stupid knock knock jokes.

Waiter, there is a fly in my soup.
That's all right, sir, he won't drink much.

Waiter, what's this fly doing in my soup?
I believe he is doing the backstroke, sir.

Waiter, this soup is terrible, please call the manager.
He won't drink it either, sir.

Patient: Doctor, my little brother is really crazy. He thinks he is a chicken.
Doctor: How long has this been going on?
Patient: About six years.
Doctor: Good heavens. Why have you waited so long to come for help?
Patient: Because we needed the eggs.

Why did the doctor take his eye chart into the classroom?
Because he wanted to check the pupils.

What did the judge give the thief who stole the calendar?
Twelve months.

What does an eagle like to write with?
A bald point pen.

What is an outspoken hot dog?
A frank frank.

What is a writing instrument used in jail?
A pen pen.

What is bought by the yard and worn by the foot?
A carpet.

What did one toe say to the other toe?
Don't look now but there is a big heel following us.

What do you have when you don't feel well?
Gloves on your hands.

105. *Doublespeak*

Here's something both you and your students can enjoy. Select in any order one word from Column A, one from Column B, and one from Column C. Now copy them on scratch paper in the order they were selected.

A	**B**	**C**
1. social	1. involvement	1. objectives
2. perceptual	2. motivation	2. activity
3. developmental	3. accelerated	3. curriculum
4. professional	4. cognitive	4. concept
5. homogeneous	5. effectiveness	5. evaluation
6. interdependent	6. maturation	6. processes
7. exceptional	7. integration	7. approach
8. instructional	8. orientation	8. articulation
9. individual	9. guidance	9. utilization
10. sequential	10. creative	10. resources
11. environmental	11. culture	11. adjustment
12. incremental	12. relationship	12. capacity

EXAMPLES: (A-10) sequential, (B-1) involvement, (C-2) activity, (A-3) developmental, (B-4) cognitive, (C-7) approach

Now that you have the hang of it, enjoy your new status by sprinkling a few common words between the phrases like this:

Social involvement objectives in today's schools are realized by combining an accelerated developmental curriculum with professional effectiveness utilization and creative instructional evaluation.

The motivation of interdependent activity in an environmental adjustment culture is not easy when one takes into account the perceptual maturation processes of the individual.

The utilization of instructional guidance resources will enable students to employ a sequential orientation approach to social integration.

After you have mastered this creative incremental approach to educationalese you will realize that happiness is social effectiveness through concept articulation. Infectious, isn't it?

The Reading Teacher's Book of Lists, Third Edition, © 1993 by Prentice Hall

If you are interested in Doublespeak, you might enjoy the book *Doublespeak* by William Lutz (Harper Row, 1981); also, the *Committee on Public Doublespeak*, NCTE, 1111 Kenyon Road, Urbana, IL 61801 publishes the *Quarterly Review of Doublespeak*, edited by William Lutz.

Used with permission from William Lutz.

106. *Spelling Game*

Here's a spelling game your students might like to do in their spare time. If they do, have them make up other similar games using other letters (and a dictionary). If you would like a little book of these games, see *Games Make Alpha-Betics Fun* by John Dean and Karol Hicks.

AN "F PLUS" PAPER

1. F plus one letter: a musical note
2. F plus two letters: cost; charge
3. F plus two letters: not many
4. F plus three letters: after three comes . . .
5. F plus three letters: to locate
6. F plus three letters: froth
7. F plus four letters: fictitious story
8. F plus four letters: before second
9. F plus four letters: case for a picture
10. F plus four letters: defect; flaw; misdeed
11. F plus five letters: celebrated; distinguished
12. F plus five letters: group of related people
13. F plus five letters: delicately
14. F plus five letters: to secure
15. F plus five letters: solidly; compactly
16. F plus six letters: untrue story
17. F plus six letters: used in swimming
18. F plus six letters: covered with water
19. F plus six letters: blooms
20. F plus six letters: other than one's own country
21. F plus six letters: cargo
22. F plus seven letters: after thirty-ninth
23. F plus seven letters: a heating fuel
24. F plus seven letters: celebration
25. F plus seven letters: having an elevated temperature
26. F plus seven letters: fleeing from danger or justice
27. F plus seven letters: the normal action of anything
28. F plus seven letters: Walt Disney movie; musical

1. ___fa___
2. _____
3. _____
4. _____
5. _____
6. _____
7. _____
8. _____
9. _____
10. _____
11. _____
12. _____
13. _____
14. _____
15. _____
16. _____
17. _____
18. _____
19. _____
20. _____
21. _____
22. _____
23. _____
24. _____
25. _____
26. _____
27. _____
28. _____

ANSWERS

1. fa	8. first	15. firmly	20. foreign			
2. fee	7. fable	14. fasten	19. flowers	24. festival	28. fantasia	
3. few	6. foam	13. finely	18. flooded	23. firewood	27. function	
4. four	5. find	11. famous	17. flipper	22. fortieth	26. fugitive	
	9. frame	12. family	16. fiction	21. freight	25. feverish	
	10. fault					

The Reading Teacher's Book of Lists, Third Edition, © 1993 by Prentice Hall

107. *Palindromes*

Palindromes are words or sentences that read the same way forward and backward. They are enjoyed by people of all ages who like to have some fun with words. Here is a starter list; your students will likely come up with several more.

Incidentally, many decades ago a physician named Samuel Orton coined the term *strepholsymbolia* to describe the error of reading or writing words backward, like *saw* for *was*.

Word Palindromes

Mom	Otto	eve	madam	rotor	nun	solos
Dad	deed	Bob	tot	sees	civic	mum
Pop	peep	refer	dud	kayak	gag	SOS
noon	ere	Anna	toot	eye	reviver	gig
level	did	radar	Hannah			

Sentence and Phrase Palindromes

Name no one man.
Step on no pets.
Never odd or even.
Able was I ere I was Elba.
Red root put up to order.
May a moody baby doom a yam?
Madam I'm Adam.
A man, a plan, a canal, Panama!
Nurses run.
Sages use gas.
We sew.
Stressed desserts.

Net ten.
Live evil.
Rats star.
Flee to me remote elf.
Cigar? Toss it in a can. It is so tragic.
Ma handed Edna ham.
Red rum, sir, is murder.
Did Hanna say as Hanna did?
Now sir, a war is won.
Was it a rat I saw?
Roy, am I mayor?

Words that Read Differently Backward and Forward

Similar to palindromes are words that give different words when read backward. These words are often used in forming phrase palindromes.

but	on	draw	deer	stab	rats	keep
no	ton	reed	gels	star	taps	pets
not	was	leg	keels	spat	naps	drawer
saw	may	sleek	parts	span	step	doc
yam	doom	strap	rat	pot	reward	time
mood	evil	tar	top	pots	cod	time
live	Leon	won	stop	peels	emit	pools
Noel	now	ten	sleep	Dennis	sloop	pals
tub	net	ward	sinned	bats	slap	peek

108. *Family Tree*

This is a fun, interesting, and educational way to develop a sense of family history and an understanding of the many family relationships students may read about. Nontraditional families abound; for example, single-parent families may be able to fill in just the maternal or paternal lines while families with second or third marriages will need additional sheets. Students can interview relatives for help in filling out the tree and then write a family history or an autobiography.

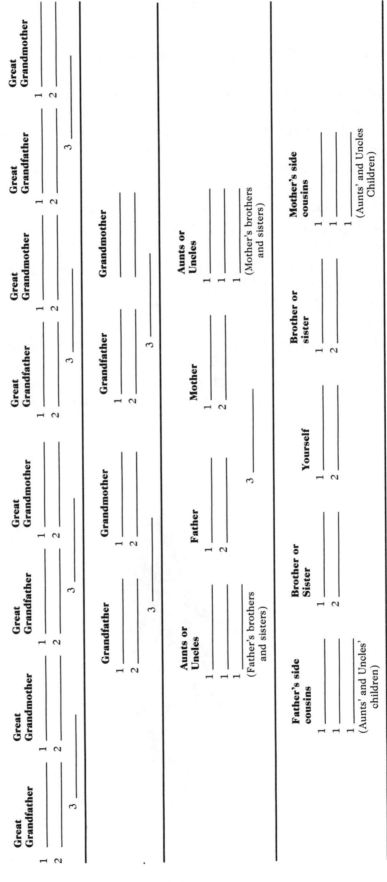

1. Put full name on first line; use maiden name for female.
2. Put year born on second line.
3. Put year married on third line.
4. Cousins are children of your aunts and uncles.
Few people can fill in all the blanks, but get some family member to help you. For half-brothers and -sisters (from second marriage) or stepbrothers and stepsisters, use a second sheet.

109. *Parent Helps*

TEN THINGS PARENTS CAN DO TO HELP THEIR CHILD READ BETTER

1. **Read to your child.** Preferably every day, from ages 1 to 12. From a wide variety of materials: classics and contemporary; fact and fiction.

2. **Encourage writing.** Encourage scribbling and pretend writing. Write letters and stories. Have writing materials available: crayons, pens, computers.

3. **Have reading material at home.** Books, children's magazines, adult magazines. For entertainment and information. Make sure some are easy.

4. **Get your child a library card.** Exchange books weekly.

5. **Encourage conversation.** Talk about animals, family problems, the world. Discuss their reading.

6. **Control TV.** It must not be on all the time. Have silent periods for reading. Watch some good shows about books, science, major events.

7. **Model reading.** Read yourself and let the child see you. Regularly read books, newspapers.

8. **Have your child read aloud.** To you, to other children. Help with mistakes. If many mistakes, select an easier book.

9. **Do many informal educational activities.** Visit zoos, museums, different places. Have your child cook, construct, observe carefully. Don't omit games and exercises.

10. **Value school and learning.** Visit your child's class. Talk to the teacher about reading progress. Praise academic achievement.

The Reading Teacher's Book of Lists, Third Edition, © 1993 by Prentice Hall

110. *Ten Great Ideas For Reading Teachers*

This is a summary of the book *The 10 Best Ideas For Reading Teachers* (Addison Wesley) in which 44 reading specialists, including some of the best-known people in the field such as Jay Samuels, James Flood, Diane Lapp, Ken and Yetta Goodman, Jeannie Chall, P. David Pearson and Wayne Otto, contributed "best ideas."

1. *Integrate* reading into the curriculum; integrate the language arts.
2. Use a variety of *methods* and strategies.
3. Give plenty of reading *practice* for fluency and automaticity.
4. Use *assessment* and diagnosis, both informal and formal.
5. Use good reading *materials:* literature, expository, and variety.
6. Teach *phonics* and decoding, especially for beginners.
7. Develop *vocabulary*, both general and in subject areas.
8. Emphasize *comprehension*.
9. Pay attention to *individual differences;* tackle problems early.
10. *Theory* is important: schema, goals, emergent literacy, text structure, motivation, and success.

SECTION X
Books

111. *All-Time Favorites*

What does it take to be an all-time favorite? A great story. Fascinating characters. Superb writing. The following selections have all three characteristics and have been enjoyed by millions of readers since they were first published. Some have been favorites of our parents, grandparents, and even our great-grandparents. Read these and see which ones will be on *your* list of all-time favorites.

Aesop's Fables. (1967) Watts.

Alcott, Louisa May. (1968) *Little Women*. Little Brown.

Andersen, Hans Christian. (1974) *The Complete Fairy Tales and Stories*. Doubleday.

Armstrong, William. (1976) *Sounder*. Harper Trophy.

Barrie, Sir James. (1957) *Peter Pan*. Random House.

Baum, L. Frank. (1956) *The Wizard of Oz*. Reilly and Lee.

Bemelmans, Ludwig. (1962) *Madeline*. Viking.

Blume, Judy. (1974) *Are You There, God? It's Me, Margaret*. Dell/Yearling.

Brown, Margaret Wise. (1947) *Goodnight Moon*. Harper & Row.

Brunhoff, Jean de. (1960) *The Story of Babar*. Random House.

Burnett, Frances Hodgson. (1921) *The Secret Garden*. J. B. Lippincott.

Carroll, Lewis. (1963) *Alice in Wonderland and Through the Looking Glass*. Grosset & Dunlap.

Chaucer, Geoffrey. (1958) *Chanticleer and the Fox*. Thomas Y. Crowell.

Dahl, Ronald. (1964) *Charlie and the Chocolate Factory*. Knopf.

Dickens, Charles. (1966) *A Christmas Carol*. Lippincott.

Farley, Walter. (1977) *The Black Stallion*. Random House.

Frank, Anne. (1967) *Diary of a Young Girl*. Doubleday.

Freeman, Don. (1976) *Corduroy*. Puffin.

Goble, Paul. (1978) *The Girl Who Loved Wild Horses*. Bradbury.

Grahame, Kenneth. (1961) *The Wind in the Willows*. Scribners.

Grimm, Jakob and Grimm, Wilhelm. (1974) *The Complete Fairy Tales*. Pantheon.

Henry, Marguerite. (1950) *Album of Horses*. Rand McNally.

Keats, Ezra Jack. (1963) *The Snowy Day*. Viking.

Kotzwinkle, William. (1983) *ET the Extra-Terrestrial Story Book*. Grosset & Dunlap.

L'Engle, Madeleine. (1976) *A Wrinkle in Time*. Dell/Laurel.

Lang, Andrew (ed). (1948) *The Blue Fairy Book*. McKay.

McCloskey, Robert. (1963) *Make Way for Ducklings*. Viking.

Milne, A. A. (1954) *Winnie-the-Pooh*. Dutton.

Potter, Beatrix. (1958) *The Tale of Peter Rabbit*. Frederick Warne.

Saint-Exupery, Antoine de. (1943) *The Little Prince*. Harcourt Brace Jovanovich.

Sendak, Maurice. (1963) *Where the Wild Things Are*. Harper.

Seuss, Dr. (1957) *The Cat in the Hat*. Random House.

Silverstein, Shel. (1981) *A Light in the Attic*. Harper & Row.

Silverstein, Shel. (1974) *Where the Sidewalk Ends*. Harper & Row.

Stevenson, Robert Louis. (1951) *A Child's Garden of Verses*. Golden Press.

Stevenson, Robert Louis. (1938) *Treasure Island*. Scribners.

Swift, Jonathan. (1961) *Gulliver's Travels*. Duel.

Tolkien, J.R.R. (1937) *The Hobbit*. Houghton.

Travers, P. L. (1962) *Mary Poppins*. Harcourt.

Twain, Mark. (1938) *The Adventures of Tom Sawyer*. Harper.

White, E. B. (1952) *Charlotte's Web*. Harper & Row.

White, E. B. (1970) *The Trumpet of the Swan*. Harper.

Wilder, Laura Ingalls. (1971) *Little House on the Prairie*. Harper Trophy.

Wilder, Laura Ingalls. (1953) *Little House in the Big Woods*. Harper.

Williams, Margery. (1926) *The Velveteen Rabbit*. Doubleday.

Wright, Blanche F. (illus.). (1916) *The Real Mother Goose*. Rand McNally.

See also List 112, Caldecott and Newbery Award Winners.

112. *Caldecott and Newbery Award Winners*

Since 1938, the Caldecott Medal has been awarded annually to the artist of the most distinguished American picture book for children published during the preceding year. It was named for Randolph Caldecott, a famous English illustrator of books for children. In cases where only one name is given, the book was written and illustrated by the same person.

CALDECOTT MEDAL WINNERS

1938 *Animals of the Bible* by Helen Dean Fish, illustrated by Dorothy P. Lathrop. Philadelphia: Lippincott.

1939 *Mei Li* by Thomas Handforth. New York: Doubleday.

1940 *Abraham Lincoln* by Ingri and Edgar Parin d'Aulaire. New York: Doubleday.

1941 *They Were Strong and Good* by Robert Lawson. New York: Viking.

1942 *Make Way for Ducklings* by Robert McCloskey. New York: Viking.

1943 *The Little House* by Virginia Lee Burton. Boston: Houghton Mifflin.

1944 *Many Moons* by James Thurber, illustrated by Louis Slobodkin. New York: Harcourt Brace Jovanovich.

1945 *Prayer for a Child* by Rachel Field, illustrated by Elizabeth Orton Jones. New York: Macmillan.

1946 *The Rooster Crows* . . . (traditional Mother Goose), illustrated by Maud and Miska Petersham. New York: Macmillan.

1947 *The Little Island* by Golden MacDonald, illustrated by Leonard Weisgard. New York: Doubleday.

1948 *White Snow, Bright Snow* by Alvin Tresselt, illustrated by Roger Duvoisin. New York: Lothrop.

1949 *The Big Snow* by Berta and Elmer Hader. New York: Macmillan.

1950 *Song of the Swallows* by Leo Politi. New York: Scribner's.

1951 *The Egg Tree* by Katherine Milhous. New York: Scribner's.

1952 *Finders Keepers* by William Lipkind, illustrated by Nicolas Mordvinoff. New York: Harcourt Brace Jovanovich.

1953 *The Biggest Bear* by Lynd Ward. Boston: Houghton Mifflin.

1954 *Madeline's Rescue* by Ludwig Bemelmans. New York: Viking.

1955 *Cinderella, or the Little Glass Slipper* by Charles Perault, translated and illustrated by Marcia Brown. New York: Scribner's.

1956 *Frog Went A-Courtin'* edited by John Langstaff, illustrated by Feodor Rojankovsky. New York: Harcourt Brace Jovanovich.

1957 *A Tree Is Nice* by Janice May Udry, illustrated by Marc Simont. New York: Harper.

1958 *Time of Wonder* by Robert McCloskey. New York: Viking.

1959 *Chanticleer and the Fox* adapted from Chaucer and illustrated by Barbara Cooney. New York: Thomas Y. Crowell.

1960 *Nine Days to Christmas* by Marie Hall Ets and Aurora Labastida, illustrated by Marie Hall Ets. New York: Viking.

1961 *Baboushka and the Three Kings* by Ruth Robbins, illustrated by Nicolas Sidjakov. New York: Parnassus.

1962 *Once a Mouse . . .* by Marcia Brown. New York: Scribner's.

1963 *The Snowy Day* by Ezra Jack Keats. New York: Viking.

1964 *Where the Wild Things Are* by Maurice Sendak. New York: Harper.

1965 *May I Bring A Friend?* By Beatrice Schenk de Regniers, illustrated by Beni Montresor. New York: Atheneum.

1966 *Always Room for One More* by Sorche Nic Leodhas, illustrated by Nonny Hogrogian. New York: Holt, Rinehart & Winston.

1967 *Sam, Bangs & Moonshine* by Evaline Ness. New York: Holt, Rinehart & Winston.

1968 *Drummer Hoff* by Barbara Emberley, illustrated by Ed Emberley. Englewood Cliffs, N J: Prentice-Hall.

1969 *The Fool of the World and the Flying Ship* by Arthur Ransome, illustrated by Uri Shulevitz. New York: Farrar, Straus & Giroux.

1970 *Sylvester and the Magic Pebble* by William Steig. New York: Windmill.

1971 *A Story—A Story* by Gail E. Haley. New York: Atheneum.

1972 *One Fine Day* by Nonny Hogrogian. New York: Macmillan.

1973 *The Funny Little Woman* retold by Arlene Mosel, illustrated by Blair Lent. New York: Dutton.

1974 *Duffy and the Devil* by Harve Zemach, illustrated by Margot Zemach. New York: Farrar, Straus & Giroux.

1975 *Arrow to the Sun* adapted and illustrated by Gerald McDermott. New York: Viking.

1976 *Why Mosquitoes Buzz in People's Ears* retold by Verna Aardema, illustrated by Leo and Diane Dillon. New York: Dial Press.

1977 *Ashanti to Zulu; African Traditions* by Margaret Musgrove, illustrated by Leo and Diane Dillon. New York: Dial Press.

1978 *Noah's Ark* by Peter Spier. New York: Doubleday.

1979 *The Girl Who Loved Wild Horses* by Paul Goble. Scarsdale, New York: Bradbury.

1980 *Ox-Cart Man* by Donald Hall. New York: Viking.

1981 *Fables* by Arnold Lobel. New York: Harper.

1982 *Jumanji* by Chris van Allsburg. Boston: Houghton Mifflin.

1983 *Shadow* translated by Blaise Cendrars, illustrated by Marcia Brown. New York: Scribner's.

1984 *The Glorious Flight Across the Channel with Louis Bleriot* by Alice and Martin Provensen. New York: Viking.

1985 *Saint George and the Dragon* as retold by Margaret Hodges, illustrated by Trina Schart Hyman. Boston: Little, Brown.

The Reading Teacher's Book of Lists, Third Edition, © 1993 by Prentice Hall

1986 *The Polar Express* by Chris van Allsburg. Boston: Houghton Mifflin.

1987 *Hey, Al* by Arthur Yorinks, illustrated by Richard Egielski. New York: Farrar, Straus & Giroux.

1988 *Owl Moon* by Jane Yolen, illustrated by John Schoenherr. New York: Philomel.

1989 *Song and Dance Man* by Karen Ackerman, illustrated by Stephen Gammell. New York: Alfred A. Knopf.

1990 *Lon Po Po* by Ed Young. New York: Philomel.

1991 *Black and White* by David Macaulay. Boston: Houghton Mifflin.

1992 *Tuesday* by David Weisner. New York: Clarion Books.

1993 *Mirette on the High Wire* by Emily Arnold McCully. New York: Putnam.

The Newbery Medal is awarded annually to the author of the most distinguished contribution to American literature for children. The award, named after John Newbery, an eighteenth-century publisher of quality children's books, has been offered since 1922 as an incentive for quality in children's books.

NEWBERY AWARD WINNERS

1922 *The Story of Mankind* by Hendrik Willem van Loon. New York: Liveright.

1923 *The Voyages of Doctor Dolittle* by Hugh Lofting. Philadelphia: J. B. Lippincott.

1924 *The Dark Frigate* by Charles Hawes. Atlantic/Little.

1925 *Tales from Silver Lands* by Charles Finger. New York: Doubleday.

1926 *Shen of the Sea* by Arthur Bowie Chrisman. New York: Dutton.

1927 *Smoky, the Cowhorse* by Will James. New York: Scribner's.

1928 *Gayneck, The Story of a Pigeon* by Dhan Gopal Mukerji. New York: Dutton.

1929 *The Trumpeter of Krakow* by Eric P. Kelly. New York: Macmillan.

1930 *Hitty, Her First Hundred Years* by Rachel Field. New York: Macmillan.

1931 *The Cat Who Went to Heaven* by Elizabeth Coatsworth. New York: Macmillan.

1932 *Waterless Mountain* by Laura Adams Armer. New York: Longman.

1933 *Young Fu of the Upper Yangtze* by Elizabeth Forman Lewis. Winston.

1934 *Invincible Louisa* by Cornelia Meigs. Boston: Little Brown.

1935 *Dobry* by Monica Shannon. New York: Viking.

1936 *Caddie Woodlawn* by Carol Brink. New York: Macmillan.

1937 *Roller Skates* by Ruth Sawyer. New York: Viking.

1938 *The White Stag* by Kate Seredy. New York:Viking.

1939 *Thimble Summer* by Elizabeth Enright. New York: Rinehart.

1940 *Daniel Boone* by James Daugherty. New York: Viking.

1941 *Call It Courage* by Armstrong Sperry. New York: Macmillan.

1942 *The Matchlock Gun* by Walter D. Edmonds. New York: Dodd.

1943 *Adam of the Road* by Elizabeth Janet Gray. New York: Viking.

1944 *Johnny Tremain* by Esther Forbes. Boston: Houghton Mifflin.

1945 *Rabbit Hill* by Robert Lawson. New York: Viking.

1946 *Strawberry Girl,* by Lois Lenski. Philadelphia: J. B. Lippincott.

1947 *Miss Hickory* by Carolyn Sherwin Bailey. New York: Viking.

1948 *The Twenty-one Balloons* by William Pene du Bois. New York: Viking.

1949 *King of the Wind* by Marguerite Henry. Chicago: Rand McNally.

1950 *The Door in the Wall* by Marguerite de Angeli. New York: Doubleday.

1951 *Amos Fortune, Free Man* by Elizabeth Yates. Aladdin.

1952 *Ginger Pye* by Eleanor Estes. New York: Harcourt Brace Jovanovich.

1953 *Secret of the Andes* by Ann Nolan Clark. New York: Viking.

1954 *. . . and now Miguel* by Joseph Krumgold. New York: Thomas Y. Crowell.

1955 *The Wheel on the School* by Meindert DeJong. New York: Harper.

1956 *Carry on, Mr. Bowditch* by Jean Lee Latham. Boston: Houghton Mifflin.

1957 *Miracles on Maple Hill* by Virginia Sorensen. New York: Harcourt Brace Jovanovich.

1958 *Rifles for Watie* by Harold Keith. New York: Thomas Y. Crowell.

1959 *The Witch of Blackbird Pond* by Elizabeth George Speare. Boston: Houghton Mifflin.

1960 *Onion John* by Joseph Krumgold. New York: Thomas Y. Crowell.

1961 *Island of the Blue Dolphins* by Scott O'Dell. Boston: Houghton Mifflin.

1962 *The Bronze Bow* by Elizabeth George Speare. Boston: Houghton Mifflin.

1963 *A Wrinkle in Time* by Madeleine L'Engle. New York: Farrar, Straus & Giroux.

1964 *It's Like This, Cat* by Emily Cheney Neville. New York: Harper.

1965 *Shadow of a Bull* by Maia Wojciechowska. New York: Atheneum.

1966 *I, Juan de Pareja* by Elizabeth Borton de Trevino. New York: Farrar, Straus & Giroux.

1967 *Up a Road Slowly* by Irene Hunt. Follett.

1968 *From the Mixed-Up Files of Mrs. Basil E. Frankweiler* by E. L. Konigsburg. New York: Atheneum.

1969 *The High King* by Lloyd Alexander. New York: Holt.

1970 *Sounder* by William H. Armstrong. New York: Harper.

1971 *Summer of the Swans* by Betsy Byars. New York: Viking.

1972 *Mrs. Frisby and the Rats of NIMH* by Robert C. O'Brien. New York: Atheneum.

1973 *Julie of the Wolves* by Jean C. George. New York: Harper.

1974 *The Slave Dancer* by Paula Fox. Bradbury.

1975 *M. C. Higgins, The Great* by Virginia Hamilton. New York: Macmillan.

1976 *The Grey King* by Susan Cooper. New York: Atheneum.

1977 *Roll of Thunder, Hear My Cry* by Mildred D. Taylor. New York: Dial Press.

1978 *Bridge to Terabithia* by Katherine Paterson. New York: Thomas Y. Crowell.

1979 *The Westing Game* by Ellen Raskin. New York: Dutton.

1980 *A Gathering of Days: A New England Girl's Journal, 1830–32* by Joan Blos. New York: Greenwillow.

The Reading Teacher's Book of Lists, Third Edition, © 1993 by Prentice Hall

1981 *Jacob Have I Loved* by Katherine Paterson. New York: Thomas Y. Crowell.

1982 *A Visit to William Blake's Inn: Poems for Innocent and Experienced Travelers* by Nancy Willard. New York: Harcourt Brace Jovanovich.

1983 *Dicey's Song* by Cynthia Voigt. New York: Atheneum.

1984 *Dear Mr. Henshaw* by Beverly Cleary. New York: Morrow.

1985 *The Hero and the Crown* by Robin McKinley. New York: Greenwillow.

1986 *Sarah, Plain and Tall* by Patricia MacLachlan. New York: Harper.

1987 *The Whipping Boy* by Sid Fleischman. New York: Greenwillow.

1988 *Lincoln: A Photobiography* by Russell Freedman. Boston: Houghton Mifflin.

1989 *Joyful Noise: Poems for Two Voices* by Paul Fleischman. New York: Harper.

1990 *Number the Stars* by Lois Lowry. Boston: Houghton Mifflin.

1991 *Maniac Magee* by Jerry Spinelli. New York: Little Brown.

1992 *Shiloh* by Phyllis Reynolds Naylor. New York: Atheneum.

1993 *Missing May* by Cynthia Rylant. New York: Orchard Books.

See also List 111, All-Time Favorites.

113. *Picture Books*

It's never too early to enjoy reading a good book, and the following books are just the thing for very young children. Wordless books allow preschoolers to "read" the stories through pictures. Early positive reading experiences through picture books can be a real boost to learning to read.

Anno, Mitsumasa. (1970) *Topsy-Turvies: Pictures to Stretch the Imagination*. John Weatherhill Pub.

Anno, Mitsumasa. (1977) *Anno's Counting Book*. Crowell/Harper Collins.

Anno, Mitsumasa. (1978) *Anno's Journey*. Philomel Pub.

Anno, Mitsumasa. (1984) *Anno's Flea Market*. Philomel Pub.

Bang, Molly. (1980) *The Grey Lady and the Strawberry Snatcher*. Four Winds.

Briggs, Raymond. (1978) *The Snowman*. Random House.

Bruna, Dick. (1978) *Another Story To Tell*. Metheun.

Burlson, Joe. (1984) *Space Colony*. Putnam's.

Carle, Eric. (1971) *Do You Want to Be My Friend?* Harper.

Collington, Peter. (1987) *The Angel and the Soldier Boy*. Knopf.

Collington, Peter. (1990) *On Christmas Eve*. Knopf.

Day, Alexandra. (1990) *Carl's Christmas*. New York: Farrar, Straus, & Giroux.

Day, Alexandra. (1989) *Carl Goes Shopping*. New York: Farrar, Straus, & Giroux.

De Groat, Diane. (1977) *Alligator's Toothache*. Crown.

De Paola, Tomie. (1978) *Pancakes for Breakfast*. Harcourt Brace Jovanovich.

Drescher, Henrik. (1987) *The Yellow Umbrella*. Bradbury.

Goodall, John. (1973) *The Midnight Adventures of Kelly, Dot and Esmeralda*. Atheneum.

Goodall, John. (1976) *Paddy Pork's Holiday*. Atheneum.

Goodall, John. (1977) *The Surprise Picnic*. Atheneum.

Goodall, John. (1975) *Creepy Castle*. Atheneum.

Gorey, Edward. (1984) *The Tunnel Calamity*. Putnam's.

Hoban, Tana. (1973) *Over, Under, Through, and Other Spacial Concepts*. Macmillan.

Hoban, Tana. (1976) *Big Ones, Little Ones*. Greenwillow.

Hoban, Tana. (1978) *Is It Red? Is It Yellow? Is It Blue?* Greenwillow.

Hutchins, Pat. (1971) *Changes, Changes*. Macmillan.

Keats, Ezra Jack. (1981) *Skates!* Scholastic.

Kitchen, Bert. (1984) *Animal Alphabet*. Dial Press.

Krahn, Fernando. (1974) *April Fools*. Dutton.

Krahn, Fernando. (1982) *The Creepy Thing*. Houghton.

Krahn, Fernando. (1983) *The Secret in the Dungeon*. Houghton.

Martin, Rafe. (1989) *Will's Mammoth*. Putnam's.

Mayer, Mercer. (1974) *Frog Goes to Dinner*. Dial Press.

The Reading Teacher's Book of Lists, Third Edition, © 1993 by Prentice Hall

Mayer, Mercer. (1975) *The Great Cat Chase*. Scholastic.

Mayer, Mercer. (1976) *Hiccup*. Dial Press.

Mayer, Mercer. (1980) *Frog, Where Are You?* Dial Press.

McCully, Emily Arnold. (1984) *Picnic*. Harper & Row/Harper Collins.

Ormerod, Jan. (1982) *Moonlight*. Lothrop, Lee, and Shepard.

Sasaki, Isao. (1982) *Snow*. Viking.

Sesame Street. (1974) *Can You Find What's Missing?* Random House.

Spier, Peter. (1981) *Peter Spier's Rain*. Doubleday.

Turk, Hanne. (1984) *Happy Birthday Max*. Alphabet Press.

Turk, Hanne. (1984) *Max Packs*. Alphabet Press.

Turk, Hanne. (1984) *Snapshot Max*. Alphabet Press.

Turkle, Brinton. (1976) *Deep in the Forest*. Dutton.

Ward, Lynd. (1973) *The Silver Pony*. Houghton Mifflin.

Winter, Paula. (1976) *The Bear and the Fly*. Crown.

The Reading Teacher's Book of Lists, Third Edition, © 1993 by Prentice Hall

See also List 100, Activities for Language Development; and List 114, Predictable Books.

114. *Predictable Books*

These books contain a lot of repetition and still maintain high interest. Some teachers use them regularly as part of beginning reading instruction.

Becker, John. *Seven Little Rabbits*. New York: Scholastic, 1973.

Bonne, Rose and Mills, Alan. *I Know an Old Lady*. New York: Rand McNally, 1961.

Brown, Marcia. *The Three Billy Goats Gruff*. New York: Harcourt Brace Jovanovich, 1957.

Burningham, John. *Hey! Get Off Our Train*. New York: Crown Publishers, 1989.

Burningham, John. *Mr. Gumpy's Outing*. New York: Scholastic Press, 1970.

Carle, Eric. *The Very Busy Spider*. New York: Philomel Books, 1984.

Carle, Eric. *The Very Hungry Caterpillar*. New York: Philomel Books, 1969.

Charlip, Remy. *Fortunately*. New York: Macmillan, 1985.

Domanska, Janina. *Busy Monday Morning*. New York: Macmillan, 1985.

Elting, Mary and Folsom, Michael. *Q is for Duck, An Alphabet Guessing Game*. New York: Houghton Mifflin, 1980.

Galdone, Paul. *Henny Penny*. New York: Seabury Press, 1968.

Galdone, Paul. *The Gingerbread Boy*. New York: Seabury Press, 1975.

Galdone, Paul. *The Little Red Hen*. New York: Seabury Press, 1973.

Galdone, Paul. *The Three Little Bears*. New York: Seabury Press, 1972.

Galdone, Paul. *The Three Little Pigs*. New York: Seabury Press, 1970.

Gelman, Rita. *More Spaghetti I Say!* New York: Scholastic, 1977.

Ginsburg, Mirra. *The Chick and the Duckling*. New York: Macmillan, 1972.

Hutchins, Pat. *Good Night, Owl*. New York: Penguin, 1982.

Hutchins, Pat. *Happy Birthday Sam*. New York: Puffin, 1985.

Hutchins, Pat. *Rosie's Walk*. New York: Macmillan, 1971.

Kellog, Steven. *Can I Keep Him?* New York: The Dial Press, 1971.

Kraus, Robert. *Where Are You Going Little Mouse?* New York: Greenwillow, 1986.

Langstaff, John. *Oh, A-Hunting We Will Go*. New York: Atheneum, 1974.

Lobel, Arnold. *A Treeful of Pigs*. New York: Greenwillow, 1979.

Mars, W. *The Old Woman and Her Pig*. New York: Western Publishing Co., 1961.

Martin, Bill. *Brown Bear, Brown Bear, What Do You See?* Newly illustrated 25th Edition by Eric Carle. New York: H. Holt, 1992.

Martin, Bill. *Polar Bear, Polar Bear, What Do You Hear?* New York: H. Holt, 1991.

McGovern, Ann. *Too Much Noise*. New York: Scholastic, 1967.

Peppe, Rodney. *The House that Jack Built*. New York: Delacorte, 1970.

Sendak, Maurice. *Chicken Soup with Rice*. New York: Scholastic, 1962.

Sendak, Maurice. *Where the Wild Things Are*. New York: Harper, 1984.

Williams, Sue. *I Went Walking*. New York: Harcourt Brace Jovanich, 1990.

Wylie, Joanne and David. *A Funny Fish Story*. Illinois: Regensteiner Publishing Enterprises, 1984.

The Reading Teacher's Book of Lists, Third Edition, © 1993 by Prentice Hall

These sets of predictable books provide many enjoyable reading experiences for students.

City Kids. Cypress; Rigby. Short comic paperbacks that include no text versions to encourage writing.

Predictable Books. Scholastic. Two sets containing 15 books each that are designed for grades K–1 and grades 1–2.

Ready to Read. Richard C. Owens. 45 paperback books from New Zealand that contain different formats and natural language. Big books available.

The Story Box. Wright Group. 117 books from New Zealand that are color coded for different levels. Big books and cassettes available.

Sunshine Books. Wright Group. Easy reading books that are short and small.

Theme Packs. Rigby. One big book and several matching small books that cover such themes as space, dinosaurs, and family.

Willie MacGurkle and Friends; Finnigan and Friends. Curriculum Associates. 10 books in each set that develop language skills through the use of rhymes, rhythm, and amusing characters.

115. Selected Book Lists

There are many different book lists. Here are a few you might enjoy.

CHILDREN'S FAVORITE BOOKS—R.I.F. LIST

1. *Charlotte's Web*, E. B. White
2. *Superfudge*, Judy Blume
3. *Where the Red Fern Grows*, Wilson Rawls
4. *Tales of a Fourth-Grade Nothing*, Judy Blume
5. *Honey, I Shrunk the Kids*, B. Hiller and E. Faucher
6. *Indian in the Cupboard*, Lynne Banks
7. *Charlie and the Chocolate Factory*, Roald Dahl
8. *James and the Giant Peach*, Roald Dahl
9. *There's a Boy in the Girls' Bathroom*, Louis Sachar
10. *Where the Sidewalk Ends*, Shel Silverstein

Source: Reading Is Fundamental survey of 300,000 children participating in RIF programs nationwide.

CHILDREN'S FAVORITE BOOKS—MOTT LIST

1. *Charlotte's Web*, E. B. White
2. The Berenstain Bears series, Stan Berenstain and Janice Berenstain
3. The Dr. Seuss series, Dr. Seuss
4. The Ramona series, Beverly Cleary
5. *Superfudge*, Judy Blume
6. *Tales of a Fourth-Grade Nothing*, Judy Blume
7. The Little House series, Laura I. Wilder
8. *Where the Red Fern Grows*, Wilson Rawls
9. The Baby Sitters series, Ann M. Martin
10. *Cinderella*, Charles Perrault

PARENTS' FAVORITE BOOKS—MOTT LIST

1. *Little Women*, Louisa May Alcott
2. The Nancy Drew series, Carolyn Keene
3. *Charlotte's Web*, E. B. White
4. The Dr. Seuss series, Dr. Seuss
5. *Cinderella*, Charles Perrault
6. *Black Beauty*, Anna Sewell
7. The Little House series, Laura I. Wilder

The Reading Teacher's Book of Lists, Third Edition, © 1993 by Prentice Hall

8. *Heidi*, Johanna Spyri
9. *Tom Sawyer*, Mark Twain
10. *The Secret Garden*, Frances H. Burnett

Source: Based on a survey of 90,000 Americans in 1970, sponsored by The Mott Foundation.

EDUCATORS' READING LIST

Preschool

Dr. Seuss series, Dr. Seuss
Mother Goose Stories
The Little Engine That Could, Watty Piper
Where the Wild Things Are, Maurice Sendak
Make Way for Ducklings, Robert McCloskey

Elementary (K–6)

The Velveteen Rabbit, Margery Williams
Alexander and the Terrible, Horrible, No Good, Very Bad Day, Judith Viorst
Ira Sleeps Over, Bernard Waber
The Tale of Peter Rabbit, Beatrix Potter
Winnie-the-Pooh, A. A. Milne
Charlotte's Web, E. B. White
Tales of a Fourth-Grade Nothing, Judy Blume
Where the Red Fern Grows, Wilson Rawls
The Laura Ingalls Wilder series, Laura Ingalls Wilder
Little Women, Louisa May Alcott

Junior High School (7–9)

Where the Red Fern Grows, Wilson Rawls
Anne Frank: Diary of a Young Girl, Anne Frank
The Red Badge of Courage, Stephen Crane
Call of the Wild, Jack London
Huckleberry Finn, Mark Twain
Treasure Island, Robert Louis Stevenson
The Outsiders, S. E. Hinton

High School (10–12)

The Grapes of Wrath, John Steinbeck
To Kill a Mockingbird, Harper Lee

Source: Recommendations of State Teachers and Principals of the Year.

The Reading Teacher's Book of Lists, Third Edition, © 1993 by Prentice Hall

Huckleberry Finn, Mark Twain
The Scarlet Letter, Nathaniel Hawthorne
A Tale of Two Cities, Charles Dickens
Macbeth, William Shakespeare
The Catcher in the Rye, J. D. Salinger

BOOKS MOST WIDELY ASSIGNED IN PUBLIC SCHOOLS, GRADES 7–12

Romeo and Juliet, William Shakespeare
Macbeth, William Shakespeare
Huckleberry Finn, Mark Twain
To Kill a Mockingbird, Harper Lee
Julius Caesar, William Shakespeare
The Pearl, John Steinbeck
The Scarlet Letter, Nathaniel Hawthorne
Of Mice and Men, John Steinbeck
Diary of a Young Girl, Anne Frank
Hamlet, William Shakespeare
Lord of the Flies, William Golding

The Reading Teacher's Book of Lists, Third Edition, © 1993 by Prentice Hall

116. *Books Most Frequently Read Aloud in Each Grade*

Most teachers read aloud to their classes every day. It's a great idea since it promotes a love of books and reading.

KINDERGARTEN

Alexander and the Terrible, Horrible, No Good, Very Bad Day, J. Viorst
Benjamin and Tulip, R. Wells
Big Orange Splot, D. Pinkwater
Charlotte's Web, E. B. White
Chicka Chicka Boom Boom, B. Martin
Crictor, T. Ungerer
Curious George, H. A. Rey
Corduroy, D. Freeman
The Giving Tree, S. Silverstein
If You Give a Mouse a Cookie, L. Numeroff

King of the Playground, P. Naylor
Jesse Bear, What Will You Wear? N. Carlstrom
Little Bear, E. Minarik
Mike Mulligan and His Steam Shovel, V. Burton
The Runaway Bunny, M. W. Brown
When Will I Read?, M. Cohen
The Snowy Day, E. J. Keats
The Story about Ping, M. Flack

FIRST GRADE

Miss Nelson Is Missing, H. Allard
Amazing Grace, M. Hoffman
Charlotte's Web, E. B. White
And to Think That I Saw It on Mulberry Street, Dr. Seuss
Where the Wild Things Are, M. Sendak
Chrysanthemum, K. Henkes
Alexander and the Terrible, Horrible, No Good, Very Bad Day, J. Viorst
Frog and Toad are Friends, A. Lobel
Fantastic Mr. Fox, R. Dahl
It's George, M. Cohen

Henry and Mudge, C. Rylant
Lyle, Lyle Crocodile, B. Waber
Millions of Cats, W. Gag
First Grade King, K. L. Williams
The Polar Express, C. Van Allsburg
The Snowy Day, E. J. Keats
The True Story of the Three Little Pigs, J. Scieszka
The Secret in the Matchbox, V. Willis
Wiley and the Hairy Man, M. Bang
Heckedy Peg, A. Wood

SECOND GRADE

Charlotte's Web, E. B. White
Madeline, L. Bemelmans
Fat Chance, Claude, J. Nixon
Ramona the Pest, B. Cleary
My Father's Dragon, R. Gannet
Molly's Pilgrim, B. Cohen

A Job for Jenny Archer, E. Conford
The Courage of Sarah Noble, A. Dalgleish
Beans on the Roof, B. Byars
Herbie Jones, S. Kline
In a Messy, Messy Room, J. Gorog
Flossie and the Fox, P. McKissack

Amelia Bedelia, P. Parish
The Cut-Ups, J. Marshall
Josie Smith, M. Nabb
James and the Giant Peach, R. Dahl

The Show and Tell War, J. L. Smith
Henry Huggins, B. Cleary
The Three Billy Goats Gruff, P. Galdone
The Stories Julian Tells, E. Cameron

THIRD GRADE

Mr. Popper's Penguins, R. Atwater
The Bad Times of Irma Baumlein, C. Brink
The Mouse and the Motorcycle, B. Cleary
Ace the Very Important Pig, R. King-Smith
The Little House on the Prairie, L. I. Wilder
The Seven Treasure Hunts, B. Byars
James and the Giant Peach, R. Dahl
Charlie and the Chocolate Factory, R. Dahl
Mrs. Piggle-Wiggle, B. MacDonald
Quentin Corn, M. Stolz
Stuart Little, E. B. White

Russell Sprouts, J. Hurwitz
Pippi Longstocking, A. Lindgren
The Boxcar Children, G. C. Warner
The Chocolate Touch, P. Catling
Did You Carry the Flag Today, Charley?
  R. Caudill
Freckle Juice, J. Blume
Encyclopedia Brown, D. J. Sobol
Ramona Quimby, Age 8, B. Cleary
Sarah, Plain and Tall, P. MacLachlan

FOURTH GRADE

Tales of a Fourth-Grade Nothing, J. Blume
Dear Mr. Henshaw, B. Cleary
The Toothpaste Millionaire, J. Merrill
Mrs. Frisby and the Rats of NIMH,
  R. C. O'Brien
The Not Just Anybody Family, B. Byars
How to Eat Fried Worms, T. Rockwell
The Best Christmas Pageant Ever,
  B. Robinson
Sideways Stories from Wayside School,
  L. Sachar
Getting Something on Maggie Marmelstein,
  M. Sharmat

Class Clown, J. Hurwitz
The Good Master, K. Seredy
Half Magic, E. Eager
Oh, Honestly Angela, N. Robinson
The Trumpet of the Swan, E. B. White
The Kid in the Red Jacket, B. Park
Unreal! Eight Surprising Stories, P. Jenning
Ida Early Comes Over the Mountain,
  R. Burch
Littlejim, G. Houston
The Light in the Attic, S. Silverstein
The BFG, R. Dahl

FIFTH GRADE

Among the Dolls, W. Sleator
Anastasia Krupnik, L. Lowery
Otherwise Known as Sheila the Great,
  J. Blume

On Meeting Witches at Wells, J. Gorog
Beetles, Lightly Toasted, P. Naylor
Bridge to Terebitha, K. Paterson

The Reading Teacher's Book of Lists, Third Edition, © 1993 by Prentice Hall

The Mixed-Up Files of Mrs. Basil E. Frankweiler, E. Konigsburg
Matilda, R. Dahl
The Pushcart War, J. Merrill
Tornado, H. Milton
On My Honor, M. Bauer
A Wrinkle in Time, M. L'Engle

The Secret Garden, F. Burnett
The Pinballs, B. Byars
Paul's Volcano, B. Gormley
Tom Sawyer, S. Clemens
The Wolves of Willoughby Chase, J. Aiken
The Cook Camp, G. Paulsen
New Kid on the Block, J. Prelutsky

SIXTH GRADE

A Darker Magic, M. Bedard
The Great Gilly Hopkins, K. Paterson
Isabelle and Little Orphan Frannie, C. Greene
Island of the Blue Dolphins, S. O'Dell
The True Confessions of Charlotte Doyle, Avi
Mrs. Frisby and the Rats of NIMH, R. C. O'Brien
Jackaroo, C. Voight
I Know What You Did Last Summer, L. Duncan

Hatchet, G. Paulsen
There's a Boy in the Girl's Bathroom, L. Sachar
Maniac Magee, J. Spinelli
Shiloh, P. Naylor
The Machine Gunners, R. Westall
Beauty, R. McKinley
Where the Red Fern Grows, W. Rawls
My Side of the Mountain, J. C. George
Roll of Thunder, Hear My Cry, M. Taylor
Weasel, C. C. DeFelice

117. *Book Interest Arousers*

1. **Library corner in your classroom.** Change frequently. Add a bulletin board with rotating themes, such as horses, history, science, favorite authors, mysteries, and so forth.

2. **New-book advertisements.** Have a teacher or student make brief reviews, oral reports, posters, or a contest with a competing book.

3. **Book fair.** Exchange an exhibit of books with another class. Show off award winners. Specialize in some types of new books, old books, picture books, Indian books, joke books, novels, and so forth.

4. **Oral reading by the teacher** or a child. Read a whole book, read interesting parts, read just the first chapter, read about a specific character. Especially read to upper-grade children. They love it.

5. **Poetry reading** by a teacher or a student. Have students memorize classic poems. Read new poems by published authors or read students poems. Read winners from a schoolwide poetry contest.

6. **Hold individual reading conferences** regularly with every student. Discuss books being read. Suggest similar books. Suggest other types of books.

7. **Visit libraries** both in school and in other classes, as well as your public library. Make sure every parent gets every student a public library card.

8. **Keep a books-read chart** for your class and for each student. Encourage progress and sometimes competition.

9. **Have book-related activities.** In art, design new book jackets or illustrations of book scenes. In drama, act out parts of a book. Discuss different endings.

10. **Tie in book with other subjects.** What was happening in history at the same time? Was the radio invented then? What causes volcanos? Are murders or sports upsets really happening today?

The Reading Teacher's Book of Lists, Third Edition, © 1993 by Prentice Hall

118. *Major Reading Journals*

To stay abreast of happenings in the field of reading instruction, read one of the professional journals. Ask to keep a subscription in your school library or better yet, in the teacher's room.

Journal of Reading (general and secondary orientation) International Reading Association. Eight issues yearly.

Journal of Reading Behavior (research orientation) National Reading Conference. Quarterly.

The Reading Teacher (elementary teacher orientation) International Reading Association. Eight issues yearly. (Formerly *Journal of Developmental Reading*.)

Reading Research Quarterly (research orientation) International Reading Association. Quarterly.

Reading World (general and college orientation) College Reading Association. Quarterly.

Language Arts (elementary teacher and language arts orientation) National Council of Teachers of English. Eight issues yearly. (Formerly *Elementary English*.)

119. *Book Words*

Good readers know how to talk about parts of a book. Here are some terms that can help you in discussing a book, its parts, and some book types. For book contents, see the Library Classifications, List 120 (Library of Congress and Dewey Decimal classifications systems). Your school or neighborhood librarian can also help you with book parts and book classification lessons.

BOOK PARTS

Jacket
Cover—soft
　　　　hard
Spine
End papers
Binding—sewn
　　　　perfect
　　　　spiral
Title page—title
　　　　author
　　　　publisher
　　　　(date)
Copyright—date
　　　　L.C. Number
　　　　Dewey Number
　　　　I.S.B.N. Number
　　　　Copying Limits
Preface
Introduction
Table of Contents
List of Figures
List of Tables
Chapters
Sub Headings
Divisions
Index—subject
　　　　author
　　　　(mixed together)
Glossary
Bibliography
References
Appendices
Series
Volume

BOOK TYPES

Reference
Trade
Text
Picture
Coffee table
Juveniles
Fiction

REFERENCE BOOKS

Dictionary
Encyclopedia
Thesaurus
Atlas
Reader's Guide
Almanac
Reading Teachers Book of Lists

TYPE FONTS (examples)

Korinna
Brush
Aster (a serif typeface)
Helvetica (a sans serif typeface)

TYPE SIZES (examples)

8 point
9 point
10 point
12 point
14 point

THE PAGE

Footnotes
Running head
Subtitles
Paragraph
Indentation
Single space
Double space
Leading
Margins (left and right)

PAPER

Newsprint
Bond
Rag
Weight (thickness)
Tint (color)
Special purpose (photocopy, ditto)

The Reading Teacher's Book of Lists, Third Edition, © 1993 by Prentice Hall

120. *Library Classifications*

Most universities, research organizations, large public libraries, and, of course, the Library of Congress use the Library of Congress classifications for organizing their book collections. Most school libraries and smaller public libraries use the Dewey Decimal System. Students should have at least a modest acquaintance with both systems.

LIBRARY OF CONGRESS CLASSIFICATION

A General Works
B Philosophy and Religion
C History of Civilization
D General History
E–F History—Americas
G Geography and Anthropology
H Social Sciences
J Political Science
K Law
L Education
M Music
N Fine Arts
P Language and Literature
PA Classical Language and Literature
PB-PH Modern European Languages
PJ-PL Oriental Language and Literature
PN General Literature
PQ French, Italian, Spanish, Portuguese Literature
PR English Literature
PS American Literature
PT German, Dutch, Scandinavian Literature
Q Science
R Medicine
S Agriculture
T Technology
U Military Science
V Naval Science
Z Bibliography

SIMPLIFIED DEWEY DECIMAL SYSTEM

000 General Works
100 Philosophy and Psychology
200 Religion
300 Social Sciences
310 Statistics
320 Political Science
330 Economics
331 Labor Economics
331.3 Labor by Age Groups
331.39 Employed Middle-aged and Aged
340 Law
350 Administration
360 Welfare and Social Institutions
370 Education
380 Public Services and Utilities
390 Customs and Folklore
400 Philology
500 Pure Science
600 Applied Science
700 Fine Arts
800 Literature
900 History

Note: Libraries that use the Dewey Decimal system classify fiction by author's last name and it is usually divided into Adult Fiction and Children's Fiction. All the books in the library are listed in the "Card Catalogue." Most books have 3 cards: an author card, a subject card, and a title card.

121. Book Report Alternatives

Once you have enticed your students to read, consult this list of alternatives for fifty exciting things to do in place of writing a book report.

1. Draw a time line to illustrate the events in the story.
2. Construct a story map to show the plot and setting.
3. Create a jacket for the book, complete with illustrations and blurbs.
4. Prepare a chart showing the characters, their relationships, and a few biographical facts about each.
5. Create a poster-sized ad for the book.
6. Have a panel discussion if several students read the same book.
7. Dramatize an incident or an important character alone or with others.
8. Do a radio announcement to publicize the book.
9. Have individual conferences with students to get their personal reactions.
10. Appoint a committee to conduct peer discussion and seminars on books.
11. Illustrate the story, take slides, coordinate music and narration, and give a multimedia presentation.
12. Write a play based on the continuation of the story or a new adventure for the characters.
13. Give a demonstration of what was learned from a how-to book.
14. Compose a telegram about the book, limited to twenty words.
15. Dramatically read a part of the book to the class to get them hooked.
16. Keep a diary of one of the characters in the story, using first person.
17. Write a letter to the author telling why you liked the book, your favorite parts, what you would have done with the plot.
18. Be a newspaper columnist; write a review for the book section.
19. Explain how the story might have ended if a key character or incident were changed.
20. Write a letter to the key character to tell him or her how to solve the problem.
21. Write a newspaper article based on an incident from the book.
22. Write a biography of the leading character, using information from the book.
23. Write an obituary article about a key character, giving an account of what he or she was best known for.
24. Give a testimonial speech citing the character for special distinctions noted in the book.
25. Compare the movie and book versions of the same story.
26. Make a diorama to show the time and setting of the story.
27. Have a character day. Dress up as your favorite character in the story and relive some of the story.
28. Rewrite the story as a TV movie, including staging directions.

The Reading Teacher's Book of Lists, Third Edition, © 1993 by Prentice Hall

The Reading Teacher's Book of Lists, Third Edition, © 1993 by Prentice Hall

29. Examine the story for the author's craft and try to write a story of your own, imitating the use of tone, setting, style, and so on.

30. Memorize your favorite lines, or write them down for future quoting.

31. Make sketches of some of the action sequences.

32. Read the story into a tape recorder so that others may listen to it.

33. Research the period of history in which the story is set.

34. Make a list of similes, metaphors, or succinct descriptions used in the book.

35. Make puppets and present a show based on the book.

36. Build a clay or papier-mâché bust of a key character.

37. Give a "chalk talk" about the book.

38. Paint a mural that shows the key incidents in the story.

39. Rewrite the story for students in a lower grade. Keep it interesting.

40. File information about the book in a classroom cross-reference. Include author, story type, list of books it is similar to, and so on.

41. Imagine a *Life* magazine story on the book you've just read. What are several scenes you think ought to be photographed? Describe the photographs and write captions for them.

42. Tell the general effect of the book on you. What made you feel the way you did?

43. Report on any new, interesting, or challenging ideas you gained through reading the book.

44. Letter the title of the book vertically; then write a brief phrase applicable to the book for each letter.

45. Tell what kind of people should read this book. Who shouldn't?

46. Explain why you would or would not recommend this book to your parents for their reading. Be specific in your references to characters, plot, and setting.

47. Explain why you think this book will/will not be read a hundred years from now. Support your viewpoint by making specific references to plot, setting, characters, and author's style.

48. Make a list of five to ten significant questions about this book that you think anyone who reads this book should be able to answer.

49. Write an original poem after you have read a book of poetry.

50. If it is a geographical book, make a map and locate places found in the book.

See also List 122, Book Report Form.

122. *Book Report Form*

This form can be duplicated and distributed for reports on short stories, plays, and books.

TITLE _____

AUTHOR _____

PUBLISHER _____

COPYRIGHT DATE _____

ILLUSTRATOR _____

THEME OR MAIN IDEA:

MAIN CHARACTERS:

SETTING:

SUMMARY:

OPINION/RECOMMENDATIONS:

The Reading Teacher's Book of Lists, Third Edition, © 1993 by Prentice Hall

See also List 121, Book Report Alternatives; List 61, Story Guide.

123. *Book List Collections*

Use this list of indexes, anthologies, collections, and recommendations to identify and locate books for the classroom, school library, or personal library. Many of these reference or resource titles can be found in your public library.

FICTION AND NONFICTION COLLECTIONS

American Library Association. *Notable Children's Books*. (annual) Chicago: ALA. Bibliographic information and plot summaries are given for the winners of an annual review of new books.

American Library Association. *Outstanding Books for the College Bound*. (annual) Chicago: ALA. A series of bibliographic lists highlighting the best in fiction, nonfiction, biographies, fine arts, and theater reading for precollege students.

Arbuthnot, May. (1976) *The Arbuthnot Anthology of Children's Literature*. New York: Lothrop. Contains a wealth of information about reading material for young children as well as book recommendations.

Barstow, Barbara, and Judith Riggle. (1989) *Beyond Picture Books*. New York: R. R. Bowker. More than 1,500 early reading books are presented with plots, evaluations, and bibliographic information. A list of 200 first-grade readers with readability information is included.

Bernstein, Joanne, and Marsha Rudman. (1988) *Books to Help Children Cope with Separation and Loss*. Volume 3. New York: R. R. Bowker. A good reference guide to more than 600 titles dealing with separation themes and appropriate for children kindergarten to junior high.

Bingham, Jane, and Grayce Scholt. (1980) *Fifteen Centuries of Children's Literature: An Annotated Chronology of British and American Works in Historical Context*. Westport, CT: Greenwood Press. A good resource for a history of children's literature.

Breen, Karen. (1988) *Index to Collective Biographies for Young Readers*. New York: R. R. Bowker. Indexes more than 1,000 collective biographies covering more than 10,000 famous people; easy to use indexes by name, field, and book title.

Children's Literature Center. (annual) *Books for Children*. Washington, DC: Library of Congress. Recommendations for good reading selected from recently published fiction and nonfiction. Books are listed by age group, and entries include bibliographic and thematic information.

Children's Literature Center. (1990) *Children and Reading: A Reading List for Parents*. Washington, DC: Library of Congress. Recommended reading lists for use by parents.

Children's Magazine Guide. Periodical. New York: R. R. Bowker. A unique source that lets children find articles on subjects of interest in more than thirty-five children's magazines.

Cole, Joanna. (1983) *Best-loved Folktales of the World*. New York: Doubleday. Anthology of 200 folktales from around the world.

Dreyer, Sharon. (1981) *The Bookfinder: A Guide to Children's Literature about the Needs and Problems of Youth Aged 2–15*. New York: American Guidance Service.

Fakih, Kimberly. (1992) *The Literature of Delight: A Critical Guide to Humorous Books for Children*. New York: R. R. Bowker. A guide to more than 1,000 fiction and nonfiction titles sure to please students, preschool through junior high.

Freeman, Judy. (1990) *Books Kids Will Sit Still For: The Complete Read-Aloud Guide*. 2nd Ed. New York: R. R. Bowker. A guide to the best fiction, poetry, folktales, and nonfiction to read aloud to students, grades preschool through 6.

Friedberg, Joan; June Mullins, and Adelaide Sukiennik. (1991) *Portraying the Disabled: A Guide to Juvenile Non-Fiction*. New York: R. R. Bowker. Annotated bibliography of more than 350 nonfiction books covering physical, sensory, cognitive, and behavioral disabilities.

Gillespie, John, and Corrinne Naden. (1990) *Best Books for Children: Preschool Through Grade 6*. New York: R. R. Bowker. Annotated bibliography of nearly 12,000 titles in 500 categories, each with recommendations from two or more notable children's book journals.

Gillespie, John. (1991) *Best Books for Junior High Readers*. New York: R. R. Bowker. Annotated bibliography of nearly 6,000 recommended titles for recreation and content-based reading for students in grades 7 through 9. An appendix of more than 750 titles for advanced students is included.

Gillis, Ruth. (1978) *Children's Books for Times of Stress: An Annotated Bibliography*. Bloomington, IN: Indiana University Press.

Hart, Carole; et al. (eds.) (1974) *Free to be You and Me*. New York: McGraw-Hill. Collection of stories, poems, and art that encourage children to excel.

Haviland, Virginia. (1972) *Children's Literature: A Guide to Reference Sources*. Washington, DC: Library of Congress. Good for school and other library collections.

Hearne, Betsy. (1990) *Choosing Books for Children: A Commonsense Guide*. Revised. New York: Delacorte Press/Delta. Helpful information about children's books, including recommendations.

International Reading Association and Children's Book Council. (annual) *Children's Choices*. Newark, DE: IRA. Results of an annual survey of 10,000 students' preferences for recently published trade books. Winning books are annotated and divided by reader's age.

International Reading Association and Children's Book Council. (1991) *99 Favorite Paperbacks 1991*. Newark, DE: IRA. A list of poetry, fiction, and nonfiction favorites for students aged twelve and under.

International Reading Association. (annual) *Young Adults' Choices*. Newark, DE: IRA. Results of an annual survey of 4,500 middle school through high school students' preferences for recently published trade books. Bibliographic information and plot summaries are included for the winners.

Kennedy, DayAnn, Stella Spangler, and Mary Ann Vanderwerf. (1990) *Science & Technology in Fact and Fiction*. A valuable source for good books on science topics for elementary-school children. Readability levels are included.

Kimmel, Margaret, and Elizabeth Segel. (1991) *For Reading Out Loud!: A Guide to Sharing Books with Children*. Revised. New York: Dell. Annotated list of books recommended for reading aloud to children preschool through grade 8.

Landsberg, Michele. (1987) *Reading for the Love of It: Best Books for Young Readers*. New York: Prentice-Hall. An annotated list of recommended books.

LiBretto, Ellen. (1990) *High/Lo Handbook: Encouraging Literacy in the 1990's*. 3rd. Ed. New York: R. R. Bowker. A guide to books, magazines, and software for reluctant or remedial readers, grades 7 through high school.

Lima, Carolyn. (1989) *A to Zoo: Subject Access to Children's Picture Books*. New York: R. R. Bowker. Annotated bibliography of 11,500 books indexed by subject, author, title, illustrator, and with bibliographic information.

Lipson, Eden. (1991) *The New York Times Parent's Guide to the Best Books for Children*. New York: Times Books. An annotated list of recommended books and other helpful information about selecting books for children.

Lynn, Ruth. (1988) *Fantasy Literature for Children and Young Adults*. 3rd. Ed. New York: R. R. Bowker. Recommendations for more than 3,000 award winning fantasy novels and collections. Titles are grouped by topics, from allegory to witchcraft and sorcery.

Miller-Lachmann, Lyn. (1991) *Our Family, Our Friends, Our World: An Annotated Guide to Significant Multicultural Books for Children and Teenagers*. New York: R. R. Bowker. A bibliographic guide to fine fiction and nonfiction focusing on the life and culture of minority people in the U.S. and Canada as well as in their native lands.

Reading Is Fundamental. (1987) *When We Were Young*. Washington, DC: Reading Is Fundamental. Favorite book recommendations from RIF kids and volunteers. Also special section listing the favorite books of famous people, including Stephen King, Michael Learned, and Billy Joel.

Schulman, L. (1990) *The Random House Book of Sports Stories*. New York: Random House. A collection of sports-related stories by some of the best modern authors.

Schwartz, Alvin (ed.) (1983) *Scary Stories to Tell in the Dark*. New York: Harper. A list of the best thrillers for children.

Sinclair, Patti. (1992) *E for Environment: An Annotated Bibliography of Children's Books with Environmental Themes*. New York: R. R. Bowker. More than 500 children's books on environmental topics are profiled and indexed. Reading levels are included.

Singer, Isaac. (1966) *Zlateh the Goat and Other Stories*. New York: Harper. A collection of folk tales from Eastern European Jewish tradition.

Stott, Jon. (1984) *Children's Literature from A to Z: A Guide for Parents and Teachers*. New York: McGraw-Hill. An annotated list of recommended books and other helpful information about selecting books for children.

The Young Adult Reader's Adviser. (1991). New York: R. R. Bowker. A substantial reference for students grades 6 through 12. The two-volume work presents introductions to and recommendations for reading about key authors and about topics from the curriculum.

Trelease, Jim. (1989) *The New Read Aloud Handbook*. Revised. New York: Penguin. Annotated list of books selected for reading to children grades preschool through 8. The book also includes chapters on the why and how to read aloud to your students.

Young Adult Library Services Association. (annual) *Best Books for Young Adults*. Chicago: American Library Association. A list of 70 recommendations of "best" recently published fiction and nonfiction titles for junior and senior high school students.

Young Adult Library Services Association. (annual) *Recommended Books for Reluctant Young Readers*. Chicago: American Library Association. A list of 27 fiction and 29 nonfiction recommendations intended to stimulate the interest of reluctant teen readers. All recommended books are at sixth grade readability or below.

POETRY COLLECTIONS

Adoff, Arnold (ed.). (1970) *I Am the Darker Brother: An Anthology of Modern Poems by Black Americans*. New York: Macmillan.

Bodecker, Nils. (1974) *"Let's Marry," Said the Cherry, and Other Nonsense Poems*. Atheneum.

Bodecker, Nils. (1983) *Snowman Sniffles and Other Verse*. Atheneum.

Elledge, Scott (ed.) (1990) *Wider Than the Sky: Poems to Grow Up With*. New York: Harper Collins.

Fishback, Margaret. (1942) *I Feel Better Now and Out of My Head*. New York: World.

McCord, David. (1977) *One at a Time*. New York: Little, Brown.

Obligato, Lillian. (1983) *Faint Frogs Feeling Feverish and Other Terrifically Tantalizing Tongue Twisters*. New York: Viking.

Silverstein, Shel. (1974) *Where the Sidewalk Ends*. New York: Harper & Row.

Silverstein, Shel. (1981) *A Light in the Attic*. New York: Harper & Row.

Wallace, Daisy. (1976) *Monster Poems*. Holiday House.

The Reading Teacher's Book of Lists, Third Edition, © 1993 by Prentice Hall

SECTION XI
Signs, Symbols, and Abbreviations

124. State Abbreviations and Capitals

The official postal abbreviations and the traditional abbreviations are listed for each state. Some of the postal abbreviations are easy to remember, such as NY and FL. Others will take a bit of concentration to get straight, such as MI, MO, MS, MA, MT, and ME. The new postal abbreviations generally are not followed by periods. Literate students need to know them just as they need to know how to spell the state names.

FULL NAME	NEW	OLD	CAPITAL
Alabama	AL	Ala.	Montgomery
Alaska	AK	Alaska	Juneau
Arizona	AZ	Ariz.	Phoenix
Arkansas	AR	Ark.	Little Rock
California	CA	Calif.	Sacramento
Colorado	CO	Colo.	Denver
Connecticut	CT	Conn.	Hartford
Delaware	DE	Del.	Dover
Florida	FL	Fla.	Tallahassee
Georgia	GA	Ga.	Atlanta
Hawaii	HI	Hawaii	Honolulu
Idaho	ID	Idaho	Boise
Illinois	IL	Ill.	Springfield
Indiana	IN	Ind.	Indianapolis
Iowa	IA	Iowa	Des Moines
Kansas	KS	Kans.	Topeka
Kentucky	KY	Ky.	Frankfort
Louisiana	LA	La.	Baton Rouge
Maine	ME	Me.	Augusta
Maryland	MD	Md.	Annapolis
Massachusetts	MA	Mass.	Boston
Michigan	MI	Mich.	Lansing
Minnesota	MN	Minn.	St. Paul
Mississippi	MS	Miss.	Jackson
Missouri	MO	Mo.	Jefferson City
Montana	MT	Mont.	Helena
Nebraska	NE	Nebr.	Lincoln
Nevada	NV	Nev.	Carson City
New Hampshire	NH	N.H.	Concord
New Jersey	NJ	N.J.	Trenton
New Mexico	NM	N.Mex.	Santa Fe
New York	NY	N.Y.	Albany
North Carolina	NC	N.C.	Raleigh
North Dakota	ND	N. Dak.	Bismarck
Ohio	OH	Ohio	Columbus
Oklahoma	OK	Okla.	Oklahoma City
Oregon	OR	Oreg.	Salem
Pennsylvania	PA	Pa.	Harrisburg
Rhode Island	RI	R.I.	Providence
South Carolina	SC	S.C.	Columbia

FULL NAME	NEW	OLD	CAPITAL
South Dakota	SD	S.D.	Pierre
Tennessee	TN	Tenn.	Nashville
Texas	TX	Tex.	Austin
Utah	UT	Utah	Salt Lake City
Vermont	VT	Vt.	Montpelier
Virginia	VA	Va.	Richmond
Washington	WA	Wash.	Olympia
West Virginia	WV	W.Va.	Charleston
Wisconsin	WI	Wisc.	Madison
Wyoming	WY	Wyo.	Cheyenne

FULL NAME	NEW/OLD	CAPITAL
District of Columbia	DC	Washington
Puerto Rico	PR	San Juan
Virgin Islands	VI	St. Thomas

The Reading Teacher's Book of Lists, Third Edition, © 1993 by Prentice Hall

125. *Common Abbreviations*

Abbreviations are so widely used that it is important to know what the common ones stand for. In addition to being an advantage in reading comprehension, knowing and using abbreviations saves time, space, and energy when we write.

The Reading Teacher's Book of Lists, Third Edition, © 1993 by Prentice Hall

acct.	account		dept.	department
A.D.	Anno Domini (in the year of our Lord)		diam.	diameter
adj.	adjective		div.	division
ad lib	ad libitum (improvise)		doz.	dozen
adv.	adverb		Dr.	Doctor, drive
AKA	also known as			
a.m.	ante meridiem (morning)		ea.	each
amt	amount		ed.	edition
anon.	anonymous		e.g.	exempli gratia (for example)
ans.	answer		elec.	electric
Apr.	April		Esq.	Esquire
arith.	arithmetic		et al.	et alii (and others)
assn.	association		etc.	et cetera (and others)
assoc.	association		ex.	example
asst.	assistant			
atty.	attorney		F	Fahrenheit
Aug.	August		Feb.	February
ave.	avenue		fem.	feminine
			fig.	figure
B.A.	Bachelor of Arts		freq.	frequency
bib.	bibliography		Fri.	Friday
biog.	biography		ft.	foot
B.C.	before Christ			
bldg.	building		g	gram
B.S.	Bachelor of Science		gal.	gallon
blvd.	boulevard		Gen.	General
			govt.	government
c	centimeter, centigrade			
cap.	capital		H.M.S.	His (Her) Majesty's Ship
Capt.	Captain		Hon.	Honorable
cc	cubic centimeter		hosp.	hospital
cert.	certificate		hr	hour
chap.	chapter		H.R.H.	His (Her) Royal Highness
Chas.	Charles		ht	height
Col.	Colonel			
conj.	conjunction		ibid.	ibidem (in the same place)
corp.	corporation		id.	idem (the same)
cu	cubic		i.e.	id est (that is)
			illus.	illustration
D.C.	District of Columbia		in.	inch
D.D.	Doctor of Divinity		inc.	incorporated
D.D.S.	Doctor of Dental Surgery		incl.	including
Dec.	December		intro	introduction

Jan.	January		pres.	president
Jour.	Journal		prin.	principal
Jr.	junior		pron.	pronoun
			pt.	pint
kg	kilogram			
			qt.	quart
lat.	latitude		recd.	received
lb.	pound		ref.	referee; reference
lieut.	lieutenant		Rev.	reverend
long.	longitude		R.N.	Registered Nurse
lt.	lieutenant			
			Sat.	Saturday
M.A.	Master of Arts		sci.	science
mag.	magazine		sec.	second
masc.	masculine		Sept.	September
math	mathematics		sgt.	sergeant
M.D.	Doctor of Medicine		sing.	singular
mdse.	merchandise		sq.	square
med.	medium		Sr.	Senior; Sister
mgr.	manager		St.	Street; Saint
min.	minute		subj.	subject
misc.	miscellaneous		Sun	Sunday
ml	milliliter		supt.	superintendent
mo.	month			
mph	miles per hour		tel.	telephone
Mr.	mister		Thurs.	Thursday
Mrs.	mistress		Tues.	Tuesday
neg.	negative		univ.	university
neut.	neuter		USA	United States of America
no.	number			
Nov.	November		vet.	veterinarian; veteran
			vocab.	vocabulary
Oct.	October		vol.	volume
opp.	opposite		vs.	versus
oz.	ounce			
			Wed.	Wednesday
p.	page		wk.	week
pd.	paid		Wm.	William
Ph.D.	Doctor of Philosophy		wt.	weight
pkg.	package			
pl.	plural		yd.	yard
p.m.	post meridiem (afternoon)		yr.	year
pop.	population			
pp.	pages			

See also List 13, Measurement; List 36, Acronyms and Initializations; and List 124, State Abbreviations and Capitals.

The Reading Teacher's Book of Lists, Third Edition, © 1993 by Prentice Hall

126. *Education Abbreviations*

The field of education has its share of abbreviations. Here are some widely known ones that you may find useful.

AASA	American Association of School Administrators
ADD/ADHD	Attention Deficit Disorder/Attention Deficit Hyperactivity Disorder
AFT	American Federation of Teachers
AP	Advanced Placement
ASCD	Association for Supervision and Curriculum Development
CEC	Council for Exceptional Children
CEEB	College Entrance Exam Board
EH	Emotionally Handicapped
ERIC	Educational Resources Information Center
ESL	English as a Second Language
ETS	Educational Testing Service
GED	General Educational Development Test (high school equivalency test)
IRA	International Reading Association
LEP	Limited English Proficiency
LD	Learning Disabled
MH	Mentally Handicapped
NAEP	National Assessment of Educational Progress
NAESP	National Association of Elementary School Principals
NASSP	National Association of Secondary School Principals
NCATE	National Council for Accreditation of Teacher Education
NCEA	National Catholic Educational Association
NCES	National Center for Educational Statistics
NCPT	National Congress of Parents and Teachers
NCTE	National Council of Teachers of English
NCTM	National Council of Teachers of Mathematics
NEA	National Education Association
NSF	National Science Foundation
NSTA	National Science Teachers Association
SAT	Scholastic Aptitude Test

127. *Dictionary Phonetic Symbols*

Dictionaries tell you how to pronounce words by using phonetic symbols. These are based on the Roman alphabet but add diacritical marks and special letter combinations. Although all dictionaries use similar phonetic symbols, they are not all identical. This list shows four of the more widely used sets of symbols.

COMMON AND UNCOMMON SPELLINGS FOR PHONEMES	THORNDIKE BARNHART (SCOTT FORESMAN)	WEBSTER-MERRIAM (AMERICAN BOOK CO.)	AMERICAN HERITAGE (HOUGHTON MIFFLIN)	RANDOM HOUSE (SILVER BURDETT & GINN)
A Short h<u>a</u>t, pl<u>ai</u>d	a	a	ă	a
A Long <u>a</u>ge, <u>ai</u>d, g<u>ao</u>l, g<u>au</u>ge, s<u>ay</u>, br<u>ea</u>k, v<u>ai</u>n, th<u>ey</u>	ā	ā	ā	ā
A ("air" sound-diphthong) c<u>a</u>re, <u>ai</u>r, wh<u>e</u>re, p<u>ea</u>r, th<u>ei</u>r	ā, er, ar	eər	âr	â(r)
A Broad f<u>a</u>ther, h<u>ea</u>rt, s<u>e</u>rgeant	ä	ä	ä	ä
B b<u>a</u>d, ra<u>bb</u>it	b	b	b	b
CH Digraph <u>ch</u>ild, wat<u>ch</u>, righ<u>te</u>ous, ques<u>ti</u>on, vir<u>tu</u>ous	ch	ch	ch	ch ‿
D <u>d</u>id, a<u>dd</u>, fille<u>d</u>	d	d	d	d
E short m<u>a</u>ny, <u>ae</u>sthetic, s<u>ai</u>d, s<u>ay</u>s, l<u>e</u>t, br<u>ea</u>d, h<u>ei</u>fer, l<u>eo</u>pard, fr<u>ie</u>nd, b<u>u</u>ry	e	ĕ	ĕ	e
E Long C<u>ae</u>sar, qu<u>ay</u>, <u>e</u>qual, t<u>ea</u>m, b<u>ee</u>, rec<u>ei</u>ve, p<u>eo</u>ple, k<u>ey</u>, mach<u>i</u>ne, bel<u>ie</u>ve, ph<u>oe</u>nix	ē	ē	ē	ē
R (or short u plus R) st<u>er</u>n, p<u>ea</u>rl, f<u>ir</u>st, w<u>or</u>d, j<u>our</u>ney, t<u>ur</u>n, m<u>y</u>rtle	ėr	ər	ûr	û(r)
F <u>f</u>at, e<u>ff</u>ort, lau<u>gh</u>, <u>ph</u>rase	f	f	f	f
G <u>g</u>o, e<u>gg</u>, <u>gh</u>ost, <u>gu</u>est, catalo<u>gue</u>	g	g	g	g
H <u>h</u>e, <u>wh</u>o	h	h	h	h

The Reading Teacher's Book of Lists, Third Edition, © 1993 by Prentice Hall

The Reading Teacher's Book of Lists, Third Edition, © 1993 by Prentice Hall

COMMON AND UNCOMMON SPELLINGS FOR PHONEMES	THORNDIKE BARNHART (SCOTT FORESMAN)	WEBSTER-MERRIAM (AMERICAN BOOK CO.)	AMERICAN HERITAGE (HOUGHTON MIFFLIN)	RANDOM HOUSE (SILVER BURDETT & GINN)
WH Digraph wheat	hw	hw	hw	hw
I Short England, been, bit, sieve, women, busy. build, hymn	i	i	ĭ	i
I Long aisle, aye, height, eye, ice, lie, buy, sky	ī	ī	ī	ī
J bridge, gradual, soldier, tragic, exaggerate, jam	j	j	j	j
K coat, account, chemistry, back, acquire, sacque, kind, liquor	k	k	k	k
L land, tell	l	l	l	l
M drachm, paradigm, calm, me, climb, common, solemn	m	m	m	m
N gnaw, knife, no, manner, pneumonia	n	n	n	n
NG Blend ink, long, tongue	ng	ng	ng	n͡g
O Short watch, hot	o	ä	ŏ	o
O Long beau, yeoman, sew, open, boat, toe, oh, brooch, soul, low	ō	ō	ō	ō
O Broad all, Utah, taught, law, order, broad, bought	ô	ȯ	ô	ô
OI Diphthong boil, boy	oi	ȯi	oi	oi
OU Diphthong house, bough, now	ou	au̇	ou	ou
P cup, happy	p	p	p	p
R run, rhythm, carry	r	r	r	r
S cent, say, scent, schism, miss	s	s	s	s

COMMON AND UNCOMMON SPELLINGS FOR PHONEMES	THORNDIKE BARNHART (SCOTT FORESMAN)	WEBSTER-MERRIAM (AMERICAN BOOK CO.)	AMERICAN HERITAGE (HOUGHTON MIFFLIN)	RANDOM HOUSE (SILVER BURDETT & GINN)
SH Digraph ocean, machine, special, sure, schist, conscience, nauseous, pshaw, she, tension, issue, mission, nation	sh	sh	sh	sh͜
T stopped, bought, tell, Thomas, button	t	t	t	t
TH (voiceless) thin	th	th	th	th͜
TH (voiced) then, breathe	ŦH	th̲	*th*	t̶h
U Short come, does, flood, trouble, cup	u	ə	ŭ	u
U Long beauty, feud, queue, few, adieu, view, use		yü	yo͞o	yo͞o
U Short wolf, good, should, full	u̇	u	o͝o	o͝o
OO Long maneuver, threw, move, shoe, food, you, rule, fruit	ü	ü	o͞o	o͞o
V of, Stephen, very, flivver	v	v	v	v
W choir, quick, will	w	w	w	w
Y (consonant) opinion, hallelujah, you	y	y	y	y
Z has, discern, scissors, Xerxes, zero, buzz	z	z	z	z
ZH garage, measure, division, azure, brazier	zh	zh	zh	zh͜
A (schwa) alone, fountain, moment, pencil, complete, cautious, circus	ə	ə	ə	ə

The Reading Teacher's Book of Lists, Third Edition, © 1993 by Prentice Hall

Diacritical Marks

(circumflex)	ôrder
(macron)	ēqual
(tilde)	cañon
(dieresis)	naïve
(cedilla)	façade
(single dot)	pu̇t
(acute accent)	attaché
(grave accent)	à la mode

See also List 48, Phonics Example Words.

128. *Foreign Alphabets*

The table of alphabets shows how some other languages are written. Your students will enjoy writing their names and other messages using the different alphabets.

Hebrew
Vowels are not represented in normal Hebrew writing, but for educational purposes they are indicated by a system of subscript and superscript dots.
The transliterations shown in parentheses apply when the letter falls at the end of a word. The transliterations with subscript dots are pharyngeal consonants, as in Arabic.
The second forms shown are used when the letter falls at the end of a word.

Greek
The superscript ' on an initial vowel or *rhō*, called the "rough breathing," represents an aspirate. Lack of aspiration on an initial vowel is indicated by the superscript ', called the "smooth breathing."
When *gamma* precedes *kappa, xi, khi,* or another *gamma*, it has the value *n* and is so transliterated. The second lower-case form of *sigma* is used only in final position.

Russian
[1]This letter, called *tvordiĭ znak*, "hard sign," is very rare in modern Russian. It indicates that the previous consonant remains hard even though followed by a front vowel.
[2]This letter, called *myakiĭ znak*, "soft sign," indicates that the previous consonant is palatalized even when a front vowel does not follow.

HEBREW

Forms	Name	Sound
א	'aleph	
ב	bĕth	b (bh)
ג	gimel	g (gh)
ד	dăleth	d (dh)
ה	hĕ	h
ו	waw	w
ז	zayin	z
ח	ḥeth	ḥ
ט	ṭeth	ṭ
י	yodh	y
כ ך	kăph	k (kh)
ל	lămedh	l
מ ם	mĕm	m
נ ן	nûn	n
ס	samekh	s
ע	'ayin	'
פ ף	pĕ	p (ph)
צ ץ	ṣadhe	ṣ
ק	qōph	q
ר	rĕsh	r
שׂ	sin	s
שׁ	shin	sh
ת	tăw	t (th)

GREEK

Forms	Name	Sound
A α	alpha	a
B β	beta	b
Γ γ	gamma	g (n)
Δ δ	delta	d
E ε	epsilon	e
Z ζ	zĕta	z
H η	ĕta	ē
Θ θ	thĕta	th
I ι	iota	i
K κ	kappa	k
Λ λ	lambda	l
M μ	mu	m
N ν	nu	n
Ξ ξ	xi	x
O o	omicron	o
Π π	pi	p
P ρ	rhō	r (rh)
Σ σ ς	sigma	s
T τ	tau	t
Υ υ	upsilon	u
Φ φ	phi	ph
X χ	khi	kh
Ψ ψ	psi	ps
Ω ω	ōmega	ō

RUSSIAN

Forms	Sound
А а	a
Б б	b
В в	v
Г г	g
Д д	d
Е е	e
Ж ж	zh
З з	z
И и Й й	i, ĭ
К к	k
Л л	l
М м	m
Н н	n
О о	o
П п	p
Р р	r
С с	s
Т т	t
У у	u
Ф ф	f
Х х	kh
Ц ц	ts
Ч ч	ch
Ш ш	sh
Щ щ	shch
Ъ ъ	''[1]
Ы ы	y
Ь ь	'[2]
Э э	e
Ю ю	yu
Я я	ya

The Reading Teacher's Book of Lists, Third Edition, © 1993 by Prentice Hall

129. *Manual Alphabet*

The manual alphabet shows one way in which deaf persons communicate. They also use a signing language that uses hand positions for whole words or concepts, and most can read lips to some extent.

MANUAL ALPHABET

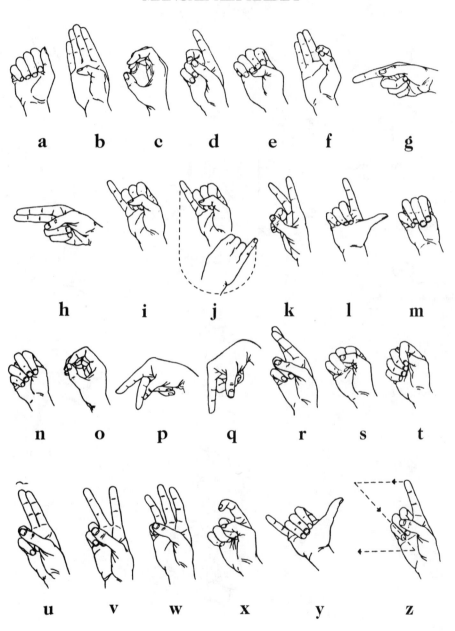

The Reading Teacher's Book of Lists, Third Edition, © 1993 by Prentice Hall

130. *Signing for the Deaf*

Words are communicated by hand positions and movement.

Go

Yes

Stupid

Stand up

Stop

Bad

Smart

Sit down

No

Good

The Reading Teacher's Book of Lists, Third Edition, © 1993 by Prentice Hall

131. *Braille Alphabet*

Blind people learn to read the alphabet by feeling raised dots with their fingers.

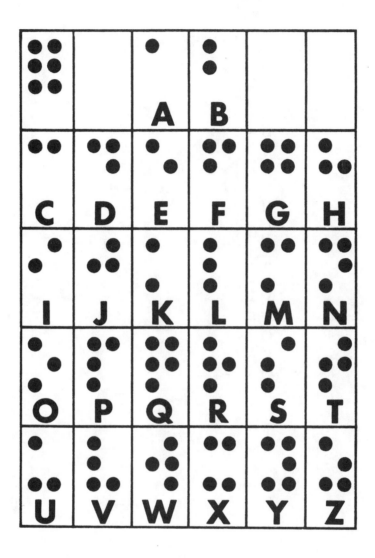

The Reading Teacher's Book of Lists, Third Edition, © 1993 by Prentice Hall

132. *Morse Code*

The Morse Code is still used by some radio hams. With practice, it is possible for amateurs to use it to send flashlight messages.

MORSE CODE

A	·—	V	···—
B	—···	W	·——
C	—·—·	X	—··—
D	—··	Y	—·——
E	·	Z	——··
F	··—·	Á	·——·—
G	——·	Ä	·—·—
H	····	É	··—··
I	··	Ñ	——·——
J	·———	Ö	———·
K	—·—	Ü	··——
L	·—··	1	·————
M	——	2	··———
N	—·	3	···——
O	———	4	····—
P	·——·	5	·····
Q	——·—	6	—····
R	·—·	7	——···
S	···	8	———··
T	—	9	————·
U	··—	0	—————
, (comma)			——··——
· (period)			·—·—·—
?			··——··
;			—·—·—·
:			———···
/			—··—·
- (hyphen)			—····—
apostrophe			·————·
parenthesis			—·——·—
underline			··——·—

The Reading Teacher's Book of Lists, Third Edition, © 1993 by Prentice Hall

133. *Radio Voice Alphabet*

This international alphabet is used by airplane pilots, ship personnel, ham radio operators, and many others who speak over the radio when they need to spell out words or give call letters.

Alfa	Hotel	Oscar	Uniform
Bravo	India	Papa	Victor
Charlie	Juliett	Quebec	Whiskey
Delta	Kilo	Romeo	Xray
Echo	Lima	Sierra	Yankee
Foxtrot	Mike	Tango	Zulu
Golf	November		

134. *General Signs and Symbols*

Many specialized fields have sets of symbols or abbreviations, such as computer science, mathematics, and chemistry, which are needed to understand and work with concepts in those fields. In addition, there are many general-use symbols that we need in everyday life.

+ plus	∟ right angle	≦ or ≤ less than or equal to	∴ therefore
− minus	△ triangle			absolute value	∵ because
± plus or minus	□ square	∪ logical sum or union	‾ vinculum (above letter)
∓ minus or plus	▭ rectangle	∩ logical product or intersection	( ) parentheses
× multiplied by	▱ parallelogram	⊂ is contained in	[ ] brackets
÷ divided by	◡ circle	ε is a member of; permittivity; mean error	{ } braces
= equal to	⌒ arc of circle	: is to; ratio	° degree
≠ or ≠ not equal to	⊥ equilateral	:: as; proportion	′ minute
≈ or ≐ nearly equal to	≙ equiangular	≑ approaches	″ second
≡ identical with	√ radical; root; square root	→ approaches limit of	△ increment
≢ not identical with	∛ cube root	∝ varies as	ω angular frequency; solid angle
⇌ equivalent	∜ fourth root	‖ parallel	Ω ohm
∼ difference	Σ sum	⊥ perpendicular	μΩ microhm
≅ congruent to	! or ⌐ factorial product	∠ angle	MΩ megohm
> greater than	∞ infinity		Φ magnetic flux
≯ not greater than	∫ integral		
< less than	ƒ function		
≮ not less than	∂ or δ differential; variation		
≧ or ≥ greater than or equal to	π pi		

℥ ounce	@ at	♃ per	' grave
ʒ dram	* asterisk	# number	~ tilde
℈ scruple	† dagger	/ virgule; slash; solidus; shilling	^ circumflex
f℥ fluid ounce	‡ double dagger	© copyright	¯ macron
fʒ fluid dram	§ section	‰ per cent	˘ breve
m minim	☞ index	℅ care of	¨ dieresis
& or ⅋ and; ampersand	′ acute	% account of	¸ cedilla
			∧ caret
Ψ dielectric flux; electrostatic flux	♓ Pisces	♀ Venus	∞ haze; dust haze
ρ resistivity	☌ conjunction	⊖ or ⊕ Earth	T thunder
Λ equivalent conductivity	☍ opposition	♂ Mars	< sheet lightning
R reluctance	△ trine	♃ Jupiter	☉ solar corona
→ direction of flow	□ quadrature	♄ Saturn	⊕ solar halo
⇌ electric current	* sextile	♅ Uranus	thunderstorm
◯ benzene ring	☊ dragon's head, ascending node	♆ Neptune	\ direction
→ yields	☋ dragon's tail, descending node	♇ Pluto	○ or ⊙ or ① annual
⇌ reversible reaction	● rain	♈ Aries	⊙⊙ or ② biennial
↓ precipitate	* snow	♉ Taurus	♃ perennial
↑ gas	⊠ snow on ground	♊ Gemini	♂ or ♂ male
‰ salinity	← floating ice crystals	♋ Cancer	♀ female
☉ or ☼ sun	▲ hail	♌ Leo	□ male (in charts)
● or ● new moon	△ sleet	♍ Virgo	○ female (in charts)
☽ first quarter	∨ frostwork	♎ Libra	℞ take (from Latin *Recipe*)
○ or ☀ full moon	⊔ hoarfrost	♏ Scorpius	ĀĀ or Ā or āā of each (doctor's prescription)
☾ last quarter	≡ fog	♐ Sagittarius	℔ pound
☿ Mercury		♑ Capricornus	
		♒ Aquarius	

See also List 124, State Abbreviations and Capitals; List 125, Common Abbreviations; and List 149, Taxonomy of Graphs.

The Reading Teacher's Book of Lists, Third Edition, © 1993 by Prentice Hall

135. *Native American Symbols*

The earliest writings of the American Indians were those of signs and symbols. These symbols are also apparent in their handicraft and jewelry.

HORSE
Journey

MAN
Human Life

SUN RAYS
Constancy

LASSO
Captivity

THUNDERBIRD
Sacred Bearer of Happiness Unlimited

CROSSED ARROWS
Friendship

ARROW
Protection

ARROWHEAD
Alertness

FOUR AGES
Infancy, Youth, Middle and Old Age

CACTUS
Sign of the Desert

GILA MONSTER
Sign of the Desert

CACTUS FLOWER
Courtship

SADDLE BAGS
Journey

BIRD
Carefree   Lighthearted

LIGHTNING SNAKE

SNAKE
Defiance, Wisdom

THUNDERBIRD TRACK
Bright Prospects

DEER TRACK
Plenty Game

BEAR TRACK
Good Omen

RATTLESNAKE JAW
Strength

HEADDRESS
Ceremonial Dance

COYOTE TRACKS

RAIN CLOUDS
Good Prospects

**LIGHTNING AND
LIGHTNING ARROW**
Swiftness

DAYS AND NIGHTS
Time

MORNING STARS
Guidance

SUN SYMBOLS
Happiness

RUNNING WATER
Constant Life

RAINDROP - RAIN
Plentiful Crops

TEPEE
Temporary Home

SKY BAND
Leading to Happiness

MEDICINE MAN'S EYE
Wise, Watchful

MOUNTAIN RANGE

HOGAN
Permanent Home

BIG MOUNTAIN
Abundance

HOUSE OF WATER

FENCE
Guarding Good Luck

**ENCLOSURE FOR
CEREMONIAL DANCES**

EAGLE FEATHERS
Chief

WARDING OFF EVIL SPIRITS

PATHS CROSSING

PEACE
(broken arrow)

BUTTERFLY
Everlasting Life

136. *Diacritical Marking System*

The Diacritical Marking System (DMS) was an experimental teaching system that provided much phonic regularity to help beginning readers pronounce words. Diacritical marks are added to the text without altering the words' traditional spellings. If you want an interesting and challenging learning experience, have your students take any printed material and add these diacritical marks.

SHORT VOWELS & REGULAR CONSONANTS (no marks)	A apple	F fish	K kitten	P penny	U umbrella
	B Bill	G girl	L Linda	Q queen (qu)	V valentine
	C cookies	H hat	M midnight	R Rickey	W window
	D Daddy	I Indian	N nest	S saw	X box (ks)
	E egg	J jar	O ox	T table	Y baby
					Z zebra

LONG VOWELS (bar over)	Ā apron	Ē ear	Ī ice cream	Ō Ocean	Ū United States

SCHWA (comma over) À ago = È enough = 'O other — can also be used when any vowel, not a u, makes a short u sound. Examples: some front

LETTER Y y in yes (consonant)   ȳ in mȳ (long vowel)   funny (Note y = E not marked)

DIPHTHONGS (underline both)	OI boil	=	OY boy	OU out	=	OW owl

BROAD O(A) (circumflex) Â all âwful âuto = Ô lông   ôr

LONG AND SHORT OO (one and two dots)	One Dot U or Short OO	U̇ put	=	Ȯ good	
	Two Dot U or Long OO	Ü June	=	Ö room	= Ë new

R-CONTROLLED VOWELS (r acts as vowel) AR far   AR vāry   IR fir   ER her   UR fur

DIGRAPHS (underline) SH shoe   CH chair   WH which   TH that (voiced)   TH thing (unvoiced)   NG sing   PH =f phone

SECOND SOUNDS OF CONSONANTS (underline) C (c = s) cent   S c = z is   G (g = j) gem

SILENT (slash) come   right   her

EXCEPTIONS (+ over) women   action   one   stopped   of

The Reading Teacher's Book of Lists, Third Edition, © 1993 by Prentice Hall

Here is a sample of a text marked with the DMS:

"Lȯøk at <u>our</u> fi<u>sh</u>," sȧi̇d Bill.

"Hē wânts ṡomȩ<u>th</u>ing.

But lȯøk at <u>th</u>is box!"

See also List 127, Dictionary Phonetic Symbols

Note: Blends such as Bk or FL are not marked because each letter retains its regular sound.

137. *Roman Numerals*

We might have taken our alphabet from the Romans but, thankfully, we did not take their number system. Roman numerals are used for formal or decorative purposes, such as on clocks and cornerstones. For fun and learning have every student write his or her date of birth in Roman Numerals. Write the principal's birthday.

ROMAN	ARABIC	ROMAN	ARABIC
I	1	XX	20
II	2	XXI	21
III	3	XXIX	29
IV	4	XXX	30
V	5	XL	40
VI	6	XLVIII	48
VII	7	IL	49
VIII	8	L	50
IX	9	LX	60
X	10	XC	90
XI	11	XCVIII	98
XII	12	IC	99
XIII	13	C	100
XIV	14	CI	101
XV	15	CC	200
XVI	16	D	500
XVII	17	DC	600
XVIII	18	CM	900
XIX	19	M	1,000
		MCMLXXXVI	1986

Note: Roman Numerals have the following basic symbols:

$$I = 1 \qquad L = 50 \qquad M = 1000$$
$$V = 5 \qquad C = 100$$
$$X = 10 \qquad D = 500$$

A smaller symbol *before* a larger symbol means *subtract* the smaller amount, thus,

$$IX = 9 \qquad CM = 900 \qquad IL = 49 \qquad XXIX = 29$$

A smaller symbol *after* a larger symbol means *add* the small amount, thus,

$$XI = 11 \qquad LI = 51 \qquad XXVIII = 28$$
$$MC = 1100 \qquad XXXI = 31 \qquad LV = 55$$

The Reading Teacher's Book of Lists, Third Edition, © 1993 by Prentice Hall

138. *Traffic Signs*

As international travel has become more common, the United States has adopted traffic signs that use pictures and symbols. These help overcome language barriers. Understanding traffic signs is important for safety for drivers and pedestrians.

Shapes have meaning. Diamond-shaped signs signify a warning; rectangular signs with the longer dimension vertical provide a traffic regulation; rectangular signs with the longer dimension horizontal contain guidance information. An octagon means stop; an inverted triangle means yield; a pennant means no passing; a pentagon shows the presence of a school, and a circle warns of a railroad crossing.

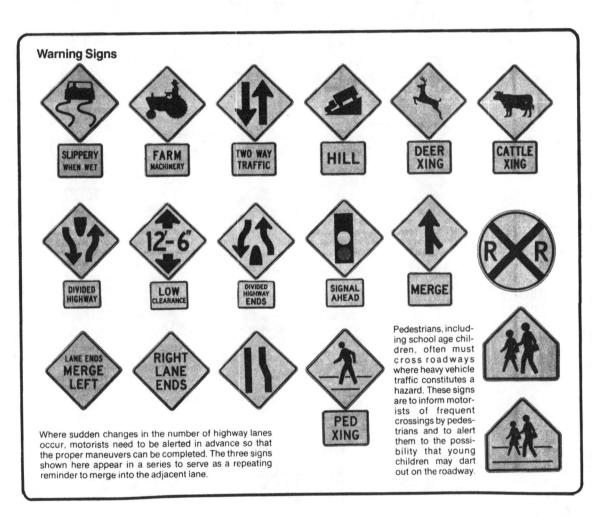

Warning Signs

SLIPPERY WHEN WET

FARM MACHINERY

TWO WAY TRAFFIC

HILL

DEER XING

CATTLE XING

DIVIDED HIGHWAY

12'-6" LOW CLEARANCE

DIVIDED HIGHWAY ENDS

SIGNAL AHEAD

MERGE

R X R

LANE ENDS MERGE LEFT

RIGHT LANE ENDS

PED XING

Where sudden changes in the number of highway lanes occur, motorists need to be alerted in advance so that the proper maneuvers can be completed. The three signs shown here appear in a series to serve as a repeating reminder to merge into the adjacent lane.

Pedestrians, including school age children, often must cross roadways where heavy vehicle traffic constitutes a hazard. These signs are to inform motorists of frequent crossings by pedestrians and to alert them to the possibility that young children may dart out on the roadway.

Regulatory Signs

Black and white signs are for posting regulations. Red signifies stop, yield or prohibition. The red circle with a diagonal slash always indicates a prohibited movement.

NO U TURN

NO LEFT TURN

NO RIGHT TURN

NO TRUCKS

KEEP RIGHT

CENTER LANE — LEFT TURN ONLY

Left turns may be allowed for traffic coming from opposing directions in the center lane of a highway. There are two types of signs used to identify these locations. One a word message and the other a symbol sign showing opposing left turn arrows with the word "Only."

ONLY

SPEED LIMIT 55

NO TURN ON RED

RIGHT TURN ON RED AFTER STOP

Turns are permitted in many States at traffic signals when the red traffic signal is on. There are two types of laws which permit this movement. One permits the turn only with posting of the sign "Right Turn on Red After Stop." The other law allows turns at any intersection unless specifically prohibited by displaying the sign "No Turn on Red."

The pennant-shaped warning sign supplements the rectangular regulatory, "Do Not Pass" sign. The pennant is located on the left side of the road at the beginning of the no-passing pavement marking.

A "Restricted Lane Ahead" sign provides advance notice of a preferential lane which has been established in many cases to conserve energy by the use of high occupancy vehicles such as buses and carpools. The diamond symbol displayed on the sign is also marked on the pavement to further identify the controlled lane.

YIELD

WRONG WAY

STOP

DO NOT ENTER

DO NOT PASS

RESTRICTED LANE AHEAD

Guide Signs

Green background signs provide directional information. Diagrams on some signs are being introduced to help motorists find the correct path through complicated interchange ramp networks. Roadside mileage markers will assist in trip planning and provide locational information. In addition mileage numbers (mile post numbers) are used to identify interchanges and exits. The number for an exit is determined from the nearest roadside mileage marker preceding the crossroad. Green signs also point the way of such items as trails for hiking and places for parking.

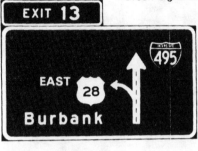

The brown background sign provides information pertaining to access routes for public parks and recreation areas.

Signs for Bicycles

Bicycles are used by many persons on portions of heavily traveled roadways. This mixing of bicycles and motor vehicles is extremely dangerous and wherever possible, separate facilities are being provided for the bicycles. The green guide sign points out the bike route. The other two signs shown here appear where bicycles are restricted from use of the roadways and where separate roadway crossings for bicycles are provided.

See also List 7, Daily Living Words; and List 8, Highway Travel Words.

Services Signs

The blue color of these signs indicates that they provide direction to motorist service facilities. Word message signs generally are used to direct motorist to areas where service stations, restaurants, and motels are available. Logo signs are optional.

Signs in Construction Areas

The color orange has a special use. It appears on signs and barricades in construction and maintenance areas as a constant warning to motorists of possible dangers

SECTION XII
Reference

139. *People to Know*

Broaden your students' reading and curricular horizons by adding gender and multicultural perspectives. The people on this list are interesting subjects for biography reading and student research papers. Their accomplishments make important additions to school curricula, elementary through high school.

Adams, Harriet Stratemeyer—1892–1982; a lifelong New Jersey resident, Harriet Adams is more readily known as Carolyn Keene, the author of the Nancy Drew mystery series. Adams also wrote the Hardy Boys, Tom Swift and other widely enjoyed juvenile fiction. Her stories of adventure and mystery have entertained generations of young readers.

Addams, Jane—1860–1935; Addams's founding of Hull House in Chicago marked the beginning of the settlement house approach to improving living and health conditions for the urban poor. It is also associated with the beginnings of the field of social work. Addams also started the American Women's Peace Party and helped organize the Women's International League for Peace and Freedom. For her efforts she was awarded the Nobel Prize for Peace in 1931.

Alcott, Louisa May—1832–1888; author of the classic family saga *Little Women;* was born in Boston, MA. She kept an "imagination book" as a child and enjoyed writing little stories and plays. She began selling her stories to help her family finances, and after *Little Women* became a success went on to write seven sequels.

Anderson, Marian—1902–   ; began her career by singing in church choirs in Philadelphia. She earned awards and scholarships to study singing, and after a successful European concert tour became the first black solo performer at New York's Metropolitan Opera House.

Attucks, Crispus—1723–1770; a former slave and sailor, Attucks led a group of colonists in an argument with British soldiers in Boston; the argument resulted in the "Boston Massacre," and Attucks was killed, making him one of the first American colonists to die during the Revolutionary War.

Banneker, Benjamin—1731–1806; a black land surveyor and mathematician, Banneker was one of the designers of the street patterns of our national capital, Washington, DC.

Barton, Clara—1821–1912; a nurse, teacher, and founder of a school, she was called the "angel of the battlefield." Barton organized food and medical-supply distribution during the Civil War; after the war, she worked to find missing soldiers, leading to her association with the International Red Cross and her founding of the American Red Cross.

Blackwell, Elizabeth—1821–1910; became the first American woman doctor, graduating from Geneva Medical College in New York in 1847. She also established a hospital and women's medical school. She is also thought of as the first woman doctor in England, where she also practiced medicine for many years.

Bourke-White, Margaret—1906–1971; an American photojournalist; became known for her photographs of the American industry and people. She also worked as a war correspondent/photographer for *Life* magazine and the U.S. Air Force during World War II and the Korean conflict.

Brooks, Gwendolyn—1918–   ; in 1950 became the first black to win a Pulitzer Prize when honored for her second book of poetry, *Annie Allen*. Brooks is known for an artful use of "black English" in her work and has written more than fifteen books of poetry.

Carson, Rachel—1907–1964; a marine biologist whose work on the effects of DDT on the ecological cycle and food chain resulted in the banning of the pesticide. Her books on nature and the sea have increased Americans' knowledge of and respect for nature.

Carver, George Washington—1864–1943; a black botanist at Tuskegee Institute; best known for his exhaustive scientific work with peanuts—he invented 300 uses for the peanut plant and peanuts, including peanut butter—Carver studied the cotton and sweet potato plants and discovered ways to add nutrients to poor soil to improve crop production.

Cassatt, Mary—1844–1926; one of the "Americans in Paris" in the 1870s, her work was shown in the Impressionist Exhibition of 1879. Her paintings of mothers and children are best known.

Ch'iu Chin—1875–1907; began her life in a traditional Chinese middle-class family. In 1900 she moved to Peking with her family and was horrified by the corruption of the ruling Manchu dynasty. She became an activist, founded a feminist newspaper, and urged the liberation of women and the overthrow of the Manchu dynasty. She organized an unsuccessful rebellion, was arrested and executed. Four years later, after the Manchu dynasty was overthrown she was honored as a heroine.

Chisholm, Shirley—1924–   ; in 1968 became the first black woman to be elected to the United States Congress. Born in Brooklyn, NY, she attended Brooklyn College and Columbia University. She was a teacher before she entered politics. She is known for her dedication to racial and sexual equality.

Comaneci, Nadia—1961–   ; at the age of 14 became the first athlete ever to earn perfect scores, 10s, in the Olympic Games. She earned 7 of them and received 3 gold medals, a silver medal, and a bronze medal for gymnastics in the 1976 Olympics.

Cotton, Donald—1939–   ; a black nuclear chemist who works for the United States to assist underdeveloped nations' energy production efforts. He invented a technique for measuring the rate that solid fuel is burned for propulsion using microwave absorption.

Curie, Marie—1867–1934; a Polish mathematician and physicist who moved to France as a young woman in order to study. In 1902 she, working with her husband Pierre, discovered the element radium. They received the Nobel Prize in Physics in 1903. She received a second Nobel Prize in 1922 for her continued work with radium.

Doxiadis, Constantinos—1913–   ; this award-winning Greek architect is world famous for his designs for the building and rebuilding of cities. His designs for new urban centers arrange living space, park areas, public and commercial buildings, and traffic routes for better living and less congestion. Some of his designs are seen in Philadelphia, Cleveland, Miami, and Louisville.

Earhart, Amelia—1897–1937; became the first woman pilot to make a solo flight across the Atlantic Ocean in 1932. In 1937, close to the end of her attempt to fly around the world, she and her plane were lost near Howland Island in the Pacific Ocean.

Eddy, Mary Baker—1821–1910; temporarily cured of persistent back pain by a faith healer, she became convinced that the mind governed health and recovery. She began to preach about the role of faith and prayer in healing and founded the Church of Christ, Scientist, and the *Christian Science Monitor* newspaper.

Estavanico—North African explorer who sailed to the New World with the Spaniards and traveled the lands around the Gulf of Mexico from 1528 to 1536 in search of Cibola, the legendary Seven Cities of Gold.

Fauset, Jessie Redmon—1882–1961; this black New Jersey woman was a prominent figure in the Harlem Renaissance, helping other black writers and poets, including Langston Hughes, gain recognition. She was a writer and a reporter, an editor and poet. She also taught Latin and French and translated the work of French-speaking Caribbean and African black writers.

Frank, Anne—1930–1945; in 1933 her family fled to Holland from Germany and were in hiding for a year before they were sent to concentration camps. During their hiding, she kept a diary of her thoughts and everyday family events. She died of typhus in the camp at Belsen. The diary was later published and has been read by more than 60 million people.

Friedan, Betty—1921–   ; sometimes called the "mother of the women's movement," she wrote a book called *The Feminine Mystique* in 1963, which argued that women should have the same opportunities for education and careers as men do. She formed the National Organization for Women (NOW) to help educate America to women's issues and equal protection of the law.

Gandhi, Indira—1917–1984; was the daughter of India's first prime minister. Because her mother had died earlier, Indira assumed the duties of "first lady" of the land and became involved in politics. In 1966 she became prime minister of India. Her career was marked by civil tensions, poverty, disease, and an insufficient food supply in her country. She was assassinated by members of a religious sect that was trying to break away from the central government and establish a separate state.

Gannett, Deborah—disguised herself as a man and joined the Colonial Army. She fought in the Revolutionary War for 18 months and was wounded.

Goodall, Jane—1934–   ; born in England and interested in nature as a child, she went to Kenya and worked with Dr. Louis Leakey, a well-known anthropologist. She is known for her in-depth study of chimpanzees and her type of research, long-term observation of animals in the wild, known as ethology.

Graham, Martha—1894–1991; often called the mother of modern dance, began her dance career as a student, then teacher. She came to New York in the 1920s and opened the School of Contemporary Dance, where she was principal dancer for several decades and an active choreographer and teacher.

Grandma Moses—1860–1961; one of America's most famous painters, she did not begin to paint until she was more than 70 years old. In the next 30 years, she produced more than 2,000 paintings, in the American Primitive style.

Grasso, Ella Tambussi—1919–1981; born in Connecticut to Italian immigrant parents, Grasso began her political career in 1952, when at age 33 she was elected to the Connecticut General Assembly. From there she served as Connecticut's Secretary of State, then represented the state in the U.S. Congress. In 1974, she became the first woman in America to be elected governor.

Greenaway, Kate—1846–1901; her watercolor illustrations of children's books were so popular that children's clothing was modeled after her character's clothes. She is best known for the illustrations in *Kate Greenaway's Almanack*, and *Birthday Book for Children*.

Handy, William C.—1873–1958; a black musician and composer; Handy, a self-taught cornetist, is often called the "Father of the Blues" and composed such famous pieces as "St. Louis Blues" and the "Memphis Blues." He is also the author of books on the Blues style.

Hao, Li Choh—1913–   ; a native of Canton, China, he spent most of his lifetime researching the human pituitary gland, the gland that produces the hormones that control growth, maturation, and reproduction. His discoveries have led to treatments for a number of serious diseases.

Henson, Matthew—1866–1955; a black explorer of the North Pole, Henson worked with Robert Peary on several expeditions and during their 1908–09 explorations planted a U.S. flag at the top of the world.

Hodgkin, Dorothy—1910–   ; an Englishwoman who, in 1964, won the Nobel Prize in Chemistry for her research on vitamin B12. She developed the procedure known as X-ray chrystallography, by which a scientist can tell the chemical structure of a substance by using X-rays to determine the molecular structure.

Hunter, Alberta—a black woman who began her career as a jazz and blues singer and songwriter; then, when middle-aged, became a nurse and worked in a hospital for nearly three decades before retiring and returning to her singing career.

Hurston, Zora Neale—1901–1960; a black woman anthropologist who was concerned that people be treated as people, not as racial stereotypes. As a result, she began writing about black life in America. She was not very successful financially and died in a state-supported home. More than 15 years after her death, her writings were collected and published, earning her well-deserved respect.

Jones, Frederick M.—1892–1961; this black inventor received more than 60 patents during his lifetime, including some that have directly influenced our day-to-day living. Jones invented the refrigeration system used by long-distance trucks, ships, and trains that enables foods to be transported without spoilage. Other Jones inventions include the automatic ticket machine used by movie theaters to dispense tickets and change and equipment to adapt silent-movie projectors to "talkies."

Lambo, Thomas Adeoye—1925–   ; Lambo, a Nigerian psychiatrist, spent his career adapting the knowledge of Western psychiatric theory to the mental-health issues and needs of African tribal life. He worked to bring harmony to the individual who was struggling to balance tribal religious tradition and Westernized economic/political demands.

Lange, Dorothea—1895–1965; beginning her career as a portrait photographer for the well-to-do, Lange's work took a very different direction during the Depression when she began to document the plight of the poor and migrant workers in California. Her documentary photographs helped convince the government to increase assistance to rural communities. She was considered to be one of the United States's finest photographers.

McCoy, Caldwell—1933–   ; a black electrical engineer who designed systems for detecting and tracking submarines. He also managed one of the largest U.S. computer networks to research the use of magnetic fusion as a means of producing usable energy.

Meir, Golda—1898–1978; A Russian Jew who grew up in America with a dream that Palestine would one day become a real Jewish homeland. She moved to Palestine in 1921, worked hard for organizations raising money and building schools, factories, and roads for Palestine. After World War II, the United Nations declared part of Palestine to be the free state of Israel. She helped Israel by serving as its ambassador, minister of labor, foreign minister, and prime minister.

Mitchell, Maria—1818–1889; a native of Nantucket, MA, was America's first woman astronomer. She was honored in 1848 for her discovery of a comet, the first one discovered with the aid of a telescope. She was also the first to take photographs of the sun's surface. She did research and taught astronomy at Vassar College.

Mother Teresa—1910–   ; born in Yugoslavia, this Roman Catholic nun has spent her life teaching and caring for the poor and sick in Calcutta. She founded an order of missionaries that now has thousands of sisters and brothers helping the sick and poor all over the world. She was awarded the Nobel Peace Prize in 1980.

Mott, Lucretia—1793–1880; a Boston schoolteacher whose feminist activities began soon after she learned that she was paid only half of what a male teacher earned. She dedicated her life to women's rights and the abolition of slavery. Refused her seat at the Anti-Slavery Society World Conference in London, she returned to the United States and launched the Women's Rights Convention, working toward a recognition of the equality of men and women.

Neruda, Pablo—1904–1973; A Chilean poet who is known for writing about common things and events in a provoking and powerful way. In his poems he expresses a range of emotion from the simple pleasure of receiving a gift to the horror of death and destruction. His work received many awards.

Nightingale, Florence—1820–1910; an Englishwoman who dedicated her life to improving health care. She opened a training school for nurses that became the model for nursing education in Europe and America.

O'Connor, Sandra Day—1930–   ; has had a distinguished career in government and law, serving as a lawyer, an assistant state attorney general, an Arizona state senator, and judge. In 1981, she was appointed by President Ronald Reagan to a seat on the Supreme Court of the United States.

O'Keeffe, Georgia—1887–1986; chose art as her life's work when she was a child and determined to study painting. Much of her work is abstract and was inspired by the New Mexican desert. Her larger-than-life flowers are widely known.

Parks, Rosa—1913–   ; a black Alabaman who unwittingly changed American civil rights history in 1955 when she refused to give up her seat on a bus to a white man. Her action was followed by a boycott of the buses by blacks. Dr. Martin Luther King, Jr. joined in the peaceful protest, and a year later the U.S. Supreme Court declared segregated buses unconstitutional.

Paul, Alice—1885–1977; a tireless organizer and supporter of women's rights, Paul was a founder of the National Women's Party and was instrumental in getting final passage of the Women's Suffrage Amendment and in adding equal gender rights to the Civil Rights Act of 1964. She was an advocate of nonviolent civil disobedience as a means to achieve national political change.

Pavlova, Anna—1882–1931; possibly the most famous Russian ballerina of all time. She began dancing at age 10, was a leading dancer at 13, and a prima ballerina by age 23. She toured the world for more than 25 years.

Ride, Sally—1951–   ; became the first American woman astronaut in 1983 as part of the crew on a six-day *Challenger* space mission. In 1984 she spent eight days in space on her second mission. She retired from her career as an astronaut in 1986 after the explosion of another *Challenger* spacecraft.

Rudolph, Wilma—1940–   ; as a young child she became ill with scarlet fever, a disease that left her weak and unable to walk. After therapy, she was able to walk on her own, but to strengthen her legs she began to play basketball and to run. By the time she was 15, she had qualified for the U.S. Olympic Track Team. She won a bronze medal in 1956. In 1960 she became the first American woman to win 3 Olympic gold medals in a single year. This black athlete continued to set world records until she retired in 1964.

Shelley, Mary Godwin—1797–1851; wrote the first science-fiction novel, *Franken-stein*, after a group of her friends decided to try to concoct tales of the supernatural.

The Reading Teacher's Book of Lists, Third Edition, © 1993 by Prentice Hall

Stokes, Rufus—1924–   ; a black Alabaman and an early advocate of clean air, he invented and patented an air-purification system to reduce the gases and ash emitted from factories and power plants. His ideas for air filtration also helped design auto-exhaust emissions controls.

Tereshkova, Valentina—1937–   ; after learning that fellow Russian Yuri Gagarin had become the first man in space in 1961, she applied for cosmonaut training. In 1963 she became the first woman to orbit the earth, circling nearly 50 times in a 3-day space mission.

Thatcher, Margaret—1925–   ; had three distinct careers: first she was a chemist, then a tax lawyer, then a politician. After serving as an elected Member of Parliament from 1959 to 1970, she became secretary of education, then leader of the Conservative Party. In 1979 she became Britain's first woman prime minister.

Ts'ai Lun—a Chinese man who pounded mulberry tree bark into thin sheets, making the first paper from plant fibers in the year 105.

Wheatley, Phillis—1753–1784; was brought to Boston, MA, as a slave. By the time she was 14 she had begun writing poetry about events of the time. A book of her poems was published in England in the 1770s—the first book published by a North American black. She was freed during the Revolutionary War.

Wilkins, J. Ernest—1923–   ; as a young black child, Ernest amazed everyone with his extraordinary academic achievements, which included earning a college degree by the age of 17 and a doctorate from the University of Chicago by the age of 19. His mathematical expertise was used in his development of models for the absorption rates for gamma rays, a necessary calculation for space and nuclear research.

Yen, Y.C. James—1893–1990; Yen dedicated his life to raising the literacy and economic level of Chinese peasants. He was born in the Szechwan Province, but attended college in the United States. He invented a basic Chinese vocabulary using a limited number of characters in order to speed the teaching of reading and writing and worked with the Mass Education Movement, a project that helped millions of his compatriots learn to read. He also worked to improve health, food production, and rural economic and civil programs. His programs were used as models for helping the poor in many parts of Asia, Africa, and South America.

140. *Nondiscriminatory Language Guidelines*

"Sticks and stones can break my bones, but words can never hurt me." Remember this childhood refrain? We knew, even at the age of six or seven, that it wasn't true and that name calling and taunts hurt. Now we know that even subtle, unintended biased or discriminatory words hurt students' self-esteem as well as their relationships with others. Make a conscious effort to use and teach nondiscriminatory language in class.

GENDER RELATED

INSTEAD OF	USE	COMMENT
The student chooses his assignments in this class.	The student chooses the assignments in this class.	Avoid gender-specific pronouns (his, her).
	Students choose their assignments in this class.	Use plural form.
	The assignments in this class are chosen by the students.	Rewrite to avoid gender reference.
Man's scientific discovery is limited only by his diligence.	Scientific discovery is limited only by our diligence.	Rewrite, using first person plural.
Man has . . . Mankind has . . .	People have . . . (humanity, human beings, humankind, the average person)	Use inclusive group words.
Manpower	Personnel, staff, workers, employees	Use inclusive group words.
Each participant should bring his own gear.	Participants should bring their own gear.	Use plural form.
The nurse will explain it to her patients.	Nurses will explain it to their patients.	Use plural; avoid the stereotype.
The male nurse said . . .	The nurse said . . .	Use inclusive term; no added gender words.
The child suffers from lack of mothering.	The child suffers from lack of nurturing (lack of parenting).	Use inclusive nonstereotype.
The chairman said . . .	The chairperson said . . . (chair, moderator, leader)	Avoid gender-specific term.
Dear Sir:	Dear Director: (Colleague, Editor, Service Manager)	Use title; avoid gender-specific term.

The Reading Teacher's Book of Lists, Third Edition, © 1993 by Prentice Hall

DISABILITY RELATED

INSTEAD OF	USE	COMMENT
The handicapped	Persons with disabilities	Emphasis on people, not disability.
The AIDS victim	Person with the HIV virus	Emphasis on person; avoid sensationalism.
The deaf use . . .	Deaf people use . . .	People are not the disability.
The deformed child	The child who has a cleft lip, etc.	Avoid emotion-laden terms.
The crippled child		
The wheelchair-bound boy . . .	The boy who uses a wheelchair . . .	Avoid emotion-laden terms.
The insane	People with mental illness	Emphasis on people.
The special student	The student with a disability	Avoid vague or euphemistic terms.

141. *One Hundred Ways to Praise*

Be free with praise for even minor successes; it will encourage larger successes. Be careful, however, never to be phony and praise when it isn't deserved; you will lose your credibility and the value of future praise.

Fantastic!
That's really nice.
That's clever.
You're right on target.
Thank you!
Wow!
That's great!
Very creative.
Very interesting.
I like the way you're working.
Good thinking.
That's an interesting way of looking at it.
It's a pleasure to teach you when you work like this.
Now you've figured it out.
Keep up the good work.
You've made my day.
Purrfect!
You're on the ball today.
This is something special.
Everyone's working so hard.
That's quite an improvement.
Much better.
Keep it up.
That's the right answer.
Exactly right!
You're on the right track now.
This is quite an accomplishment.
I like how you've tackled this assignment.
A powerful argument!
That's coming along nicely.
I like the way you've settled down to work.
You've shown a lot of patience with this.
I noticed that you got right down to work.
You've really been paying attention.
It looks like you've put a lot or work into this.
You've put in a full day today.
This is prize-winning work.
An A-1 paper!
I like your style.
Pulitzer-prize-winner in training.
Your style has spark.
Your work has such personality.
That's very perceptive.

This is a moving scene.
Your remark shows a lot of sensitivity.
This really has flair.
Clear, concise, and complete!
A well-developed theme!
You are really in touch with the feeling here.
This piece has pizzazz!
A splendid job!
You're right on the mark.
Good reasoning.
Very fine work.
You really scored here.
Outstanding!
This is a winner!
Go to the head of the class.
Superb!
Super!
Superior work.
Great going!
Where have you been hiding all this talent?
I knew you could do it!
You're really moving.
Good job.
What neat work!
You really outdid yourself today.
That's a good point.
That's a very good observation.
That's certainly one way of looking at it.
This kind of work pleases me very much.
Congratulations! You got _____ more correct today.
That's right. Good for you.
Terrific!
I bet your parents will be proud to see the job you did on this.
That's an interesting point of view.
You're really going to town.
You've got it now.
Nice going.
You make it look so easy.
This shows you've been thinking.
You're becoming an expert at this.
Topnotch work!
This gets a four-star rating.

The Reading Teacher's Book of Lists, Third Edition, © 1993 by Prentice Hall

Beautiful.
I'm very proud of the way you worked today.
Excellent work.
I appreciate your help.
Very good. Why don't you show the class?
The results were worth all your hard work.
You've come a long way with this one.
I appreciate your cooperation.

Thank you for getting right to work.
Marvelous.
I commend you for your quick thinking.
I like the way you've handled this.
That looks like it's going to be a good report.
I like the way you are working today.
My goodness, how impressive!

See also List 121, Book Report Alternatives.

142. *Readability Graph*

The Readability Graph is included on the next page so you will have it on hand when you need it. Use it to help judge the difficulty level of the materials your students use so that you can better match reading selections to students' reading abilities.

1. Randomly select three sample passages and count out exactly 100 words beginning with the beginning of a sentence. Count proper nouns, initializations, and numerals.

2. Count the number of sentences in the hundred words estimating length of the fraction of the last sentence to the nearest 1/10th.

3. Count the total number of syllables in the 100-word passage. If you don't have a hand counter available, an easy way is to put a mark above every syllable over one in each word, and then when you get to the end of the passage, count the number of marks and add 100. Small calculators also can be used as counters by pushing numeral "1," then push the "+" sign for each word or syllable when counting.

4. Enter graph with *average* sentence length and *average* number of syllables; plot a dot where the two lines intersect. The area where a dot is plotted will give you the approximate grade level.

5. If a great deal of variability is found in syllable count or sentence count, putting more samples into the average is desirable.

6. A word is defined as a group of symbols with a space on either side; thus, "Joe," "IRA," "1945," and "&" are each one word.

7. A *syllable* is defined as a phonetic syllable. Generally, there are as many syllables as vowel sounds. For example, *stopped* is one syllable and *wanted* is two syllables. When counting syllables for numerals and initializations, count one syllable for each symbol. For example, *1945* is four syllables, and *IRA* is three syllables, and & is one syllable.

Example

	SYLLABLES	SENTENCES
1st hundred words	124	6.6
2nd hundred words	141	5.5
3rd hundred words	158	6.8
AVERAGE	141	6.3

READABILITY 7th GRADE (see dot plotted on graph)

See also List 93, Writeability Checklist.

The Reading Teacher's Book of Lists, Third Edition, © 1993 by Prentice Hall

The Reading Teacher's Book of Lists, Third Edition, © 1993 by Prentice Hall

GRAPH FOR ESTIMATING READABILITY —EXTENDED

by Edward Fry, Rutgers University Reading Center, New Brunswick, N.J. 08904

Average number of syllables per 100 words

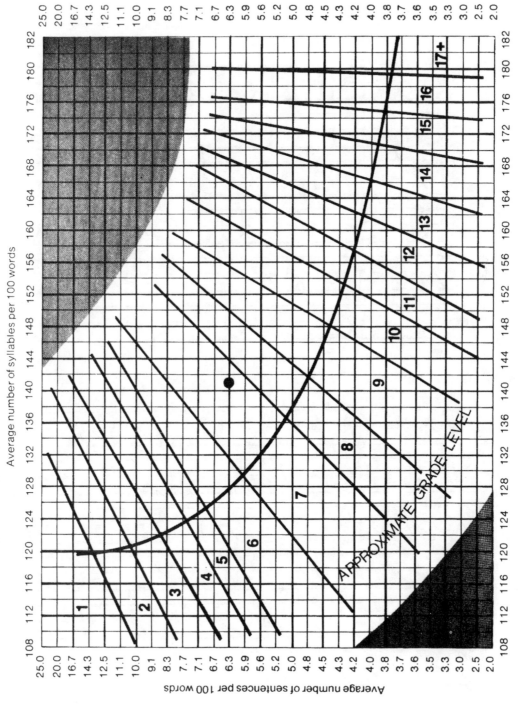

Average number of sentences per 100 words

143. *Handwriting Charts*

Have you ever needed a handwriting chart for a special student and couldn't quickly locate one? The Zaner-Bloser and D'Nealian manuscript and cursive alphabet charts are here to help you out in just such a situation.

Zaner-Bloser MANUSCRIPT ALPHABET

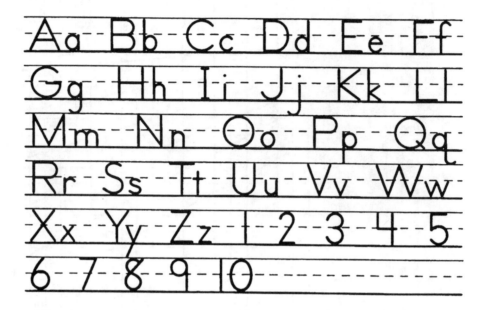

Zaner-Bloser CURSIVE ALPHABET

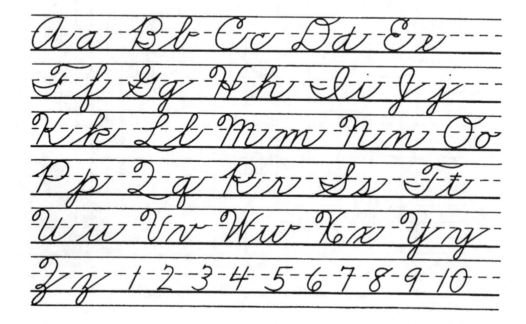

Used with permission from *Handwriting: Basic Skills and Application*. Copyright © 1984, Zaner-Bloser, Inc., Columbus, OH.

The Reading Teacher's Book of Lists, Third Edition, © 1993 by Prentice Hall

D'Nealian® Manuscript Alphabet

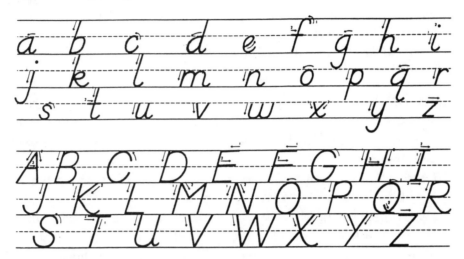

D'Nealian® Cursive Alphabet

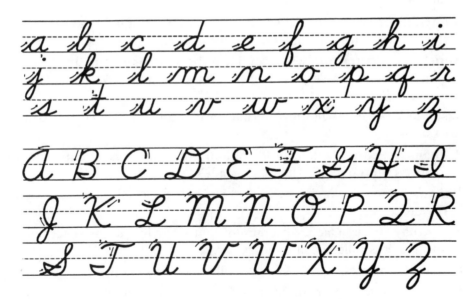

D'Nealian® Numbers

Used with permission from D'Nealian® *Home/School Activities: Manuscript Practice for Grades 1–3*, Copyright © 1986 Scott, Foresman and Company.

The Reading Teacher's Book of Lists, Third Edition, © 1993 by Prentice Hall

144. *Literary Terms*

Every area of knowledge has its own specialized vocabulary—literature included. Knowing these terms and their meanings will help students recognize the use of these elements in literature. These terms are basic to discussions about an author's skilled use of language. Many of them can also be used to help beginning writers improve or add interest to their writing.

Accented. A part of a word, phrase, or sentence spoken with greater force or a stronger tone.

Act. Part or section of a play, similar to a book chapter. Acts are usually made up of groups of scenes.

Allegory. Links the objects, characters, and events of a story with meanings beyond the literal meaning of the story.

Alliteration. Occurs when two or more words have the same beginning sound. Example: *Mike mixed some malt in his milk.*

Anadiplosis. The use of the ending word of a phrase or clause as the beginning or base word for the next one. Example: *Pleasure might cause her to read, reading might cause her to know, knowledge might win piety, and piety might grace obtain.*

Analysis. Occurs when we look at and try to understand the parts of something so that we can better understand the whole thing.

Antithesis. Contrasting words or ideas by asserting something and denying its contrary or by parallel or balanced phrases. Example: *This soup should be eaten cold, not hot.*

Assonance. Occurs when an internal vowel sound is repeated in two or more words. Example: *He feeds the deer.*

Author's purpose. Authors write for four main purposes: to entertain, to inform, to express their opinions, and to persuade.

Ballad. A long poem that tells a story. Ballads usually have strong rhythm and rhyme.

Biography. Gives a factual account of someone's life. If the writer tells of his or her own life, it is called an autobiography.

Cast of characters. List of names of all the characters in a play.

Cause and effect. Sometimes an event or circumstance makes another event or circumstance happen. The first one is called the cause or reason for the second one. The second one is called the effect or result.

Characters. People or animals in a story or other writing.

Chiasmus. Change of word order to get the reader's attention and to highlight something. Example: *Down he fell.*

Chronological order. The telling of a group of events in the time order in which they happened.

Comparison. Points out the ways in which two or more things are alike or similar.

Conclusions. A decision made after considering several pieces of information. The information may include facts from the reading and ideas that the reader already had.

The Reading Teacher's Book of Lists, Third Edition, © 1993 by Prentice Hall

Conflict. The problem the characters face in the plot. The conflict can be a problem between two characters or between a character and something in nature or society. Sometimes the conflict makes a character choose between two important ideas.

Contrast. Points out the ways in which two or more things are different.

Description. A group of details the writer gives that helps the reader imagine a person, place, or object or event. The details help create a picture in the reader's mind.

Dialogue. A conversation between characters in a story or play.

Drama. A story written to be acted out in front of an audience. Another word for drama is play.

Epic. A long narrative poem about the deeds of a hero.

Fact. A statement that can be proven.

Fantasy. A story that has imagined characters, settings, or other elements that could never really exist.

Fiction. A form of literature that tells stories about characters, settings, and events that the writer invents. Fiction may be based on some real places, people, or events, but it is not a true, factual story about them.

Folk tale. A story about people or animals that has been handed down from one generation to the next. Folk tales often explain something that exists in nature or they tell about a hero.

Form. The structure or arrangement of elements in literature. Example: *The form of traditional poetry is lines of poetry in groups called stanzas.*

Free verse. Poetry that does not rhyme or use strict patterns of rhythm.

Generalization. A statement about a whole group that is made based on information about part of the group.

Historical fiction. Uses details about real places, events, and times from history as the setting for an imagined story.

Hyperbole. An exaggeration. Example: *He must have been nine feet tall.*

Idiom. An expression that cannot be understood from the literal meaning of its words. Example: *Tom is barking up the wrong tree.*

Imagery. The author's use of description and words to create vivid pictures or images in the reader's mind. Example: *A blanket of soft snow covered the sleeping tractors.*

Inference. A guess or conclusion based on known facts and hints or evidence. Sometimes readers use information from experience to help make inferences about what they are reading.

Irony. The use of tone, exaggeration, or understatement to suggest the opposite of the literal meaning of the words used. Example: *I didn't mind waiting two hours; it was restful.*

Kenning. A short metaphor for a thing that is not actually named. Example: *Sky candle is a kenning for the word sun.*

Litote. An understatement or assertion made by denying or negating its opposite. Example: *He wasn't unhappy about winning the bet.*

The Reading Teacher's Book of Lists, Third Edition, © 1993 by Prentice Hall

Main idea. The one idea that all the sentences in a paragraph tell about. Sometimes the main idea is stated in a topic sentence; sometimes it is not stated but is implied.

Metaphor. The comparison of two things without using the words "like" or "as." Example: *Habits are first cobwebs, then cables.*

Sense metaphor. Relates one of the five senses to an object or situation. Example: *a cool reception.*

Frozen metaphor. A metaphor so frequently used that it has become an idiom or an expression with understood but not literal meaning. Example: *head of the class.*

Humanistic metaphor. Gives inanimate objects human qualities or humans inanimate qualities. Example: *a user-friendly computer; her porcelain skin.*

Inanimate metaphor. Pairs the quality of an inanimate object with another inanimate object. Example: *The walls were paper.*

Abstract metaphor. Links an abstract concept with an object. Example: *Death is the pits.*

Animal metaphor. Associates the characteristics of an animal with a human or object. Example: *What a teddy bear he is!*

Incarnation metaphor. Links the attributes of a deceased person to another person or entity. Example: *He is a modern George Washington.*

Metonymy. The use of a related word in place of what is really being talked about. Example: *"pen"* instead of *"writing."*

Moral. The lesson that a story or fable teaches. Sometimes the moral of a fable is stated at the end of the story.

Motive. A reason a character does something.

Narrative poetry. Poetry that tells a story.

Narrator. The teller of the story.

Nonfiction. Writing that tells about real people, places and events.

Novel. A long work of fiction.

Ode. A poem written in praise of someone or something.

Onomatopoeia. Words in which the sounds suggest the meaning of the words. Example: *Ouch.*

Opinion. A statement of someone's idea or feelings. An opinion cannot be proven. An opinion can be based on facts.

Oxymoron. The use of words with contradictory or clashing ideas next to one another. Example: *free slaves.*

Personification. The linking of a human quality or ability to an animal, object, or idea. Example: *The wind whispered through the night.*

Plot. Or storyline. The group of events that happen in order to solve the problem or conflict in the story.

Poetry. An expression of ideas or feeling in words. Poetry usually has form, rhythm, and rhyme.

Point of view. Refers to how a story is narrated. If a story is narrated from the first-person point of view, the narrator is a character in the story and uses

The Reading Teacher's Book of Lists, Third Edition, © 1993 by Prentice Hall

the first-person pronouns I, me, mine, we, and our. If the story is narrated from the third-person point of view, the narrator is not part of the story and uses the third-person pronouns he, him, she, her, them.

Predictions. The use of facts in the story and other information you know about the world to guess what will happen.

Rhyme. Two or more words that have the same ending sound.

Rhythm. A pattern of accented and unaccented syllables.

Science fiction. A type of story that is based on science-related ideas. Some of the scientific "facts" and developments in science fiction are not real and may never be possible.

Sequence. The order in which events occur or ideas are presented.

Setting. The time and place in which the story happens.

Simile. A comparison of two things using the words "like" or "as." Example: *She felt as limp as a rag doll*.

Solution. The turning point in a storyline or plot. It is the part in which a decision or important discovery is made or an important event happens that will solve the story's problem or end the conflict. The solution is also called the resolution or the climax of the plot.

Stage directions. What tells actors how to perform their parts of a play. They describe movements, tone, use of props, lighting, and other details.

Stanza. A group of related lines in a poem.

Theme. The message about life or nature that the author wants the reader to get from the story, play, or poem.

EDITH BALLINGER PRICE

145. *Computer Terms*

This is a list of terms commonly known by computer users. Since most students and workers in all fields are increasing their use of computers, or will be, this list is a good place to start for "computer literacy."

Alphanumeric. A set of characters that consists of letters (A-Z), numbers (0-9), and sometimes other special symbols.

BASIC. Beginner's All-Purpose Symbolic Code. A computer language that is widely used in schools, businesses, and in personal-use programming.

Baud. The rate in bits per second (bps) at which data can be transferred between two devices. One baud is one bit per second, and 10 baud is approximately 1 character per second. Thus, 300 baud would be approximately 30 characters per second. Baud is important in selecting a modem or telephone data transfer peripheral because it is the measure of speed of receiving or sending.

Binary Code. Code using "0's" and "1's" to represent data. The binary number system is based on the number 2, with each place representing a power of 2.

Bit. Binary digit. The smallest unit of data. It has a value of either "0" or "1." It typically represents "on/off" or "true/false."

Bomb. An error that causes the computer to stop working. Information in "RAM" is lost.

Boot. Inserting a disk and/or loading information into a computer.

Bug. Error, usually in the software or its use. Not all "bugs" cause "bombs."

Byte. The fundamental unit of data that can be processed by a computer. In most microcomputers, a byte consists of eight bits. Characters are normally represented by a byte. For example, a Mac Apple Classic II has a 4 meg (4 million) byte memory.

CAD/CAM. Computer-aided design and computer-aided manufacturing. Involves manipulating pictorial representations that appear on the computer screen.

CAI. Computer Assisted Instruction. The direct use of computers in the instructional process for drill and practice, tutorials, dialogue, games, and simulations.

CD-ROM. See Optical disk.

Chip. A small rectangle of silicon material on which thousands or millions of electronic circuits have been implanted.

CMI. Computer Managed Instruction for record keeping of individuals and suggested teaching and diagnosis.

COBOL. Common Business-Oriented Language. A higher level computer language used for business applications.

Command. A single instruction to the computer that is executed as soon as it is received.

Computer language. An organized set of rules, codes, and procedures used to communicate with the computer. Examples are BASIC, FORTRAN, COBAL, and LISP.

CPU. Central Processing Unit. The central unit of the computer that contains the memory, logic, and arithmetical procedures necessary to process data and perform computations. The CPU also directs functions of input, output, and memory devices. CPUs in personal computers are imprinted with microcomputer chips.

CRT. Cathode Ray Tube. Display screen like that of a TV. Also called a monitor. Most common computer display technology.

Cursor. Movable indicator appearing on the monitor (often flashing) that shows where the next character to be typed will appear.

Data. Information such as words, symbols, or pictures put into the computer. For example, the story in your word-processing program is data.

Database. An organized collection of related information from which data can be retrieved.

Debug. Process of locating and correcting errors.

Disk drive. A device that reads information from and records information on a floppy diskette.

Diskette (disk). See Floppy diskette.

Documentation. The written description of software or hardware. For example, the manual that comes with a program.

DOS. Disk Operating System. The operating system common with 1980s IBM PC's. For example, Mac's have a different operating system so they can't usually use the same programs.

Dot Matrix Printer. A printer that generates characters that are composed of small dots.

Drill and Practice. A common type of CAI that gives the student practice and enrichment, but not initial instruction in an area.

Electronic bulletin board. Computerized bulletin boards that enable users to send and receive electronic mail, transfer data, and read informational bulletins.

Electronic mail. A method of sending and receiving messages via electronic devices.

File. A block of information; for example, a story that can be stored as a unit.

File server. The central computer in a computer network that controls a hard disk, printer, and other peripheral devices.

Floppy diskette. A paper-thin flexible disk that can store information in a manner similar to a magnetic tape. The 5 1/4-inch diskette is in an envelope that is flexible, and when you shake the envelope the disk "flops." The 3 1/2-inch diskette is in a rigid shell.

Fortran. Formula translation. A higher-level computer language used in scientific applications.

G, Gigabyte. A large amount of memory. 1 million megabytes.

GIGO. Garbage in, Garbage Out.

Hard copy. Computer output produced on a paper by a printer.

Hard disk. A permanent data-storage device that is faster in loading and saving files than is a floppy diskette. It also holds more information.

Hardware. The physical components of a computer system (exclusive software).

Hypermedia. A computer-based technology that allows the user to navigate interactively through an information base that combines a variety of media such as film, video, computer graphics, sound, music, and text. Usually involves several technologies (e.g., CD-ROM) linked to a personal computer.

I/O. Input/Output. The use of peripheral devices (e.g., keyboard, printer, or disk drive) to enter, store, or retrieve information.

Joystick. A hand-control device that allows the user to control input to the computer without a keyboard. Frequently used in games. Similar to a "mouse."

Keyboarding. Using the keyboard to input information into the computer; typing skill. This should be taught to all students.

K. Kilobyte. It represents 2 to the 10th power or 1,024 bytes and is used to describe a computer's memory capacity. For example, a computer with 48K has 48 × 1024, or 49,152 bytes of memory.

LAN. Local Area Network. A network in which computers and/or other computing equipment in a local area (room, building, etc.) are linked so that they can share memory, software, data, printers, etc. See File Server.

Laser printer. A printer that uses laser technology to produce text and graphics that are very clear. It has the added advantage of being fast and quiet.

Light pen. A hand-held penlike pointer that is sensitive to the light emitted from a computer monitor and can be used to select, move, or draw objects on the screen.

Load. Put information into the computer. See Boot.

LOGO. A higher-level language that permits easy interaction and problem solving with a computer. Often used as a first computer language for children.

M. See Meg or Megabyte.

Mainframe computer. A large and powerful computer usually used by corporations, government offices, and universities that process large volumes of data. Highly trained specialists are usually required to oversee its operation.

Meg or megabyte. Refers to a memory of 1 million bytes. This is about 200,000 English words or 4 1/2 books.

Memory. That part of the computer that stores information and instructions. Memory capacity is described in "K," "M," or "G." See also Disk, RAM, and ROM.

Menu. A list of options, such as a choice of programs on a disk, or a choice of routines in a program. The menu is usually displayed on the monitor.

Microcomputer. A computer using a chip for its CPU. Can usually be operated by relatively inexperienced people.

Modem. Modulator/Demodulator. A device that permits computers to transmit information over regular telephone lines.

Monitor. A kind of TV (CRT) screen that provides a video display of computer output.

Mouse. A hand-held input device that, when moved over a flat surface such as a tabletop can move the cursor on the screen.

Optical disk. A high-density storage disk that requires a special (laser) disk drive. An optical disk can store 1/2 a gigabyte, which is 500 megabytes. Also called CD-ROM.

Optical scanner. A peripheral device for inputting words, numbers, graphics, etc., to the computer without the use of a keyboard.

The Reading Teacher's Book of Lists, Third Edition, © 1993 by Prentice Hall

Peripheral. A device, such as a printer or disk drive, that is used to transfer information to and from the central processing unit. Devices added to the computer.

Personal computer. See Microcomputer.

Program. A set of instructions in a computer language that a computer can execute. For example, a Word Processing Program causes the computer to act like an intelligent typewriter.

RAM. Random Access Memory. Computer memory that holds information put there by the user. This information can be erased and changed as frequently as necessary. It is the working memory. Information can be lost if the computer is turned off. To avoid this, store information on a disk.

ROM. Read Only Memory. Computer memory that cannot be altered by the user. It usually contains the operating system and sometimes a computer language such as BASIC. It might be used for just information retrieval, such as the encyclopedia on an optical disk.

Software. Computer programs.

Spreadsheet. Computer software used for working with data (both numbers and words) in rows and columns.

Terminal. A device that allows the user to communicate with a computer. It usually consists of a keyboard and a monitor.

Tutorial. CAI lessons that provide initial instructions as opposed to drill and practice.

Word processor. Computer software used for typing and editing manuscripts.

Write-protect. Use of a small label placed over the cut-out edge of a disk to prevent writing additional information onto the disk. Information may still be read from the disk; and if the label is removed, information can once again be written onto the disk. This helps prevent accidental erasing or altering.

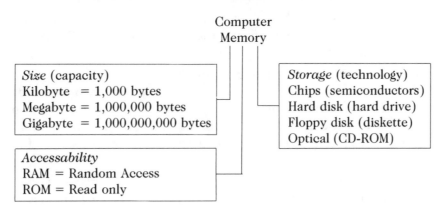

See also List 13, Measurement; and Lists 15–18, Science Vocabulary.

146. Testing Terms

Most school districts give tests. Most teachers get the results of those tests. What do those test scores mean? How do you interpret them? One place to start is with an understanding of the terminology that test makers use. Familiarity with these terms will help you to explain test results to interested and sometimes anxious students and parents.

Achievement tests. Tests that measure how much students have learned in a particular subject area.

Aptitude tests. Tests that attempt to predict how well students will do in learning new subject matter in the future.

CEEB test scores. College Entrance Examination Board test scores. This type of score is used by exams such as the Scholastic Aptitude Test. It has a mean of 500 and a standard deviation of 100.

Correlation coefficient. A measure of the strength and direction (positive or negative) of the relationship between two things.

Criterion-referenced tests. Tests for which the performance of the test taker is compared with a fixed standard or criterion. The primary purpose is to determine if the test taker has mastered a particular unit sufficiently to proceed to the next unit.

Diagnostic tests. Tests that are used to identify individual students' strengths and weaknesses in a particular subject area.

Grade equivalent scores. The grade level for which a score is the real or estimated average. For example, a grade equivalent score of 3.5 is the average score of students halfway through the third grade.

Mean. The arithmetical average of a group of scores.

Median. The middle score in a group of scores.

Mode. The score that was obtained by the largest number of test takers.

Normal distribution. A bell-shaped distribution of test scores in which scores are distributed symmetrically around the mean and where the mean, median, and mode are the same.

Norming population. The group of people to whom the test was administered in order to establish performance standards for various age or grade levels. When the norming population is composed of students from various sections of the country, the resulting standards are called *national norms*. When the norming population is drawn from a local school or school district, the standards are referred to as *local norms*.

Norm-referenced tests. Tests for which the results of the test taker are compared with the performance of others (the norming population) who have taken the test.

Percentile rank. A comparison of an individual's raw score with the raw score of others who took the test (usually this is a comparison with the norming population). This comparison tells the test taker the percentage of other test takers whose scores fell below his or her own score.

Raw score. The initial score assigned to test performance. This score usually is the number correct; however, sometimes it may include a correction for guessing.

Reliability. A measure of the extent to which a test is consistent in measuring whatever it purports to measure. Reliability coefficients range from 0 to 1. In order to be considered highly reliable a test should have a reliability coefficient of 0.90 or above. There are several types of reliability coefficients: *parallel-form* reliability (the correlation of performance on two different forms of a test), *test-retest* reliability (the correlation of test scores from two different administrations of the same test to the same population), *split-half* reliability (the correlation between two halves of the same test), and *internal consistency* reliability (a reliability coefficient computed using a Kuder-Richardson formula).

Standard deviation. A measure of the variability of test scores. If most scores are close to the mean, the standard deviation will be small. If the scores have a wide range, then the standard deviation will be large.

Standard error of measurement (SEM). An estimate of the amount of measurement error in a test. This provides an estimate of how much a person's actual test score may vary from his or her hypothetical true score. The larger the SEM, the less confidence can be placed in the score as a reflection of an individual's true ability.

Standardized tests. Tests that have been given to groups of students under standardized conditions and for which norms have been established.

Stanine scores. Whole number scores between 1 and 9 which have a mean of 5 and a standard deviation of 2.

True score. The score that would be obtained on a given test if that test were perfectly reliable. This is a hypothetical score.

Validity. The extent to which a test measures what it is supposed to measure. Two common types of validity are *content validity* (the extent to which the content of the test covers situations and subject matter about which conclusions will be drawn) and *predictive validity* (the extent to which predictions made from the test are confirmed by evidence gathered at some later time).

See also List 75, Test and Workbook Words; List 76, Essay Test Words; and List 77, Important Modifiers.

147. *Reading Organizations*

The four organizations listed below publish many useful journals, monographs, and research reports. They also organize and sponsor many local and regional conferences. They are excellent sources of current information in the field.

International Reading Association (IRA)*
Box 8139
Newark, DE 19711
Annual meeting, late April or early May.

College Reading Association (CRA)
3340 South Danbury Avenue
Springfield, MO 65807
Annual meeting, October.

National Reading Conference (NRC)
1070 Silbey Tower
Rochester, NY 14604
Annual meeting, early December.

National Council of Teachers of English (NCTE)**
1111 Kenyon Road
Urbana, IL 61801
Annual meeting, mid-November.

---

*Note: Many state and local councils and national affiliates of the International Reading Association hold regular meetings and publish either journals or newsletters on reading. A complete list of them can be obtained without charge from the IRA.

**NCTE has many state organizations.

IRA PRESIDENTS

1955–56	William S. Gray	1975-76	Thomas C. Barrett
1956–57	Nancy Larrick	1976–77	Walter H. MacGinitie
1957–58	Albert J. Harris	1977–78	William Eller
1958–59	George D. Spache	1978–79	Dorothy Strickland
1959–60	A. Sterl Artley	1979–80	Roger Farr
1960–61	Mary C. Austin	1980–81	Olive S. Niles
1961–62	William D. Sheldon	1981–82	Kenneth S. Goodman
1962–63	Morton Botel	1982–83	Jack Cassidy
1963–64	Nila Banton Smith	1983–84	Ira E. Aaron
1964–65	Theodore Clymer	1984–85	Bernice C. Cullinan
1965–66	Dorothy K. Bracken	1985–86	Joan C. Manning
1966–67	Mildred A. Dawson	1986–87	Roselmina Indrisano
1967–68	H. Alan Robinson	1987–88	Philliss Adams
1968–69	Leo Fay	1988–89	Patricia S. Koppman
1969–70	Helen Huus	1989–90	Dale Johnson
1970–71	Donald L. Cleland	1990–91	Carl Braun
1971–72	Theodore L. Harris	1991–92	Judith N. Thelen
1972–73	William K. Durr	1992–93	Marie M. Clay
1973–74	Millard H. Black	1993–94	Doris Roettger
1974–75	Constance M. McCullough	1994–95	Susan Glazer

The Reading Teacher's Book of Lists, Third Edition, © 1993 by Prentice Hall

NRC PRESIDENTS

1952–59	Oscar Causey	1982–84	Irene Athey
1960–61	William Eller	1985	Lenore Ringler
1962–64	George Spache	1986	P. David Pearson
1964–65	Albert Kingston	1987	Jerome Harste
1967–68	Paul Berg	1988	M. Trika Smith-Burke
1969–70	Alton Raygor	1989	James Hoffman
1971	Wendell Weaver	1990	Gerald Duffy
1972–74	Earl Rankin	1991	Robert Tierney
1974–76	Edward Fry	1992	Donna Alverman
1976–78	Jaap Tuinman	1993	Rebecca Barr
1978–80	Harry Singer	1994	James Flood
1980–82	Frank Greene		

148. *Publishers of Reading Curriculum Materials and Tests*

This list of publishers' addresses will come in handy in requesting current catalogues and in ordering curriculum materials.

For a complete up-to-date list of all major U.S. publishers, including trade book publishers for children, see *Literary Market Place*, which is published annually and can be found in most libraries.

Addison Wesley
P.O. Box 10888
Palo Alto, CA 94303

Allyn & Bacon
160 Gould Street
Needham Heights, MA 02194

American School Publishers
A Macmillan/McGraw-Hill Company
11 West 19th Street
New York, NY 10011

Amsco School Publications, Inc.
315 Hudson Street
New York, NY 10013

Apple Computer, Inc.
20525 Mariani
Cupertino, CA 95014

Barnell Loft
155 North Wacker Drive
Chicago, IL 60606

CTB/McGraw-Hill
Del Monte Research Park
Monterey, CA 93940

The Continental Press, Inc.
520 East Bainbridge Street
Elizabethtown, PA 17022

Curriculum Associates, Inc.
5 Esquire Road
No. Billerica, MA 01862

DLM Publishing
One DLM Park
Allen, TX 75002

EDL, Inc.
P.O. Box 210726
Columbia, SC 29221

Educators Publishing Service
75 Moulton Street
Cambridge, MA 02138

ERIC Clearinghouse on Reading and
  Communication Skills
Indiana University
Smith Research Center
2805 East Tenth Street
Bloomington, IN 47405

Fearon/Janus/Quercus
500 Harbor Boulevard
Belmont, CA 94002

Ginn Publishing Canada, Inc.
160 Gould St.
Needham Heights, MA 02194

Globe Book Company
240 Frisch Court
Paramus, NJ 07652

Good Apple
1204 Buchanan
Carthage, IL 60656

Harcourt Brace Jovanovich School
  Department
6277 Sea Harbor Drive
Orlando, FL 32887

Harper Collins Children's Books
10 East 53rd Street
New York, NY 10022

D.C. Heath and Company
125 Spring Street
Lexington, MA 02173

Highlights for Children
2300 West 5th Avenue
P.O. Box 269
Columbus, OH 43216-0269

Henry Holt and Company
115 West 18th Street
New York, NY 10011

Houghton Mifflin Company
Elementary School Division
One Beacon Street
Boston, MA 02108

IBM Corporation
1133 Westchester Avenue
White Plains, NY 10604

International Reading Association
Regional Conferences
800 Barksdale Road
P.O. Box 8139
Newark, DE 19714-8139

Jamestown Publishers
P.O. Box 9168
Providence, RI 02940

Judy/Instructo
1204 Buchanan
Carthage, IL 62321

Kendall/Hunt Publishing Company
2460 Kerper Boulevard
Dubuque, IA 52001

Lakeshore Curriculum Materials
P.O. Box 6261
Carson, CA 90749

Laguna Beach Educational Books
245 Grandview
Laguna Beach, CA 92651

Macmillan/McGraw-Hill School
Publishing Company
866 Third Avenue
New York, NY 10022

Macmillan/Merrill Publishing Company
866 Third Avenue
New York, NY 10022

McDougal, Littell/ALM
P.O. Box 1667
Evanston, IL 60204

Midwest Publications/Critical Thinking Press
P.O. Box 448
Pacific Grove, CA 93950

Milliken Publishing Company
1100 Research Boulevard
St. Louis, MO 63132

Modern Curriculum Press, Inc.
13900 Prospect Road
Cleveland, OH 44136

National Council of Teachers of English
1111 Kenyon Road
Urbana, IL 61801

Open Court Publishing Company
315 Fifth Street
Peru, IL 61354

Richard C. Owen Publishers, Inc.
135 Katonah Avenue
Katonah, NY 10536

The Perfection Form Company
1000 North Second Avenue
Logan, IA 51546

Phoenix Learning Resources
468 Park Avenue South
New York, NY 10016

Prentice Hall School Division
Route 9W
Englewood Cliffs, NJ 07632

The Psychological Corporation
555 Academic Court
San Antonio, TX 78204

Random House, Inc.
225 Park Avenue South
New York, NY 10003

Reading Is Fundamental, Inc.
600 Maryland Avenue S.W.
Suite 500
Washington, DC 20024

Riverside Publishing Company
8420 Bryn Mawr Avenue
Chicago, IL 60631

Frank Schaffer Publications
P.O. Box 2853
Torrance, CA 90509-2853

Scholastic, Inc.
730 Broadway
New York, NY 10003

Science Research Associates (SRA)
155 N. Wacker Drive
Chicago, IL 60606

Scott, Foresman
1900 East Lake Avenue
Glenview, IL 60025

Silver Burdett & Ginn
250 James Street
Morristown, NJ 07960

Steck-Vaughn Company
P.O. Box 26015
Austin, TX 78755

Teachers College Press
1234 Amsterdam Avenue
New York, NY 10027

The Wright Group
19201 120th Ave. NE
Bothell, WA 98011

Zaner-Bloser, Inc.
1459 King Avenue
P.O. Box 16764
Columbus, OH 43216-6764

149. *Taxonomy of Graphs*

This is a simplified version of a more complete taxonomy of graphs. Its purpose is to show some of the varieties of graphical expression used by writers and read by readers. Teachers should encourage students to use graphs to express ideas and to supplement writing. Graph comprehension can be taught using many of the same questions used to teach paragraph comprehension (main idea, inference, sequence, etc.).

1. Lineal
    a. Simple   story

    b. Multiple   history

    c. Complex
       Hierarchy   organization

       Flow   computer

       Process   chemicals

       Sociogram   friendship

2. Quantitative
    a. Frequency polygon   growth

    b. Bar graph   production

    c. Scattergram   test scores

    d. Status graph   scheduling

    e. Pie graph   percentage

    f. Dials   clock

From "Graphical Literacy" by Edward Fry. *Journal of Reading*, Feb. 1981. Also see "Theory of Graphs" ERIC #ED 240/528.

The Reading Teacher's Book of Lists, Third Edition, © 1993 by Prentice Hall

3. Spatial
  a. Two dimensions
     (single plane)

  b. Three dimensions
     (multiplane)

4. Pictorial
  a. Realistic

  b. Semipictorial

  c. Abstract

5. Hypothetical
  a. Conceptual

  b. Verbal

6. Near Graphs
  a. High verbal outline

     Main idea
     a. Detail
     b. Another detail

  b. High numerical

  c. Symbols

  d. Decorative Design

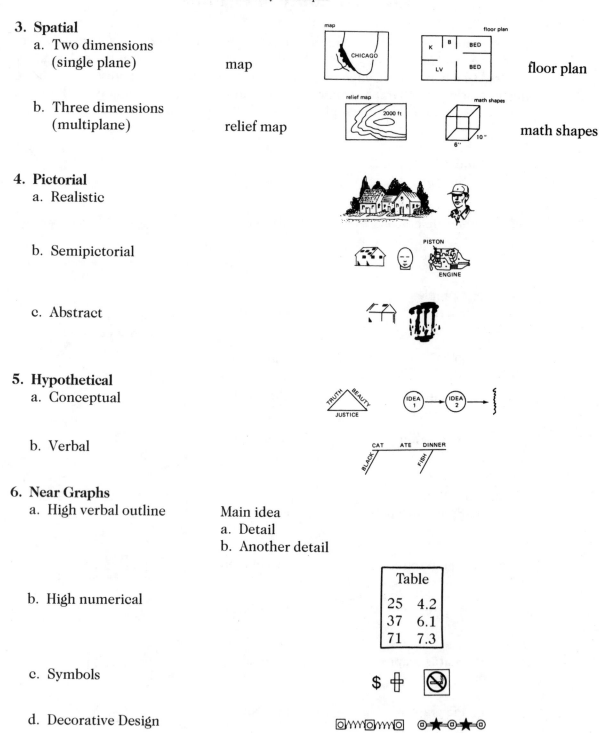

map

floor plan

relief map

math shapes

See also List 60, Story Graphs; and List 101, Games and Methods of Teaching.

150. *The Normal Distribution Curve*

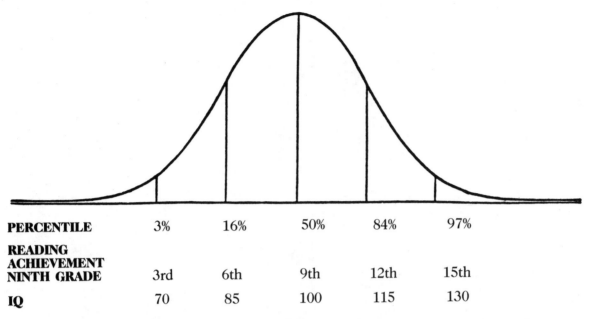

PERCENTILE	3%	16%	50%	84%	97%
READING ACHIEVEMENT NINTH GRADE	3rd	6th	9th	12th	15th
IQ	70	85	100	115	130

There is a strong but far from perfect correlation between Reading Achievement scores and IQ. In other words, on average a ninth grader with an IQ of 85 tends to read about at the sixth-grade level.

TYPICAL READING ABILITIES FOUND IN A FOURTH-GRADE CLASS

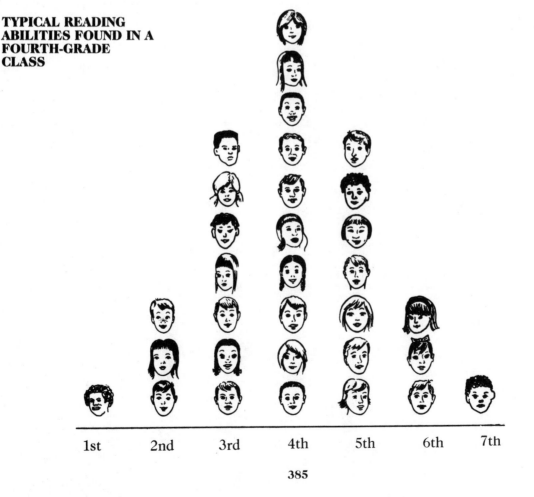

| 1st | 2nd | 3rd | 4th | 5th | 6th | 7th |

Index